bought at Cokesbury Bookstore
Nashville TN
6/17/02
Mari, Barbara & me

GOSPEL PARALLELS

A Comparison of the Synoptic Gospels

With alternative readings
from the Manuscripts and Noncanonical Parallels

Text used is the New Revised Standard Version, 1989

The arrangement follows
the Huck-Lietzmann *Synopsis,* Ninth Edition, 1936

Edited by Burton H. Throckmorton, Jr.

Publishers Since 1798

THOMAS NELSON PUBLISHERS
Nashville • Atlanta • London • Vancouver

For
Ansley Coe Throckmorton
with
love, admiration, and gratitude

Fifth Edition

Published in Nashville, Tennessee, by Thomas Nelson, Inc.

Printed in the United States of America.

Library of Congress Cataloging-in-Publication Data

Bible. N.T. Gospels. English. New Revised Standard. 1992
Gospel parallels : a synopsis of the first three gospels, with alternative readings from the manuscripts and noncanonical parallels / edited by Burton H. Throckmorton, Jr. — 5th ed.
"Text used is the New Revised Standard Version, 1989. The arrangement follows the Huck-Lietzmann Synopsis, 9th edition, 1936."
Includes bibliographical references and index.
ISBN 0-8407-7484-2
I. Throckmorton, Burton Hamilton, 1921– . II. Title.
BS2560.T48 1992
226′.1—dc20 92-29948
CIP

22 23 24 25 02 01

PREFACE TO THE SECOND EDITION

A THOROUGH STUDY OF THE GOSPELS is possible only when they are printed in parallel columns for comparison. Therefore, the American Standard Bible Committee requested a sub-committee to prepare a synopsis based on the Revised Standard Version so that the new version might better meet the needs of students. Before the work was undertaken, advice was sought from representative college and seminary professors in order to obtain their ideas on the features which should be included. The principles of arrangement in this volume were adopted on the basis of the suggestions which were made.

It seemed advisable, first of all, to compile a synopsis of the English text which could be used conveniently with a Greek synopsis. The obvious choice was the latest edition of Albert Huck's *Synopsis of the First Three Gospels* (9th ed. by Hans Lietzmann; English by Frank Leslie Cross, 1936). This edition is available to American students through the American Bible Society. During the two generations since "Huck" first appeared (1892), it has steadily come into ever wider use, until now it is known by New Testament students the world over. It prints each gospel in order (with quite minor exceptions); it repeats each gospel when out of order, and contains adequate subdivisions without being too complex. Hence, we have used the same section numbers and a similar marginal apparatus in order that the books may be used in the same class, where some can profitably follow the Greek and others only the English text.

Gospel Parallels offers two advantages never before available in a synopsis in English. First, the noncanonical parallels are given in full in addition to the parallels in the other canonical gospels. Most students do not have immediate access to the Gospel according to the Hebrews or to the quotations and gospel allusions in the Church Fathers. Yet these are a valuable part of our tradition about Jesus. Second, in connection with variant readings, the chief manuscript support has been cited. We believe that students who know no Greek can learn the significance of the most important manuscript witnesses. We have included all of the variants noted in the Revised Standard Version and have added others which seemed important enough to bring to the attention of serious Bible students.

The titles of some section headings have been changed from those used in the latest edition of "Huck." In some cases this was required by the new translation. Another difference will be found in the printing of the parallels from the Gospel of John, except where a very long passage is involved.

The Hazen Foundation made a generous subsidy toward the cost of the plates in order that the book might be available to students at as reasonable a price as possible. The committee supervising the preparation of the Synopsis was composed of Henry J. Cadbury, Harvard University Divinity School, Frederick C. Grant, Union Theological Seminary, and the late Clarence T. Craig, formerly of Yale University Divinity School and later Dean of Drew Theological Seminary. The detailed work of preparing the present volume was done by Burton H. Throckmorton, Jr., then instructor in New Testament at Union Theological Seminary and lecturer at Columbia University, now Professor of New Testament at Bangor Theological Seminary, Bangor, Maine. In the typing of the manuscript, the verification of references, and the completion of the manuscript citations, he has made an indispensable contribution. Professor Kendrick Grobel of the Vanderbilt University School of Religion kindly assisted in reading the proof.

It has been eight years since *Gospel Parallels* was first published. Its use of the Revised Standard Version, its arrangement following that of Huck's synopsis, and its fairly extensive footnotes—the three major features of this particular "harmony" or "synopsis"—have apparently proved useful to a large number of students. It is therefore reappearing in a second edition.

In spite of much proofreading, the first edition contained a number of errors. Most of these have been eliminated in subsequent printings; and it is our hope that in this edition all initial mistakes have been corrected.

The major change in this edition, however, is in the form of an addition. It has been increasingly evident that the references used in the footnotes required a more adequate explanation than what has been provided. The significance of the Greek manuscripts, the versions, the Church Fathers, and the noncanonical gospels referred to has in no way been indicated. Manuscript support for various readings is cited in the footnotes; but the book has not revealed what combinations of manuscripts constituted strong support for any given reading. In other words, without consulting a number of different sources, the student has not been able to use the apparatus satisfactorily. It has therefore seemed advisable to prepare an introduction to the references made in the footnotes.

The following introductory material deals only with writers or documents which are referred to in the footnotes of this book. It is intended to help the non-specialist appreciate the meaning and significance of these notes; and it is hoped that some, at least, will be led to inquire further.

PREFACE TO THE THIRD EDITION

BECAUSE OF THE CONTINUING AND WIDESPREAD USE of *Gospel Parallels* it has seemed important that it be published in a third edition, primarily to correct and supplement the footnote references which have proved to be one of the more helpful aspects of the book. In this edition I have for the first time included references to the Gospel of Thomas, in some cases quoting the whole saying or logion, in others indicating only the logion number. (Numbers of the logia are taken from *The Gospel According to Thomas,* translated by A. Guillaument, *et al.,* Harper & Brothers, 1959.)

A detailed checking of the textual apparatus disclosed a number of errors which have been corrected in this edition. I have also included support from four papyri not formerly referred to: P^{1}, P^{25}, P^{67}, and P^{75}. A few additional corrections and improvements have been made throughout the book, and the "Introduction to Footnote References" has been brought up to date.

I am extremely grateful to Mrs. Bernice C. Rich of Thomas Nelson & Sons whose discernment has brought to light a number of errors and inconsistencies. I should like also to thank Edwin B. Chatfield for his interest and helpfulness in the preparation of this edition.

PREFACE TO THE FOURTH EDITION

THE TEXT OF THE GOSPELS HAS BEEN BROUGHT into conformity with the second edition of the Revised Standard Version, and an index has been added. Also, additions have been made in the introductory and footnote materials, and text corrections have been made throughout.

Burton H. Throckmorton, Jr.
Bangor, Maine, 1979

PREFACE TO THE FIFTH EDITION

IT WAS FORTY-SIX YEARS AGO, in the summer of 1946, that I began work, without air conditioning, at Union Theological Seminary in New York, on the first edition of *Gospel Parallels*. That was also the year when the first edition of the New Testament of the Revised Standard Version was published. *Gospel Parallels* finally came out in 1949. No one then had any idea, least of all me, that almost a half-century later that same book would have gone through four editions and thirty-five printings, and would be in wide use throughout the whole English-speaking world.

In 1990 the successor of the Revised Standard Version of the Bible—the New Revised Standard Version—was published; and because of the apparent usefulness of *Gospel Parallels*, it seemed appropriate, perhaps even necessary, to prepare an altogether new edition based on the NRSV. The text of this fifth edition of *Gospel Parallels* is based entirely on the NRSV. That is the primary, all-important, and very significant change that has been incorporated in this fifth edition.

The reader of this new edition will also find many other changes and improvements, chief among which are the following:

- All the gospel material that appears *out of order* is now printed in italics. Formerly, only the *headings* of such pericopes were italicized, but in this edition the whole column is italicized. If, then, what one is reading is in *italics*, one knows immediately that one is reading material out of its context in the gospel in which it appears; but one can still find the pericope in its context elsewhere in the book. That information is given in parentheses in the heading. A note about the biblical references found at the top of each page: In the center of the page, in boldface type, one finds reference to the verses of each gospel on that page which occur in their own order in their respective gospels. In the inner margin of the page, in regular type, one finds reference to the last verse cited of each gospel in the order of that gospel, as well as the section number and page where that verse may be found. By following these references at the top of the page one can find any verse, in any of the gospels, in its own order and context.

- All the footnotes have been retranslated in inclusive language. Footnotes, however, that incorporate texts from the NRSV quote it verbatim.

- Parallels to the canonical gospels that are found in the Gospel of Thomas have been greatly supplemented in this edition so that all the major parallels from that gospel are now included in full in the footnotes.

- Many noncanonical parallels from other writings, not included in earlier editions of *Gospel Parallels*, have been added to this edition.

- Much of the introductory material has been rewritten, in part so as to reflect views of contemporary scholarship.

- Many of the headings found in the book and in the index have been rewritten.

- When one is reading a pericope which is in its own order in the gospel, but which has been separated from what precedes or follows it, one is told at the beginning of the pericope where the preceding verse is to be found, and one is told at the end of the pericope where the next verse may be found. See, for example, §45 for an illustration of both situations.

- When a column contains verses in addition to those stipulated in the heading, that fact is indicated by a + sign in the heading. See, for example, the Mark and Luke headings of §16.

- Where there is a parallel of sorts, not necessarily literary, and not printed in the columns, it will nevertheless often be indicated. For example, early in Luke's gospel the reader is told about Herod's imprisonment of John the Baptist. §5 contains Luke's account of that, but does not print the account of the same event found much later in Matthew and Mark, and in language very different from Luke's (see §111); but §5 does indicate where in Matthew and Mark the event is narrated, and where in *Gospel Parallels* the reader may find their accounts.
- There are six kinds of footnotes. A small sign or indicator, placed at the beginning of each type of footnote, separates the notes from each other, thus facilitating finding and reading them.

(1–4)	Numbers are used for footnotes which quote parallels from the synoptic gospels or, occasionally, from other New Testament writings.
✧	Indicates quotations from or allusions to an Old Testament writing.
✦	Indicates either textual variants and their textual support, or alternate translations of the text, or explanations of the text.
●	Indicates parallels in non-synoptic New Testament writings.
◗	Indicates parallels in non-canonical writings.
[ ]	Brackets indicate that words have been omitted from or added to the verse or that whole verses have been omitted.

Great credit and thanks for the appearance of this book go to Mark Anthony Langdon, who typeset the body of the work and is responsible for most of the meticulous verbal parallelism not only of the entire text, but even of the footnotes. Thanks are expressed also to Tricia Ann Padilla for her assiduous checking of details. Finally, I want to express my great appreciation to Mark E. Roberts, Editor of Biblical Reference Books at Thomas Nelson, for his zealous overseeing of the final production of this book.

NOMENCLATURE

Guide to Pronunciation

Alexandrinus	(âl îg zân drī ' nës)
Bezae	(bā ' zē)
Bohairic	(bō hī ' rîk)
Caesarean	(sês ë rē ' ën)
Clement	(klê ' mënt)
Curetonian	(kūr ë tōn' ēën)
Cyprian	(sî ' prē ën)
Diatessaron	(dī ë tês' ë rôn)
Didache	(dî ' dë kā)
Didymus	(dîd' ë mës)
Ebionites	(êb' ē ën īts)
Ephraemi	(êf rî ē ' mē)
Epiphanius	(êp î fān' ē ës)
Eusebius	(ū sē ' bē ës)
Fayum	(fī ' ūm)
Ferrar	(fêr' rër)
Hippolytus	(hîp ôl' î tës)
Ignatius	(îg nā ' shës)
Irenaeus	(ī rë nē ' ës)
Koridethi	(kōr î dā ' thē)
Logion	(lō' gē ôn)
minuscule	(mîn' ës kūl)
Naasenes	(nã ' ã sēns)
Nazaraeans	(nâ zë rē ' ëns)
Oxyrhynchus	(ôk sî rîng' kës)
palimpsest	(pâl' împ sêst)
Peshitta	(pë shē ' të)
papyrus	(pë pī ' rës)
Sahidic	(së hî ' dîk)
Sinaitic	(sīn ë ît' îk)
Sinaiticus	(sīn ë ît' ë kës)
Tatian	(tā ' shën)
Theodotus	(thē ôd' ë tës)
uncial	(ûn' shël)
Vaticanus	(vât î kā ' nës)

Key to Pronunciation

â *as in* fact
ā *as in* able
ã *as in* art
ê *as in* get
ē *as in* equal
î *as in* if, big
ī *as in* kite
ô *as in* box
ō *as in* over
û *as in* up
ū *as in* use, cute

Used in unaccented syllables:
ë = a *as in* alone
ë = e *as in* system
ë = i *as in* easily
ë = o *as in* gallop
ë = u *as in* circus

Greek Manuscripts Cited

S Codex Sinaiticus
(4th, or perhaps 5th century)

A Codex Alexandrinus
(5th century)

B Codex Vaticanus
(4th century)

C Codex Ephraemi
(5th century)

D Codex Bezae Cantabrigiensis
(6th century, perhaps 5th)

W Washington (Freer) Manuscript
(5th century)

Θ Koridethi Gospels
(7th to 9th century)

λ The "Lake Group"
(minuscules 1, 118, 131, 209, etc.)

ø The "Ferrar Group"
(minuscules 13, 69, 124, 346, etc.)

𝔎 The "Koine" or "Byzantine" text
(E, F, G, H, etc. and most minuscules)

P^{1} Philadelphia Papyrus
(3rd century)

P^{3} Vienna Papyrus
(6th–7th century)

P^{4} Paris Papyrus
(3rd century)

P^{25} Berlin Papyrus
(4th century)

P^{37} Ann Arbor Papyrus
(3rd–4th century)

P^{45} Dublin Papyrus
(3rd century, Chester Beatty Collection)

P^{67} Barcelona Papyrus
(*ca.* 200 A.D.)

P^{75} Geneva Papyrus
(*ca.* 200 A.D., Bodmer Collection)

Versions Cited

it Itala (the Old Latin version, as reconstructed by Adolf Jülicher)

vg Vulgate (ed. by Wordsworth and White, 1889–98)

sy^{c} The Old Syriac (ed. by Cureton, 1858)

sy^{s} The Sinaitic Syriac (discovered in 1892)

sy^{p} The Peshitta Syriac version (ed. by G. H. Gwilliam, 1901)

sa The Sahidic version (ed. by G. Horner, 1911 ff.)

bo The Bohairic version (ed. by G. Horner, 1898 ff.)

Terms Used

Uncial — refers to capital letters; manuscripts written in capital letters are "uncials" and predominated until the ninth century A.D.

Minuscule — refers to manuscripts written in small, cursive letters, often joined to each other. Minuscules and uncials overlapped during the ninth and tenth centuries, and only minuscules occur from the eleventh century onward.

Cursive — refers to small, joined, "longhand" letters used in minuscules.

Palimpsest — a manuscript which has been written on twice, the first writing having been erased or rubbed off.

Roll — refers to the way in which a book was put together. If a book were a "roll," the writing material was rolled—sometimes, in the few cases of expensive books, on rollers. To be read, the manuscript had to be unrolled with the right hand and re-rolled with the left. There were no "pages" and, even in the case of the Bible, no chapter and verse divisions; so references could not be made except to rolls themselves, or to works appearing in a roll. Titles and authors were noted at the end of the roll, which was somewhat inconvenient. Greek rolls seldom exceeded 35 feet and were usually closer to 25 feet; a gospel such as Matthew or Luke would have used about 32–35 feet. The material was written in a series of columns about two to three inches wide; there were usually 25 to 45 lines to a column depending on the width of the roll and the size of the letters. Sometimes the rolls were wrapped in parchment for protection. When rolled up, they were about 9 or 10 inches tall and an inch to an inch and a half in diameter. Words were not separated and there was little punctuation.

Codex — a bound book. With the introduction of codices, page references could be given, and much more material could be included in one book. The codex was introduced into Christian usage well before 100 A.D., and the gospels surely appeared together in codex form in the second century. One does not know why it was that Christians adopted the use of codices immediately, and universally, but all eleven Christian manuscripts of the second century are in codex form, and on papyrus. The earliest extant example of the gospels in codex form comes from the third century. The codex played a neglible role in non-Christian manuscripts of the second century. Of 304 pagan manuscripts of the third century, 275 are papyrus rolls, 26 are papyrus codices, and 3 are vellum codices.

Papyrus — refers to a very durable writing material, and to the writing itself. Papyrus was used surely from the sixth century B.C. Single sheets usually did not exceed 13 by 19 inches. Papyrus was used to make both codices and rolls. To make a roll, pieces were glued together end to end. Writing was usually done on only one side of the papyrus (the recto) where the fibers ran horizontally; sometimes, however, the other side (the verso) was also used. In the fourth century A.D. the use of papyrus declined, probably because larger codices than papyrus could provide were needed, and because the manufacture of vellum was improved, but papyrus was still being used in Egypt in the sixth century A.D.

Vellum — skins of cattle, sheep, and goats, seldom of pigs and asses. These skins were washed, scraped, rubbed with pumice, and chalked. They made an excellent writing material. The two earliest vellum documents known were found at Dura in Mesopotamia, and date from 190–189 and 196–195 B.C. But vellum was rare this early. All references in Roman literature as far as the end of the first century A.D. are to papyrus. But toward the end of the first century A.D. vellum was fairly common outside of Rome, although it had by no means displaced papyrus. In the fourth century vellum displaced papyrus both in the roll and in the codex. Vellum books, some of which were the most beautiful books ever made, were used for about a thousand years.

Types of Text

Before we take up the manuscripts themselves we must remember that more important than the manuscripts are the types of text or "families" they represent. None of the original manuscripts of the New Testament have survived nor, presumably, any direct copies of the original manuscripts. What we have are copies of copies. Into these copies crept errors; moreover additions and "corrections" were sometimes made by the copyists, for the only Bible of the early church was the Old Testament, and it was not imperative to copy the gospels and epistles—still "uncanonized"—exactly word for word. The manuscripts of the New Testament can be classified by groups or families, descended from common ancestors and supporting distinctive types of text. Indeed, the chief value of the majority of manuscripts is not their approximation to the original text of the New Testament, but their support of one or another of these groups or families. No manuscript can be better than that from which it was copied. Textual criticism since the publication of Bengel's study of the New Testament in 1734 has shown that manuscripts, like animals, can be classified into families, which families are related to each other in varying degrees of intimacy. It is the family, then, that is far more significant than the manuscript, and one manuscript copied from a good family gives far more support to a reading than a hundred manuscripts, no matter how accurately copied, from a poor family which *as a family* is late or inaccurate. First must be asked, how good is the family? and second, how accurate is the copy or text at hand?

How did these families, or types of text, arise? It is quite obvious that errors, corrections, and additions made in Rome would be perpetuated in manuscripts copied at Rome, and not at Alexandria or Antioch or Caesarea. Each religious center in the church would preserve and add to its own peculiar readings and gradually the texts in and around the various leading communities took on their own characteristics. Moreover, when bishops and scholars edited New Testament texts for local use by copying from the various manuscripts in their own communities, the character of the text in these communities became the more fixed; so that today, with the help of the early versions (translations into other languages) and quotations from the Church Fathers, we can assign manuscripts to their proper families. There are, of course, cases in which manuscripts seem to fit more than one family, and there is always the possibility of a new family being isolated by the discovery of new manuscripts or by the re-arrangement of old ones. Textual criticism is by no means a closed study! It should be added in conclusion that because we are dealing now primarily with differences among the manuscripts, they loom far larger than their actual significance should allow. The fact is that in about 90 per cent of the New Testament the manuscripts all agree; the differences occur in a small percentage of passages, and do not affect fundamental Christian doctrine.

The Main Types of Text Now Recognized

(1) ***The Alexandrian text*** (called "Neutral" by Westcott and Hort because of their belief that it was uncontaminated) represented chiefly by **B, S,** and the Coptic versions. It is identified by the absence of aberrations found in other groups. Its center was Alexandria, hence its name; but it was

found throughout the Eastern church. As it is represented by the oldest extant uncials, **B** and **S,** this type of text is very significant.

(2) ***The Byzantine text,*** also called Syrian, Antiochene, Koine, and Received (*Textus Receptus*), originated in the late third century around Antioch—hence its designation as Antiochene and Syrian. It was adopted in Constantinople and so predominated in the Byzantine world. It is also referred to as the "Received text," or ***Textus Receptus***, because it was this text which was found in almost all late manuscripts and so became the basis of the first printed editions of the Greek New Testament in the sixteenth century, beginning with Erasmus' edition of 1516. Through these editions, it was the text which was first translated into the modern European tongues. Our King James (Authorized) Version is a translation of this type of text. The oldest and best manuscripts of this text are **A** and parts of **C** in the Gospels; **W** in Matthew and most of Luke, and often the Peshitta; then follow most of the late uncials and minuscules. By the eighth century it was practically the only Greek text being used. It is characterized by conflations (combinations of readings from other manuscripts) and revisions in the interest of smoothness and intelligibility. The late uncial and minuscule manuscripts of this text are referred to by the German capital 𝔎, the first letter of the Greek word *koine,* "common," which term is often used to refer to this family.

(3) The term ***"Western text"*** was once used to refer to all pre-Byzantine, non-Alexandrian readings, but it more properly refers to the Graeco-Latin manuscripts of western Europe such as **D**; to the Old Latin version; and to quotations from western Church Fathers such as Cyprian. Other non-Alexandrian, pre-Byzantine readings must be classified in another way. This type of text is marked by omissions and insertions sometimes the length of several verses, and by eccentric readings. The text originated in the middle of the second century, and so its readings cannot easily be dismissed. The so-called "Western non-interpolations," chiefly found in the last three chapters of Luke, are readings found in all but the Western manuscripts and believed by Hort to be late; hence they were not interpolated in (or added to) Western manuscripts. This designation begs the question of the authenticity of the readings: it implies that they were not in the original autographs but were interpolated in the non-Western manuscripts, or not interpolated in the Western manuscripts. It would seem wise not to consider the readings as a unit, but to decide on the authenticity of each one separately, on other grounds. The Western text probably originated in North Africa or Egypt, in Greek, and was early translated into Latin.

(4) ***The Syriac text,*** to be distinguished from the Syrian (Byzantine), was once thought to belong to the Western text but is now considered by many scholars to be an independent text. It was originally associated with the Western type of text, but it was also closely akin to the Alexandrian type. Its Western readings probably came by way of Tatian's *Diatessaron,* which was written in Rome but was widely circulated in Syria in the Syriac language. The Syriac family is represented primarily by the manuscripts sy^{c} and sy^{s}. It was later revised by Rabbula under Byzantine influence and became the Peshitta (sy^{p}) which is the authorized Bible of the Syrian Church.

(5) ***The Caesarean text*** is found in Θ, λ, ø, **W** (in Mark), P^{45}, and quotations in the later works of Origen and in the works of Eusebius. It was used in Caesarea (hence its name), but the discovery of the third century P^{45} in Egypt, together with the knowledge that Origen used this type of text in Alexandria as well as in Caesarea, makes it probable that it originated in Egypt, perhaps as early as the second century. This text lies between the Alexandrian and the Western. It is as significant a group as we possess because it is as early as the Alexandrian type, but lacks the extravagant readings of the Western.

Greek Manuscripts of the New Testament Referred to in the Footnotes

S—***Codex Sinaiticus,*** middle fourth century; included both the Old and New Testaments plus the Epistle of Barnabas and the Shepherd of Hermas. The text is Alexandrian. It often agrees with **B**, but not always, for it has been influenced by another tradition similar to the Western. Among the versions, the Bohairic comes nearest to it, with much support coming also from the Sahidic. The manuscript may have originated in Palestine or in Alexandria.

The story of its discovery is one of the most fascinating true stories of modern times. In 1844 Constantin von Tischendorf made his first visit to St. Catherine's Convent on Mount Sinai, looking for manuscripts. While browsing around the library, he saw a large basket full of parts of old manuscripts containing fragments of the Old Testament in Greek. As they were in a basket whose contents, according to the librarian, had already twice been burned as fuel, Tischendorf asked and received permission to take the leaves to his room. He might as well have them, as far as the librarian was concerned, because they were about to be burned anyway. But when the librarian became aware of the fact that the leaves were valuable, he refused Tischendorf permission to see the source from which these comparatively few sheets had been taken. So Tischendorf took back the sheets, forty-three in all, to the University of Leipzig, and gave them the name of the reigning king of Saxony, Frederick Augustus. These leaves remain to this day in the University library, catalogued as Codex Friderico-Augustanus, and containing several chapters of I Chronicles, some of II Esdras, all of Esther, part of Tobit, most of Jeremiah, and about half of Lamentations.

In spite of all the publicity which these sheets received, Tischendorf managed not to disclose the place where they had been found. He was determined to return to that convent and secure the other fragments, whatever they might be. In 1853 he did return, but in vain; for no information was given him. In 1859 he returned for the third time under the auspices of the Czar of Russia. Again he looked through the library but found nothing like the forty-three leaves he had taken back to Leipzig. On February 4th while he and the steward were taking a walk around the convent garden, they discussed the Septuagint and various texts of it which they had seen. When they returned to the convent, the steward invited Tischendorf to join him in his cell for some refreshments. From a corner he took an object wrapped in a cloth, which he placed before Tischendorf on a table. Tischendorf unwrapped the cloth, and before him lay Codex Sinaiticus—"the Bible of Sinai." He soon noticed that the whole New Testament was there. Having received permission to take this treasure to his room, Tischendorf was so filled with emotion that he could neither sleep nor even lie down on a bed; and so in a cold room, by the light of a small lamp, he spent the night copying the Epistle of Barnabas. "All my boldest dreams," he writes, "were surpassed. I was certain of having found the most important manuscript in the whole world—a veritable pillar to sustain Divine Truth."* Not successful in obtaining permission to take the manuscript to Cairo, he nevertheless went to Egypt without it; and by playing a little game of politics, he succeeded in getting it sent to him there. In 1869 these leaves, 347 in all, were "given" to Czar Alexander II of Russia in exchange for money amounting to about $7000—a gift which was somewhat slow in arriving but was finally presented to the monastery at Mount Sinai and the affiliated convent of Mount Tabor. In addition to this money, some Russian decorations were awarded to certain Sinai fathers. In the 1930's when the Soviet government was in need of funds—and not particularly

---

* This quotation, as well as the story narrated, may be found in Tischendorf's own record of his discovery of Sinaiticus read by him at a meeting of the Royal Society of Literature, February 15, 1865, and entitled: *Mémoire sur la Découverte et l'Antiquité du Codex Sinaïticus.*

interested in biblical manuscripts—a group of Americans was asked to consider the purchase of the new manuscript from the Soviet government. The figure proposed was a million dollars; but due to the Depression it could not be raised. In 1933 the British people and government bought the famous manuscript from the Soviet government for £100,000, and it was moved to the British Museum in London, where it may now be seen. In addition to the leaves at the University of Leipzig, there is a small fragment of the manuscript in the Library of the Society of Ancient Literature in Leningrad. As Tischendorf considered this the oldest extant manuscript of the Bible, he referred to it by the sign א *(Aleph)*, which is the first letter in the Hebrew alphabet. The letter A had already been used to designate Codex Alexandrinus. In this book the letter **S** is used as more significant than *Aleph* to students who do not know the Hebrew language.

A — ***Codex Alexandrinus,*** first half of fifth century; contained originally both the Old and New Testaments, plus I and II Clement (see p. xxii) and the Psalms of Solomon, which follow the Book of Revelation. Matthew 1:1—25:6 (most of this gospel) is lost; also missing from the New Testament are John 6:50—8:52 and II Corinthians 4:13—12:6. The text is Byzantine in the gospels and Alexandrian in the Pauline epistles.

The manuscript is said to have been given to the patriarchate of Alexandria in 1098. In 1621 it was perhaps taken from Alexandria to Constantinople by Cyril Lucar who left Alexandria as patriarch to take up the same position in Constantinople. Cyril Lucar offered the codex as a gift to James I of England, through Sir Thomas Roe, the English ambassador to Turkey; but James having died in 1627 when the codex arrived in England, it was received by Charles I who deposited it in the Royal Library. When George II presented that Library to the nation in 1757, the codex passed into the possession of the British Museum. The Byzantine text of Alexandrinus in the gospels is the earliest representative of this text (sometimes called "Syrian") which, as early as the fourth century, had come to predominate over all other texts. The Authorized (King James) Version is the English equivalent of this type of text. In the Acts and Epistles, however, the text of this codex is of the Alexandrian type, the chief exponents of which are Sinaiticus and Vaticanus. In the Book of Revelation the text is also Alexandrian and is, with the possible exception of P^{47}, the best extant text of that book.

B — ***Codex Vaticanus,*** fourth century; contained originally both the Old and New Testaments, but Hebrews 9:14—13:25, the Pastoral Epistles, Philemon, and the Apocalypse—and perhaps, as in **S** and **A**, parts of the Apostolic Fathers—have now been lost. The text is Alexandrian. It was considered by Westcott and Hort, and after them by many other scholars, to be the best single extant text of the New Testament. The text of the gospels and Acts is the best Alexandrian text we have, but there is a considerable Western element in the text of the Pauline epistles. Vaticanus and Sinaiticus are textually closely related, but their common birthplace cannot now be determined.

This codex appears in the earliest catalogue of the Vatican library, published in 1475, but no one knows when it was taken there or any of its earlier history. There is, then, no interesting story in connection with a "discovery" of this manuscript, as it has been preserved in the Vatican for almost five hundred years. But the way in which it was guarded by Vatican authorities is interesting. For hundreds of years nobody in the outside world knew what Vaticanus' text was like, as no one was allowed to copy it or to study a section long enough to remember it. It was first made known in 1553 when a correspondent of Erasmus, one Sepulveda, sent him some selected readings from it. In 1669 a collation (or list of its various readings) was made by Bartolocci, a Vatican librarian, but it was never published and no one knew anything more of it for a hundred and fifty years. Napoleon carried the manuscript off to Paris as a victory prize, and while there it was studied by Hug. He was the first to make known its great age and supreme importance (1810). In 1815 it was returned to its home as were the many other treasures which Napoleon had robbed from the various libraries of Europe. Again it became practically inaccessible to scholars. In 1843, after waiting for several months, Tischendorf was finally permitted to look at it for six hours. In 1844 de Muralt was allowed to examine it for nine hours. In the next year the great English scholar, Tregelles, was permitted to see it on condition that he would not copy a word. And so before he entered the precinct where the manuscript was kept, his pockets were searched for all potential writing materials; and when he seemed to be looking too intently at any particular passages, the two guards who stood next to him snatched the manuscript away. Meanwhile in 1857 Cardinal Mai published an edition of the work, and in 1866 Tischendorf again applied for the opportunity to study it. His request was granted on condition that he examine it for no longer than three hours a day, and not copy any of it. By the end of eight days, however, he had managed to copy out eight whole pages. His permission was then revoked, but on special entreaty it was renewed for a period of six days. This gave Tischendorf enough time to enable him to publish, in 1867, the best edition of the manuscript then available. Finally, in 1889–90 a photographic copy was made of the whole manuscript and it became the common property of all scholars.

C — ***Codex Ephraemi,*** first half of fifth century; a palimpsest containing parts of both the Old and New Testaments. The text is Alexandrian in general but has many other mixed readings, so it is not so important as the texts of Sinaiticus, Alexandrinus, and Vaticanus, because it does not represent as consistently any one type of text.

In the twelfth century a scribe expunged the biblical text and re-used the vellum to record the thirty-eight discourses of Ephraem (a Syrian Father [d. 373] often referred to as Ephraem Syrus) translated into Greek. It was therefore very difficult to recover the original biblical text but most of it has now been deciphered by the use of chemicals. The first complete edition of the manuscript was published by Tischendorf in 1843–45. He was able to read almost every word of it, and had even discovered several notes by some of the correctors of the text. The manuscript seems to have been brought from the East to Florence in the time of Lorenzo de' Medici by a Greek named Andrew John Lascar. When Lascar died in 1535 the manuscript, together with all his library, was bought by Pietro Strozzi. It then belonged to Cardinal Niccolò Ridolfi, of Florence, of the de' Medici family, and later Queen Catherine de' Medici owned it. As she was the wife of King Henry II of France, the codex was brought to Paris and became part of the Bibliothèque Royale (now the Bibliothèque Nationale).

D — ***Codex Bezae,*** late fifth century or early sixth; a bilingual manuscript of the gospels and Acts, written in Greek on the left page and in Latin on the right, and the oldest known manuscript written in two languages. The text is Western.

The Bishop of Clermont borrowed the manuscript from the Monastery of St. Irenaeus in Lyons to take to the Council of Trent in 1546. It was then returned to the monastery whence it was rescued when Lyons was sacked by the Huguenots in 1562. In some way it got into the hands of Théodore de Bèze, the Geneva scholar and reformer; and he presented it to the University of Cambridge in 1581. Since then it has been called by his name, the letter **D** being used to refer to it. See under "Types of Text" for a discussion of its textual characteristics.

W — ***Washington Codex,*** fifth century or perhaps late fourth; includes Deuteronomy, Joshua, the gospels, and the Pauline epistles, with two small lacunae in the gospels, Mark 15:13–38 and John 14:25—16:7.

The manuscript is unusually interesting because it contains four types of text, not corresponding to the four gospels: the Alexandrian type of text is found in Luke 1:1—8:12 and in the Gospel of John; the Byzantine type is found in the rest of Luke and in Matthew; the Western type is found in Mark 1:1—5:30; and the Caesarean in the rest of Mark. The manuscript is quite independent with regard to its reading; for this reason its origins are difficult to determine. An addition following Mark 16:14, the so-called Freer Logion, is of special interest because it is rather lengthy and is not to be found in any other known manuscript. A translation of this addition follows:

> And they excused themselves, saying, "This age of lawlessness and unbelief is under Satan, who does not allow the truth and power of God to prevail over the unclean things of the spirits. Therefore reveal your righteousness now"—thus they spoke to Christ. And Christ replied to them, "The term of years of Satan's power has been fulfilled, but other terrible things draw near. And for those who have sinned I was handed over to death, that they may return to the truth and sin no more; that they may inherit the spiritual and imperishable glory of righteousness that is in heaven."

If these words are inserted between verses 14 and 15 of Mark 16, it will be seen that they fit well into the context. Apparently they were inserted by a scribe to soften the reference to Jesus' strong rebuke of the disciples in verse 14. The "quotation" from Jesus was probably composed ad hoc somewhere around the end of the second century or the beginning of the third. The first part of this reading is quoted by Jerome in his treatise against the Pelagians (ii. 15).

The manuscript was bought by Charles L. Freer from an Arab dealer named Ali in Gizeh, near Cairo, on December 19, 1906. It was taken to Detroit and later deposited in the Freer Gallery of Art in Washington, D.C.; hence the letter **W** refers to it. It had once been located, perhaps, in the Monastery of the Vinedresser, which was situated near the third pyramid in Egypt, until the monastery was destroyed between 1208 and 1441. What happened to the manuscript between this date and 1906 we do not know, but when Professor H.A. Sanders of the University of Michigan began to study it, he found sand in the wrinkles and encrusted on the outside. It had apparently not been opened for centuries.

Θ — ***Koridethi Codex,*** probably ninth, perhaps seventh century. It is difficult to date because no other specimen of the same kind of writing has yet been found. It contains only the gospels and is referred to as *Theta,* **Θ,** the eighth letter of the Greek alphabet. The text is Caesarean in Mark and Byzantine in the other gospels.

Colonel Bartholomée discovered it in Swanetia on the slopes of the Caucasus in 1853. In 1869 it was taken to St. Petersburg by the military governor of Kutais; but it was later taken back to the Caucasus and sent to the Gelaty convent near Kutais. It was then forgotten for about thirty years; and in 1901 was rediscovered by Bishop Kirion in the treasure room of St. Andrew's Cathedral, in which were preserved the codices belonging to the Gelaty monastery. Bishop Kirion then took the manuscript to Tiflis in Russia where it is now to be found. Scholars were first informed of its existence by von Soden in 1906, in the prolegomena to his edition of the New Testament. It takes its name from the monastery of Koridethi, near the Caspian, to which it formerly belonged. It was edited in 1913 by Gustav Beermann and Caspar René Gregory.

λ — ***The Lake Group*** (Family 1)

We are now dealing not with one manuscript, but with families or groups of manuscripts which have so much in common that they are presumably derived from a common ancestor. Moreover, these manuscripts are not uncials but minuscules, and are known by their numbers as they stand in the commonly accepted catalogue of minuscule manuscripts of the Greek New Testament. We shall consider only two—Families 1 and 13. Family 1 was isolated for separate examination and edited by Kirsopp Lake in 1902 (hence its name). This group, also referred to by the Greek letter *Lambda,* λ, consists of several manuscripts, numbers 1, 118, 131, 209, etc. of which Codex 1 is the most important. The family is known by the number (1) of this codex as well as by the name of the scholar who edited it. Codex 1 is a Basel manuscript dated in the tenth to twelfth centuries. It is impossible to establish a place of origin for any of these manuscripts.

ø — ***The Ferrar Group*** (Family 13)

The other group of manuscripts is the Ferrar Group named after W.H. Ferrar who helped edit them, and known by the Greek letter *Phi*, ø. In 1877 T. K. Abbot published *A Collation of Four Important Manuscripts of the Gospels,* which manuscripts had been examined by Abbot and Ferrar and were published after the latter's death. Many peculiar readings had been found which pointed to a common parent. The four manuscripts studied were related to each other but not to any other known family; so it was thought that they belonged to a separate family of manuscripts which in turn were derived perhaps from an uncial. These four manuscripts are minuscules, written in the twelfth, thirteenth, and fifteenth centuries. They are: codex 13 (12th or 13th century, in the Bibliothèque Nationale, Paris); codex 69 (the Leicester Codex, 15th century, in possession of the borough of Leicester, England); codex 124 (12th century, Imperial Library, Vienna); and codex 346 (12th century, Ambrosian Library, Milan). The parent of these manuscripts has never been found, but other manuscripts, similar to them, have since been seen to be additional members of the same family. They are codices 543 (12th century); 788 (11th century); 826 (12th century); 828 (12th century), etc. Most of these manuscripts seem to have an Italian-Sicilian origin and their texts are Caesarean in character. Codex 69, however, was written in England.

ℜ — ***Koine*** — see under the Byzantine text, page xiii.

The Papyri

The papyri referred to in this book are as follows:

P^{1} — at the University of Pennsylvania, Philadelphia, Pennsylvania; third century; containing Matthew 1:1–9, 12–20, 23.

P^{3} — in the Österreichische Nationalbibliothek, Vienna; sixth-seventh century; from a lectionary; containing Luke 7:36–45; 10:38–42; the text is Alexandrian.

P^{4} — in the Bibliothèque Nationale, Paris; third century; from a lectionary; containing Luke 1:58–59; 1:62—2:1, 6, 7; 3:8—4:2, 29–32, 34–35; 5:3–8; 5:30—6:16; the text is Alexandrian.

P^{25} — at the State Museum, Berlin; late fourth century; containing Matthew 18:32–34; 19:1–3, 5–7, 9–10.

P^{37} — in the University of Michigan Library, Ann Arbor, Michigan; third-fourth century; containing Matthew 26:19–52.

P^{45} — in the Chester Beatty Library, Dublin, and the Österreichische Nationalbibliothek, Vienna: known as Chester Beatty Papyrus 1; third century; contains parts of all the gospels and Acts; the text is chiefly Caesarean in Mark, Alexandrian and Western elsewhere—very mixed. This collection of gospel papyri represents a large collection of biblical manuscripts acquired around 1930 from a dealer in Egypt by A. Chester Beatty, an American collector of manuscripts. These leaves of both the Old and New Testaments vary in age from the second to the fourth centuries and are believed to have been found on the banks of the Nile near Memphis.

P^{64} — in Oxford; from about 200 A.D. See P^{67}.

P^{67} — at the Fundación San Lucas Evangelista, Barcelona; *ca.* 200 A.D.; belongs with P^{64}; contains Matthew 3:9, 15; 5:20–22, 25–28.

P^{75} — Bodmer Papyrus XIV and XV, in the Bodmer Library, Geneva; *ca.* 200 A.D.; containing Luke 3:18—18:18; 22:4—24:53 with lacunae; also John 1:1—15:8 with lacunae.

The Oxyrhynchus Papyri, became known in 1897 when B.P. Grenfell and A.S. Hunt published a fragment of papyrus found in Oxyrhynchus, Egypt, probably dating from the middle of the second century and containing some sayings of Jesus.

The numbers used in this text (1, 654, 655, 1224) refer to the numbers of the documents as numbered by Grenfell and Hunt. Number 1 is found in vol. 1 of this edition of the papyri; numbers 654 and 655 are found in vol. IV; number 1224 is found in vol. X.

The Greek sayings that are found in these papyri are the same as, or similar to the sayings of the Coptic Gospel of Thomas that was found later, about 1945, at Nag Hammadi. Though the Oxyrhynchus papyri fragments do not all derive from the same book, they undoubtedly represent the Greek original of the Copic version preserved in the Gospel of Thomas. The sayings of both the Oxyrhynchus papyri and the Gospel of Thomas are similar, in varying degrees, to the canonical form of the sayings found in Matthew, Mark, and Luke, but they also usually represent a later form of the sayings, having their own particular characteristics.

The Egerton Papyrus 2, dated around 150, or perhaps even earlier, is the second oldest specifically Christian manuscript yet discovered. (The oldest is the John Rylands Papyrus, P^{52}, showing parts of John 18:31–33, 37–38, and dating from around 125.) Its provenance is unknown because it was bought from a dealer, along with many other manuscripts. Oxyrhynchus, however, is not an unlikely possibility. It has affiliations with all four canonical gospels, but the author apparently reproduced verses from our canonical gospels from memory, and did not have them before him. This papyrus has been edited by H.I. Bell and T.C. Skeat in *Fragments of an Unknown Gospel,* British Museum, 1935, with three other Egerton papyri.

The Fayum Fragment (Fragment Fajjumense) is a fragment of a gospel containing words similar to those found in Mark 14:27–30, but with no words corresponding to v. 28. The fragment comes from the third century. It was discovered by G. Brickell in Vienna in 1885, in the great papyrus collection of the Archduke Rainer. There is a question as to whether it comes from the text of a gospel or is a homiletical paraphrase of Mark 14:27–30.

Versions of the New Testament

In the beginning the church read what was to become its New Testament altogether in the Greek language in which it had been written; but when the gospel was taken to people who did not speak Greek, it had to be translated immediately into the language of its new hearers. These early translations from the Greek are known as "versions," and this book refers to three of them: the Latin, the Syriac, and the Coptic (Sahidic and Bohairic). We shall deal with them in this order. Other versions of less value from a textual point of view are the Ethiopic, the Gothic, the Armenian, the Georgian, the Arabic, the Slavonic, and the Persian.

The Latin Versions (**it vg**) The Latin version is divided into two groups—the Itala (it) and the Vulgate (vg). The Itala (also known as the Old Latin) refers to all the Old Latin manuscripts which are not derived from Jerome's Latin translation known as the Vulgate. Jerome tells us that Pope Victor (*ca.* 190) was the first person to write theological treatises in Latin; and Tertullian, who died around

223, also wrote in Latin. Latin then became more and more the language of the Roman Empire, and the New Testament had to be translated into that language. In 383, in his preface to his revised Latin text of the gospels, Jerome wrote that he had compiled one Latin text because there were so many floating around which differed both among themselves and from the Greek manuscripts; and Jerome's contemporary, Augustine, in his *De Doctrina Christiana,* attests the same wide variety of Latin interpretations. It was in order to give the church what he considered the best available Latin text and to rid the Latin New Testament of its variety of readings, that Jerome, at the behest of Pope Damasus, published his edition of the gospels in 383. This was followed by the rest of the Bible, completed in 405. It was Jerome's edition of the Bible which in the eighth century became standard in the Roman Catholic Church. There is a question as to whether the extant Vulgate of the Acts, the Epistles, and the Apocalypse goes back to Jerome; but at present there seems to be no better explanation of them.

It is the earlier Latin manuscripts with their great variety of readings to which we refer as the Itala, or the Old Latin. We have no whole Bibles in the Old Latin, but only groups of books or fragments, dating from the fourth to the thirteenth centuries. There are also quotations from the Itala in the Latin Church Fathers which sometimes amount to whole chapters. These date from the second century on.

The Old Latin manuscripts may be roughly divided into three groups:

(1) The African manuscripts, such as ***k, e.***
(2) The European manuscripts, such as ***a, b, i.***
(3) The Italic manuscripts, such as ***f, q.***

It is probably group number 3 which Jerome took as the basis for his own revision, and which may itself be a modification of number 2. Number 1, the African group, represented by manuscripts ***k*** and ***e,*** is extremely important because it is the same type of text as that used in Africa by Tertullian and Cyprian in the second and third centuries. Hence the tradition is at least that old, although the manuscripts ***k*** and ***e*** are later, ***e*** coming from the fourth or fifth century and ***k*** from the fifth or sixth. In parts of the gospels, then, we can recover a Latin text which existed in the second century.

In order to arrive at the Greek text which this Latin represents, the Latin manuscripts must be retranslated back into Greek; and before this can be done, the translator must decide whether the Latin has itself been translated from the Greek literally or in paraphrase. For a literal Latin to Greek translation of a Latin manuscript which often paraphrased the Greek it translated, will not get us back very close to the original Greek! In addition to this difficulty we must try to decide whether the Latin manuscript with which we are dealing is itself a translation of a Greek manuscript or an edition of another Latin manuscript. These are some of the difficulties which accompany all the versions—Latin, Syriac, Coptic, etc.

We do not know what Greek manuscripts Jerome used, but they were apparently of an Alexandrian rather than a Western type. As the years went on, however, Jerome's Vulgate text itself became corrupt, being made to conform to Old Latin texts which died hard; and as a result there is scarcely an Old Latin reading which cannot be found in some manuscript of the Vulgate. There were numerous commentators who preferred the Itala, and its many surviving manuscripts testify to its having been in use centuries after Jerome had made his great revision. Indeed it was still being used in Bohemia at the close of the Middle Ages. As, then, the Vulgate was corrupted by the Old Latin and by many and sundry "improvements," it likewise had to be revised. This was done as early as the sixth century by Cassiodorus. Later Charlemagne, aware of the confusion of texts in his day, asked an Englishman, Alcuin, Abbot of St. Martin at Tours, to revise the Latin Bible; and on Christmas day in the year 801, Alcuin presented the Emperor with his revision. Other revisions followed and finally Pope Sixtus V (1585–90) published a text in 1590, accompanied by a bull declaring it alone to be trustworthy. Three months later he died. The College of Cardinals then called in all copies of the Sixtine edition, which had many errors, and in 1592 Pope Clement VIII (1592–1605) issued his own edition of the Vulgate (the Clementine Vulgate), but under the names of both Sixtus and Clement. The bull which accompanied Clement's Vulgate established it as the standard Roman text, and the third edition of the *Clementina* of 1598 is still the official Latin text of the Bible of the Roman Catholic Church. No verses were to be altered and no variant readings were to be put in the margin; so that officially, at any rate, textual criticism within the Roman Church was apparently proscribed from that date. No text of the New Testament has been so influential and significant in the Western church as the Vulgate. It was from the Vulgate that the Bible was read throughout western Europe for a thousand years; and it was the Vulgate that missionaries carried with them throughout the world and later translated into the vernacular of those to whom they had borne the gospel. The first complete book to be printed from a press in Europe was a text of the Vulgate, published in 1455 at Mainz by Gutenberg and Fust; the first complete English Bible was a translation from the Vulgate, made by Wycliffe; it was in the Vulgate text that the present chapter divisions of the Bible were worked out, probably by Stephen Langton, later Archbishop of Canterbury, *ca.* 1228.

The Syriac Versions **(sy^c sy^s sy^p)** As in the Latin there is an old text (the Old Latin, represented by many manuscripts) and an authorized text (the Vulgate versions), so in the Syriac there is an old text (the Old Syriac, represented by two manuscripts) and an authorized text (the Peshitta—sy^p). In the eighteenth century, the Peshitta was the only Syriac text known; but scholars like Griesbach felt certain that an Old Syriac text lay behind it. This Old Syriac text is represented by two manuscripts discovered since Griesbach's time—the Curetonian and the Sinaitic Syriac (sy^c and sy^s). In 1842 a Syriac manuscript of the gospels arrived at the British Museum from the library of a monastery in the Nitrian Desert in Egypt. William Cureton, the English Syriac scholar and an officer of the Museum, edited the leaves which were published in 1858 and are known by his name. They come from the middle of the fifth century and were erroneously believed by Dr. Cureton to contain the words of Jesus just as he spoke them, language and all! He stated that the original of his version was made before the original of the Peshitta. This was hotly disputed by advocates of the Peshitta but it has since been generally recognized to be true.

A second aid in getting at the Old Syriac text was made available in 1836 when the Armenians of the Mechitarist Monastery of San Lazzaro, Venice, published a commentary on Tatian's *Diatessaron* by Ephraem, the Syrian Father of the fourth century, which they possessed in an Armenian translation. This was not widely known until 1876, but since then Zahn and others have reconstructed the text on which this commentary, originally in Syriac, was based. In addition to the commentary, an Arabic translation of the *Diatessaron* was subsequently found in the Vatican Library; and after that still another Arabic translation was found in Egypt. From these two manuscripts the *Diatessaron* was edited in 1888. One should not leave the *Diatessaron* without also mentioning the Dura Fragment which was found on the site of Dura-Europos, a Roman fortified city captured by the Persians in 256 A.D. One of the vellum fragments from this site proved to be fourteen imperfect lines of the *Diatessaron* in Greek. Scholars are still uncertain whether Tatian wrote his *Diatessaron* in Greek or in Syriac—we have an Arabic translation and a Syriac commentary on it in an Armenian translation—but we now know that it existed in Greek, in Mesopotamia, in the early third century.

Finally, in 1892, two Cambridge women, Mrs. A.S. Lewis and her sister, Mrs. M.D. Gibson, discovered some palimpsest leaves of a Syriac manuscript of the gospels in the same monastery of St. Catherine on Mount Sinai where Tischendorf had found his great Greek uncial, Sinaiticus. The gospel text underlay a Syriac treatise dated in the year 778 and was itself of the early fifth century. It was later photographed at Sinai and the photographs were published in 1894 containing about three-fourths of the gospels. Known as Sinaitic Syriac (sy^S), the manuscript is still at Sinai, and along with other manuscripts there, has been rephotographed by an expedition from the American Schools of Oriental Research at Jerusalem.

The Old Syriac version, to which sy^c and sy^s belong, probably originated in the late second century or early third, and was akin to the text of Sinaiticus and Vaticanus, with Western readings inserted under the influence of the *Diatessaron*. It has been observed that the two manuscripts do not represent exactly the same text. There is a great deal more difference between them than there is, for instance, between two copies of the Peshitta; and of the two manuscripts the Sinaitic Syriac represents the earlier text. It is the oldest text of the Syriac that is known. But only the gospels survive in the Old Syriac version; the rest of the New Testament first appears in the Syriac language in the Peshitta.

The Peshitta (common language) version of the Syriac New Testament was increasingly used in the Syrian church from the end of the fifth century. Its origin is not certain. Until recently it was generally believed that this text was edited under the direction of Rabbula, Bishop of Edessa in 411–435, but perhaps it existed before Rabbula, originating in Antioch as an attempt to make the Syriac text conform more closely to the Greek. The Peshitta still remains the basis of the authorized Syriac text. It has two early, significant revisions, one by Philoxenus, Bishop of Mabug (Hierapolis), in 508, known as the Philoxenian Syriac; and the other by Thomas of Harkel (Heraclea) at Alexandria, in 616, known as the Harclean Syriac.

***The Coptic Versions* (sa, bo)** The New Testament spread to Greek-speaking people in Egypt, thence to natives who spoke Coptic in various dialects, chief of which were the Sahidic and the Bohairic.

The Sahidic — The Sahidic or Thebaic version was current in Upper (southern) Egypt whose chief city was Thebes, and its existence was not known until the end of the eighteenth century. It is found only in numerous fragments from which, however, most of the New Testament can be put together. Many fragments date from the fifth century, some from the fourth. The text is preponderantly Alexandrian but contains some Western readings, especially in Mark and Luke. The version is dated early in the third century.

The Bohairic — The Bohairic or Memphitic version, which alone of the Coptic has the complete New Testament, was current in Lower (northern) Egypt. Bohairic, the most developed of Egyptian dialects, ultimately superseded all other dialects, until "Coptic" came to mean "Bohairic." Over a hundred manuscripts, all late, have been found. Three date from the twelfth century; the oldest, containing the gospels, is at Oxford and is dated 1173–74 A.D. The remaining manuscripts are later; but a single leaf of Ephesians may be dated in the fifth century. The text is mainly Alexandrian, and the version is dated in the first half of the third century, a little after the Sahidic.

Church Fathers

I Clement — a letter written from the church at Rome to the church at Corinth by Clement, a leading presbyter of Rome, *ca.* 95 A.D. It admonishes the Corinthians to lead a godly life and then exhorts them to obey their presbyters who have received their leadership from the apostles. It is an early indication of Rome's initiative among the churches.

II Clement — a sermon, probably originating in Alexandria or Corinth *ca.* 150 A.D., not by Clement, but receiving its name from him because of an early association with his letter. It follows I Clement in the manuscripts.

Ignatius — bishop of Antioch in Syria who, at the beginning of the second century, *ca.* 110–117, while being led through western Asia Minor to his execution as a martyr in Rome, wrote a letter to each of six churches exhorting unity among the believers. The basis of this unity was the threefold ministry of bishop, presbyter, and deacon. The churches written to were at Ephesus, Magnesia, Tralles, Rome, Philadelphia, Smyrna; and one personal note to Polycarp, bishop of Smyrna.

Didache — otherwise known as the "Teaching of the Twelve Apostles" first appeared *ca.* 100–110 A.D. as a brief formulation of the rules of conduct Christians should observe.

Barnabas — the Epistle of Barnabas written *ca.* 130 A.D. probably in Alexandria, offered Christians a compromise solution to the problem of the proper significance for them of the Hebrew law. This compromise held that the Hebrew scriptures were true, not literally as the Jews believed, but allegorically. The Epistle was accepted as scripture by Clement and Origen, and is found in the manuscript Sinaiticus.

Marcion — a Christian heretic, excommunicated *ca.* 144 A.D. (He is cited in this book only as giving manuscript support.) He was antilegalistic, rejecting the Old Testament and its God, substituting a docetic Christ and a New Testament canon composed of St. Paul's epistles (not the Pastorals) and the Gospel of Luke considerably excised. This was the first New Testament canon to be drawn up as far as is known.

Justin — called the Martyr from his testimony unto death in Rome *ca.* 165 A.D., was born in Samaria of non-Christian parents. A student of philosophy, he was gradually converted to Christianity as the oldest, truest, and most divine of all philosophies. In its defense he wrote his *Apology* (for Christianity) *ca.* 155, addressed to the Emperor Antoninus Pius and his colleagues; and his *Dialogue with Trypho,* shortly after, which defends Christianity against the attacks of Judaism by means of a discussion between Justin and a Jew named Trypho.

Tatian — from Syria or Assyria, writing in the middle of the second century. Known chiefly for his *Diatessaron* which interweaves the four gospels into one continuous narrative.

Irenaeus — born in Asia Minor, probably in the second quarter of the second century; made bishop of Lyons, which post he held till his death, *ca.* 200. Known chiefly for his book refuting various Gnostic schools, *Refutation of Gnosticism,* or *Against Heresies*—the oldest surviving work in which the church repudiated heresy—he also wrote several other books and many letters which must have been almost treatises. His *Refutation* is known mostly from an early Latin translation.

Theodotus — late second century; a follower of the Gnostic heretic, Valentinus of Alexandria; excerpts from his writings have been recorded by Clement.

Tertullian — born in Carthage *ca.* 150–55, studied law; converted to Christianity *ca.* 190–95, but broke with the "Catholic" Church *ca.* 207 in favor of the asceticism of the Montanists. Father of Latin theology, he wrote in Latin; when he died *ca.* 223, he had left the Montanists and founded a sect of his own. His chief polemical work was *Against Marcion* in five books written over a period of about twelve years, 200–12.

Clement of Alexandria — successor of Pantaenus as head of the Alexandrian catechetical school from *ca.* 200 till his death about 215; he was also a presbyter in the Alexandrian church. Perhaps not a great theologian, Clement was a kind of Greek puritan who understood philosophy to be a servant of Christianity, having led the Greeks to Christ. Four of his more important surviving works are: the *Exhortation to the Heathen;* the *Protrepticus,* or *Address,* designed to convert pagans; the *Instructor,* the first treatise on Christian conduct; and the *Stromateis,* or *Miscellanies* which is a scrapbook of many thoughts Clement wished to preserve.

Origen — born in 184–85, lived mostly in Alexandria where he headed the catechetical school, and in Caesarea where he probably died in 254 during the Decian persecution. He was the greatest Christian scholar and the most prolific Christian writer of antiquity, having written thousands of scrolls about the length of the Gospel of Matthew. He was a biblical critic and exegete, interpreting scripture allegorically. He wrote numerous commentaries and doctrinal works including *On Prayer;* a great apology, *Contra Celsum* (Against Celsus), which is a defense of Christianity against the attacks of the pagan Celsus; and what may perhaps be considered Christianity's first systematic theology, *De Principiis* (On First Principles), in four books. He was also the compiler of the famous Hexapla which contained the Old Testament in six columns—the Hebrew, a Greek transliteration of the Hebrew, the Septuagint, and the Greek translations of Aquila, Theodotion, and Symmachus. This must have been about nine thousand pages long.

Hippolytus — born *ca.* 170, spent most of his life in Rome where he was a presbyter, and bishop for about seven years (222–23 to 230) when he split with Calixtus who had been elected bishop. He was sent into exile to the mines of Sardinia in 235 and died there or in Rome probably the following year; he was buried on the road to Tivoli. He wrote many books but is known chiefly for his *Refutation of All Heresies* which seeks to show that the heresies had their source in Greek philosophy and in paganism.

Cyprian — cited in this book only as giving manuscript support. Born probably in Carthage *ca.* 200–210; spent all his life there; was bishop of Carthage from 248–49 till his death as a martyr in 258, when he was beheaded.

Eusebius of Caesarea — born *ca.* 260, probably in Palestine; bishop of Caesarea from *ca.* 315 till his death in 340. Played a prominent part at the Council of Nicea; known chiefly for his *Church History* in ten books, written between 323 and 325; also wrote *Theophany,* a brief exposition of the meaning of Christ, toward the end of his life.

Didymus — a disciple of Origen; blinded in early youth; one of the last presidents of the catechetical school at Alexandria; died *ca.* 398. Noted chiefly for his exegesis of biblical books and his three books, *On the Trinity.* Also surviving is a treatise on the Holy Spirit in a Latin translation.

Epiphanius of Salamis — born in Palestine between 310 and 320; an ascetic; became bishop of Salamis, capital of Cyprus, in 367; spent life hunting heretics and died at sea on his way from Constantinople to Cyprus in 403. He wrote the *Ancoratus,* which is a defense of Christian doctrine, in 373; and, most important, the *Panarion*—his work against heresies—between 374 and 377. In this he tracks down eighty heresies, twenty of which precede the time of Christ, and the first of which is barbarism, from Adam to the Flood.

Jerome — born in Stridon, Dalmatia, between 331 and 342; educated in Rome where he was baptized *ca.* 370, becoming an ascetic. In 385 he left Rome for Jerusalem where he presided over a monastery till his death in 420. His supreme gift to Christendom was the Vulgate—his translation of the whole Bible into Latin (*cf.* p. xix). Also of great importance are his many commentaries on biblical books; his dialogue against the Pelagians in three books (415 A.D.); and *On Illustrious Men,* written in 392 and 393, which is a list of ecclesiastical writers from the apostles to his own times, with their main works. Many of his letters are also preserved.

Augustine — cited in this book only as giving manuscript support; born in North Africa in 354, died in August, 430. Chiefly known for his *Confessions, City of God,* commentaries, etc. Tremendous influence on subsequent theology.

Peter of Laodicea — a bishop (although not always so acknowledged) of Laodicea, in the seventh century, who wrote commentaries on the four gospels.

Peter of Riga — author of the poem, *Aurora,* written in the late twelfth century. In the thirteenth century McClean manuscript of this poem, bequeathed to the Fitzwilliam Museum, are many marginal notations in Latin. One such notation which is an answer to the question asked in the text, "Why did not the buyers and sellers resist our Lord?" is found in this book.

Noncanonical Gospels

Gospel of the Ebionites — written in the first half of the second century. It was apparently an abridged and altered form of the Gospel of Matthew, which Epiphanius incorrectly refers to as the "Gospel of the Hebrews" or the "Hebrew Gospel." Written in Greek and assuming all three of the synoptic gospels, this gospel was used by the Jewish Christian sect known as the Ebionites, who denied the virgin birth, and believed that Jesus' sonship to God rested entirely on the union of the Holy Spirit with Jesus that was made at Jesus' baptism. The seven extant fragments of the work are found in Epiphanius' *Against Heresies XXX, 13–22.*

Gospel of the Hebrews — written in the first half of the second century, for Greek-speaking Jewish Christian circles. It probably originated in Egypt—one reason for this supposition being that its main witnesses are the Alexandrians, Clement and Origen. The gospel is apparently not a development from any of the four canonical gospels. It contains traditions of Jesus' pre-existence and coming into the world.

Gospel of the Egyptians — probably from the first half of the second century, it was used by Christians in Egypt perhaps as their only "life of Jesus." Though it was influenced by Gnosticism, it was quoted by II Clement. Clement of Alexandria also quoted it *(Miscellanies, Book III)*, and not as heresy; but Origen regarded this gospel as heretical. It is ascetic on sexual matters.

Gospel of the Naassenes — quoted by Hippolytus in Book V of his *Refutation of All Heresies.* The origin of the Naassenes, or Ophites, i.e., Serpent-Worshipers, is unknown, but they practiced heathen rites and were considered heretics by Hippolytus.

Gospel of the Nazaraeans — appeared in the first half of the second century, in Syrian, Jewish Christian circles. It is apparently an Aramaic translation of a Greek form of the Gospel of Matthew. It is first quoted by Hegesippus *ca.* 180, and probably originated in Syria.

Gospel of Peter — coming from the middle of the second century, it is a development in a Gnostic direction of the four canonical gospels. It is not, however, a full-blown Gnostic work. It was known by reference only (i.e., there were no extant quotations from it) until the winter of 1886-87 when a fragment of it, coming from the eighth or ninth century, was found at Akhmim in Upper Egypt. The gospel began with Pilate's washing of his hands and ended with a unique description of Jesus' resurrection.

Acts of Philip — a fourth century Gnostic work which we know from fragments of later revisions.

Gospel of Thomas — a late fourth or early fifth century "gospel," consisting of sayings of Jesus, but no narrative, that was found *ca.* 1945 near the village of Nag Hammadi, up the Nile River in Egypt. The sayings, written in Sahidic Coptic, almost certainly originated in Greek, *ca.* 140. An early Greek form of some of the sayings appears in the Oxyrhynchus papyrus fragments.

INDEX OF NONCANONICAL PARALLELS

INDEX OF THE GOSPEL PARALLELS

Introductory Note

The Index of Parallels which follows is a double one. The first set of references (in bold face) contains the main passages; the second set contains those sections which may be regarded as parallels apart from context considerations. The *italics* in the second set of references denote those passages in the Synopsis indicated only by cross-references (i.e., without the printing of the text).

THE INFANCY NARRATIVES

The Matthean Infancy Narrative (Matthew 1, 2)

		PAGE
A. The Genealogy of Jesus	1: 1–17	1
B. The Birth of Jesus	18–25	2
C. The Visit of the Wise Men	2: 1–12	3
D. The Flight into Egypt. The Killing of the Babies. The Return from Egypt	13–23	3

The Lucan Infancy Narrative (Luke 1, 2)

E. The Prologue to the Gospel	1: 1–4	4
F. The Promise of the Baptist's Birth	5–25	4
G. The Annunciation	26–38	5
H. Mary's Visit to Elizabeth	39–56	6
I. The Birth of the Baptist	57–80	7
J. The Birth of Jesus	2: 1–20	8
K. The Circumcision of Jesus and the Presentation in the Temple	21–40	9
L. Jesus at Twelve Years	41–52	10

THE GALILEAN SECTION (Matthew 3—18 = Mark 1—9 = Luke 3:12—9:50)

§		MAT	MAR	LUK	Parallels and Doublets MAT	MAR	LUK	Pg
1	John the Baptist	**3: 1–6**	**1: 1–6**	**3: 1–6**	*11:10*	*1:15*	*7:27*	11
2	John's Preaching of Repentance	**7–10**	—	**7–9**	*7:19*			12
3	John's Preaching to Special Groups	—	—	**10–14**				13
4	John's Preaching about the Coming One	**11–12**	**7–8**	**15–18**				13
5	John's Imprisonment	—	—	**19–20**	*14:3–4*	*6:17–18*		13
6	The Baptism of Jesus	**13–17**	**9–11**	**21–22**				14
7	The Genealogy of Jesus	—	—	**23–38**	1:1–16			15
8	The Temptation	**4:1–11**	**12–13**	**4:1–13**				16
9	The First Preaching in Galilee	**12–17**	**14–15**	**14–15**				17
10	The Rejection at Nazareth	—	—	**16–30**	13:54–58	6:1–6a		18
11	The Call of the First Disciples	**18–22**	**16–20**	—			*5:1–11*	20
12	Jesus in the Synagogue at Capernaum	—	**21–28**	**31–37**	7:28–29			20
13	The Healing of Peter's Mother-in-Law	—	**29–31**	**38–39**	8:14–15			21
14	The Sick Healed at Evening	—	**32–34**	**40–41**	*4:24;* 8:16–17; 12:16	3:10–11		22
15	Jesus Departs from Capernaum	—	**35–38**	**42–43**				22

§		MAT	MAR	LUK	Parallels and Doublets MAT	Parallels and Doublets MAR	Parallels and Doublets LUK	Pg
16	A Preaching Journey in Galilee	**23–25**	**39**	**44**	*8:16;* 9:35 12:15; 14:35	3:7, 8, 10 6:54–55	6:17–19	23
17	The Miraculous Catch of Fish	—	—	**5:1–11**	*4:18–22*	*1:16–20*		24

The Sermon on the Mount (Matthew 5—7)

§		MAT	MAR	LUK	MAT	MAR	LUK	Pg
18	Introduction	**5:1–2**	—	—		*3:13*	6:12, 20	24
19	The Beatitudes	**3–13**	—	—			6:20–23	25
20	The Parables of Salt and Light	**13–16**	—	—		4:21; 9:50	8:16; 11:33 14:34–35	26
21	Words of Jesus on the Law	**17–20**	—	—	*24:35*	*13:31*	16:17 21:33	26
22	On Anger	**21–26**	—	—			12:57–59	27
23	On Adultery	**27–30**	—	—	18:8–9	9:43–48		28
24	On Divorce	**31–32**	—	—	19:9	10:11, 12	16:18	28
25	On Swearing	**33–37**	—	—	*23:16–22*			29
26	On Retaliation	**38–42**	—	—			6:29–30	29
27	On Love of One's Enemies	**43–48**	—	—			6:27–28, 32–36	29
28	On Almsgiving	**6:1–4**	—	—				30
29	On Prayer	**5–8**	—	—				31
30	The Lord's Prayer	**9–15**	—	—	*18:35*	11:25 [26]	11:2–4	31
31	Words of Jesus on Fasting	**16–18**	—	—				32
32	On Treasures	**19–21**	—	—			12:33–34	32
33	The Sound Eye	**22–23**	—	—			11:34–36	33
34	Words of Jesus on Serving Two Masters	**24**	—	—			16:13	33
35	On Anxiety	**25–34**	—	—			12:22–31	33
36	On Judging	**7:1–5**	—	—		4:24	6:37–38, 41–42	34
37	On Profaning the Holy	**6**	—	—				35
38	God's Answering of Prayer	**7–11**	—	—			11:9–13	35
39	"The Golden Rule"	**12**	—	—			6:31	36
40	The Narrow Gate	**13–14**	—	—			13:23–24	36
41	The Test of a Good Person	**15–20**	—	—	*3:10* 12:33–35		*3:9* 6:43–45	36
42	On Self-Deception	**21–23**	—	—			6:46 13:26–27	37
43	Hearers and Doers of the Word	**24–27**	—	—			6:47–49	38
44	The End of the Sermon	**28–29**	—	—		1:21, 22	4:31–32 *7:1a*	38
45	The Healing of a Leper	**8:1–4**	**1:40–45**	**5:12–16**		*1:35*	*4:42*	38
46	The Centurion's Servant	**5–13**	—	—			7:1–10	39
47	The Healing of Peter's Mother-in-Law	**14–15**	—	—		*1:29–31*	*4:38–39*	41
48	The Sick Healed at Evening	**16–17**	—	—		*1:32–34*	*4:40–41*	41
49	Would-Be Followers of Jesus	**18–22**	—	—		*4:35*	9:57–60	41
50	Calming the Storm	**23–27**	—	—		*4:35–41*	*8:22–25*	41
51	The Gadarene Demoniacs	**28–34**	—	—		*5:1–20*	*8:26–39*	42
52	The Healing of the Paralytic	**9:1–8**	**2:1–12**	**17–26**				42
53	The Call of Levi	**9–13**	**13–17**	**27–32**			*15:1–2*	44
54	The Question about Fasting	**14–17**	**18–22**	**33–39**				45
55	Jairus' Daughter and a Woman's Faith	**18–26**	—	—		*5:21–43* *10:52*	*7:50;* *8:40–56* *18:42*	46
56	Two Blind Men Healed	**27–31**	—	—	*20:29–34*	*10:46–52*	18:35–43	46
57	The Healing of a Demoniac Who Was Mute	**32–34**	—	—	12:22–24	3:22	11:14–15	46
58	The Sending Out of the Twelve	**35– 10:16**	—	—	4:23; 15:24	3:13–19 6:6b–11, 34	6:13–16 *8:1;* 9:1–5 10:1–12	47

§		MAT	MAR	LUK	Parallels and Doublets MAT	MAR	LUK	Pg
59	Coming Persecutions	**10:17–25**	—	—	24:9, 13	13:9–13	6:40 12:11–12 21:12–17, 19	51
60	Exhortation to Fearless Confession	**26–33**	—	—		4:22; 8:38	8:17; 9:26 12:2–9 21:18	52
61	Division in Households	**34–36**	—	—			12:51–53	53
62	Conditions of Discipleship	**37–39**	—	—	16:24–25	8:34–35	9:23–24 14:26–27 17:33	53
63	End of the Discourse	**40–11:1**	—	—	18:5	9:37, 41	9:48; 10:16	54
64	John's Question to Jesus	**11:2–6**	—	—			7:18–23	55
65	Jesus' Words about John	**7–19**	—	—	*21:32*	*1:2; 9:13*	7:24–35 16:16	55
66	Woes to Unrepentant Cities	**20–24**	—	—			10:13–15	57
67	Jesus' Thanksgiving to the Father	**25–27**	—	—			10:21–22	57
68	Comfort for the Weary	**28–30**	—	—				58
69	Plucking Heads of Grain on the Sabbath	**12:1–8**	**23–28**	**6:1–5**				58
70	The Healing of the Man with the Withered Hand	**9–14**	**3:1–6**	**6–11**			13:15–16 14:3, 5	59
71	Jesus Heals the Multitudes	**15–21**	**7–12**		4:24–25 14:36	6:56	6:17–19 4:41	60
72	The Call of the Twelve	—	**13–19**	**12–16**	*5:1;* 10:1–4	6:7	9:1, 2	62

The Sermon on the Plain (Luke 6:20–49)

§		MAT	MAR	LUK	Parallels and Doublets MAT	MAR	LUK	Pg
73	The Beatitudes	—	—	**6:20–23**	5:3, 4, 6, 11, 12			63
74	The Woes	—	—	**24–26**				63
75	On Love of One's Enemies	—	—	**27–36**	5:39–42, 44–48; 7:12			64
76	On Judging	—	—	**37–42**	7:1–5 10:24–25 15:14	4:24		65
77	The Test of a Good Person	—	—	**43–46**	7:16–21 12:33–35			65
78	Hearers and Doers of the Word	—	—	**47–49**	7:24–27			66
79	The Centurion's Slave	—	—	**7:1–10**	*7:28a;* *8:5–13*			67
80	The Widow's Son at Nain	—	—	**11–17**				67
81	John's Question to Jesus	—	—	**18–23**	*11:2–6*			68
82	Jesus' Words about John	—	—	**24–35**	*11:7–19* 21:32	*1:2*		68
83	The Woman with the Ointment	—	—	**36–50**	*9:22* *26:6–13*	*5:34; 10:52* *14:3–9*		69
84	The Ministering Women	—	—	**8:1–3**	*4:23; 9:35* *27:55*	*15:41; 16:9*		69
85	Accusations against Jesus	**12:22–24**	**3:19b–22**	—	*9:32f;* 9:34		11:14–16	70
86	A House Divided	**25–37**	**23–30**	—	7:16–20	9:40	6:43–45 9:50 11:17–23 12:10	70
87	Against Seeking for Signs	**38–42**	—	—	16:1, 2, 4	8:11–12	11:29–32	72
88	The Return of the Unclean Spirit	**43–45**	—	—			11:24–26	73
89	Jesus' True Relatives	**46–50**	**31–35**	—			8:19–21	73
90	The Parable of the Sower	**13:1–9**	**4:1–9**	**4–8**			*5:1–3*	74

§		MAT	MAR	LUK	Parallels and Doublets			Pg
					MAT	MAR	LUK	
91	The Reason for Speaking in Parables	**10–15**	**10–12**	**9–10**		*4:25*	*8:18b*	75
92	The Blessedness of the Disciples	**16–17**	—	—			10:23–24	76
93	The Interpretation of the Parable of the Sower	**18–23**	**13–20**	**11–15**				76
94	The Purpose of Parables	—	**21–25**	**16–18**	5:15; 7:2 10:26		6:38; 11:33 12:2	77
95	The Parable of the Seed Growing Secretly	—	**26–29**	—				78
96	The Parable of the Weeds	**24–30**	—	—				78
97	The Parable of the Mustard Seed	**31–32**	**30–32**	—			13:18–19	78
98	The Parable of the Yeast	**33**	—	—			13:20–21	79
99	Jesus' Use of Parables	**34–35**	**33–34**	—				79
100	The Interpretation of the Parable of the Weeds	**36–43**	—	—				79
101	The Parables of the Hidden Treasure and of the Pearl	**44–46**	—	—				80
102	The Parable of the Net	**47–50**	—	—				80
103	Treasures New and Old	**51–52**	—	—				80
104	Jesus' True Relatives	—	—	**19–21**	*12:46–50*	*3:31–35*		80
105	The Stilling of the Storm	—	**35–41**	**22–25**	8:18, 23–27			81
106	The Gerasene Demoniac	—	**5:1–20**	**26–39**	8:28–34			81
107	Jarius' Daughter and a Woman's Faith	—	**21–43**	**40–56**	9:18–26			83
108	Jesus Is Rejected at Nazareth	**13:53–58**	**6:1–6a**	—			*4:16–30*	86
109	The Sending out of the Twelve	—	**6b–13**	**9:1–6**	9:35; 10:1, 9–11, 14	3:14–15	*10:1–12*	86
110	Herod Thinks Jesus Is John, Raised	**14:1–2**	**14–16**	**7–9**				87
111	The Death of John	**3–12**	**17–29**	—			3:19–20	88
112	The Return of the Twelve, and the Feeding of the Five Thousand	**13–21**	**30–44**	**10–17**	9:36 *15:32–39*	*8:1–10*	10:17	89
113	The Walking on the Water	**22–33**	**45–52**	—				91
114	Healings at Gennesaret	**34–36**	**53–56**	—	4:24	*1:32f.*; 3:10	*4:40f.* *6:18–19*	92
115	What Defiles a Person	**15:1–20**	**7:1–23**	—			6:39	92
116	The Syrophoenician Woman	**21–28**	**24–30**	—				94
117	The Healing of Many Sick People (Matthew) and of the Deaf Person with a Speech Impediment (Mark)	**15:29–31**	**7:31–37**	—				95
118	The Feeding of the Four Thousand	**32–39**	**8:1–10**	—	*14:13–21*	*6:30–44*	*9:10–17*	95
119	The Pharisees Seek a Sign	**16:1–4**	**11–13**	—	12:38–39		11:16, 29 12:54–56	96
120	The Yeast of the Pharisees and of Herod	**5–12**	**14–21**	—			12:1	97
121	The Blind Man of Bethsaida	—	**22–26**	—				98
122	The Confession at Caesarea Philippi and the First Prediction of the Passion	**13–23**	**27–33**	**9:18–22**	18:18			99
123	The Conditions of Discipleship	**24–28**	**34–9:1**	**23–27**	10:33, 38–39		12:9; 14:27 17:33	100
124	The Transfiguration	**17:1–8**	**9:2–8**	**28–36**				101
125	The Coming of Elijah	**9–13**	**9–13**	—			*9:37*	102
126	The Healing of the Boy with a Spirit	**14–21**	**14–29**	**37–43a**	*17:9;* 21:21	*9:9* 11:22–23	17:6	103
127	The Second Prediction of the Passion	**22–23**	**30–32**	**43b–45**				105
128	The Temple Tax	**24–27**	—	—				105
129	The Dispute about Greatness	**18:1–5**	**33–37**	**46–48**	10:40 20:26–27 23:11–12	10:15, 43–44	*10:16* 14:11 18:14, 17 22:26	106
130	Another Exorcist	—	**38–41**	**49–50**	10:42 12:30		11:23	107
131	On Temptations	**6–9**	**42–48**	—	5:29–30		17:1–2	107

					Parallels and Doublets			
§		MAT	MAR	LUK	MAT	MAR	LUK	Pg
132	Concerning Salt	—	**49–50**	—	5:13		14:34–35	108
133	The Parable of the Lost Sheep	**10–14**	—	—			15:3–7	109
134	On Reproving Another Believer	**15–20**	—	—	16:19		17:3	109
135	On Forgiveness	**21–22**	—	—			17:4	110
136	The Parable of the Unmerciful Servant	**23–35**	—	—	6:15			110

LUKE'S SPECIAL SECTION (Luke 9:51—18:14)

§		MAT	MAR	LUK	MAT	MAR	LUK	Pg
137	The Samaritan Villagers	—	—	**9:51–56**				111
138	Would-Be Followers of Jesus	—	—	**57–62**	8:19–22			111
139	The Sending out of the Seventy	—	—	**10:1–16**	9:37–38 10:7–16, 40 11:21–23 *18:5*	*6:6–11* *9:37*	*9:1–5, 48*	112
140	The Return of the Seventy	—	—	**17–20**		*6:30* *16:17–18*	*9:10*	113
141	Jesus' Gratitude to the Father	—	—	**21–22**	11:25–27			114
142	The Blessedness of the Disciples	—	—	**23–24**	13:16–17			114
143	The Lawyer's Question	—	—	**25–28**	22:34–40	12:28–31		114
144	The Parable of the Good Samaritan	—	—	**29–37**				115
145	Martha and Mary	—	—	**38–42**				116
146	The Lord's Prayer	—	—	**11:1–4**	6:9–13			116
147	The Friend at Midnight	—	—	**5–8**				117
148	The Answer to Prayer	—	—	**9–13**	7:7–11			117
149	The Beelzebul Controversy	—	—	**14–23**	9:32–34 12:22–30 *12:38; 16:1*	3:22–27 *9:40; 8:11*	*9:50; 11:29*	117
150	The Return of the Unclean Spirit	—	—	**24–26**	12:43–45			119
151	True Blessedness	—	—	**27–28**				119
152	The Sign of Noah	—	—	**29–32**	12:38–42 16:1, 2, 4	8:11–12	*11:16*	119
153	The Light of the Body	—	—	**33–36**	5:15 6:22–23	*4:21*	*8:16*	120
154	Discourse against the Pharisees	—	—	**37–12:1**	*15:1ff.* *16:6, 12* 23:4–36	*7:1ff.; 8:15* 12:38, 39	20:46	120
155	Exhortation to Fearless Confession	—	—	**12:2–12**	10:19–20, 26–33 12:32	3:28–29 4:22; 8:38 13:11	8:17; 9:26 21:14, 15	122
156	The Parable of the Rich Fool	—	—	**13–21**				124
157	On Anxiety	—	—	**22–34**	6:19–21, 25–33			125
158	Watchfulness and Faithfulness	—	—	**35–46**	24:43–51 *25:1–13*	13:35–36		126
159	The Slave's Wages	—	—	**47–48**			*17:7–10*	127
160	Jesus the Cause of Division	—	—	**49–56**	10:34–36 16:2–3	10:38		127
161	Settling with One's Accuser	—	—	**57–59**	5:25–26			128
162	Repentance or Destruction	—	—	**13:1–9**				128
163	The Healing of the Crippled Woman	—	—	**10–17**	12:11–12		*14:1–6* 14:5	128
164	The Parables of the Mustard Seed and the Yeast	—	—	**18–21**	13:31–33	4:30–32		129

§		MAT	MAR	LUK	Parallels and Doublets MAT	MAR	LUK	Pg
165	The Narrow Door	—	—	**22–30**	7:13–14, 22–23 8:11–12 25:10–12 19:30 20:16	10:31		130
166	The Departure from Galilee	—	—	**31–33**				131
167	The Lament over Jerusalem	—	—	**34–35**	23:37–39			131
168	The Healing of a Man with Dropsy	—	—	**14:1–6**	*12:9–14*	*3:1–6*	*6:6–11* *13:10–17*	131
169	Teaching on Humility	—	—	**7–14**	*18:4; 23:12*		*18:14*	132
170	The Parable of the Great Dinner	—	—	**15–24**	22:1–10			132
171	The Cost of Discipleship	—	—	**25–35**	*5:13* 10:37–38 16:24	8:34; *9:50*	9:23	133
172	The Parables of the Lost Sheep and the Lost Coin	—	—	**15:1–10**	*9:10–11* 18:12–14	*2:15–16*	*5:29–30*	134
173	The Parable of the Prodigal Son and His Brother	—	—	**11–32**				135
174	The Unjust Steward	—	—	**16:1–13**	6:24			136
175	The Hypocrisy of the Pharisees	—	—	**14–15**				137
176	About the Law and about Divorce	—	—	**16–18**	5:18, 32 11:12–13 *19:9*	*10:11, 12*		137
177	The Rich Man and Lazarus	—	—	**19–31**				137
178	On Causing Sin	—	—	**17:1–2**	18:6–7	9:42		138
179	On Forgiveness	—	—	**3–4**	18:15, 21–22			138
180	On Faith	—	—	**5–6**	17:20 21:21	11:22–23		139
181	The Slave's Wages	—	—	**7–10**				139
182	The Healing of Ten Lepers	—	—	**11–19**				139
183	On the Kingdom of God	—	—	**20–21**	24:33	13:21		140
184	The Day of the Son of Man	—	—	**22–37**	10:39 16:25 24:17–18, 26–28, 37–41	8:35 13:15–16	9:24	140
185	The Parable of the Widow and the Unjust Judge	—	—	**18:1–8**				141
186	The Parable of the Pharisee and the Tax Collector	—	—	**9–14**	*18:4* *23:12*		*14:11*	142

THE JUDEAN SECTION (Matthew 19—27 = Mark 10—15 = Luke 18:15—23:40)

The Journey to Jerusalem (Matthew 19—20 = Mark 10 = Luke 18:15—19:27)

187	Marriage and Divorce	**19:1–12**	**10:1–12**	—	5:32		16:18	143
188	Jesus Blesses the Children	**13–15**	**13–16**	**18:15–17**	18:3			144
189	The Rich Young Man	**16–30**	**17–31**	**18–30**	*20:16*		13:30 22:28–30	145
190	The Parable of the Laborers in the Vineyard	**20:1–16**	—	—	*19:30*			147
191	The Third Prediction of the Passion	**17–19**	**32–34**	**31–34**				148
192	Jesus and the Sons of Zebedee	**20–28**	**35–45**	—	*23:11*	*9:35*	*9:48b 12:50* 22:24–27	148

					Parallels and Doublets			
§		MAT	MAR	LUK	MAT	MAR	LUK	Pg
193	The Healing of Bartimaeus	**29–34**	**46–52**	**35–43**	*9:27–31*			149
194	Zacchaeus	—	—	**19:1–10**				150
195	The Parable of the Pounds	—	—	**11–27**	*13:12* 25:14–30	*4:25*	*8:18*	151

The Days in Jerusalem (Matthew 21—25 = Mark 11—13 = Luke 19:28—21:7)

§		MAT	MAR	LUK	MAT	MAR	LUK	Pg
196	The Entry into Jerusalem	**21:1–9**	**11:1–10**	**19:28–38**				153
197	Prediction of the Destruction of Jerusalem	—	—	**39–44**	*21:14–16*			154
198	Jesus Cleanses the Temple	**10–17**	**11**	**45–46**		*11:15–19*	*19:39–40*	154
199	The Cursing of the Fig Tree	**18–19**	**12–14**	—				155
200	The Cleansing of the Temple	—	**15–19**	**47–48**	21:12–13 *22:33*		19:45–46 *21:37*	156
201	The Lesson from the Withered Fig Tree	**20–22**	**20–25** **[26]**	—	6:14, 15 17:20		17:6	156
202	The Question about Jesus' Authority	**23–27**	**27–33**	**20:1–8**				157
203	The Parable of the Two Sons	**28–32**	—	—			7:29–30	158
204	The Parable of the Wicked Tenants	**33–46**	**12:1–12**	**9–19**	*22:22*			158
205	The Parable of the Wedding Banquet	**22:1–14**	—	—			14:16–24	160
206	The Question of Paying Taxes to Caesar	**15–22**	**13–17**	**20–26**		*12:12*		161
207	The Question about the Resurrection	**23–33**	**18–27**	**27–40**	*22:46*	*11:18* *12:32, 34*		162
208	The Great Commandment	**34–40**	**28–34**	—	*22:46*		10:25–28 *20:39, 40*	163
209	About David's Son	**41–46**	**35–37a**	**41–44**		*12:34*	*20:40*	164
210	Jesus Denounces Scribes and Pharisees	**23:1–36**	**37b–40**	**45–47**	*3:7* *20:26, 27*	*9:35* *10:43, 44*	*3:7; 9:48* 11:39–52 *14:11 18:4, 14 22:26*	165
211	The Lament over Jerusalem	**37–39**	—	—			13:34–35	168
212	The Widow's Gift	—	**41–44**	**21:1–4**				169
213	Prediction of the Destruction of the Temple	**24:1–3**	**13:1–4**	**5–7**				169

The Synoptic Apocalypse (Matthew 24:4–36 = Mark 13:5–37 = Luke 21:8–36)

§		MAT	MAR	LUK	MAT	MAR	LUK	Pg
214	The Signs of the End of the Age	**24:4–8**	**13:5–8**	**21:8–11**	*24:23–26*	*13:21–22*	*17:23*	170
215	The Coming of Persecution	**9–14**	**9–13**	**12–19**	10:17–22, 30		12:7, 11, 12	170
216	The Desolating Sacrilege	**15–22**	**14–20**	**20–24**			17:31	172
217	False Messiahs Will Arise	**23–25**	**21–23**	—			*17:21*	173
218	The Day of the Son of Man	**26–28**	—	—			17:23–24, 37	173
219	The Coming of the Son of Man	**29–31**	**24–27**	**25–28**				173
220	The Lesson of the Fig Tree	**32–33**	**28–29**	**29–31**				174
221	The Day and Hour Are Unknown Except to God	**34–36**	**30–32**	**32–33**	*5:17* *16:28*	*9:1*	*9:27* *16:17*	174
222	The Necessity of Watchfulness	—	**33–37**	—	24:42 25:13–14, 15b		12:38, 40 19:12–13	175
223	Luke's Ending to the Discourse	—	—	**34–36**				175
224	The Suddenness of the Coming of the Son of Man	**37–41**	—	—			17:26–27, 34–35	176
225	The Watchful House Owner	**42–44**	—	—		*13:33, 35*	12:39–40	176
226	The Faithful and Wise Slave	**45–51**	—	—			12:42–46	177

§		MAT	MAR	LUK	Parallels and Doublets MAT	MAR	LUK	Pg
227	The Parable of the Ten Bridesmaids	**25:1–13**	—	—		*13:35–37*	12:35–36 13:25	177
228	The Parable of the Talents	**14–30**	—	—	*13:12*	*4:25* *13:34*	*8:18* 19:12–27	178
229	The Last Judgment	**31–46**	—	—				179
230	A Summary of the Days Spent in Jerusalem	—	—	**37–38**	*21:17*	*11:19*		180

The Passion Narrative (Matthew 26—27 = Mark 14—15 = Luke 22—23)

§		MAT	MAR	LUK	MAT	MAR	LUK	Pg
231	The Conspiracy against Jesus	**26:1–5**	**14:1–2**	**22:1–2**				181
232	The Anointing at Bethany	**6–13**	**3–9**	—			*7:36–50*	181
233	Judas Agrees to Betray Jesus	**14–16**	**10–11**	**3–6**				182
234	Preparation for the Passover	**17–19**	**12–16**	**7–13**				182

The Last Supper (Matthew 26:20–29 = Mark 14:17–25 = Luke 22:14–38)

§		MAT	MAR	LUK	MAT	MAR	LUK	Pg
235	The Traitor	**26:20–25**	**14:17–21**	**22:14**			22:21–23	183
236	The Institution of the Lord's Supper	**26–29**	**22–25**	**15–20**				184
237	Last Words	—	—	**21–38**				185
	a) The Betrayal Foretold	—	—	**21–23**	*26:21–25*	*14:18–21*		185
	b) Greatness in the Kingdom of God	—	—	**24–30**	19:28 20:25–28	*9:35* 10:42–45	*9:48b*	185
	c) Peter's Denial Predicted	—	—	**31–34**	*26:30–35*	*14:26–31*		186
	d) Purse, Bag, and Sword	—	—	**35–38**				186
238	Peter's Denial Predicted	**30–35**	**26–31**	**39**			22:31–34	187
239	Jesus in Gethsemane	**36–46**	**32–42**	**40–46**				188
240	Jesus Taken Captive	**47–56**	**43–52**	**47–53**				189
241	Jesus before the Council. Peter's Denial	**57–75**	**53–72**	**54–71**	*27:1*	*15:1*		190
242	Jesus Delivered to Pilate	**27:1–2**	**15:1**	**23:1**			22:66	193
243	The Death of Judas	**3–10**	—	—				194
244	The Trial before Pilate	**11–14**	**2–5**	**2–5**				194
245	Jesus before Herod	—	—	**6–16**	*27:12*	*15:3*		195
246	The Sentence of Death	**15–26**	**6–15**	**17–25**				195
247	The Mocking of the Soldiers	**27–31**	**16–20**	—			*23:26*	197
248	Simon of Cyrene Carries Jesus' Cross	**32**	**21**	**26–32**	*27:38*	*15:27*		198
249	The Crucifixion	**33–44**	**22–32**	**33–43**	*27:48*	*15:36*		199
250	The Death on the Cross	**45–56**	**33–41**	**44–49**			*8:3 23:36*	201
251	The Burial of Jesus	**57–61**	**42–47**	**50–56**		*16:1*		203
252	The Guard at the Tomb	**62–66**	—	—				204
253	The Empty Tomb	**28:1–10**	**16:1–8**	**24:1–12**				204

APPEARANCES OF THE RISEN LORD

The Matthean Narrative (28:11–20)

PAGE

AA. The Bribing of the Soldiers 28:11–15 206
BB. The Commissioning of the Disciples 28:16–20 207

The Lucan Narrative (24:13–53)

CC. The Road to Emmaus 24:13–35 207
DD. Jesus Appears to the Disciples 24:36–49 208
EE. The Ascension 24:50–53 209

The Longer Ending of Mark (16:9–20) 209

THE INFANCY NARRATIVES

The Matthean Infancy Narrative

Matthew 1–2

§ A THE GENEALOGY OF JESUS

MAT 1:1–17	MAR	Δ *LUK 3:23–34* (*§ 7, p. 15*)
1 An account of the genealogy of Jesus the Messiah, the son		(In reverse order.)
of David, the son of Abraham.		
2 Abraham was the father of Isaac,		34 *Abraham*
and Isaac the father of Jacob,		*Isaac*
and Jacob the father of Judah and his brothers,		*Jacob*
3 and Judah the father of Perez and Zerah by Tamar,		33 *Judah*
and Perez the father of Hezron,		*Perez*
and Hezron the father of Aram,		*Hezron, Arni, Admin,*
4 and Aram the father of Aminadab,		
and Aminadab the father of Nahshon,		*Amminadab*
and Nahshon the father of Salmon,		32 *Nahshon*
5 and Salmon the father of Boaz by Rahab,		*Sala*
and Boaz the father of Obed by Ruth,		*Boaz*
and Obed the father of Jesse,		*Obed*
6 and Jesse the father of King David.		*Jesse*
And David was the father of Solomon by the wife of Uriah,		31 *David*
7 and Solomon the father of Rehoboam,		
and Rehoboam the father of Abijah,		*Nathan*
and Abijah the father of Asaph,[A]		*Mattatha*
8 and Asaph[A] the father of Jehoshaphat,		*Menna*
and Jehoshaphat the father of Joram,		*Melea*
and Joram the father of Uzziah,		30 *Eliakim*
9 and Uzziah the father of Jotham,		*Jonam*
and Jotham the father of Ahaz,		*Joseph*
and Ahaz the father of Hezekiah,		*Judah*
10 and Hezekiah the father of Manasseh,		*Simeon*
and Manasseh the father of Amos,[B]		29 *Levi*
and Amos[B] the father of Josiah,		*Matthat*
11 and Josiah the father of Jechoniah and his brothers, at		*Jorim*
the time of the deportation to Babylon.		*Eliezer, Joshua,* 28 *Er,*
		Elmadam, Cosam, Addi,
12 And after the deportation to Babylon: Jechoniah was the		*Melchi,* 27 *Neri*
father of Salathiel,		
and Salathiel the father of Zerubbabel,		*Shealtiel*
13 and Zerubbabel the father of Abiud,		*Zerubbabel*
and Abiud the father of Eliakim,		

✧ MAT 1:2–6 — 1CH 2:1–15. ✧ MAT 1:3–6 — RTH 4:18–22. ✧ MAT 1:7–12 — 1CH 3:10–19.

✦ [A] text: P^{1} S B C ø it (some MSS.) sa bo; *Asa*: W ℜ it (some MSS.) vg sy^{c} sy^{s} sy^{p} ✦ [B] text: S B C Θ λ it sa bo; *Amon*: W ø ℜ vg sy^{c} sy^{s} sy^{p}.

and Eliakim the father of Azor,
14 and Azor the father of Zadok,
and Zadok the father of Achim,
and Achim the father of Eliud,
15 and Eliud the father of Eleazar,
and Eleazar the father of Matthan,

and Matthan the father of Jacob,
16 and Jacob the father of Joseph the husband of
Mary, of whom Jesus was born, who is called the
Messiah.[C] 17 So all the generations from Abraham to David
are fourteen generations; and from David to the deportation
to Babylon, fourteen generations; and from the deportation to Babylon to the Messiah, fourteen generations.

Rhesa
Joanan
26 *Joda*
Josech
Semein
Mattathias
Maath, 25 *Naggai, Esli,*
Nahum, Amos, Mattathias,
24 *Joseph, Jannai,*
Melchi, Levi, Matthat, 23 *Heli*
Joseph

§ B THE BIRTH OF JESUS

MAT 1:18–25	MAR	LUK
18 Now the birth of Jesus[D] the Messiah took place in this way. When his mother Mary had been engaged to Joseph, but before they lived together, she was found to be with child from the Holy Spirit. 19 Her husband Joseph, being a righteous man and unwilling to expose her to public disgrace, planned to dismiss her quietly. 20 But just when he had resolved to do this, an angel of the Lord appeared to him in a dream and said, "Joseph, son of David, do not be afraid to take Mary as your wife, for the child conceived in her is from the Holy Spirit. 21 She will bear a son, and you are to name him Jesus, for he will save his people from their sins." 22 All this took place to fulfill what had been spoken by the Lord through the prophet: 23 "Look, the virgin shall conceive and bear a son, and they shall name him Emmanuel," which means, "God is with us." 24 When Joseph awoke from sleep, he did as the angel of the Lord commanded him; he took her as his wife, 25 but had no marital relations with her until she had borne a son;[E] and he named him Jesus.		

✧ MAT 1:23 — ISA 7:14; 8:8.

✦ [C] text: P^1 S B C W λ 𝔑 it (some MSS.) vg sy^p sa Tert.; *Jacob the father of Joseph, to whom the virgin Mary having been betrothed bore Jesus who is called Christ*: Θ ø it (some MSS.); *Jacob the father of Joseph. Joseph, to whom was betrothed the virgin Mary, was the father of Jesus who is called the Christ*: sy^s; *Jacob the father of Joseph, to whom was betrothed the virgin Mary who* (fem.) *bore Jesus the Christ*: sy^c; *Jacob the father of Joseph the husband of Mary who bore Jesus who is called Christ*: bo.
✦ [D] text: P^1 S C Θ λ ø 𝔑 sy^p sa bo; *Christ Jesus*: B; *Christ*: it vg sy^c sy^s; *Jesus*: W. ✦ [E] text: S B λ ø it sy^c sa bo; *her firstborn son*: C D W 𝔑 vg sy^p; *and she bore him a son*: sy^s.

§ C THE VISIT OF THE WISE MEN

MAT 2:1–12	MAR	LUK

1 In the time of King Herod, after Jesus was born in Bethlehem of Judea, wise men
from the East came to Jerusalem, 2 asking, "Where is the child who has been born
king of the Jews? For we observed his star at its rising, and have come to pay him
homage." 3 When King Herod heard this, he was frightened, and all Jerusalem
with him; 4 and calling together all the chief priests and scribes of the people, he
inquired of them where the Messiah was to be born. 5 They told him,
"In Bethlehem of Judea; for so it has been written by the prophet:

6 'And you, Bethlehem, in the land of Judah,
are by no means least among the rulers of Judah;
for from you shall come a ruler
who is to shepherd my people Israel.' "

7 Then Herod secretly called for the wise men and learned from them the exact time
when the star had appeared. 8 Then he sent them to Bethlehem, saying, "Go and
search diligently for the child; and when you have found him, bring me word so
that I may also go and pay him homage." 9 When they had heard the king, they
set out; and there, ahead of them, went the star that they had seen at its rising,
until it stopped over the place where the child was. 10 When they saw that the star
had stopped, they were overwhelmed with joy. 11 On entering the house, they saw
the child with Mary his mother; and they knelt down and paid him homage. Then,
opening their treasure chests, they offered him gifts of gold, frankincense, and
myrrh. 12 And having been warned in a dream not to return to Herod, they left for
their own country by another road.

§ D THE FLIGHT INTO EGYPT, THE KILLING OF THE BABIES, THE RETURN FROM EGYPT

MAT 2:13–23	MAR	LUK

13 Now after they had left, an angel of the Lord appeared to Joseph in a dream and
said, "Get up, take the child and his mother, and flee to Egypt, and remain there
until I tell you; for Herod is about to search for the child, to destroy him." 14 Then
Joseph got up, took the child and his mother by night, and went to Egypt, 15 and
remained there until the death of Herod. This was to fulfill what had been spoken
by the Lord through the prophet, "Out of Egypt I have called my son." 16 When
Herod saw that he had been tricked by the wise men, he was infuriated, and he
sent and killed all the children in and around Bethlehem who were two years old
or under, according to the time that he had learned from the wise men. 17 Then
was fulfilled what had been spoken through the prophet Jeremiah:

✧ MAT 2:2 — NUM 24:17. ✧ MAT 2:6 — MIC 5:2. ✧ MAT 2:11 — ISA 60:6. ✧ MAT 2:15 — HOS 11:1. ✧ MAT 2:18 — JER 31:15.

◗ To MAT 2:15 *cf.* **Gospel of the Nazaraeans** (in Jerome, *On Illustrious Men 3*). — "Out of Egypt have I called my son" and "For he shall be called a Nazaraean." ◗ To MAT 2:15 *cf.* margin of codex 1424. — This was to fulfill what the Lord had spoken by the prophet, "Out of Egypt have I called my son."

18 "A voice was heard in Ramah,
wailing and loud lamentation,
Rachel weeping for her children;
she refused to be consoled,
because they are no more."

19 When Herod died, an angel of the Lord suddenly appeared in a dream to Joseph
in Egypt and said, 20 "Get up, take the child and his mother, and go to the land of
Israel, for those who were seeking the child's life are dead." 21 Then Joseph got
up, took the child and his mother, and went to the land of Israel. 22 But when he
heard that Archelaus was ruling over Judea in place of his father Herod, he was
afraid to go there. And after being warned in a dream, he went away to the district
of Galilee. 23 There he made his home in a town called Nazareth, so that what had
been spoken through the prophets might be fulfilled, "He will be called a Na-
zorean."

The Lucan Infancy Narrative

Luke 1–2

§ E THE PROLOGUE TO THE GOSPEL

MAT	MAR	LUK 1:1–4

1 Since many have undertaken to set down an orderly account of the events that
have been fulfilled among us, 2 just as they were handed on to us by those who
from the beginning were eyewitnesses and servants of the word, 3 I too decided,
after investigating everything carefully from the very first, to write an orderly
account for you, most excellent Theophilus, 4 so that you may know the truth
concerning the things about which you have been instructed.

§ F THE PROMISE OF THE BAPTIST'S BIRTH

MAT	MAR	LUK 1:5–25

5 In the days of King Herod of Judea, there was a priest named Zechariah,[F] who
belonged to the priestly order of Abijah. His wife was a descendant of Aaron, and
her name was Elizabeth. 6 Both of them were righteous before God, living blame-
lessly according to all the commandments and regulations of the Lord. 7 But they had
no children, because Elizabeth was barren, and both were getting on in years. 8
Once when he was serving as priest before God and his section was on duty, 9 he
was chosen by lot, according to the custom of the priesthood, to enter the sanctuary
of the Lord and offer incense. 10 Now at the time of the incense offering, the whole
assembly of the people was praying outside. 11 Then there appeared to him an angel
of the Lord, standing at the right side of the altar of incense. 12 When Zechariah

---

◇ MAT 2:23 — ISA 11:1 (in Hebrew). ◇ LUK 1:5 — 1CH 24:10.

✦ [F] Greek: *Zacharias*.

saw him, he was terrified; and fear overwhelmed him. 13 But the angel said to
him, “Do not be afraid, Zechariah, for your prayer has been heard. Your wife
Elizabeth will bear you a son, and you will name him John.

14 You will have joy and gladness,
and many will rejoice at his birth,

15 for he will be great in the sight of the Lord.
He must never drink wine or strong drink;
even before his birth he will be filled with the Holy Spirit.

16 He will turn many of the people of Israel to the
Lord their God.

17 With the spirit and power of Elijah he will go before him,
to turn the hearts of parents to their children,
and the disobedient to the wisdom of the righteous,
to make ready a people prepared for the Lord.”

18 Zechariah said to the angel, “How will I know that this is so? For I am an old
man, and my wife is getting on in years.” 19 The angel replied, “I am Gabriel. I
stand in the presence of God, and I have been sent to speak to you and to bring you
this good news. 20 But now, because you did not believe my words, which will
be fulfilled in their time, you will become mute, unable to speak, until the day
these things occur.” 21 Meanwhile the people were waiting for Zechariah, and
wondered at his delay in the sanctuary. 22 When he did come out, he could not
speak to them, and they realized that he had seen a vision in the sanctuary. He
kept motioning to them and remained unable to speak. 23 When his time of service
was ended, he went to his home.
24 After those days his wife Elizabeth conceived, and for five months she remained
in seclusion. She said, 25 “This is what the Lord has done for me when he looked
favorably on me and took away the disgrace I have endured among my people.”

§ G THE ANNUNCIATION

MAT	MAR	LUK 1:26–38

26 In the sixth month the angel Gabriel was sent by God to a town in Galilee called
Nazareth, 27 to a virgin engaged to a man whose name was Joseph, of the house of
David. The virgin’s name was Mary. 28 And he came to her and said, “Greetings,
favored one! The Lord is with you.”[G] 29 But she was much perplexed by his
words and pondered what sort of greeting this might be. 30 The angel said to her,
“Do not be afraid, Mary, for you have found favor with God. 31 And now, you
will conceive in your womb and bear a son, and you will name him Jesus.

✧ LUK 1:15 — NUM 6:3; 1SM 1:11. ✧ LUK 1:17 — MAL 4:5–6; Ecclesiasticus 48:10. ✧ LUK 1:18 — GEN 15:8. ✧ LUK 1:31 — ISA 7:14.

✦ [G] text: S B W λ sa bo; add: *Blessed are you among women!* A C D Θ ø ℜ it vg sy[p].

32 He will be great, and will be called the Son of the Most High,
and the Lord God will give to him the throne of his ancestor David.

33 He will reign over the house of Jacob forever,
and of his kingdom there will be no end."

34 Mary said to the angel, "How can this be, since I am a virgin?" 35 The angel
said to her,

"The Holy Spirit will come upon you,
and the power of the Most High will overshadow you;
therefore the child to be born[H] will be holy; he will be called Son of God.

36 And now, your relative Elizabeth in her old age has also conceived a son; and
this is the sixth month for her who was said to be barren. 37 For nothing will be
impossible with God." 38 Then Mary said, "Here am I, the servant of the Lord;
let it be with me according to your word." Then the angel departed from her.

§ H MARY'S VISIT TO ELIZABETH

MAT	MAR	LUK 1:39–56

39 In those days Mary set out and went with haste to a Judean town in the hill country,
40 where she entered the house of Zechariah and greeted Elizabeth. 41 When
Elizabeth heard Mary's greeting, the child leaped in her womb. And Elizabeth
was filled with the Holy Spirit 42 and exclaimed with a loud cry, "Blessed are you
among women, and blessed is the fruit of your womb. 43 And why has this
happened to me, that the mother of my Lord comes to me? 44 For as soon as I
heard the sound of your greeting, the child in my womb leaped for joy. 45 And
blessed is she who believed that there would be a fulfillment[I] of what was spoken
to her by the Lord." 46 And Mary[J] said,

"My soul magnifies the Lord,
47 and my spirit rejoices in God my Savior,
48 for he has looked with favor on the lowliness of his servant.
Surely, from now on all generations will call me blessed;
49 for the Mighty One has done great things for me,
and holy is his name.
50 His mercy is for those who fear him
from generation to generation.
51 He has shown strength with his arm;
he has scattered the proud in the thoughts of their hearts.
52 He has brought down the powerful from their thrones,

✧ LUK 1:32–33 — ISA 9:6–7; 2SM 7:12–16. ✧ LUK 1:37 — GEN 18:14. ✧ LUK 1:46–55 — 1SM 2:1–10. ✧ LUK 1:47 — HAB 3:18. ✧ LUK 1:48 — 1SM 1:11. ✧ LUK 1:48b — GEN 30:13. ✧ LUK 1:49b — PSA 111:9. ✧ LUK 1:50 — PSA 103:17. ✧ LUK 1:51 — PSA 89:10. ✧ LUK 1:52 — Ecclesiasticus 10:14; EZE 21:31.

✦ [H] text: S A B D W ø ℜ it (some MSS.) vg sa bo; add: *of you*: C Θ λ it (some MSS.) sy[p]. ✦ [I] Or, *believed, for there will be a fulfillment.* ✦ [J] *Elizabeth* instead of *Mary* in Origen, and some MSS. of the Itala.

and lifted up the lowly;
53 he has filled the hungry with good things,
and sent the rich away empty.
54 He has helped his servant Israel,
in remembrance of his mercy,
55 according to the promise he made to our ancestors,
to Abraham and to his descendants forever."

56 And Mary remained with her about three months and then returned to her home.

§ I THE BIRTH OF THE BAPTIST

MAT	MAR	LUK 1:57–80

57 Now the time came for Elizabeth to give birth, and she bore a son. 58 Her
neighbors and relatives heard that the Lord had shown his great mercy to her, and
they rejoiced with her. 59 On the eighth day they came to circumcise the child, and
they were going to name him Zechariah after his father. 60 But his mother said,
"No; he is to be called John." 61 They said to her, "None of your relatives has this
name." 62 Then they began motioning to his father to find out what name he wanted
to give him. 63 He asked for a writing tablet and wrote, "His name is John." And
all of them were amazed. 64 Immediately his mouth was opened and his tongue
freed, and he began to speak, praising God. 65 Fear came over all their neighbors,
and all these things were talked about throughout the entire hill country of Judea.
66 All who heard them pondered them and said, "What then will this child become?"
For, indeed, the hand of the Lord was with him.

67 Then his father Zechariah was filled with the Holy Spirit and spoke this prophecy:

68 "Blessed be the Lord God of Israel,
for he has looked favorably on his people and redeemed them.
69 He has raised up a mighty savior for us
in the house of his servant David,
70 as he spoke through the mouth of his holy prophets from of old,
71 that we would be saved from our enemies
and from the hand of all who hate us.
72 Thus he has shown the mercy promised to our ancestors,
and has remembered his holy covenant,
73 the oath that he swore to our ancestor Abraham, to grant us
74 that we, being rescued from the hands of our enemies,
might serve him without fear,
75 in holiness and righteousness before him all our days.
76 And you, child, will be called the prophet of the Most High;
for you will go before the Lord to prepare his ways,
77 to give knowledge of salvation to his people

✧ LUK 1:53 — PSA 107:9. ✧ LUK 1:54 — ISA 41:8–9; PSA 98:3. ✧ LUK 1:55 — MIC 7:20; 2SM 22:51. ✧ LUK 1:59 — LEV 12:3. ✧ LUK 1:68 — PSA 41:13; 111:9. ✧ LUK 1:69 — PSA 18:2; 132:17. ✧ LUK 1:71 — PSA 106:10; 18:17. ✧ LUK 1:72a — MIC 7:20. ✧ LUK 1:72b — PSA 105:8; 106:45. ✧ LUK 1:73 — JER 11:5. ✧ LUK 1:76 — MAL 3:1; ISA 40:3.

by the forgiveness of their sins.
78 By the tender mercy of our God,
the dawn from on high will break upon[K] us,
79 to give light to those who sit in darkness and in the shadow of death,
to guide our feet into the way of peace."

80 The child grew and became strong in spirit, and he was in the wilderness until
the day he appeared publicly to Israel.

§ J THE BIRTH OF JESUS

MAT	MAR	LUK 2:1–20

1 In those days a decree went out from Emperor Augustus that all the world should
be registered. 2 This was the first registration and was taken while Quirinius was
governor of Syria. 3 All went to their own towns to be registered. 4 Joseph also
went from the town of Nazareth in Galilee to Judea, to the city of David called
Bethlehem, because he was descended from the house and family of David. 5 He
went to be registered with Mary, to whom he was engaged and who was expecting
a child. 6 While they were there, the time came for her to deliver her child. 7
And she gave birth to her firstborn son and wrapped him in bands of cloth, and laid
him in a manger, because there was no place for them in the inn.
8 In that region there were shepherds living in the fields, keeping watch over their
flock by night. 9 Then an angel of the Lord stood before them, and the glory of
the Lord shone around them, and they were terrified. 10 But the angel said to them,
"Do not be afraid; for see—I am bringing you good news of great joy for all the
people: 11 to you is born this day in the city of David a Savior, who is the Messiah,
the Lord.[L] 12 This will be a sign for you: you will find a child wrapped in bands
of cloth and lying in a manger." 13 And suddenly there was with the angel a
multitude of the heavenly host, praising God and saying,

14 "Glory to God in the highest heaven,
and on earth peace among those whom he favors!"[M]

15 When the angels had left them and gone into heaven, the shepherds said to one
another, "Let us go now to Bethlehem and see this thing that has taken place, which
the Lord has made known to us." 16 So they went with haste and found Mary and
Joseph, and the child lying in the manger. 17 When they saw this, they made
known what had been told them about this child; 18 and all who heard it were
amazed at what the shepherds told them. 19 But Mary treasured all these words
and pondered them in her heart. 20 The shepherds returned, glorifying and praising God for all they had heard and seen, as it had been told them.

✧ LUK 1:79a — PSA 107:10. ✧ LUK 1:79b — ISA 59:8.

✦ [K] text: S B W Θ sy^{s} sy^{p} sa bo; *broke upon us*: P^{47} A C D λ ø ℜ it vg. ✦ [L] text: S A B D Θ λ ø ℜ it vg sa bo; *the Lord Christ*: W sy^{s} sy^{p}; *Christ of the Lord*: two MSS. of the Itala and two Syriac versions. ✦ [M] text: S A B D W it vg sa Irenaeus, Origen; *peace, goodwill among people*: Θ λ ø ℜ bo; *peace and goodwill among people*: sy^{s}; *peace and good hope to people*: sy^{p}.

§ K THE CIRCUMCISION OF JESUS AND THE PRESENTATION IN THE TEMPLE

MAT	MAR	LUK 2:21–40

21 After eight days had passed, it was time to circumcise the child; and he was
called Jesus, the name given by the angel before he was conceived in the womb.
22 When the time came for their purification according to the law of Moses, they
brought him up to Jerusalem to present him to the Lord 23 (as it is written in the
law of the Lord, "Every firstborn male shall be designated as holy to the Lord"),
24 and they offered a sacrifice according to what is stated in the law of the Lord, "a
pair of turtledoves or two young pigeons." 25 Now there was a man in Jerusalem
whose name was Simeon; this man was righteous and devout, looking forward to
the consolation of Israel, and the Holy Spirit rested on him. 26 It had been revealed
to him by the Holy Spirit that he would not see death before he had seen the Lord's
Messiah. 27 Guided by the Spirit,[N] Simeon came into the temple; and when the
parents brought in the child Jesus, to do for him what was customary under the law,
28 Simeon took him in his arms and praised God, saying,

29 "Master, now you are dismissing your servant in peace,
according to your word;
30 for my eyes have seen your salvation,
31 which you have prepared in the presence of all peoples,
32 a light for revelation to the Gentiles
and for glory to your people Israel."

33 And the child's father and mother were amazed at what was being said about him.
34 Then Simeon blessed them and said to his mother Mary,

"This child is destined for the falling and the rising of many in Israel,
and to be a sign that will be opposed
35 so that the inner thoughts of many will be revealed—
and a sword will pierce your own soul too."

36 There was also a prophet, Anna the daughter of Phanuel, of the tribe of Asher.
She was of a great age, having lived with her husband seven years after her
marriage, 37 then as a widow to[O] the age of eighty-four. She never left the temple
but worshiped there with fasting and prayer night and day. 38 At that moment she
came, and began to praise God and to speak about the child to all who were looking
for the redemption of Jerusalem.
39 When they had finished everything required by the law of the Lord, they returned
to Galilee, to their own town of Nazareth. 40 The child grew and became strong,[P]
filled with wisdom; and the favor of God was upon him.

✧ LUK 2:22 — LEV 12:6. ✧ LUK 2:23 — EXO 13:2, 12, 15. ✧ LUK 2:24 — LEV 12:8. ✧ LUK 2:30 — ISA 52:10. ✧ LUK 2:31 — ISA 40:5. ✧ LUK 2:32 — ISA 49:6.

✦ [N] Or, *And in the Spirit*. ✦ [O] text: A B vg sy^{s} sa bo; read: *of* for *to*: D it; *widow of about eighty-four*: W Θ λ sy^{p}; *widow until she was seventy-four*: S. ✦ [P] text: S B D W it vg sy^{s} sa bo; add: *in spirit*: A Θ λ ø ℜ sy^{p}.

§ L JESUS AT TWELVE YEARS

MAT	MAR	LUK 2:41–52
		41 Now every year his parents went to Jerusalem for the festival of the Passover. 42 And when he was twelve years old, they went up as usual for the festival. 43 When the festival was ended and they started to return, the boy Jesus stayed behind in Jerusalem, but his parents did not know it. 44 Assuming that he was in the group of travelers, they went a day's journey. Then they started to look for him among their relatives and friends. 45 When they did not find him, they returned to Jerusalem to search for him. 46 After three days they found him in the temple, sitting among the teachers, listening to them and asking them questions. 47 And all who heard him were amazed at his understanding and his answers. 48 When his parents saw him they were astonished; and his mother said to him, "Child, why have you treated us like this? Look, your father and I have been searching for you in great anxiety." 49 He said to them, "Why were you searching for me? Did you not know that I must be in my Father's house?" 50 But they did not understand what he said to them. 51 Then he went down with them and came to Nazareth, and was obedient to them. His mother treasured all these things in her heart. 52 And Jesus increased in wisdom and in years,[Q] and in divine and human favor.

✦ [Q] Or, *stature.*

THE GALILEAN SECTION

Matthew 3—18; Mark 1—9; Luke 3:1—9:50

§ 1 JOHN THE BAPTIST

MAT 3:1–6	MAR 1:1–6	LUK 3:1–6
	1 The beginning of the good news of Jesus Christ, the Son of God.[R]	
1 In those days		1 In the fifteenth year of the reign of Emperor Tiberius, when Pontius Pilate was governor of Judea, and Herod was ruler of Galilee, and his brother Philip ruler of the region of Ituraea and Trachonitis, and Lysanias ruler of Abilene, 2 during the high priesthood of Annas and Caiaphas, the word of God
John the Baptist appeared in the wilderness of Judea, proclaiming,	*Cf.* 1:15 (§ 9, p. 17)	came to John son of Zechariah in the wilderness. 3 He went into all the region around the Jordan, proclaiming
2 "Repent, for the kingdom of heaven has come near."	*Cf.* 1:4	a baptism of repentance for the forgiveness of sins,
3 This is the one of whom the prophet Isaiah spoke when he said,	2 As it is written in the prophet[S] Isaiah, "See, I am sending my messenger ahead of you, who will prepare your way;	4 as it is written in the book of the words of the prophet Isaiah,
Cf. 11:10 (§ 65, p. 55)		*Cf.* 7:27 (§ 82, p. 68)
"The voice of one crying out in the wilderness: 'Prepare the way of the Lord, make his paths straight.' "	3 the voice of one crying out in the wilderness: 'Prepare the way of the Lord, make his paths straight,' "	"The voice of one crying out in the wilderness: 'Prepare the way of the Lord, make his paths straight. 5 Every valley shall be filled, and every mountain and hill shall be made low, and the crooked shall be made straight, and the rough ways made smooth;

✧ MAT 3:3; MAR 1:3; LUK 3:4 *cf.* MAT 11:10 (§ 65, p. 55) — ISA 40:3. ✧ MAR 1:2 — MAL 3:1. ✧ LUK 3:5–6 — ISA 40:4–5.

✦ [R] text: A B D W λ ø ℜ it vg sy[p] sa bo; omit: *the Son of God*: S Θ. ✦ [S] text: S B D Θ λ it vg sy[p] sa bo; *the prophets* (minus, *Isaiah*): A W ø ℜ.

◗ To MAT 3:1 *cf.* **Gospel of the Ebionites** (in Epiphanius, *Against Heresies, XXX.13:6*). — In the days of Herod, king of Judea, when Caiaphas was high priest, a certain man named John came baptizing with a baptism of repentance in the river Jordan. He was said to be of the family of Aaron the priest, son of Zechariah and Elizabeth, and all went out to him.

MAT	MAR	LUK
		6 and all flesh shall see the salvation of God.' "
	4 John the baptizer appeared in[T] the wilderness, proclaiming a baptism of repentance for the forgiveness of sins.	*Cf.* 3:3b
4 Now John wore clothing of camel's hair with a leather belt around his waist, and his food was locusts and wild honey.	*Cf.* 1:6	
5 Then the people of Jerusalem and all Judea	5 And people from the whole Judean countryside and all the people of Jerusalem	
were going out to him, and all the region along the Jordan,	were going out to him,	
6 and they were baptized by him in the river Jordan, confessing their sins.	and were baptized by him in the river Jordan, confessing their sins.	*Cf.* 3:3a
Cf. 3:4	6 Now John was clothed with camel's hair, with a leather belt around his waist,[U] and he ate locusts and wild honey.	

§ 2 JOHN'S PREACHING REPENTANCE

MAT 3:7–10	MAR	LUK 3:7–9
7 But when he saw many Pharisees and Sadducees coming for baptism, he said to them,		7 John said to the crowds that came out to be baptized by him,
"You brood of vipers! Who warned you to flee from the wrath to come? 8 Bear fruit worthy of repentance. 9 Do not presume to say to yourselves, 'We have Abraham as our ancestor'; for I tell you, God is able from these stones to raise up children to Abraham.		"You brood of vipers! Who warned you to flee from the wrath to come? 8 Bear fruits worthy of repentance. Do not begin to say to yourselves, 'We have Abraham as our ancestor'; for I tell you, God is able from these stones to raise up children to Abraham.
10 Even now the ax is lying at the root of the trees; every tree therefore that does not bear good fruit is cut down and thrown into the fire."[1]		9 Even now the ax is lying at the root of the trees; every tree therefore that does not bear good fruit is cut down and thrown into the fire."[1]

[1] *Cf.* MAT 7:19 (§41, p. 36).

✦ [T] text: S B bo; *John was baptizing in*: A D W Θ λ φ 𝔐 it vg sy^{p} sa. ✦ [U] Omit, *with a leather girdle around his waist*: D it.

▸ To MAT 3:4–5 *cf.* **Gospel of the Ebionites** (in Epiphanius, *Against Heresies, XXX.13:4*). — John was baptizing; and Pharisees went out to him and were baptized, and all Jerusalem. Now John wore a garment of camel's hair, and a leather girdle around his waist; his food was wild honey, tasting like manna, like a cake in olive oil.

§ 3 JOHN'S PREACHING TO SPECIAL GROUPS

MAT	MAR	LUK 3:10–14
		10 And the crowds asked him, "What then should we do?" 11 In reply he said to them, "Whoever has two coats must share with anyone who has none; and who- ever has food must do likewise." 12 Even tax collectors came to be baptized, and they asked him, "Teacher, what should we do?" 13 He said to them, "Collect no more than the amount prescribed for you." 14 Soldiers also asked him, "And we, what should we do?" He said to them, "Do not extort money from anyone by threats or false accusation, and be satisfied with your wages."

§ 4 JOHN'S PREACHING ABOUT THE COMING ONE

MAT 3:11–12	MAR 1:7–8	LUK 3:15–18
11 "I baptize you with water for repentance, but one who is more powerful than I is coming after me; I am not worthy to carry his sandals. He will baptize you with the Holy Spirit and fire. 12 His win- nowing fork is in his hand, and he will clear his threshing floor and will gather his wheat into the granary; but the chaff he will burn with unquenchable fire."	7 He proclaimed, "The one who is more powerful than I is coming after me; I am not worthy to stoop down and untie the thong of his sandals. 8 I have baptized you with water; but he will baptize you with the Holy Spirit."	15 As the people were filled with expectation, and all were question- ing in their hearts concerning John, whether he might be the Messiah, 16 John answered all of them by saying, "I baptize you with water; but one who is more powerful than I is coming; I am not worthy to untie the thong of his sandals. He will baptize you with the Holy Spirit and fire. 17 His win- nowing fork is in his hand, to clear his threshing floor and to gather the wheat into his granary; but the chaff he will burn with unquenchable fire." 18 So, with many other exhorta- tions, he proclaimed the good news to the people.

§ 5 JOHN'S IMPRISONMENT

MAT	MAR	LUK 3:19–20
Cf. 14:3–4 (§ 111, p. 88)	*Cf.* 6:17–18 (§ 111, p. 88)	19 But Herod the ruler, who had been rebuked by him because of Herodias, his brother's wife, and because of all the evil things that Herod had done, 20 added to them all by shutting up John in prison.

• To MAT 3:11; MAR 1:7; LUK 3:16 *cf.* ACT 13:25. — And as John was finishing his work, he said, "What do you suppose that I am? I am not he. No, but one is coming after me; I am not worthy to untie the thong of the sandals on his feet." *Cf.* ACT 1:5; 11:16; 19:4. • To MAT 3:11–12 *cf.* JOH 1:24–28. • To LUK 3:15 *cf.* JOH 1:19–25.

§ 6 THE BAPTISM OF JESUS

MAT 3:13–17	MAR 1:9–11	LUK 3:21–22
13 Then Jesus came from Galilee to John at the Jordan, to be baptized by him. 14 John would have prevented him, saying, "I need to be baptized by you, and do you come to me?" 15 But Jesus answered him, "Let it be so now; for it is proper for us in this way to fulfill all righteousness." Then he consented.[V]	9 In those days Jesus came from Nazareth of Galilee	
		21 Now when all the people were baptized,
16 And when Jesus had been baptized,	and was baptized by John in the Jordan.	and when Jesus also had been baptized and was praying,
just as he came up from the water, suddenly	10 And just as he was coming up out of the water,	
the heavens were opened[W] to him and he saw the Spirit of God descending	he saw the heavens torn apart and the Spirit descending	the heaven was opened, 22 and the Holy Spirit descended upon him in bodily form
like a dove and alighting on him.	like a dove on him.	like a dove.
17 And a voice from heaven said, "This is my Son,[X] the Beloved, with whom I am well pleased."	11 And a voice came from heaven, "You are my Son,[X] the Beloved; with you I am well pleased."	And a voice came from heaven, "You are my Son,[X] the Beloved; with you I am well pleased."[Y]

✧ MAT 3:17; MAR 1:11 *cf.* ISA 42:1; 44:2.

✦ [V] MAT 3:15 — *Then he consented; and when he was baptized a huge light shone from the water so that all who were near were frightened.* Two manuscripts of the Itala. ✦ [W] text: C D W λ ø ℜ it vg sy^{p} bo; omit: *to him*: S B sy^{c} sy^{s} sa.
✦ [X] Or, *my Son, my* (or *the*) *Beloved.* ✦ [Y] text: P^{4} S A B W Θ λ ø ℜ vg sy^{s} sy^{p} sa bo; *You are my son; today I have begotten you* (Psalm 2:7): D it Justin, Clement, Origen, Augustine, Gospel of the Ebionites.

● To § 6 *cf.* JOH 1:29–34.

◗ To MAT 3:13 *cf.* **Gospel according to the Hebrews** (in Jerome, *Against Pelagius III.2*). — The mother of the Lord and his brothers said to him, "John the Baptist baptizes for the forgiveness of sins; let us go and be baptized by him." But he said to them, "In what way have I sinned that I should go and be baptized by him? Unless, perhaps, what I have just said is a sin of ignorance."
◗ To MAT 3:13–17 *cf.* **Gospel of the Ebionites** (in Epiphanius, *Against Heresies, XXX.13:7–8*). — After the people were baptized, Jesus also came and was baptized by John. And when Jesus came up from the water, the heavens were opened, and Jesus saw the Holy Spirit descend in the form of a dove and enter into him. And a voice from heaven said, "You are my beloved Son; with you I am well pleased." And again, "Today I have begotten you." And immediately a great light shone around the place; and John, seeing it, said to Jesus, "Who are you, Lord?" And again a voice from heaven said to him, "This is my beloved Son, with whom I am well pleased." Then John, falling down before Jesus, said, "I beseech you, Lord, baptize me!" But Jesus forbade John, saying, "Let it be so; for thus it is fitting that all things be fulfilled." ◗ To MAT 3:16–17 *cf.* **Gospel according to the Hebrews** (in Jerome, *Commentary on Isaiah 11:2*). — When the Lord ascended from the water, the whole fount of the Holy Spirit descended and rested upon him, and said to him, "My son, in all the prophets I was waiting for you, that you might come, and that I might rest in you. For you are my rest; and you are my firstborn son, who reigns forever."

§ 7 THE GENEALOGY OF JESUS

Δ *MAT 1:1–16* (*§ A, p. 1*)

1 An account of the genealogy of Jesus the Mes-
siah, the son of David, the son of Abraham.
2 Abraham was the father of Isaac, and Isaac
the father of Jacob, and Jacob the father of
Judah and his brothers, 3 and Judah the father
of Perez and Zerah by Tamar, and Perez the
father of Hezron, and Hezron the father of
Aram, 4 and Aram the father of Aminadab,
and Aminadab the father of Nahshon, and
Nahshon the father of Salmon, 5 and Salmon
the father of Boaz by Rahab, and Boaz the
father of Obed by Ruth, and Obed the father of
Jesse, 6 and Jesse the father of King David.
And David was the father of Solomon by the
wife of Uriah, 7 and Solomon the father of Re-
hoboam, and Rehoboam the father of Abijah,
and Abijah the father of Asaph, 8 and Asaph
the father of Jehoshaphat, and Jehoshaphat
the father of Joram, and Joram the father of
Uzziah, 9 and Uzziah the father of Jotham,
and Jotham the father of Ahaz, and Ahaz the
father of Hezekiah, 10 and Hezekiah the father
of Manasseh, and Manasseh the father of
Amos, and Amos the father of Josiah, 11 and
Josiah the father of Jechoniah and his brothers,
at the time of the deportation to Babylon.
12 And after the deportation to Babylon:
Jechoniah was the father of Salathiel, and
Salathiel the father of Zerubbabel, 13 and
Zerubbabel the father of Abiud, and Abiud the
father of Eliakim, and Eliakim the father of
Azor, 14 and Azor the father of Zadok, and
Zadok the father of Achim, and Achim the fa-
ther of Eliud, 15 and Eliud the father of Eleazar,
and Eleazar the father of Matthan, and Mat-
than the father of Jacob, 16 and Jacob the
father of Joseph the husband of Mary, of whom
Jesus was born, who is called the Messiah.

MAR

LUK 3:23–38

23 Jesus was about thirty years old when he
began his work. He was the son (as was
thought) of Joseph son of Heli, 24 son of Matthat, son of Levi, son of Melchi, son of
Jannai, son of Joseph, 25 son of Mattathias,
son of Amos, son of Nahum, son of Esli, son
of Naggai, 26 son of Maath, son of Mattathias,
son of Semein, son of Josech, son of Joda,
27 son of Joanan, son of Rhesa, son of Zerubbabel, son of Shealtiel, son of Neri, 28 son of
Melchi, son of Addi, son of Cosam, son of
Elmadam, son of Er, 29 son of Joshua, son of
Eliezer, son of Jorim, son of Matthat, son of
Levi, 30 son of Simeon, son of Judah, son of
Joseph, son of Jonam, son of Eliakim, 31 son
of Melea, son of Menna, son of Mattatha, son
of Nathan, son of David, 32 son of Jesse, son
of Obed, son of Boaz, son of Sala, son of
Nahshon, 33 son of Amminadab, son of Admin,
son of Arni, son of Hezron, son of Perez, son
of Judah, 34 son of Jacob, son of Isaac, son of
Abraham, son of Terah, son of Nahor, 35 son
of Serug, son of Reu, son of Peleg, son of
Eber, son of Shelah, 36 son of Cainan, son of
Arphaxad, son of Shem, son of Noah, son of
Lamech, 37 son of Methuselah, son of Enoch,
son of Jared, son of Mahalaleel, son of Cainan,
38 son of Enos, son of Seth, son of Adam, son
of God.

✧ LUK 3:27 — 1CH 3:17. ✧ LUK 3:31–34 — 1CH 2:1–15. ✧ LUK 3:32–33 — RTH 4:18–22. ✧ LUK 3:34–35 — 1CH 1:24–27. ✧ LUK 3:36–38 — 1CH 1:1–4.

◗ To LUK 3:23 *cf.* **Gospel of the Ebionites** (in Epiphanius, *Against Heresies XXX.13:2*). — "There was a man named Jesus, about thirty years old, who chose us." ◗ To LUK 3:23 *cf.* Justin, *Dialogue 88:3*. — When Jesus went down to the water, fire was kindled in the Jordan; and when Jesus came up from the water, the Holy Spirit came upon him like a dove. The apostles of our Christ wrote this.

§ 8 THE TEMPTATION

MAT 4:1–11	MAR 1:12–13	LUK 4:1–13
1 Then Jesus was led up by the Spirit into the wilderness to be tempted by the devil.	12 And the Spirit immediately drove him out into the wilderness. 13 He was in the wilderness forty days, tempted by Satan;	1 Jesus, full of the Holy Spirit, returned from the Jordan and was led by the Spirit in the wilderness, 2 where for forty days he was tempted by the devil.
2 He fasted forty days and forty nights, and afterwards he was famished.		He ate nothing at all during those days, and when they were over, he was famished.
	and he was with the wild beasts;	
3 The tempter came and said to him, "If you are the Son of God, command these stones to become loaves of bread." 4 But he answered, "It is written, 'One does not live by bread alone, but by every word that comes from the mouth of God.' "		3 The devil said to him, "If you are the Son of God, command this stone to become a loaf of bread." 4 Jesus answered him, "It is written, 'One does not live by bread alone.' "
5 Then the devil took him to the holy city and placed him on the pinnacle of the temple, 6 saying to him, "If you are the Son of God, throw yourself down; for it is written, 'He will command his angels concerning you,' and 'On their hands they will bear you up, so that you will not dash your foot against a stone.' " 7 Jesus said to him, "Again it is written, 'Do not put the Lord your God to the test.' "		*Cf.* 4:9–12
8 Again, the devil took him to a very high mountain and showed him all the kingdoms of the world and their splendor; 9 and he said to him, "All these I will give you, if you will fall down and worship me." 10 Jesus said to him, "Away with you, Satan! for		5 Then the devil led him up and showed him in an instant all the kingdoms of the world. 6 And the devil said to him, "To you I will give their glory and all this authority; for it has been given over to me, and I give it to anyone I please. 7 If you, then, will worship me, it will all be yours." 8 Jesus answered him,

◆ MAT 4:4; LUK 4:4 — DEU 8:3b. ◆ MAT 4:6; LUK 4:10–11 — PSA 91:11–12. ◆ MAT 4:7; LUK 4:12 — DEU 6:16. ◆ MAT 4:10; LUK 4:8 — DEU 6:13.

▸ To MAT 4:5 *cf.* **Gospel of the Nazaraeans.** — The Jewish Gospel has not: *to the holy city*, but: *to Jerusalem.*

▸ To MAT 4:8 *cf.* **Gospel according to the Hebrews** (in Origen, *Commentary on John 2:12* and *Homily on Jeremiah 15:4*). — And if any accept the Gospel of the Hebrews, here the Savior says: "Even so did my mother, the Holy Spirit, take me by one of my hairs, and carry me to the great Mount Tabor." Jerome also records these words in Latin in his commentaries on MIC 7:6, ISA 40:9*ff*., and EZE 16:13.

it is written, 'Worship the Lord your God, and serve only him.' ”		“It is written, 'Worship the Lord your God, and serve only him.' ”
Cf. 4:5–7		9 Then the devil took him to Jerusalem, and placed him on the pinnacle of the temple, saying to him, “If you are the Son of God, throw yourself down from here, 10 for it is written, 'He will command his angels concerning you, to protect you,' 11 and 'On their hands they will bear you up, so that you will not dash your foot against a stone.' ” 12 Jesus answered him, “It is said, 'Do not put the Lord your God to the test.' ” 13 When the devil had finished every test,
11 Then the devil left him,		he departed from him until an opportune time.
and suddenly angels came and waited on him.	and the angels waited on him.	

§ 9 THE FIRST PREACHING IN GALILEE

MAT 4:12–17	MAR 1:14–15	LUK 4:14–15
		14 Then Jesus, filled with the power of the Spirit,
12 Now when Jesus heard that John had been arrested,	14 Now after John was arrested,	
he withdrew to Galilee.	Jesus came to Galilee,	returned to Galilee,
13 He left Nazareth and made his home in Capernaum by the sea, in the territory of Zebulun and Naphtali, 14 so that what had been spoken through the prophet Isaiah might be fulfilled: 15 “Land of Zebulun, land of Naphtali, on the road by the sea, across the Jordan, Galilee of the Gentiles— 16 the people who sat in darkness have seen a great light, and for those who sat in the region and shadow of death light		

✧ MAT 4:15–16 — ISA 9:1–2.

• To MAT 4:11; MAR 1:13 *cf.* JOH 1:51. — And he said to him, [Jesus said to Nathanael] “Very truly, I tell you, you will see heaven opened and the angels of God ascending and descending upon the Son of Man.”

• To MAT 4:12; MAR 1:14; LUK 4:14 *cf.* JOH 4:1–3. — 1 Now when Jesus learned that the Pharisees had heard, “Jesus is making and baptizing more disciples than John” — 2 although it was not Jesus himself but his disciples who baptized — 3 he [Jesus] left Judea and started back to Galilee. *Cf.* JOH 4:43; 2:12.

has dawned."		
		and a report about him spread through all the surrounding country. 15 He began to
17 From that time Jesus began to proclaim, "Repent, for	proclaiming the good news[Z] of	teach in their synagogues
the kingdom of heaven has come near."	God, 15 and saying, "The time is fulfilled, and the kingdom of God has come near; repent, and be- lieve in the good news."	
		and was praised by everyone.

§ 10 THE REJECTION AT NAZARETH

Δ *MAT 13:54–58* (*§ 108, p. 86*)	Δ *MAR 6:1–6a* (*§ 108, p. 86*)	**LUK 4:16–30**
54 *He came to* *his hometown*	1 *He left that place and came to* *his hometown,* *and his disciples followed him.*	16 When he came to Nazareth, where he had been brought up,
and began to teach the people *in their synagogue,*	2 *On the sabbath he began to teach* *in the synagogue,*	he went to the synagogue on the sabbath day, as was his custom. He stood up to read, 17 and the scroll of the prophet Isaiah was given to him. He unrolled the scroll and found the place where it was written: 18 "The Spirit of the Lord is upon me, because he has anointed me to bring good news to the poor. He has sent me to pro- claim release to the captives and recovery of sight to the blind, to let the oppressed go free, 19 to pro- claim the year of the Lord's favor." 20 And he rolled up the scroll, gave it back to the attendant, and sat down. The eyes of all in the syna- gogue were fixed on him. 21 Then he began to say to them, "Today this scripture has been fulfilled in your hearing." 22 All spoke well of
so that they were astounded	*and many* *who heard him were astounded.*	him and were amazed at the gra- cious words that came from his mouth. They said,
and said, "Where *did this man get*	*They said, "Where* *did this man get all this? What is*	

✧ LUK 4:18–19 — ISA 61:1–2; 58:6.

✦ [Z] text: S B Θ λ φ it (some MSS.) sy^s sa bo; *gospel of the kingdom of God:* A D W 𝔐 it (some MSS.) vg sy^p.

• To MAT 13:54; MAR 6:2 *cf.* JOH 7:15. — The Jews were astonished at it, saying, "How does this man have such learning, when he has never been taught?"

this wisdom
and these deeds of power?
55 *Is not this*
the carpenter's son? Is not his
mother called Mary? And are not
his brothers James and Joseph
and Simon and Judas? 56 *And are*
not all his sisters with us? Where
then did this man get all this?"
57 *And they took offense*[A] *at him.*

But Jesus said to them,
"Prophets are not without honor
except in their own country
and in their own house."
58 *And he did not do many deeds of*
power there,
because of their unbelief.

---

this wisdom that has been given to
him? What deeds of power are be-
ing done by his hands! 3 *Is not this*
the carpenter,
the son of Mary and
brother of James and Joses
and Judas and Simon, and are
not his sisters here with us?"
And they took offense[A] *at him.*

4 *Then Jesus said to them,*
"Prophets are not without honor,
except in their hometown, and
among their own kin,
and in their own house."
5 *And he could do no deed of*
power there, except that he laid his
hands on a few sick people and
cured them. 6 *And he was amazed*
at their unbelief. Then he went
about among the villages teaching.

"Is not this
Joseph's son?"

23 He said to them, "Doubtless you
will quote to me this proverb,
'Doctor, cure yourself!' And you
will say, 'Do here also in your
hometown the things that we have
heard you did at Capernaum.' "
24 And he said, "Truly I tell you,
no prophet is accepted
in the prophet's hometown.

25 But the truth is, there were many
widows in Israel in the time of Elijah, when the heaven was shut up
three years and six months, and
there was a severe famine over all
the land; 26 yet Elijah was sent to
none of them except to a widow at
Zarephath in Sidon. 27 There were
also many lepers in Israel in the time
of the prophet Elisha, and none of
them was cleansed except Naaman
the Syrian." 28 When they heard
this, all in the synagogue were
filled with rage. 29 They got up,
drove him out of the town, and led
him to the brow of the hill on which
their town was built, so that they

✧ LUK 4:25 — 1KI 17:1; 18:1–2. ✧ LUK 4:26 — 1KI 17:8–9. ✧ LUK 4:27 — 2KI 5:14.

✦ [A] Or, *stumbled.*

● To MAT 13:57; MAR 6:4; LUK 4:24 *cf.* JOH 4:44. — For Jesus himself had testified that a prophet has no honor in the prophet's own country.

◗ To LUK 4:24 *cf. Oxyrhynchus Papyrus 1, Logion 6.* — "Prophets are not acceptable in their own country, neither do physicians heal those who know them." ◗ To LUK 4:24 *cf.* **Gospel of Thomas, Logion 31.** — "No prophets are acceptable in their hometowns; no physicians heal those who know them."

		might hurl him off the cliff. 30 But
		he passed through the midst of them
		and went on his way.

§ 11 THE CALL OF THE FIRST DISCIPLES

MAT 4:18–22	MAR 1:16–20	LUK
18 As he walked by the Sea of Galilee,	16 As Jesus passed along the Sea of Galilee,	*Cf.* 5:1–11
he saw two brothers, Simon, who is called Pe-	he saw Simon	(§ 17, p. 24)
ter, and Andrew his brother, casting a net into	and his brother Andrew casting a net into	
the sea—for they were fishermen. 19 And	the sea—for they were fishermen. 17 And	
he said to them, "Follow me, and I will make	Jesus said to them, "Follow me and I will make	
you fish for people." 20 Immediately they	you fish for people." 18 And immediately they	
left their nets and followed him. 21 As he went	left their nets and followed him. 19 As he went	
from there, he saw two other brothers,	a little farther, he saw	
James son of Zebedee and his brother John,	James son of Zebedee and his brother John,	
in the boat with their father Zebedee, mending	who were in their boat mending	
their nets, and he called them.	the nets. 20 Immediately he called them; and	
22 Immediately they left the boat and their father,	they left their father Zebedee in the boat	
and followed him.	with the hired men, and followed him.	
▼ 4:23–25 (§ 16, p. 23)		

§ 12 JESUS IN THE SYNAGOGUE AT CAPERNAUM

Δ *MAT 7:28–29 (§ 44, p. 38)*	MAR 1:21–28	LUK 4:31–37
28 *Now when Jesus*	21 They went to Capernaum; and	31 He went down to Capernaum, a
		city in Galilee, and
	when the sabbath came, he	
had finished saying these things,	entered the synagogue and taught.	was teaching them on the sabbath.
the crowds were astounded at his	22 They were astounded at his	32 They were astounded at his
teaching, 29 *for he taught them as*	teaching, for he taught them as	teaching, because he spoke
one having authority, and not as	one having authority, and not as	with authority.
their scribes.	the scribes. 23 Just then	
	there was in their synagogue a man	33 In the synagogue there was a man
	with an unclean spirit,	who had the spirit of an unclean
	24 and he cried out,	demon, and he cried out with a loud

✧ MAR 1:24; LUK 4:34 — JDG 11:12; 1KI 17:18.

• To § 11 *cf.* JOH 1:35–42. • To MAT 7:28; MAR 1:22; LUK 4:32 *cf.* JOH 7:46. — The police answered, "Never has anyone spoken like this!"

◗ To MAT 4:18–22 and parallels (and 9:9 and parallels, as well as 10:2–5 and parallels) *cf.* **Gospel of the Ebionites** (in Epiphanius, *Against Heresies, XXX.13:2–3*). — There was a man named Jesus, about thirty years old, who chose us. (*Cf.* LUK 3:23, § 7, p. 15.) Coming to Capernaum, Jesus entered the house of Simon, who is called Peter, and said, "As I passed by the lake of Tiberias, I chose John and James, sons of Zebedee, and Simon, Andrew, Thaddaeus, Simon the Zealot, Judas Iscariot; and you, Matthew, sitting at the tax booth, I called and you followed me. You, therefore, I desire to be twelve apostles, as a witness to Israel."

		voice, 34 "Let us alone!
	"What have you to do with us, Jesus of Nazareth? Have you come to destroy us? I know who you are, the Holy One of God."	What have you to do with us, Jesus of Nazareth? Have you come to destroy us? I know who you are, the Holy One of God."
	25 But Jesus rebuked him, saying, "Be silent, and come out of him!"	35 But Jesus rebuked him, saying, "Be silent, and come out of him!"
	26 And the unclean spirit, convulsing him and crying with a loud voice, came out of him.	When the demon had thrown him down before them, he came out of him without having done him any harm.
	27 They were all amazed, and they kept on asking one another, "What is this? A new teaching—with authority! He commands even the unclean spirits, and they obey him."	36 They were all amazed and kept saying to one another, "What kind of utterance is this? For with authority and power he commands the unclean spirits, and out they come!"
	28 At once his fame began to spread throughout the surrounding region of Galilee.	37 And a report about him began to reach every place in the region.

§ 13 THE HEALING OF PETER'S MOTHER-IN-LAW

Δ *MAT 8:14–15* *(§ 47, p. 41)*	**MAR 1:29–31**	**LUK 4:38–39**
14 When Jesus entered Peter's house,	29 As soon as they[B] left the synagogue, they entered the house of Simon and Andrew, with James and John.	38 After leaving the synagogue he entered Simon's house.
he saw his mother-in-law lying in bed with a fever;	30 Now Simon's mother-in-law was in bed with a fever, and they told him about her at once.	Now Simon's mother-in-law was suffering from a high fever, and they asked him about her.
15 he touched her hand,	31 He came and took her by the hand and lifted her up.	
		39 Then he stood over her and rebuked the fever, and
and the fever left her, and she got up and began to serve him.	Then the fever left her, and she began to serve them.	it left her. Immediately she got up and began to serve them.

✦ [B] text: S A C ℜ vg sy^s sy^p bo; *he*: B D W Θ λ φ it.

§ 14 THE SICK HEALED AT EVENING

Δ *MAT 8:16–17 (§ 48, p. 41)*	MAR 1:32–34	LUK 4:40–41
16 That evening they brought to him many who were possessed with demons;	32 That evening, at sundown, they brought to him all who were sick or possessed with demons.	40 As the sun was setting, all those who had any who were sick with various kinds of diseases brought them to him;
	33 And the whole city was gathered around the door.	
and he cast out the spirits with a word, and cured all who were sick.	34 And he cured many who were sick with various diseases, and cast out many demons;[1]	and he laid his hands on each of them and cured them.
		41 Demons also came out of many, shouting, "You are the Son of God!" But he rebuked them
	and he would not permit the demons to speak, because they knew him.[2]	and would not allow them to speak, because they knew that he was the Messiah.[2]
17 This was to fulfill what had been spoken through the prophet Isaiah, "He took our infirmities and bore our diseases."		

§ 15 JESUS DEPARTS FROM CAPERNAUM

MAT	MAR 1:35–38	LUK 4:42–43
	35 In the morning, while it was still very dark, he got up and went out to a deserted place, and there he prayed.	42 At daybreak he departed and went into a deserted place.
	36 And Simon and his companions hunted for him.	And the crowds were looking for him; and
	37 When they found him, they said to him, "Everyone is searching for you."	when they reached him, they wanted to prevent him from leaving them.
	38 He answered, "Let us go on to the neighboring towns, so that I may proclaim the message there also; for that is what I came out to do."	43 But he said to them, "I must proclaim the good news of the kingdom of God to the other cities also; for I was sent for this purpose."

[1] MAR 3:10–11 (§ 71, p. 60): 10 for he [Jesus] had cured many, so that all who had diseases pressed upon him to touch him. 11 Whenever the unclean spirits saw him, they fell down before him and shouted, "You are the Son of God!"
Cf. MAT 4:24 (§ 16, p. 23).

[2] MAT 12:16 (§ 71, p. 60): and he [Jesus] ordered them not to make him known.
MAR 3:12 (§ 71, p. 60): But he [Jesus] sternly ordered them not to make him known.

✧ MAT 8:17 — ISA 53:4.

§ 16 A PREACHING JOURNEY IN GALILEE

MAT 4:23–25	MAR 1:39 +	LUK 4:44 +
23 Jesus went throughout Galilee, teaching in their synagogues and	39 And he went throughout Galilee,	44 So he continued
proclaiming the good news of the kingdom and	proclaiming the message	proclaiming the message
	in their synagogues and	in the synagogues of Judea.[C]
curing every disease and every sickness among the people.[1] 24 So his fame spread throughout all Syria, and they brought to him all the sick,[2] those who were afflicted with various diseases and pains,	casting out demons.	Δ 6:18, 19, 17 (§ 71, p. 60) *18 They had come to hear him and to be healed of their diseases; and those who were troubled*
demoniacs, epileptics, and paralytics, and he cured them.	Δ 3:10, 7, 8 (§ 71, p. 61) *10 for he had cured many, so that all who had diseases pressed upon him to touch him.*	*with unclean spirits were cured.* *19 And all in the crowd were trying to touch him, for power came out from him and healed all of them.*
	7 Jesus departed with his disciples to the sea,	*17 He came down with them and stood on a level place, with a great crowd of his disciples*
25 And great crowds followed him[3] from Galilee, the Decapolis,	*and a great multitude from Galilee followed him;*	*and a great multitude of people*
	8 hearing all that he was doing, they came to him in great numbers	
Jerusalem, Judea, and from beyond the Jordan.	*from Judea, Jerusalem, Idumea, beyond the Jordan, and the region around Tyre and Sidon.*	*from all Judea, Jerusalem, and the coast of Tyre and Sidon.*
	▼ 1:40–45 (§ 45, p. 38)	

[1] MAT 9:35 (§ 58, p. 47): Then Jesus went about all the cities and villages, teaching in their synagogues, and proclaiming the good news of the kingdom, and curing every disease and every sickness.

[2] MAT 14:35 (§ 114, p. 92): After the people of that place recognized him [Jesus], they sent word throughout the region and brought all who were sick to him.

MAR 6:54–55 (§ 114, p. 92): 54 When they got out of the boat, people at once recognized him [Jesus], 55 and rushed about that whole region and began to bring the sick on mats to wherever they heard he was.

[3] MAT 12:15 (§ 71, p. 60): When Jesus became aware of this, he departed. Many crowds followed him, and he cured all of them.

✦ [C] text: P[75] S B C λ sy[s] sa bo; *Galilee*: A D Θ ø ℜ it vg sy[p]; *synagogues of the Jews*: W.

§ 17 THE MIRACULOUS CATCH OF FISH

MAT	MAR	LUK 5:1–11
Cf. 4:18–22 (§ 11, p. 20)	*Cf.* 1:16–20 (§ 11, p. 20)	1 Once while Jesus was standing beside the lake of Gennesaret, and the crowd was pressing in on him to hear the word of God, 2 he saw two boats there at the shore of the lake; the fishermen had gone out of them and were washing their nets. 3 He got into one of the boats, the one belonging to Simon, and asked him to put out a little way from the shore. Then he sat down and taught the crowds from the boat.[1] 4 When he had finished speaking, he said to Simon, "Put out into the deep water and let down your nets for a catch." 5 Simon answered, "Master, we have worked all night long but have caught nothing. Yet if you say so, I will let down the nets." 6 When they had done this, they caught so many fish that their nets were beginning to break. 7 So they signaled their partners in the other boat to come and help them. And they came and filled both boats, so that they began to sink. 8 But when Simon Peter saw it, he fell down at Jesus' knees, saying, "Go away from me, Lord, for I am a sinful man!" 9 For he and all who were with him were amazed at the catch of fish that they had taken; 10 and so also were James and John, sons of Zebedee, who were partners with Simon. Then Jesus said to Simon, "Do not be afraid; from now on you will be catching people." 11 When they had brought their boats to shore, they left everything and followed him. ▼ 5:12–16 (§ 45, p. 38)

The Sermon on the Mount

Matthew 5—7

§ 18 INTRODUCTION

MAT 5:1–2	MAR	Δ *LUK 6:12, 20* (*§ 72, p. 62; § 73, p. 63*)
1 When Jesus saw the crowds, he went		*12 Now during those days he went*
up the mountain; and	*Cf.* 3:13 (§ 72, p. 62)	*out to the mountain to pray; and he spent the* *night in prayer to God.*
after he sat down, his disciples came to him.		*[13–19] 20 Then he looked up at his disciples*
2 Then he began to speak,		
and taught them, saying:		*and said:*

[1] *Cf.* MAT 13:1–2; MAR 4:1.

§ 19 THE BEATITUDES

MAT 5:3–12	MAR	Δ *LUK 6:20–23 (§ 73, p. 63)*
3 "Blessed are the poor in spirit, for theirs is the kingdom of heaven.		*20 "Blessed are you who are poor, for yours is the kingdom of God.*
4 "Blessed are those who mourn, for they will be comforted.		
5 "Blessed are the meek, for they will inherit the earth.		
6 "Blessed are those who hunger and thirst for righteousness, for they will be filled.		*21 "Blessed are you who are hungry now, for you will be filled. "Blessed are you who weep now, for you will laugh.*
7 "Blessed are the merciful, for they will receive mercy.		
8 "Blessed are the pure in heart, for they will see God.		
9 "Blessed are the peacemakers, for they will be called children of God.		
10 "Blessed are those who are persecuted for righteousness' sake, for theirs is the kingdom of heaven.		
11 "Blessed are you when people revile you and persecute you and utter all kinds of evil against you falsely on my account.		*22 "Blessed are you when people hate you, and when they exclude you, revile you, and defame you on account of the Son of Man.*
12 Rejoice and be glad, for your reward is great in heaven, for in the same way they persecuted the prophets who were before you."		*23 Rejoice in that day and leap for joy, for surely your reward is great in heaven; for that is what their ancestors did to the prophets."*

✧ MAT 5:5 — PSA 37:11. ✧ MAT 5:8 — PSA 24:4.

▸ To MAT 5:3; LUK 6:20 *cf.* **Gospel of Thomas, Logion 54.** — Jesus said, "Blessed are the poor, for yours is the kingdom of heaven." ▸ To MAT 5:5 *cf.* Clement of Alexandria, *Protrepticus X.94:4.* — For which reason the scripture is proclaimed to those who believe, "And the saints of the Lord shall inherit the glory of God and God's power." ▸ To MAT 5:6; LUK 6:21 *cf.* **Gospel of Thomas, Logion 69b.** — "Blessed are the hungry, for the stomach of one who desires will be filled."
▸ To MAT 5:10 *cf.* **Gospel of Thomas, Logion 69a.** — "Blessed are those who have been persecuted in their heart, for they are the ones who have truly known the Father." ▸ To MAT 5:11; LUK 6:22 *cf.* **Gospel of Thomas, Logion 68.** — "Blessed are you when you are hated and persecuted, and no place will be found where you have been persecuted."

§ 20 THE PARABLES OF SALT AND LIGHT

MAT 5:13–16	**MAR**	Δ *LUK 14:34–35* (*§ 171, p. 133*) +
13 "You are the salt of the earth;		34 *"Salt is good;*
but if salt has lost its taste, how can its saltiness	*Cf.* 9:50	*but if salt has lost its taste, how can its saltiness*
be restored?[1] It is	(§ 132, p. 108)	*be restored?*[1] 35 *It is*
no longer good for anything,		*fit neither for the soil nor for the manure pile;*
but is thrown out and trampled under foot.		*they throw it away.*
		Let anyone with ears to hear listen!"
14 "You are the light of the world. A city built		
on a hill cannot be hid.		Δ *11:33 (§ 153, p. 120)*
15 No one after lighting a lamp puts it		33 *"No one after lighting a lamp puts it*
under the bushel basket, but on the lampstand,		*in a cellar, but on the lampstand*
and it gives light to all in the house.[2]		*so that those who enter may see the light."*
16 In the same way, let your light shine before		
others, so that they may see your good works		
and give glory to your Father in heaven."		

§ 21 WORDS OF JESUS ON THE LAW

MAT 5:17–20	**MAR**	**LUK**
17 "Do not think that I have come to abolish the law or the prophets; I have come not to abolish but to fulfill. 18 For truly I tell you, until heaven and earth pass away, not one letter, not one stroke of a letter, will pass from the law until all is accomplished.[3] 19 Therefore, whoever breaks one of the least of these command- ments, and teaches others to do the same, will be called least in the kingdom of heaven; but whoever does them and teaches them will be called great in the kingdom of heaven. 20 For I tell you, unless your righteousness exceeds that of the scribes and Pharisees, you will never enter the kingdom of heaven."		

---

[1] MAR 9:50 (§ 132, p. 108): "Salt is good; but if salt has lost its saltiness, how can you season it? Have salt in yourselves, and be at peace with one another."

[2] MAR 4:21 (§ 94, p. 77): He [Jesus] said to them, "Is a lamp brought in to be put under the bushel basket, or under the bed, and not on the lampstand?"

LUK 8:16 (§ 94, p. 77): "No one after lighting a lamp hides it under a jar, or puts it under a bed, but puts it on a lampstand, so that those who enter may see the light."

[3] LUK 16:17 (§ 176, p. 137): "But it is easier for heaven and earth to pass away, than for one stroke of a letter in the law to be dropped." *Cf.* MAT 24:35 = MAR 13:31 = LUK 21:33 (§ 221, p. 174).

▸ To MAT 5:14 *cf. Oxyrhynchus Papyrus 1, Logion 7.* — Jesus says, "A city built on the top of a high mountain and established can neither fall nor be hidden." ▸ To MAT 5:14 *cf.* **Gospel of Thomas, Logion 32.** — "A city built on a high mountain and fortified can neither fall nor be hidden." ▸ To MAT 5:17 *cf.* **Gospel of the Ebionites** (in Epiphanius, *Against Heresies, XXX.16:5*). — "I have come to destroy sacrifices; and if you do not stop making sacrifices, the wrath (of God) will not leave you." ▸ To MAT 5:17 *cf.* **Gospel of the Egyptians** (in Clement of Alexandria, *Miscellanies III.9:63*). — "I have come to destroy the works of the female." *Cf.* MAT 19:12 (§ 187, p. 143).

§ 22 ON ANGER

MAT 5:21–26

21 "You have heard that it was said to those of ancient times, 'You shall not murder'; and 'whoever murders shall be liable to judgment.'
22 But I say to you that if you are angry with a brother[D] or sister, you will be liable to judgment; and if you insult[E] a brother or sister, you will be liable to the council; and if you say, 'You fool,' you will be liable to the hell[F] of fire.
23 So when you are offering your gift at the altar, if you remember that your brother or sister has something against you,
24 leave your gift there before the altar and go; first be reconciled to your brother or sister, and then come and offer your gift.
25 Come to terms quickly with your accuser while you are on the way to court with him, or your accuser may hand you over to the judge, and the judge to the guard, and you will be thrown into prison.
26 Truly I tell you, you will never get out until you have paid the last penny."

MAR

Δ *LUK 12:57–59* *(§ 161, p. 128)*

57 *"And why do you not judge for yourselves what is right?*
58 *Thus, when you go with your accuser before a magistrate, on the way make an effort to settle the case, or you may be dragged before the judge, and the judge hand you over to the officer, and the officer throw you in prison.*
59 *I tell you, you will never get out until you have paid the very last penny."*

✧ MAT 5:21 — EXO 20:13; DEU 5:17.

✦ [D] text: $P^{67?}$ S B vg Justin, Origen; add: *without cause*: D W Θ λ ø ℜ it sy^{c} sy^{s} sy^{p} sa bo. ✦ [E] Greek: *says Raca to*, (an obscure term of abuse). ✦ [F] Greek: *Gehenna.*

◗ To MAT 5:22 *cf.* **Gospel of the Nazaraeans**. — The words, "without cause," are not inserted in some copies, or in the Jewish Gospel. ◗ To MAT 5:23 *cf.* **Gospel according to the Hebrews** (in Jerome, *Commentary on Ezekiel 18:7*). — And in the Gospel according to the Hebrews, which the Nazaraeans are accustomed to read, one of the greatest sins is "To grieve the spirit of one's brother or sister." And Jerome, on Ephesians 5:4 writes: As also we read in the Hebrew Gospel that the Lord spoke to his disciples: "And never," he said, "be joyful except when you look on your brother or sister with love."

§ 23 ON ADULTERY

MAT 5:27–30	MAR	LUK
27 “You have heard that it was said, ‘You shall not commit adultery.’ 28 But I say to you that everyone who looks at a woman with lust has already committed adultery with her in his heart. 29 If your right eye causes you to sin, tear it out and throw it away; it is better for you to lose one of your members than for your whole body to be thrown into hell.[G] 30 And if your right hand causes you to sin, cut it off and throw it away; it is better for you to lose one of your members than for your whole body to go into hell.”[1+G]		

§ 24 ON DIVORCE

MAT 5:31–32	*Δ MAT 19:9 (§ 187, p. 143)*	*Δ MAR 10:11–12 (§ 187, p. 143)*	*Δ LUK 16:18 (§ 176, p. 137)*
31 “It was also said, ‘Whoever divorces his wife, let him give her a certificate of divorce.’			
32 But I say to you that anyone who divorces his wife, except on the ground of unchastity,	*9 “And I say to you, whoever divorces his wife, except for unchastity,*[H]	*11 He said to them, “Whoever divorces his wife*	*18 “Anyone who divorces his wife*
	and marries another	*and marries another*	*and marries another*
causes her to commit adultery;	*commits adultery.”*[I]	*commits adultery against her;*	*commits adultery,*
and whoever marries a divorced woman commits adultery.”			*and whoever marries a woman divorced from her husband commits adultery.”*
		12 and if she divorces her husband and marries another, she commits adultery.”	

[1] MAT 18:8–9 (§ 131, p. 107): 8 “If your hand or your foot causes you to stumble, cut it off and throw it away; it is better for you to enter life maimed or lame than to have two hands or two feet and to be thrown into the eternal fire.	MAR 9:43–48 (§ 131, p. 107): 43 “If your hand causes you to stumble, cut it off; it is better for you to enter life maimed than to have two hands and to go to hell, to the unquenchable fire. {44} 45 And if your foot causes you to stumble, cut it off; it is better for you to enter life lame than to have two feet and to be thrown into hell. {46} 47 And
9 And if your eye causes you to stumble, tear it out and throw it away; it is better for you to enter life with one eye than to have two eyes and to be thrown into the hell of fire.”	if your eye causes you to stumble, tear it out; it is better for you to enter the kingdom of God with one eye than to have two eyes and to be thrown into hell, 48 where their worm never dies, and the fire is never quenched.”

✧ MAT 5:27 — EXO 20:14; DEU 5:18. ✧ MAT 5:31 — DEU 24:1.

✦ [G] Greek: *Gehenna.* ✦ [H] text: S W Θ 𝔐 vg sy^{s} sy^{p}; *except on the ground of unchastity, and marries another, commits adultery* (against her: sy^{c}): D ø it sy^{c} sa; *except on the ground of unchastity, makes her commit adultery*: $P^{25?}$ B λ bo; *except for unchastity, and marries another, makes her commit adultery*: C. ✦ [I] text: S D it (some MSS.) sy^{c} sy^{s} sa; add: *And whoever marries a divorced woman commits adultery*: P^{25} B C W Θ λ ø 𝔐 it (some MSS.) vg sy^{p} bo. *Cf.* MAT 5:32.

§ 25 ON SWEARING

MAT 5:33–37	MAR	LUK
(*Cf.* MAT 23:16–22, § 210, p. 165) 33 "Again, you have heard that it was said to those of ancient times, 'You shall not swear falsely, but carry out the vows you have made to the Lord.' 34 But I say to you, Do not swear at all, either by heaven, for it is the throne of God, 35 or by the earth, for it is his footstool, or by Jerusalem, for it is the city of the great King. 36 And do not swear by your head, for you cannot make one hair white or black. 37 Let your word be 'Yes, Yes' or 'No, No'; anything more than this comes from the evil one."		

§ 26 ON RETALIATION

MAT 5:38–42	MAR	Δ *LUK 6:29–30* *(§ 75, p. 64)*
38 "You have heard that it was said, 'An eye for		
an eye and a tooth for a tooth.' 39 But I say to		
you, Do not resist an evildoer. But		
if anyone strikes you		*29 "If anyone strikes you*
on the right cheek, turn the other also; 40 and		*on the cheek, offer the other also; and*
if anyone wants to sue you and		*from anyone who*
take your coat,		*takes away your coat*
give your cloak as well;		*do not withhold even your shirt.*
41 and if anyone forces you to go one mile,		
go also the second mile.		
42 Give to everyone who begs from you, and		*30 Give to everyone who begs from you; and*
do not refuse anyone		
who wants to borrow from you."		
		if anyone takes away your goods,
		do not ask for them again."

§ 27 ON LOVE OF ONE'S ENEMIES

MAT 5:43–48	MAR	Δ *LUK 6:27–28, 32–36* *(§ 75, p. 64)*
43 "You have heard that it was said, 'You shall		
love your neighbor and hate your enemy.'		
44 But I say to you, Love		*27 "But I say to you that listen, Love*
your enemies and		*your enemies, do good to those who hate you,*
		28 bless those who curse you,

✧ MAT 5:33 — LEV 19:12. ✧ MAT 5:34–35 — ISA 66:1. ✧ MAT 5:35 — PSA 48:2. ✧ MAT 5:38 — EXO 21:24; DEU 19:21; LEV 24:20. ✧ MAT 5:43 — LEV 19:18 (minus "and hate your enemy").

▸ To MAT 5:42; LUK 6:30 *cf.* **Gospel of Thomas, Logion 95.** — Jesus said, "If you have money, do not lend it at interest, but give it to a person from whom you will not get it back." ▸ To MAT 5:44 *cf. Oxyrhynchus Papyrus 1224, fol. 2 recto, col 1.* — "and pray for your enemies."

pray for those who persecute you,
45 so that you may be children of your Father in heaven; for he makes his sun rise on the evil and on the good, and sends rain on the righteous and on the unrighteous.
46 For if you love those who love you, what reward do you have? Do not even the tax collectors do the same?
47 And if you greet only your brothers and sisters, what more are you doing than others? Do not even the Gentiles do the same?
48 Be perfect, therefore, as your heavenly Father is perfect."

pray for those who abuse you.

32 *"If you love those who love you, what credit is that to you? For even sinners love those who love them.*
33 *If you do good to those who do good to you, what credit is that to you? For even sinners do the same.*
34 *If you lend to those from whom you hope to receive, what credit is that to you? Even sinners lend to sinners, to receive as much again.*
35 *But love your enemies, do good, and lend, expecting nothing in return.*[J] *Your reward will be great, and you will be children of the Most High; for he is kind to the ungrateful and the wicked.*
36 *Be merciful, just as your Father is merciful."*

§ 28 ON ALMSGIVING

MAT 6:1–4	MAR	LUK
1 "Beware of practicing your piety[K] before others in order to be seen by them; for then you have no reward from your Father in heaven. 2 "So whenever you give alms, do not sound a trumpet before you, as the hypocrites do in the synagogues and in the streets, so that they may be praised by others. Truly I tell you, they have received their reward. 3 But when you give alms, do not let your left hand know what your right hand is doing, 4 so that your alms may be done in secret; and your Father who sees in secret will reward you."[L]		

✧ MAT 5:48 — DEU 18:13.

✦ [J] text: A B D Θ λ ø ℜ it vg sa bo; *despairing of no one*: S W sy^{s} sy^{p}. ✦ [K] text: S B D λ it vg sy^{s} sy^{p}; *beware of giving your alms before others*: W Θ ø ℜ. ✦ [L] text: S B D λ ø it (some MSS.) vg sy^{c} sa bo; add: *openly*: W Θ ℜ it (some MSS.) sy^{s} sy^{p}.

◗ To MAT 5:46 *cf.* **II Clement 13:4**. — Whenever people hear from us that God says, "It is no credit to you if you love those who love you, but it is a credit to you if you love your enemies and those who hate you" — whenever people hear this, they wonder at this extraordinary goodness; but when they see that we not only do not love those who hate us, but not even those who love us, they laugh at us, and the name is blasphemed. ◗ To MAT 6:3 *cf.* **Gospel of Thomas, Logion 62**. — Jesus said, "I tell my mysteries to those (who are worthy of my) mysteries. Do not let your left hand know what your right hand is doing."

§ 29 ON PRAYER

MAT 6:5–8	**MAR**	**LUK**
5 "And whenever you pray, do not be like the hypocrites; for they love to stand and pray in the synagogues and at the street corners, so that they may be seen by others. Truly I tell you, they have received their reward. 6 But whenever you pray, go into your room and shut the door and pray to your Father who is in secret; and your Father who sees in secret will reward you.[M] 7 When you are praying, do not heap up empty phrases as the Gentiles do; for they think that they will be heard because of their many words. 8 Do not be like them, for your Father knows what you need before you ask him."		

§ 30 THE LORD'S PRAYER

MAT 6:9–15	Δ *MAR 11:25–26 (§ 201, p. 156)*	Δ *LUK 11:2–4 (§ 146, p. 116)*
9 "Pray then in this way: Our Father in heaven, hallowed be your name. 10 Your kingdom come. Your will be done, on earth as it is in heaven. 11 Give us this day our daily bread.[O] 12 And forgive us our debts, as we also have forgiven our debtors. 13 And do not bring us to the time of trial, but rescue us from the evil one.[P]		*2 He said to them, "When you pray, say: Father,[N] hallowed be your name. Your kingdom come.* *3 Give us each day our daily bread.[O] 4 And forgive us our sins, for we ourselves forgive everyone indebted to us. And do not bring us to the time of trial."*
14 For if you forgive others their trespasses, your heavenly Father will also	*25 "Whenever you stand praying, forgive, if you have anything against anyone; so that your Father in heaven may also*	

✧ MAT 6:6 — ISA 26:20

✦ [M] text: S B D λ it (some MSS.) vg sy[c] sy[s] sa bo; add: *openly*: W Θ ø ℜ it (some MSS.) sy[p]. ✦ [N] text: P[75] S B λ vg sy[s] Marcion, Origen; *Our Father in heaven*: A C D W Θ ø ℜ it sy[c] sy[p] sa bo. *Cf.* MAT 6:9. ✦ [O] Or, *our bread for the morrow.* ✦ [P] text: S B D λ it vg bo; add: *For the kingdom and the power and the glory are yours forever. Amen*: W Θ ø ℜ sy[p]; add: *For the power and the glory are yours forever. Amen*: sa; add: *For the kingdom and the glory are yours forever. Amen*: sy[c].

● To MAT 6:8 — *cf.* MAT 6:32.

◗ To MAT 6:5–13 *cf.* **Didache 8:1–2.** — 1 Do not fast with the hypocrites, for they fast on Mondays and Thursdays, but you are to fast on Wednesdays and Fridays. 2 And do not pray like the hypocrites, but as the Lord commanded in the gospel: "Our Father in heaven, hallowed be your name. Your kingdom come. Your will be done, on earth as it is in heaven. Give us this day our daily bread. And forgive us our debt, as we forgive our debtors. And do not bring us to the time of trial, but rescue us from the evil one. For the power and the glory are yours forever." ◗ To MAT 6:11 *cf.* **Gospel of the Nazaraeans** (in Jerome, *Commentary on Matthew 6:11*). — In the so-called Gospel according to the Hebrews, for "bread essential to existence" I found "mahar," which means "of tomorrow"; so the sense is: our bread for tomorrow, that is, of the future, give us this day.

forgive you;[1] 15 but if you do not forgive others,[Q] neither will your Father forgive your trespasses."	*forgive you your trespasses."*[R] {26}	

§ 31 WORDS OF JESUS ON FASTING

MAT 6:16–18	MAR	LUK
16 "And whenever you fast, do not look dismal, like the hypocrites, for they disfigure their faces so as to show others that they are fasting. Truly I tell you, they have received their reward. 17 But when you fast, put oil on your head and wash your face, 18 so that your fasting may be seen not by others but by your Father who is in secret; and your Father who sees in secret will reward you."		

§ 32 ON TREASURES

MAT 6:19–21	MAR	Δ *LUK 12:33–34* *(§ 157, p. 125)*
		33 *"Sell your possessions, and give alms.*
19 "Do not store up for yourselves treasures on earth, where moth and rust[S] consume and where thieves break in and steal;		
20 but store up for yourselves treasures in heaven, where neither moth nor rust[S] consumes and where thieves do not break in and steal.		*Make purses for yourselves that do not wear out, an unfailing treasure in heaven, where no thief comes near and no moth destroys.*
21 For where your treasure is, there your heart will be also."		34 *For where your treasure is, there your heart will be also."*

---

[1] *Cf.* MAT 18:35 (§ 136, p. 110).

✦ [Q] text: S D λ it vg sy[p] bo (some MSS.) Augustine; add after; *others: their trespasses*: B W Θ ø ℜ sy[c] sa bo (some MSS.).
✦ [R] text: S B W sy[s] sa bo; add verse 26: *"But if you do not forgive, neither will your Father who is in heaven forgive your trespasses"*: A C D Θ λ ø ℜ it vg sy[p] Cyprian. ✦ [S] Or, *worm.*

◗ To MAT 6:16 *cf. Oxyrhynchus Papyrus 1, Logion 2.* — Jesus says, "If you do not fast to the world, you will not find the kingdom of God; and if you do not keep the sabbath, you will not see the Father." ◗ To MAT 6:16–18 *cf.* **Didache 8:1**. — Do not let your fasts be with the hypocrites, for they fast on Mondays and Thursdays. But you are to fast on Wednesdays and Fridays.
◗ To MAT 6:19–21 *cf.* **Gospel of Thomas, Logion 76**. — Jesus said, "The kingdom of the Father is like a merchant who possessed merchandise and found a pearl. That merchant was shrewd, selling the merchandise and buying the pearl to keep it. You, too, are to seek for the treasure that does not fail, but that endures, where no moth comes near to devour and no worm destroys."

§ 33 THE SOUND EYE

MAT 6:22–23	MAR	Δ *LUK 11:34–36* (§ 153, p. 120)
22 "The eye is the lamp of the body. So, if your eye is healthy, your whole body will be full of light; 23 but if your eye is unhealthy, your whole body will be full of darkness. If then the light in you is darkness, how great is the darkness!"		34 *"Your eye is the lamp of your body.* *If your eye is healthy, your whole body* *is full of light; but if* *it is not healthy, your body* *is full of darkness.* 35 *Therefore consider* *whether the light in you is not darkness.* 36 *If then your whole body is full of* *light, with no part of it in darkness, it will* *be as full of light as when a lamp gives you* *light with its rays."*

§ 34 WORDS OF JESUS ON SERVING TWO MASTERS

MAT 6:24	MAR	Δ *LUK 16:13* (§ 174, p. 136)
24 "No one can serve two masters; for a slave will either hate the one and love the other, or be devoted to the one and despise the other. You cannot serve God and wealth."		13 *"No slave can serve two masters;* *for a slave will either hate the one and love the* *other, or be devoted to the one and despise the* *other. You cannot serve God and wealth."*

§ 35 ON ANXIETY

MAT 6:25–34	MAR	Δ *LUK 12:22–31* (§ 157, p. 125)
25 "Therefore I tell you, do not worry about your life, what you will eat or what you will drink,[T] or about your body, what you will wear. Is not life more than food, and the body more than clothing? 26 Look at the birds of the air; they neither sow nor reap nor gather into barns, and yet your heavenly Father feeds them. Are you not of more value than they? 27 And can any of you by worrying add a single hour to your span of life?[U]		22 *He said to his disciples,* *"Therefore I tell you, do not worry about* *your life, what you will eat,* *or about* *your body, what you will wear.* 23 *For life is more than food, and the body* *more than clothing.* 24 *Consider the* *ravens: they neither sow nor reap,* *they have neither storehouse nor barn, and yet* *God feeds them.* *Of how much more value are you than the birds!* 25 *And can any of you by worrying add a single* *hour to your span of life?*[U]

✦ [T] text: B W ø it (some MSS.) sa (some MSS.) bo; *what you shall eat and what you shall drink*: Θ ℜ sy[p]; omit: *or what you shall drink*: S λ it (some MSS.) vg sy[c] sa (some MSS.). ✦ [U] Or, *add one cubit to your height.*

◗ To MAT 6:25*ff*. *cf*. *Oxyrhynchus Papyrus 655 I a, b.* — "(Take no thought) from morning until evening or from evening until morning, either for your food, what you will eat, or for your clothing, what you will wear. You are far better than the lilies which grow but do not spin. Having one piece of clothing, what do you (lack)?... Who could add to your span of life? God will give you your clothing."

28 And why do you worry about clothing?
Consider the lilies of the field, how they grow;
they neither toil nor spin, 29 yet I tell you, even
Solomon in all his glory was not clothed like
one of these. 30 But if God so clothes the grass
of the field, which is alive today and tomorrow
is thrown into the oven, will he not much more
clothe you—you of little faith? 31 Therefore
do not worry, saying, 'What will we eat?'
or 'What will we drink?' or 'What will we
wear?' 32 For it is the Gentiles
who strive for all these things;
and indeed your heavenly Father knows that
you need all these things.
33 But strive first for the kingdom of God and
his righteousness, and all these things will
be given to you as well.
34 "So do not worry about tomorrow, for tomorrow will bring worries of its own. Today's
trouble is enough for today."

26 If then you are not able to do so small a thing
as that, why do you worry about the rest?
27 Consider the lilies, how they grow:
they neither toil nor spin;[V] yet I tell you, even
Solomon in all his glory was not clothed like
one of these. 28 But if God so clothes the grass
of the field, which is alive today and tomorrow
is thrown into the oven, how much more will
he clothe you—you of little faith! 29 And
do not keep striving for what you are to eat
and what you are to drink, and do not keep
worrying. 30 For it is the nations
of the world that strive after all these things,
and your Father knows that
you need them.
31 Instead, strive for his[W] kingdom, and
these things will
be given to you as well."

§ 36 ON JUDGING

MAT 7:1–5

1 "Do not judge, so that you may not be judged.
2 For with the judgment you make
you will be judged,
and the measure you give will be the
measure you get.[1] 3 Why do you
see the speck in your neighbor's eye, but do not
notice the log in your own eye? 4 Or how can
you say to your neighbor, 'Let me take
the speck out of your eye,'

MAR

Δ *LUK 6:37–38, 41–42 (§ 76, p. 65)*

37 "Do not judge, and you will not be judged;
do not condemn,
and you will not be condemned. Forgive, and
you will be forgiven; 38 give, and it will be
given to you. A good measure, pressed down,
shaken together, running over, will be put into
your lap; for the measure you give will be the
measure you get back.[1] [39–40] 41 Why do you
see the speck in your neighbor's eye, but do not
notice the log in your own eye? 42 Or how can
you say to your neighbor, 'Friend, let me take
out the speck in your eye,'

---

[1] MAR 4:24 (§ 94, p. 77): And he [Jesus] said to them, "Pay attention to what you hear; the measure you give will be the measure you get, and still more will be given you." *Cf.* MAT 6:33; LUK 12:31.

✦ [V] text: P^{45} P^{75} S A B W Θ λ ø 𝔎 it (some MSS.) vg sy^{p} sa bo; *lilies, how they neither spin nor weave*: D sy^{c} sy^{s}; *how they grow; they neither toil nor spin nor weave*: it (some MSS.). ✦ [W] text: S B D sa bo; *God's*: P^{45} A W Θ λ ø 𝔎 it vg sy^{c} sy^{s} sy^{p}; *the kingdom*: P^{75}.

◗ To MAT 6:33 *cf.* Origen, *On Prayer 2:2, 14:1.* — "Ask for the great things, and the small things will be yours as well; and ask for the heavenly things, and the earthly things will be yours as well." *Cf.* Clement of Alexandria, *Miscellanies*, I.24:158.

◗ To MAT 7:1 (also MAT 5:7; 6:14; LUK 6:31, 37–38) *cf.* **I Clement 13:2**. — "Be merciful, that you may obtain mercy. Forgive that you may be forgiven. As you do, so shall it be done to you. As you give, so shall it be given to you. As you judge, so shall you be judged. The kindness you show will be shown you. The measure you give will be the measure you get."

while the log is in your own eye? 5 You hypocrite, first take the log out of your own eye, and then you will see clearly to take the speck out of your neighbor's eye."		*when you yourself do not see the log in your* *own eye? You hypocrite, first take the log* *out of your own eye, and then you will see* *clearly to take the speck out of your neighbor's* *eye."*

§ 37 ON PROFANING THE HOLY

MAT 7:6	MAR	LUK
6 "Do not give what is holy to dogs; and do not throw your pearls before swine, or they will trample them under foot and turn and maul you."		

§ 38 GOD'S ANSWERING OF PRAYER

MAT 7:7–11	MAR	Δ *LUK 11:9–13* *(§ 148, p. 117)*
7 "Ask, and it will be given you; search, and you will find; knock, and the door will be opened for you. 8 For every- one who asks receives, and everyone who searches finds, and for everyone who knocks, the door will be opened. 9 Is there anyone among you who, if your child asks for bread, will give a stone? 10 Or if the child asks for a fish, will give a snake? 11 If you then, who are evil, know how to give good gifts to your children, how much more will your Father in heaven give good things to those who ask him!"		*9 "So I say to you, Ask, and it will be given* *you; search, and you will find; knock, and* *the door will be opened for you. 10 For every-* *one who asks receives, and everyone who* *searches finds, and for everyone who knocks,* *the door will be opened.* *11 Is there anyone among you who,* *if your child asks for*[X] *a fish,* *will give a snake instead of a fish?* *12 Or if the child asks for an egg,* *will give a scorpion?* *13 If you then, who are evil, know how to give* *good gifts to your children, how much more* *will the heavenly Father give* *the Holy Spirit to those who ask him!"*

✦ [X] text P^{45} P^{75} B sy^s sa; add: *bread, will give a stone; or if your child asks for*: S A C D W Θ λ ø ℜ it vg sy^c sy^p bo.

◗ To MAT 7:5 *cf.* **Gospel of the Nazaraeans**. — The Jewish Gospel reads here: "If you are in my bosom and do not do the will of my Father who is in heaven, I will cast you away from my bosom." ◗ To MAT 7:5; LUK 6:42 *cf. Oxyrhynchus Papyrus 1, Logion 1.* — "And then you will see clearly to take out the speck that is in your neighbor's eye." ◗ To MAT 7:6 *cf.* **Didache 9:5**. — But do not let anyone eat or drink of your Eucharist, except those who have been baptized in the name of the Lord; for concerning this the Lord has said, "Do not give what is holy to dogs." *Cf.* Epiphanius, *Against Heresies, XXIV.5:2.*
◗ To MAT 7:6 *cf.* **Gospel of Thomas, Logion 93**. — Jesus said, "Do not give what is holy to dogs, lest they throw it on the dung-heap. Do not throw pearls to swine, least they grind it ( )." ◗ To MAT 7:7 *cf. Oxyrhynchus Papyrus 654, Logion 1.* — "Those who seek will not give up until they find; and having found, they will marvel; and having marveled, they will reign; and having reigned, they will rest." *cf.* **Gospel according to the Hebrews**, (in Clement of Alexandria, *Miscellanies V.14:96*).
◗ To MAT 7:7 *cf.* **Gospel of Thomas, Logion 2**. — Jesus said, "Let those who seek not give up until they find, and when they find they will be troubled, and when they have been troubled they will marvel and they will reign over the All."

§ 39 THE GOLDEN RULE

MAT 7:12	MAR	Δ *LUK 6:31* (*§ 75, p. 64*)
12 "In everything do to others as you would have them do to you; for this is the law and the prophets."		*31 "Do to others as you would have them do to you."*

§ 40 THE NARROW GATE

MAT 7:13–14	MAR	Δ *LUK 13:23–24* (*§ 165, p. 130*)
13 "Enter through the narrow gate; for the gate is wide and the road is easy[Y] that leads to destruction, and there are many who take it. 14 For the gate is narrow and the road is hard that leads to life, and there are few who find it."		*23 Someone asked him, "Lord, will only a few be saved?" He said to them, 24 "Strive to enter through the narrow door; for many, I tell you, will try to enter and will not be able."*

§ 41 THE TEST OF A GOOD PERSON

MAT 7:15–20	MAR	Δ *LUK 6:43–45* (*§ 77, p. 65*)
15 "Beware of false prophets, who come to you in sheep's clothing but inwardly are ravenous wolves. 16 You will know them by their fruits. Are grapes gathered from thorns, or figs from thistles? 17 In the same way, every good tree bears		

✧ MAT 7:12 — Tobit 4:15; Ecclesiasticus 31:15.

✦ [Y] text: B C W Θ λ ø ℜ it (some MSS.) vg sy[c] sy[p] sa bo; *for the way is wide and easy*: S it (some MSS.) Clement, Origen.

◗ To MAT 7:12 *cf.* **Didache 1:2**. — "Whatever you would not have done to yourself, do not do to another." ◗ To MAT 7:15 *cf.* Justin, *Dialogue, 35:3*. — For, he says, "Many will come in my name, clothed in sheepskins, but inwardly they are ravenous wolves"; and "there will be divisions and heresies."

good fruit, but the bad tree bears bad fruit.[1]
18 A good tree cannot bear bad fruit, nor
can a bad tree bear good fruit.
19 Every tree that does not bear good fruit is cut
down and thrown into the fire.[2]
20 Thus you will know them by their fruits."

Cf. 12:35 (§ 86, p. 70)

43 "No good tree bears bad fruit, nor
again does a bad tree bear good fruit;

44 for each tree is known by its own fruit.[1] Figs
are not gathered from thorns, nor are grapes
picked from a bramble bush. 45 The good per-
son out of the good treasure of the heart
produces good, and the evil person out of evil
treasure produces evil; for it is out of the abun-
dance of the heart that the mouth speaks."

§ 42 ON SELF-DECEPTION

MAT 7:21–23	MAR	Δ LUK 6:46 (§ 77, p. 65) +
21 "Not everyone who says to me, 'Lord, Lord,'		*46 "Why do you call me 'Lord, Lord,'*
will enter the kingdom of heaven, but only the one who does the will of my Father in heaven.		*and do not do what I tell you?"*
		Δ *13:26–27 (§ 165, p. 130)*
22 On that day many will say to me,		*26 "Then you will begin to say,*
'Lord, Lord, did we not prophesy in your name, and cast out demons in your name, and do many deeds of power in your name?'		*'We ate and drank with you, and you taught in our streets.'*
23 Then I will declare to them,		*27 But he will say,*
'I never knew you;		*'I do not know where you come from;*
go away from me, you evildoers.' "		*go away from me, all you evildoers!' "*

---

[1] MAT 12:33–35 (§ 86, p. 70): 33 "Either make the tree good, and its fruit good; or make the tree bad, and its fruit bad; for the tree is known by its fruit. 34 You brood of vipers! How can you speak good things, when you are evil? For out of the abundance of the heart the mouth speaks. 35 The good person brings good things out of a good treasure, and the evil person brings evil things out of an evil treasure."
[2] *Cf.* MAT 3:10; LUK 3:9 (§ 2, p. 12).

⟡ MAT 7:23; LUK 13:27 — PSA 6:8.

▸ To MAT 7:21 *cf.* **II Clement 4:2.** — For he says, "Not every one who says to me, 'Lord, Lord,' will be saved; but the one who practices piety." ▸ To MAT 7:22–23 *cf.* **II Clement 4:5.** — The Lord said, "If you are gathered together with me in my bosom, and do not obey my commandments, I will cast you out and say to you, Depart from me; I do not know where you come from, you evildoers." *Cf.* LUK 13:25*ff.*

§ 43 HEARERS AND DOERS OF THE WORD

MAT 7:24–27	MAR	Δ *LUK 6:47–49* (§ 78, p. 66)
24 "Everyone then who hears these words of mine and acts on them will be like a wise man who built his house on rock. 25 The rain fell, the floods came, and the winds blew and beat on that house, but it did not fall, because it had been founded on rock. 26 And everyone who hears these words of mine and does not act on them will be like a foolish man who built his house on sand. 27 The rain fell, and the floods came, and the winds blew and beat against that house, and it fell— and great was its fall!"		*47 "I will show you what someone is like who comes to me, hears my words, and acts on them. 48 That one is like a man building a house, who dug deeply and laid the foundation on rock; when a flood arose, the river burst against that house but could not shake it, because it had been well built.*[Z] *49 But the one who hears and does not act is like a man who built a house on the ground without a foundation. When the river burst against it, immediately it fell, and great was the ruin of that house."*

§ 44 THE END OF THE SERMON

MAT 7:28–29	MAR	LUK
28 Now when Jesus had finished saying these things, the crowds were astounded at his teaching, 29 for he taught them as one having authority, and not as their scribes.[1]		*Cf.* 7:1a (§ 79, p. 67)

§ 45 THE HEALING OF A LEPER

MAT 8:1–4	MAR 1:40–45	LUK 5:12–16
1 When Jesus had come down from the mountain, great crowds followed him;	▲ 1:39 (§ 16, p. 23)	▲ 5:1–11 (§ 17, p. 24) 12 Once, when he was in one of the cities, there

[1] MAR 1:21–22 (§ 12, p. 20): 21 They went to Capernaum; and when the sabbath came, he [Jesus] entered the synagogue and taught. 22They were astounded at his teaching, for he taught them as one having authority, and not as the scribes.

LUK 4:31–32 (§ 12, p. 20): 31 He [Jesus] went down to Capernaum, a city in Galilee, and was teaching them on the sabbath. 32They were astounded at his teaching, because he spoke with authority.

✦ [Z] text: $P^{75?}$ S B W sa bo; *because it had been founded on rock*: A C D Θ λ ø ℜ it vg sy^{p}; omit phrase: $P^{45?}$ sy^{s}.

● To § 44 *cf.* JOH 7:46. — The police answered, "Never has anyone spoken like this!"

2 and there was a leper who came to
him and knelt before him,
saying,
"Lord, if you choose, you can
make me clean."
3 He stretched out his hand
and touched him, saying,
"I do choose. Be made clean!"
Immediately his leprosy
was cleansed.
4 Then Jesus said to him,
"See that you say nothing to anyone; but go, show yourself
to the priest, and offer
the gift that Moses commanded,
as a testimony to them."

40 A leper came to
him begging him, and kneeling
he said to him,
"If you choose, you can
make me clean." 41 Moved with
pity, Jesus[A] stretched out his hand
and touched him, and said to him,
"I do choose. Be made clean!"
42 Immediately the leprosy
left him, and he was made clean.
43 After sternly warning him he sent
him away at once, 44 saying to him,
"See that you say nothing to anyone; but go, show yourself
to the priest, and offer for your
cleansing what Moses commanded,
as a testimony to them." 45 But
he went out and began to proclaim
it freely, and to spread the word,
so that Jesus[A] could no longer go
into a town openly, but stayed out
in the country;[1] and people came to
him from every quarter.

▼ 2:1–12 (§ 52, p. 42)

was a man covered with leprosy.
When he saw Jesus, he bowed with
his face to the ground and
begged him,
"Lord, if you choose, you can
make me clean." 13 Then
Jesus[A] stretched out his hand,
touched him, and said,
"I do choose. Be made clean."
Immediately the leprosy
left him.
14 And he ordered him to tell no one.
"Go," he said, "and show yourself
to the priest, and,
as Moses commanded, make an
offering for your cleansing,
for a testimony to them." 15 But
now more than ever the word about
Jesus spread abroad;
many crowds would gather to hear
him and to be cured of their diseases. 16 But he would withdraw
to deserted places and pray.[1]

▼ 5:17–26 (§ 52, p. 42)

§ 46 THE CENTURION'S SERVANT

MAT 8:5–13

5 When he entered Capernaum,
a centurion came to him, appealing to him
6 and saying, "Lord, my servant is lying at

MAR

Δ LUK 7:1–10 *(§ 79, p. 67) +*

1 After Jesus had finished all his sayings in the
hearing of the people, he entered Capernaum.
2 A centurion there

---

[1] *Cf.* MAR 1:35; LUK 4:42 (§ 15, p. 22).

✧ MAT 8:4; MAR 1:44; LUK 5:14 — LEV 13:49, 14:2*ff.*

✦ [A] Greek: *he.*

● To § 46 *cf.* JOH 4:46–53.

◗ To MAT 8:2–4 and parallels, *cf. Egerton Papyrus 2.* — A person with leprosy came up to Jesus and said, "Master Jesus, journeying with leprous people and eating with them in the inn, I also became leprous. If, therefore, you will, I can be made clean." Then the Lord answered, "I will; be clean." And immediately the leprosy departed; and the Lord said, "Go and show yourself to the priests."

home paralyzed, in terrible distress." 7 And
he said to him, "I will come and cure him."

8 The centurion answered, "Lord,
I am not worthy to have
you come under my roof;

but only speak the word, and
my servant will be healed. 9 For I also am a
man under
authority, with soldiers under me;
and I say to one, 'Go,' and he goes,
and to another, 'Come,' and he comes,
and to my slave, 'Do this,' and the slave
does it." 10 When Jesus heard him, he
was amazed and
said to those who followed him,
"Truly I tell you, in no one[B] in Israel
have I found such faith.
11 I tell you, many will come from east and west
and will eat with

Abraham and Isaac and Jacob
in the kingdom of heaven,
12 while the heirs of the kingdom will be thrown
into the outer darkness, where there will be
weeping and gnashing of teeth."

13 And to the centurion Jesus said, "Go; let it
be done for you according to your faith." And
the servant was healed in that hour.[C]

had a slave whom he valued highly, and
who was ill and close to death.

3 When he heard about Jesus, he sent some
Jewish elders to him, asking him to come and
heal his slave. 4 When they came to Jesus,
they appealed to him earnestly, saying, "He is
worthy of having you do this for him, 5 for he
loves our people, and it is he who built our
synagogue for us." 6 And Jesus went with
them, but when he was not far from the house,
the centurion sent friends to say to him,
"Lord, do not trouble yourself, for
I am not worthy to have
you come under my roof;
7 therefore I did not presume to come to you.
But only speak the word, and
let my servant be healed. 8 For I also am
man set under
authority, with soldiers under me;
and I say to one, 'Go,' and he goes,
and to another, 'Come,' and he comes,
and to my slave, 'Do this,' and the slave
does it." 9 When Jesus heard this he
was amazed at him, and turning
to the crowd that followed him, he said,
"I tell you, not even in Israel
have I found such faith."

Δ *13:28–30 (§ 165, p. 130)*
28 "There will be weeping and gnashing of teeth
when you see Abraham and Isaac and Jacob
and all the prophets in the kingdom of God,
and you yourselves thrown
out.
29 Then people will come from east and west,
from north and south, and will eat in the king-
dom of God. 30 Indeed, some are last who will
be first, and some are first who will be last."
7:10 When those who had been sent returned to

the house, they found the slave in good health.

✧ MAT 8:11; LUK 13:29 — PSA 107:3.

✦ [B] text: B W λ it (some MSS.) sy^{c} sa bo; *not even in Israel*: S C Θ ø ℜ it (some MSS.) vg sy^{s} sy^{p}. ✦ [C] text: B W ø ℜ it vg sy^{c} sy^{s} sy^{p} sa bo; *and when the centurion returned to his house in that hour he found the servant well*: S C Θ λ. *Cf.* LUK 7:10.

§ 47 THE HEALING OF PETER'S MOTHER-IN-LAW

MAT 8:14–15	MAR	LUK
14 When Jesus entered Peter's house, he saw his mother-in-law lying in bed with a fever; 15 he touched her hand, and the fever left her, and she got up and began to serve him.	*Cf.* 1:29–31 (§ 13, p. 21)	*Cf.* 4:38–39 (§ 13, p. 21)

§ 48 THE SICK HEALED AT EVENING

MAT 8:16–17	MAR	LUK
16 That evening they brought to him many who were possessed with demons; and he cast out the spirits with a word, and cured all who were sick. 17 This was to fulfill what had been spoken through the prophet Isaiah, "He took our infirmities and bore our diseases."	*Cf.* 1:32–34 (§ 14, p. 22)	*Cf.* 4:40–41 (§ 14, p. 22)

§ 49 WOULD-BE FOLLOWERS OF JESUS

MAT 8:18–22	MAR	Δ *LUK 9:57–60 (§ 138, p. 111)*
18 Now when Jesus saw great crowds around him, he gave orders to go over to the other side.	*Cf.* 4:35 (§ 105, p. 81)	
		57 As they were going along the road, *someone said to him,*
19 A scribe then approached and said, "Teacher, I will follow you wherever you go." 20 And Jesus said to him, "Foxes have holes, and birds of the air have nests; but the Son of Man has nowhere to lay his head."		*"I will follow you wherever you go." 58 And* *Jesus said to him, "Foxes have holes, and* *birds of the air have nests; but the Son of Man* *has nowhere to lay his head."* *59 To another he said, "Follow me."* *But he said,*
21 Another of his disciples said to him, "Lord, first let me go and bury my father." 22 But Jesus said to him, "Follow me, and let the dead bury their own dead."		*"Lord, first let me go and bury my father."* *60 But Jesus said to him,* *"Let the dead bury their own dead; but as for* *you, go and proclaim the kingdom of God."*

§ 50 CALMING THE STORM

MAT 8:23–27	MAR	LUK
23 And when he got into the boat, his disciples followed him. 24 A windstorm arose on the sea, so great that the boat was being swamped by the waves; but he was asleep. 25 And they went and woke him up, saying, "Lord, save us! We are	*Cf.* 4:35–41 (§ 105, p. 81)	*Cf.* 8:22–25 (§ 105, p. 81)

✧ MAT 8:17 — ISA 53:4.

◗ To MAT 8:14 *cf.* **Gospel of the Ebionites**, p. 20.

MAT	MAR	LUK
perishing!" 26 And he said to them, "Why are you afraid, you of little faith?" Then he got up and rebuked the winds and the sea; and there was a dead calm. 27 They were amazed, saying, "What sort of man is this, that even the winds and the sea obey him?"		

§ 51 THE GADARENE DEMONIACS

MAT 8:28–34	MAR	LUK
28 When he came to the other side, to the country of the Gadarenes,[D] two demoni- acs coming out of the tombs met him. They were so fierce that no one could pass that way. 29 Suddenly they shouted, "What have you to do with us, Son of God? Have you come here to torment us before the time?" 30 Now a large herd of swine was feeding at some distance from them. 31 The demons begged him, "If you cast us out, send us into the herd of swine." 32 And he said to them, "Go!" So they came out and entered the swine; and suddenly, the whole herd rushed down the steep bank into the sea and perished in the water. 33 The swineherds ran off, and on going into the town, they told the whole story about what had happened to the demoniacs. 34 Then the whole town came out to meet Jesus; and when they saw him, they begged him to leave their neighborhood.	*Cf.* 5:1–20 (§ 106, p. 81)	*Cf.* 8:26–39 (§ 106, p. 81)

§ 52 THE HEALING OF THE PARALYTIC

MAT 9:1–8	MAR 2:1–12	LUK 5:17–26
	▲ 1:40–45 (§ 45, p. 38)	▲ 5:12–16 (§ 45, p. 38)
1 And after getting into a boat he crossed the sea and came to	1 When he returned to	17 One day, while he was teaching, Pharisees and teachers of the law were sitting near by (they had come from every village of Galilee and Judea and from Jerusalem); and the power of the Lord was with him to heal.[E]
his own town.	Capernaum after some days, it was reported that he was at home. 2 So many gathered around that there was no longer room for them, not even in front of the door; and he was speaking the word to them.	
2 And just then some people were carrying a paralyzed man lying on a bed.	3 Then some people came, bringing to him a paralyzed man, carried by four of them. 4 And when they could not bring him to Jesus	18 Just then some men came, carrying a paralyzed man on a bed. They were trying to bring him in and lay him before Jesus;[F]

✦ [D] text: S B C Θ sy[s] sy[p]; *Gergesenes*: W λ ø 𝔐 bo; *Gerasenes*: it vg sa. ✦ [E] text: S B W sa; *was present to heal them*: A C D Θ λ ø 𝔐 it vg sy[p] bo; *was for healing*: sy[s]. ✦ [F] Greek: *him*.

	because of the crowd, they removed the roof above him; and after having dug through it, they let down the mat on which the para- lytic lay.	19 but finding no way to bring him in because of the crowd, they went up on the roof and let him down with his bed through the tiles into the middle of the crowd in front of Jesus.
When Jesus saw their faith, he said to the paralytic, "Take heart, son; your sins are forgiven." 3 Then some of the scribes said to themselves,	5 When Jesus saw their faith, he said to the paralytic, "Son, your sins are forgiven." 6 Now some of the scribes were sitting there, questioning in their hearts, 7 "Why does this fellow speak in this way?	20 When he saw their faith, he said, "Friend, your sins are forgiven you." 21 Then the scribes and the Pharisees began to question, "Who is this who is speaking
"This man is blaspheming."	It is blasphemy! Who can forgive sins but God alone?"	blasphemies? Who can forgive sins but God alone?"
4 But Jesus, perceiving[G] their thoughts, said, "Why do you think evil in your hearts? 5 For which is easier, to say, 'Your sins are forgiven,'[H] or to say, 'Stand up and walk'? 6 But so that you may know that the Son of Man has authority on earth to forgive sins"—he then said to the paralytic— "Stand up, take your bed and go to your home." 7 And he stood up and	8 At once Jesus perceived in his spirit that they were discussing these questions among themselves; and he said to them, "Why do you raise such questions in your hearts? 9 Which is easier, to say to the paralytic, 'Your sins are forgiven,' or to say, 'Stand up and take your mat and walk'? 10 But so that you may know that the Son of Man has authority on earth to forgive sins"—he said to the paralytic— 11 "I say to you, stand up, take your mat and go to your home." 12 And he stood up, and	22 When Jesus perceived their questionings, he answered them, "Why do you raise such questions in your hearts? 23 Which is easier, to say, 'Your sins are forgiven you,' or to say, 'Stand up and walk'? 24 But so that you may know that the Son of Man has authority on earth to forgive sins"—he said to the one who was paralyzed—"I say to you, stand up and take your bed and go to your home." 25 Immediately he stood up
went to his home.	immediately took the mat and went out before all of them; so that	before them, took what he had been lying on, and went to his home, glorifying God.
8 When the crowds saw it, they were filled with awe, and they glorified God,	they were all amazed and glorified God,	26 Amazement seized all of them, and they glorified God and were filled with awe,
	saying, "We have never seen anything like this!"	saying, "We have seen strange things today."
who had given such authority to human beings.		

✦ [G] text: B Θ λ sy^{p} sa; *seeing*: S C D W ø 𝔐 it vg bo. ✦ [H] text: S B D vg sa bo; *have been forgiven*: C W Θ λ 𝔐 it.

• To MAT 9:6–7 and parallels, *cf.* JOH 5:8–9. — 8 Jesus said to him, "Stand up, take your mat and walk." 9 At once the man was made well, and he took up his mat and began to walk.

§ 53 THE CALL OF LEVI

MAT 9:9–13	MAR 2:13–17	LUK 5:27–32
	13 Jesus went out again beside the sea; the whole crowd gathered around him, and he taught them.	27 After this he went out
9 As Jesus was walking along, he saw a man called Matthew sitting at the tax booth; and he said to him, “Follow me.” And he got up and followed him.	14 As he was walking along, he saw Levi[I] son of Alphaeus sitting at the tax booth, and he said to him, “Follow me.” And he got up and followed him.	and saw a tax collector named Levi, sitting at the tax booth; and he said to him, “Follow me.” 28 And he got up, left everything, and followed him.
10 And as he sat[J] at dinner in the house, many tax collectors and sinners came and were sitting with him and his disciples.	15 And as he sat at dinner in Levi’s house, many tax collectors and sinners were also sitting with Jesus and his disciples—for there were many who followed him.	29 Then Levi gave a great banquet for him in his house; and there was a large crowd of tax collectors and others sitting[J] at the table with them.
11 When the Pharisees saw this, they said to his disciples, “Why does your teacher eat with tax collectors and sinners?”	16 When the scribes of[K] the Pharisees saw that he was eating with sinners and tax collectors, they said to his disciples, “Why does he eat[L] with tax collectors and sinners?”	30 The Pharisees and their scribes were complaining to his disciples, saying, “Why do you eat and drink with tax collectors and sinners?”[1]
12 But when he heard this, he said, “Those who are well have no need of a physician, but those who are sick.	17 When Jesus heard this, he said to them, “Those who are well have no need of a physician, but those who are sick;	31 Jesus answered, “Those who are well have no need of a physician, but those who are sick;
13 Go and learn what this means, ‘I desire mercy, not sacrifice.’		
For I have come to call not the righteous but sinners.”	I have come to call not the righteous but sinners.”	32 I have come to call not the righteous but sinners to repentance.”

[1] To LUK 5:29–30 *cf.* LUK 15:1–2 (§ 172, p. 134).

✧ MAT 9:13 = MAT 12:7 — HOS 6:6.

✦ [I] text: S A B C W λ ℜ vg sy^p sa bo; *James*: D Θ ø it. *Cf.* MAT 10:3 and parallels, § 58, p. 47. ✦ [J] Greek: *reclined* (*reclining*). ✦ [K] text: S B W; *and*: A C D Θ λ ø ℜ it vg sy^p sa bo. ✦ [L] text: B D W Θ it; *eat and drink*: A λ ℜ sy^p; *Why does your teacher eat*: S; *Why does your teacher eat and drink*: C ø vg sa bo.

◗ To MAR 2:16–17 *cf.* *Oxyrhynchus Papyrus 1224, fol. 2 verso, col. 2.* — When the scribes and the Pharisees and priests saw him, they became indignant, because he reclined in the midst of sinners. But when Jesus heard them, he said, “Those who are well have no need of a physician...(but those who are sick).” ◗ To LUK 5:32 *cf.* Justin, *Apology I.15:8.* — after “to repentance” it is added: “for your heavenly Father prefers the repentance of sinners to their punishment.”

§ 54 THE QUESTION ABOUT FASTING

MAT 9:14–17	MAR 2:18–22	LUK 5:33–39
14 Then the disciples of John	18 Now John's disciples and the Pharisees were fasting;	
came to him, saying, "Why do we and the Pharisees fast[M] often,	and people came and said to him, "Why do John's disciples and the disciples of the Pharisees fast,	33 Then they said to him, "John's disciples, like the disciples of the Pharisees, frequently fast and pray,
but your disciples do not fast?"	but your disciples do not fast?"	but your disciples eat and drink.
15 And Jesus said to them, "The wedding guests cannot mourn as long as the bridegroom is with them, can they?	19 Jesus said to them, "The wedding guests cannot fast while the bridegroom is with them, can they? As long as they have the bridegroom with them, they cannot fast.	34 Jesus said to them, "You cannot make wedding guests fast while the bridegroom is with them, can you?
The days will come when the bridegroom is taken away from them, and then they will fast.	20 The days will come when the bridegroom is taken away from them, and then they will fast on that day.	35 The days will come when the bridegroom will be taken away from them, and then they will fast in those days."
		36 He also told them a parable:
16 No one sews a piece of unshrunk cloth on an old cloak, for the patch pulls away from the cloak,	21 "No one sews a piece of unshrunk cloth on an old cloak; otherwise, the patch pulls away from it,	"No one tears a piece from a new garment and sews it on an old garment; otherwise the new will be torn, and the piece from the new will not match the old.
	the new from the old,	
and a worse tear is made.	and a worse tear is made.	
17 Neither is new wine put into old wineskins; otherwise, the skins burst, and the wine is spilled, and the skins are destroyed;	22 And no one puts new wine into old wineskins; otherwise, the wine will burst the skins, and the wine is lost, and so are the skins;	37 And no one puts new wine into old wineskins; otherwise the new wine will burst the skins and will be spilled, and the skins will be destroyed.
but new wine is put into fresh wineskins, and so both are preserved."	but one puts new wine into fresh wineskins."[N]	38 But new wine must be put into fresh wineskins.
		39 And no one after drinking old wine desires new wine, but says, 'The old is good.' "[O]
	▼ 2:23–28 (§ 69, p. 58)	▼ 6:1–5 (§ 69, p. 58)

✦ [M] text: C D W Θ λ ø ℜ it vg sy^s sy^p sa bo; omit: *often*: S B. ✦ [N] text: S A B C W Θ λ ø ℜ vg sy^s sy^p sa bo; omit: *but one puts new wine into fresh wineskins*: D it. ✦ [O] text: P^4 $P^{75?}$ S B W sy^p sa bo; *better*: A C Θ λ ø ℜ it (some MSS.) vg. Omit verse 39: D it (some MSS.) Marcion, Irenaeus, Eusebius.

◗ To MAR 2:18 *cf.* **Didache 8:1.** — Do not fast with the hypocrites, for they fast on the second and fifth days of the week (i.e., Mondays and Thursdays); but you should fast on the fourth day and on the day of Preparation (i.e., Wednesdays and Fridays).
◗ To MAR 2:19–20 *cf.* **Gospel of Thomas, Logia 27 and 104b.** — 27 Jesus said, "If you do not fast from the world you will not find the kingdom; if you do not keep the sabbath as sabbath you will not see the Father." 104*b* "When the bridegroom comes out of the bridal chamber, then let them fast and let them pray." ◗ To LUK 5:39 *cf.* **Gospel of Thomas, Logion 47b.**

§ 55 JAIRUS' DAUGHTER AND A WOMAN'S FAITH

MAT 9:18–26	MAR	LUK
18 While he was saying these things to them, suddenly a leader of the synagogue	*Cf.* 5:21–43	*Cf.* 8:40–56
came in and knelt before him, saying, "My daughter has just died; but come and	(§ 107, p. 83)	(§ 107, p. 83)
lay your hand on her, and she will live." 19 And Jesus got up and followed him,		
with his disciples.		
20 Then suddenly a woman who had been suffering from hemorrhages for twelve		*Cf.* 7:50
years came up behind him and touched the fringe of his cloak, 21 for she said to		(§ 83, p. 69)
herself, "If I only touch his cloak, I will be made well." 22 Jesus turned, and	*Cf.* 5:34	*Cf.* 8:48
seeing her he said, "Take heart, daughter; your faith has made you well." And	(§ 107, p. 83)	(§ 107, p. 83)
instantly the woman was made well.	*Cf.* 10:52	*Cf.* 18:42
23 When Jesus came to the leader's house and saw the flute players and the crowd	(§ 193, p. 149)	(§ 193, p. 149)
making a commotion, 24 he said, "Go away; for the girl is not dead but sleeping."		
And they laughed at him. 25 But when the crowd had been put outside, he went		
in and took her by the hand, and the girl got up. 26 And the report of this spread		
throughout that district.		

§ 56 TWO BLIND MEN HEALED

(*Cf.* MAT 20:29–34 = MAR 10:46–52 = LUK 18:35–43, § 193, p. 149)

MAT 9:27–31	MAR	LUK
27 As Jesus went on from there, two blind men followed him, crying loudly, "Have		
mercy on us, Son of David!" 28 When he entered the house, the blind men came		
to him; and Jesus said to them, "Do you believe that I am able to do this?" They		
said to him, "Yes, Lord." 29 Then he touched their eyes and said, "According to		
your faith let it be done to you." 30 And their eyes were opened. Then Jesus		
sternly ordered them, "See that no one knows of this." 31 But they went away and		
spread the news about him throughout that district.		

§ 57 THE HEALING OF A DEMONIAC WHO WAS MUTE

MAT 9:32–34	MAR	LUK
32 After they had gone away, a demoniac who was mute was brought to him.		
33 And when the demon had been cast out, the one who had been mute spoke; and		
the crowds were amazed and said, "Never has anything like this been seen in		

Israel." 34 But the Pharisees said, "By the ruler of the demons he casts out the demons."[1 + P]

§ 58 THE SENDING OUT OF THE TWELVE

MAT 9:35—10:16	Δ *MAR 6:6b* (§ 109, p. 86) +	Δ *LUK 9:1* (§ 109, p. 86) +	Δ *LUK 10:1–12* (§ 139, p. 112) +
			1 *After this the Lord appointed seventy others and sent them on ahead of him in pairs to every town and place where he himself intended to go.*
35 Then Jesus went about all the cities and villages, teaching in their synagogues, and proclaiming the good news of the kingdom, and curing every disease and every sickness.[2]	6b *Then he went about among the villages teaching.*	C*f.* 8:1 (§ 84, p. 69)	
36 When he saw the crowds, he had compassion for them, because they were harassed and helpless, like sheep without a shepherd.	Δ *6:34 (§ 112, p. 89)* 34 *As he went ashore, he saw a great crowd; and he had compassion for them, because they were like sheep without a shepherd; and he began to teach them many things.*		
37 Then he said to his disciples, "The harvest is plentiful, but the laborers are few; 38 therefore ask the Lord of the harvest to send out laborers into his harvest."	Δ *6:7 (§ 109, p. 86)*		2 *He said to them, "The harvest is plentiful, but the laborers are few; therefore ask the Lord of the harvest to send out laborers into his harvest."*

1 MAT 12:22–24 (§ 85, p. 70): 22 Then they brought to him [Jesus] a demoniac who was blind and mute; and he cured him, so that the one who had been mute could speak and see. 23 All the crowds were amazed and said, "Can this be the Son of David?"	MAR 3:22 (§ 85, p. 70): And	LUK 11:14–15 (§ 149, p. 117): 14 Now he [Jesus] was casting out a demon that was mute; when the demon had gone out, the one who had been mute spoke, and the crowds were amazed.
24 But when the Pharisees heard it, they said, "It is only by Beelzebul, the ruler of the demons, that this fellow casts out the demons."	the scribes who came down from Jerusalem said, "He has Beelzebul, and by the ruler of the demons he casts out demons."	15 But some of them said, " He casts out demons by Beelzebul, the ruler of the demons."

2 MAT 4:23 (§ 16, p. 23): Jesus went throughout Galilee, teaching in their synagogues and proclaiming the good news of the kingdom and curing every disease and every sickness among the people.

✧ MAT 9:36 — NUM 27:17; 1KI 22:17.

✦ P text: S B C λ ø 𝔎 it (some MSS.) vg syp sa bo; omit verse 34: D it (some MSS.) sys Diatessaron.

● To MAT 9:37 *cf.* JOH 4:35. — "Do you not say, 'Four months more, then comes the harvest'? But I tell you, look around you, and see how the fields are ripe for harvesting."

10:1 Then Jesus summoned his twelve disciples and	*7 He called the twelve and began to send them out two by two, and*	*1 Then Jesus called the twelve together and*	▼ 10:3 (§ 58, p. 47)
gave them authority over unclean spirits, to cast them out,	*gave them authority over the unclean spirits.*	*gave them power and authority over all demons*	
and to cure every disease and every sickness.		*and to cure diseases,*	
	Δ 3:13–19 (§ 72, p. 62) *13 He went up the mountain and called to him those whom he wanted, and they came to him. 14 And he appointed twelve,[Q] whom he also named apostles, to be with him, and to be sent out to proclaim the message, 15 and to have authority to cast out demons.*		
		Δ 6:13–16 (§ 72, p. 62) *13 And when day came,*	Δ ACT 1:13 *13 When they had entered the city, they went to the room upstairs where they were staying,*
2 These are the names of the twelve apostles: first,	*16 So he appointed the twelve:[R]*	*he called his disciples and chose twelve of them, whom he also named apostles:*	
Simon, also known as Peter, and his brother Andrew;	*Simon (to whom he gave the name Peter);*	*14 Simon, whom he named Peter, and his brother Andrew,*	*Peter, and John, and James, and Andrew,*
James son of Zebedee, and his brother John;	*17 James son of Zebedee and John the brother of James (to whom he gave the name Boanerges, that is, Sons of Thunder); 18 and Andrew, and*	*and James, and John, and*	
3 Philip and Bartholomew; Thomas and Matthew	*Philip, and Bartholomew, and Matthew, and Thomas,*	*Philip, and Bartholomew, 15 and Matthew, and Thomas,*	*Philip and Thomas, Bartholomew and Matthew,*

✦ [Q] text: S B C? W Θ sa bo; omit: *whom he also named apostles*: A D λ 𝔐 it vg sy^s sy^p. ✦ [R] text: S B C ; omit: *So he appointed the twelve*: A D λ ø 𝔐 it vg sy^s sy^p sa bo.

● To MAT 10:2 and parallels, *cf.* JOH 1:42. — He brought Simon to Jesus, who looked at him and said, "You are Simon son of John. You are to be called Cephas" (which is translated Peter).

◗ To MAT 10:1*ff.* and parallels, *cf.* **Gospel of the Ebionites 1**. — A man named Jesus, about thirty years old, appeared, and chose us. And having come to Capernaum, he entered the house of Simon, whose surname was Peter, and said: "As I passed along the Lake of Tiberias I chose John and James, the sons of Zebedee, and Simon and Andrew and Thaddaeus and Simon the Zealot and Judas Iscariot. And I called you, Matthew, as you sat at the tax booth, and you followed me. I want you to be twelve apostles for a witness to Israel."

the tax collector;	*and*	*and*	
James son of Alphaeus,	*James son of Alphaeus,*	*James son of Alphaeus,*	*James son of Alphaeus,*
and Thaddaeus;[S]	*and Thaddaeus,*[T] *and*	*and*	*and*
4 Simon	*Simon*	*Simon, who was called*	*Simon*
the Cananaean,	*the Cananaean,*	*the Zealot,*	*the Zealot,*
		16 and Judas son of James,	*and Judas son of James.*
and Judas Iscariot,	*19 and Judas Iscariot,*	*and Judas Iscariot,*	
the one who betrayed him.	*who betrayed him.*	*who became a traitor.*	
	Then he went home;	∆ *9:2-5 (§ 109, p. x1x)*	
5 These twelve Jesus sent out with the following instructions: "Go nowhere among the Gentiles, and enter no town of the Samaritans, 6 but go rather to the lost sheep of the house of Israel.[1]		*2 and he sent them out*	
7 As you go, proclaim the good news, 'The kingdom of heaven has come near.'		*to proclaim the kingdom of God*	
8 Cure the sick, raise the dead, cleanse the lepers, cast out demons. You received without payment; give without payment.		*and to heal.*	Cf. 10:9 (§ 58, p. 47)
9 Take no gold, or silver, or copper in your belts,	∆ *6:8–11 (§ 109, p. 86)*		
	8 He ordered them to take nothing for their journey except a staff;	*3 He said to them, "Take nothing for your journey, no staff,*	∆ *LUK 10:4–12, 3* *4 Carry no*
10 no bag for your journey,	*no bread, no bag,*	*nor bag, nor bread,*	*purse, no bag,*
	no money in their belts;	*nor money—*	
	9 but to wear sandals and		*no sandals; and greet no one on the road.*
or two tunics, or sandals, or a staff; for laborers deserve their food.	*not to put on two tunics.*	*not even an extra tunic.*	
	10 He said to them,		
11 Whatever	*"Wherever*	*4 Whatever*	*5 Whatever*
town or village you enter,	*you enter a house,*	*house you enter,*	*house you enter,*
find out who in it is worthy, and stay there	*stay there*	*stay there,*	
until you leave.	*until you leave the place.*	*and leave from there.*	

[1] MAT 15:24 (§ 116, p. 93): He [Jesus] answered, "I was sent only to the lost sheep of the house of Israel."

✦ [S] text: S B ø it (some MSS.) vg sa bo; *Lebbaeus*: D; *Lebbaeus called Thaddaeus*: C? W Θ λ ℜ sy[p]; *Judas Zelotes*: it (some MSS.); add: *Judas the son of James* after "Cananaean" in verse 4: sy[s]. ✦ [T] text: S A B C Θ λ ø ℜ it (some MSS.) vg sy[s] sy[p] sa bo; *Lebbaeus*: D it (some MSS.).

● To MAT 10:10 *cf.* 1TI 5:18b. — for the scripture says, "The laborer deserves to be paid" (S: *deserves his food*). *Cf.* 1CO 9:14. — In the same way, the Lord commanded that those who proclaim the gospel should get their living by the gospel.

◗ To MAT 10:10 *cf.* **Didache 13:1.** — All true prophets who wish to settle among you deserve their food.

12 As you enter
the house, greet it.
13 If the house is worthy,
let your peace come upon
it; but if
it is not worthy, let
your peace return to you.
14 If anyone will not
welcome you or
listen to your words,
shake off the dust from
your feet as you leave that
house or town.
15 Truly I tell you, it
will be more tolerable for
the land of Sodom and
Gomorrah on the day of
judgment
than for that town.
16 "See, I am sending you
out like sheep into the
midst of wolves;
so be wise as serpents and
innocent as doves.

11 If any place will not
welcome you and
they refuse to hear you,
as you leave,
shake off the dust
that is on your feet as a
testimony against
them."

5 Wherever
they do not
welcome you,
as you are leaving that
town shake the dust off
your feet as a
testimony against
them."

first
say, 'Peace to this house!'
6 And if anyone is there
who shares in peace,
your peace will rest on
that person; but if
not,
it will return to you.
7 Remain in the same
house, eating and drink-
ing whatever they provide,
for the laborer deserves to
be paid. Do not move
about from house to
house. 8 Whenever you
enter a town and its peo-
ple welcome you, eat
what is set before you; 9
cure the sick who are
there, and say to them,
'The kingdom of God has
come near to you.'
10 But whenever you enter
a town and they do not
welcome you, go
out into its streets and say,
11 'Even the
dust of your town that
clings to our feet, we
wipe off in protest against
you. Yet know this: the
kingdom of God has come
near.' 12 I tell you,
on that day it
will be more tolerable for
Sodom
than for that town.
3 Go on your way.
See, I am sending you
out like lambs into the
midst of wolves.

▸ To MAT 10:16 *cf.* **II Clement 5:2–4.** — 2 The Lord said, "You will be as lambs in the midst of wolves." 3 And Peter answered, "But what if the wolves tear the lambs to pieces?" 4 Jesus answered Peter, "Do not let the lambs fear the wolves after they die; and do not fear those who kill you and are not able to do anything more to you. But fear the one who, after you die, has power over your soul and body, to cast them into the hell of fire." ▸ To MAT 10:16 *cf.* **Gospel of the Nazaraeans.** The Jewish Gospel has: — (wise) more than serpents. ▸ To MAT 10:16 *cf.* **Gospel of Thomas, Logion 39.** — Jesus said, "The Pharisees and the scribes have received the keys of knowledge, and have hidden them. They themselves did not enter, and they did not allow those to enter who wished to. But you, become as wise as serpents and as innocent as doves."

§ 59 COMING PERSECUTIONS

MAT 10:17–25 [1]	MAR	LUK
17 "Beware of them, for they will hand you over to councils and flog you in their synagogues; 18 and you will be dragged before governors and kings because of me, as a testimony to them and the Gentiles. 19 When they hand you over, do not worry about how you are to speak or what you are to say; for what you are to say will be given to you at that time; 20 for it is not you who speak, but the Spirit of your Father speaking through you.[2] 21 Brother will betray brother to death, and a father his child, and children will rise against parents and have them put to death; 22 and you will be hated by all because of my name. But the one who endures to the end will be saved. 23 When they persecute you in one town, flee to the next; for truly I tell you, you will not have gone through all the towns of Israel before the Son of Man comes. 24 A disciple is not above the teacher, nor a slave above the master; 25 it is enough for the disciple to be like the teacher,[3] and the slave like the master. If they have called the master of the house Beelzebul, how much more will they malign those of his household!"		

[1] MAT 24:9, 13 (§ 215, p. 170): 9 "Then	MAR 13:9–13 (§ 215, p. 170): 9 "As for yourselves, beware; for	LUK 21:12–17, 19 (§ 215, p. 170): 12 "But before all this occurs, they will arrest you and persecute you;
they will hand you over to be tortured and will put you to death, and	they will hand you over to councils; and you will be beaten in synagogues; and you will stand before governors and kings because of me,	they will hand you over to synagogues and prisons, and you will be brought before kings and governors because of my name. 13 This will give you
	as a testimony to them. 10 And the good news must first be proclaimed to all nations.	an opportunity to testify.
	11 When they bring you to trial and hand you over, do not worry beforehand about what you are to say; but say whatever is given you at that time, for it is not you who speak, but the Holy Spirit.	14 So make up your minds not to prepare your defense in advance; 15 for I will give you words and a wisdom that none of your opponents will be able to withstand or contradict.
	12 Brother will betray brother to death, and a father his child, and children will rise against parents and have them put to death;	16 You will be betrayed even by parents and brothers, by relatives and friends; and they will put some of you to death.
you will be hated by all nations because of my name. [10–12] 13 But the one who endures to the end will be saved."	13 and you will be hated by all because of my name. But the one who endures to the end will be saved."	17 You will be hated by all because of my name. (verse 18, see MAT 10:30) [18] 19 By your endurance you will gain your souls."

[2] LUK 12:11–12 (§ 155, p. 122): 11 "When they bring you before the synagogues, the rulers, and the authorities, do not worry about how you are to defend yourselves or what you are to say; 12 for the Holy Spirit will teach you at that very hour what you ought to say."

[3] LUK 6:40 (§ 76, p. 65): "A disciple is not above the teacher, but everyone who is fully qualified will be like the teacher."

✧ MAT 10:21, 35 — MIC 7:6.

• To MAT 10:21 *cf.* verse 35. • To MAT 10:19–20 *cf.* JOH 14:26. — "But the Advocate, the Holy Spirit, whom the Father will send in my name, will teach you everything, and remind you of all that I have said to you." • To MAT 10:24 *cf.* JOH 13:16. — "Very truly, I tell you, servants are not greater than their master, nor are messengers greater than the one who sent them." Also *cf.* JOH 15:20. — "Remember the word that I said to you, 'Servants are not greater than their master.' "

§ 60 EXHORTATION TO FEARLESS CONFESSION

MAT 10:26–33

26 "So have no fear of them; for nothing is
covered up that will not be uncovered, and
nothing secret that will not become known.[1]
27 What I say to you
in the dark, tell in the light; and
what you hear whispered,
proclaim from the housetops.
28 Do not fear those who
kill the body
but cannot kill the soul;
rather fear him
who can destroy both soul and body
in hell.[U]
29 Are not two sparrows sold for a penny?
Yet not one of them
will fall to the ground apart from your Father.
30 And even the hairs of your head are all
counted.[2] 31 So do not be afraid; you are of
more value than many sparrows.
32 Everyone therefore who acknowledges
me before others, I also will
acknowledge before my Father in heaven;
33 but whoever denies me before others,
I also will deny before my Father in heaven."[3]

MAR

Δ *LUK 12:2–9* (*§ 155, p. 122*)

2 "Nothing is
covered up that will not be uncovered, and
nothing secret that will not become known.[1]
3 Therefore whatever you have said
in the dark will be heard in the light, and
what you have whispered behind closed doors
will be proclaimed from the housetops.
4 I tell you, my friends, do not fear those who
kill the body,
and after that can do nothing more. 5 But I
will warn you whom to fear: fear him who,
after he has killed, has authority to cast
into hell.[U] *Yes, I tell you, fear him!*
6 Are not five sparrows sold for two pennies?
Yet not one of them
is forgotten in God's sight.
7 But even the hairs of your head are all
counted.[2] *Do not be afraid; you are of*
more value than many sparrows.
8 And I tell you, everyone who acknowledges
me before others, the Son of Man also will
acknowledge before the angels of God;
9 but whoever denies me before others
will be denied before the angels of God."[3]

---

[1] MAR 4:22 (§ 94, p. 77): "For there is nothing hidden, except to be disclosed; nor is anything secret, except to come to light." | LUK 8:17 (§ 94, p. 77): "For nothing is hidden that will not be disclosed, nor is anything secret that will not become known and come to light."

[2] LUK 21:18 (§ 215, p. 170): "But not a hair of your head will perish."

[3] MAR 8:38 (§ 123, p. 100): "Those who are ashamed of me and of my words in this adulterous and sinful generation, of them the Son of Man will also be ashamed when he comes in the glory of his Father with the holy angels." | LUK 9:26 (§ 123, p. 100): "Those who are ashamed of me and of my words, of them the Son of Man will be ashamed when he comes in his glory and the glory of the Father and of the holy angels."

✦ [U] Greek: *Gehenna.*

▸ To MAT 10:26 *cf. Oxyrhynchus Papyrus 654, Logion 4.* — Jesus said, "Everything that is not before you, and what is hidden from you will be revealed to you. For there is nothing hidden that will not be revealed, nor buried, that will not be raised."
▸ To MAT 10:26 *cf.* **Gospel of Thomas, Logia 5 and 6.** — 5 Jesus said, "Know what is in your sight, and what is hidden from you will be revealed to you. For there is nothing hidden that will not be manifest." 6 "There is nothing hidden that will not be revealed, and there is nothing covered that will remain without being uncovered." ▸ To MAT 10:28 *cf.* **II Clement 5:2–4.** — See note to Mat 10:16, p. 50.

§ 61 DIVISION IN HOUSEHOLDS

MAT 10:34–36	MAR	Δ *LUK 12:51–53* *(§ 160, p. 127)*
34 "Do not think that I have come to bring peace to the earth; I have not come to bring peace, but a sword.		*51 "Do you think that I have come to bring peace to the earth? No, I tell you, but rather division!*
35 For I have come to set a		*52 From now on five in one household will be divided, three against two and two against three; 53 they will be divided:*
man against his father, and a		*father against son and son against father,*
		mother against daughter and
daughter against her mother, and a		*daughter against mother,*
		mother-in-law against her daughter-in-law
daughter-in-law against her mother-in-law;		*and daughter-in-law against mother-in-law."*
36 and one's foes will be members of one's own household."		

§ 62 CONDITIONS OF DISCIPLESHIP

MAT 10:37–39	MAR	Δ *LUK 14:26–27* *(§ 171, p. 133)* +
37 "Whoever		*26 "Whoever comes to me and*
loves father or mother more than me		*does not hate father and mother,*
is not worthy of me; and whoever loves son or daughter more than me is not worthy of me; 38 and whoever does not take up the cross and follow me		
		wife and children, brothers and sisters, yes, and even life itself,
is not worthy of me.		*cannot be my disciple.*
		27 Whoever does not carry the cross and follow me cannot be my disciple.
		Δ *17:33 (§ 184, p. 140)*

◇ MAT 10:35–36 = LUK 12:53 — MIC 7:6.

● To MAT 10:35–36 = LUK 12:53 *cf.* MAT 10:21.

◗ To MAT 10:37–38 = LUK 14:26–27 *cf.* **Gospel of Thomas, Logia 55 and 101.** — 55 "Whoever does not hate father and mother will not be able to be my disciple; and whoever does not hate brothers and sisters and does not take up the cross in my way will not be worthy of me." 101 "Whoever does not hate father and mother in my way will not be able to be my disciple, for my mother (gave me falsehood ?), but (my true mother ?) gave me life."

MAT	MAR	LUK
39 Those who find their life will lose it, and those who lose their life for my sake will find it."[1]		*33 Those who try to make their life secure* *will lose it,* *but those who lose their life* *will keep it."*[1]

§ 63 END OF THE DISCOURSE

MAT 10:40—11:1	MAR	LUK
40 "Whoever welcomes you welcomes me, and whoever welcomes me welcomes the one who sent me.[2] 41 Whoever welcomes a prophet in the name of a prophet will receive a prophet's reward; and whoever welcomes a righteous person in the name of a righteous person will receive the reward of the righteous; 42 and whoever gives even a cup of cold water to one of these little ones in the name of a disciple —truly I tell you, none of these will lose their reward."[3] 11:1 Now when Jesus had finished instructing his twelve disciples, he went on from there to teach and proclaim his message in their cities.		

---

[1] MAT 16:24b–25 (§ 123, p. 100): 24b "If any want to become my followers, let them deny themselves and take up their cross and follow me. 25 For those who want to save their life will lose it, and those who lose their life for my sake will find it."	MAR 8:34b–35 (§ 123, p. 100): 34b "If any want to become my followers, let them deny themselves and take up their cross and follow me. 35 For those who want to save their life will lose it, and those who lose their life for my sake, and for the sake of the gospel, will save it."	LUK 9:23b–24 (§ 123, p. 100): 23b "If any want to become my followers, let them deny themselves and take up their cross daily and follow me. 24 For those who want to save their life will lose it, and those who lose their life for my sake will save it."
[2] MAT 18:5 (§ 129, p. 106): "Whoever welcomes one such child in my name welcomes me."	MAR 9:37 (§ 129, p. 106): "Whoever welcomes one such child in my name welcomes me, and whoever welcomes me welcomes not me but the one who sent me."	LUK 9:48b (§ 129, p. 106): "Whoever welcomes this child in my name welcomes me, and whoever welcomes me welcomes the one who sent me; for the least among all of you is the greatest." LUK 10:16 (§ 139, p. 112): "Whoever listens to you listens to me, and whoever rejects you rejects me, and whoever rejects me rejects the one who sent me."

[3] MAR 9:41 (§ 130, p. 107): "For truly I tell you, whoever gives you a cup of water to drink because you bear the name of Christ will by no means lose the reward."

• To MAT 10:39 *cf.* JOH 12:25. — "Those who love their life lose it, and those who hate their life in this world will keep it for eternal life." • To MAT 10:40 *cf.* JOH 12:44b–45. — 44b Whoever believes in me believes not in me but in him who sent me. 45 And whoever sees me sees him who sent me." Also *cf.* JOH 13:20. — "Very truly, I tell you, whoever receives one whom I send receives me; and whoever receives me receives him who sent me."

§ 64 JOHN'S QUESTION TO JESUS

MAT 11:2–6	MAR	Δ *LUK 7:18–23* (§ 81, p. 68)
2 When John heard in prison what the Messiah was doing, he sent word by his disciples 3 and said to him, "Are you the one who is to come, or are we to wait for another?"		*18 The disciples of John reported all these things to him. So John summoned two of his disciples 19 and sent them to the Lord to ask, "Are you the one who is to come, or are we to wait for another?" 20 When the men had come to him, they said, "John the Baptist has sent us to you to ask, 'Are you the one who is to come, or are we to wait for another?'" 21 Jesus had just then cured many people of diseases, plagues, and evil spirits, and had given sight to many who were blind.*
4 Jesus answered them, "Go and tell John what you hear and see: 5 the blind receive their sight, the lame walk, the lepers are cleansed, the deaf hear, the dead are raised, and the poor have good news brought to them. 6 And blessed is anyone who takes no offense at me."		*22 And he answered them, "Go and tell John what you have seen and heard: the blind receive their sight, the lame walk, the lepers are cleansed, the deaf hear, the dead are raised, the poor have good news brought to them. 23 And blessed is anyone who takes no offense at me."*

§ 65 JESUS' WORDS ABOUT JOHN

MAT 11:7–19	MAR	Δ *LUK 7:24–35* (§ 82, p. 68) +
7 As they went away, Jesus began to speak to the crowds about John: "What did you go out into the wilderness to look at? A reed shaken by the wind? 8 What then did you go out to see? Someone [V] dressed in soft robes? Look, those who wear soft robes are in royal palaces. 9 What then did you go out to see? A prophet? [W] Yes, I tell you, and more than a prophet. 10 This is the one about whom it is written, 'See, I am sending my messenger ahead of you, who will prepare your way before you.'	Cf. 1:2 (§ 1, p. 11)	*24 When John's messengers had gone, Jesus began to speak to the crowds about John: "What did you go out into the wilderness to look at? A reed shaken by the wind? 25 What then did you go out to see? Someone dressed in soft robes? Look, those who put on fine clothing and live in luxury are in royal palaces. 26 What then did you go out to see? A prophet? Yes, I tell you, and more than a prophet. 27 This is the one about whom it is written, 'See, I am sending my messenger ahead of you, who will prepare your way before you.'*

✧ MAT 11:5 *cf.* LUK 4:18 — ISA 29:18–19; 35:5–6, 61:1. ✧ MAT 11:10 = LUK 7:27 — MAL 3:1.

✦ [V] Or, *Why then did you go out? To see someone...* ✦ [W] text: B? C D Θ λ ø ℜ it vg sy^{c} sy^{s} sy^{p} sa; *Why then did you go out? To see a prophet?*: S W bo.

● To MAT 11:5 = LUK 7:22 *cf.* LUK 4:18.

◗ To MAT 11:8 *cf.* **Gospel of Thomas, Logion 78.** — Jesus said, "Why did you come out into the desert? To see a reed shaken by the wind? And to see a man wearing soft clothing? See, your kings and your great ones are those who are wearing soft clothing, and they will not be able to know the truth."

11 Truly I tell you, among those born of women
no one has arisen greater than John the Baptist;
yet the least in the kingdom of heaven is greater
than he.

Cf. 21:32 (§ 203, p. 158)

12 From the days of John the Baptist

until now
the kingdom of heaven has suffered violence,[X]

and the violent take it by force.
13 For all the prophets and the law prophesied
until John came; 14 and if you are willing to
accept it, he is Elijah who is to come. 15 Let
anyone with ears[Y] listen!
16 But to what will I compare
this generation?

It is like children sitting in the
marketplaces and calling to one another,
17 'We played the flute for you, and you did not
dance; we wailed, and you did not mourn.'
18 For John came
neither eating nor drinking,
and they say, 'He has a demon'; 19 the Son of
Man came eating and drinking, and they
say, 'Look, a glutton and a drunkard, a friend
of tax collectors and sinners!'
Yet wisdom is vindicated
by her deeds."[Z]

Cf. 9:13 (§ 125, p. 102)

28 I tell you, among those born of women
no one is greater than John;
yet the least in the kingdom of God is greater
than he."
29 (And all the people who heard this, including
the tax collectors, acknowledged the justice of
God, because they had been baptized with
John's baptism. 30 But by refusing to be bap-
tized by him, the Pharisees and the lawyers
rejected God's purpose for themselves.)
Δ 16:16 (§ 176, p. 137)
16 "The law and the prophets were in effect
until John came;

since then the good news of the kingdom of God
is proclaimed,
and everyone tries to enter it by force."

7:31 "To what then will I compare
the people of this generation, and
what are they like?
32 They are like children sitting in the
marketplace and calling to one another,
'We played the flute for you, and you did not
dance; we wailed, and you did not weep.'
33 For John the Baptist has come
eating no bread and drinking no wine,
and you say, 'He has a demon'; 34 the Son of
Man has come eating and drinking, and you
say, 'Look, a glutton and a drunkard, a friend
of tax collectors and sinners!'
35 Nevertheless, wisdom is vindicated
by all her children."

✧ MAT 11:14 — MAL 4:5.

✦ [X] Or, *has been coming violently.* ✦ [Y] text: B D sy[s]; *ears to hear*: S C W Θ λ ø ℜ it vg sy[c] sy[p] sa bo. ✦ [Z] text: S B W ø sy[p] bo; *children* (LUK 7:35) C D Θ λ ℜ it vg sy[c] sy[s] sa.

◗ To MAT 11:11 *cf.* **Gospel of Thomas, Logion 46.** — Jesus said, "From Adam to John the Baptist, no one born of woman is greater than John the Baptist, so that his eyes will not (...). But I have said that anyone among you who becomes as a child will know the kingdom, and will become greater than John." ◗ To MAT 11:12 *cf.* **Gospel of the Nazaraeans.** — The Jewish Gospel has: "(the kingdom of heaven) is plundered."

§ 66 WOES TO UNREPENTANT CITIES

MAT 11:20–24

20 Then he began to reproach the cities in which
most of his deeds of power had been done,
because they did not repent.
21 "Woe to you, Chorazin! Woe to you,
Bethsaida! For if the deeds of power done in
you had been done in Tyre and Sidon, they
would have repented long ago
in sackcloth and ashes. 22 But I tell you,
on the day of judgment it will be more tolerable
for Tyre and Sidon than for you. 23 And you,
Capernaum, will you be exalted to heaven?
No, you will be brought down to Hades.
For if the deeds of power done in you had been
done in Sodom, it would have remained until
this day. 24 But I tell you that on the day of
judgment it will be more tolerable for the land
of Sodom than for you."

MAR

Δ *LUK 10:13–15* (§ 139, p. 113)

13 "Woe to you, Chorazin! Woe to you,
Bethsaida! For if the deeds of power done in
you had been done in Tyre and Sidon, they
would have repented long ago,
sitting in sackcloth and ashes. 14 But
at the judgment it will be more tolerable
for Tyre and Sidon than for you. 15 And you,
Capernaum, will you be exalted to heaven?
No, you will be brought down to Hades."

C*f*. 10:12 (§ 139, p. 113)

§ 67 JESUS' THANKSGIVING TO THE FATHER

MAT 11:25–27

25 At that time
Jesus said,
"I thank you, Father, Lord of heaven and
earth, because you have hidden these things
from the wise and the intelligent and have revealed them to infants; 26 yes, Father, for such
was your gracious will.[A] 27 All things have
been handed over to me by my Father; and no
one knows the Son except the Father,
and no one knows the Father except the Son and
anyone to whom the Son chooses to reveal
him."

MAR

Δ *LUK 10:21–22* (§ 141, p. 114)

21 At that same hour
Jesus rejoiced in the Holy Spirit and said,
"I thank you, Father, Lord of heaven and
earth, because you have hidden these things
from the wise and the intelligent and have re-
vealed them to infants; yes, Father, for such
was your gracious will.[A] 22 All things have
been handed over to me by my Father; and no
one knows who the Son is except the Father,
or who the Father is except the Son and
anyone to whom the Son chooses to reveal
him."

✧ MAT 11:23 = LUK 10:15 — ISA 14:13, 15.

✦ [A] Or, *for so it was well-pleasing in your sight.*

● To MAT 11:27; LUK 10:22 c*f*. JOH 3:35. — The Father loves the Son and has placed all things in his hands. C*f*. JOH 7:29 — "I know him, because I am from him, and he sent me." C*f*. JOH 10:14–15; 17:2.

◗ To MAT 11:25 c*f*. **Gospel of Thomas, Logion 4.** — Jesus said, "The person old in days will not hesitate to ask a little child of seven days about the place of life, and the person will live. For many who are first will become last, and they will become a single one."

§ 68 COMFORT FOR THE WEARY

MAT 11:28–30	MAR	LUK
28 "Come to me, all you that are weary and are carrying heavy burdens, and I will give you rest. 29 Take my yoke upon you, and learn from me; for I am gentle and humble in heart, and you will find rest for your souls. 30 For my yoke is easy, and my burden is light."		

§ 69 PLUCKING HEADS OF GRAIN ON THE SABBATH

MAT 12:1–8	MAR 2:23–28	LUK 6:1–5
	▲ 2:18–22 (§ 54, p. 45)	▲ 5:33–39 (§ 54, p. 45)
1 At that time Jesus	23 One sabbath he	1 One sabbath[B] while Jesus
went through the grainfields	was going through the grainfields;	was going through the grainfields,
	and as they made their way	
on the sabbath;		
his disciples were hungry, and	his disciples	his disciples
they began to pluck heads of grain	began to pluck heads of grain.	plucked some heads of grain,
		rubbed them in their hands,
and to eat.		and ate them.
2 When the Pharisees saw it,	24 The Pharisees	2 But some of the Pharisees
they said to him,	said to him,	said,
"Look, your disciples are doing	"Look, why are they doing	"Why are you doing
what is not lawful to do	what is not lawful	what is not lawful
on the sabbath."	on the sabbath?"	on the sabbath?"
3 He said to them, "Have you	25 And he said to them, "Have you	3 Jesus answered, "Have you
not read what David did when he	never read what David did when he	not read what David did when he
and his companions were hungry?	and his companions were hungry	and his companions were hungry?
	and in need of food?	
4 He entered the house of God	26 He entered the house of God,	4 He entered the house of God and
	when Abiathar was high priest,[C]	
and ate the bread of the	and ate the bread of the	took and ate the bread of the
Presence, which it was not lawful	Presence, which it is not lawful	Presence, which it is not lawful

---

✧ MAT 11:28–29 — Ecclesiasticus 51:23–27. ✧ MAT 11:29 — JER 6:16. ✧ MAT 12:1 and parallels — DEU 23:25. ✧ MAT 12:2 and parallels — EXO 20:10; DEU 5:14. ✧ MAT 12:3–4 and parallels — 1SM 21:1–7. ✧ MAT 12:4b and parallels — LEV 24:7–9.

✦ [B] text: P^{4} $P^{75?}$ S B W λ it (some MSS.) sy^{p} sa bo; *on the second first sabbath* (on the second sabbath after the first): A C D Θ ø ℜ it (some MSS.) vg. ✦ [C] text: S A B C Θ λ ø ℜ it (some MSS.) vg sy^{p} sa bo; omit: *when Abiathar was high priest*: D W it (some MSS.) sy^{s}.

● To MAR 2:24 and parallels, *cf.* JOH 5:10. — So the Jews said to the man who had been cured, "It is the sabbath; it is not lawful for you to carry your mat."

◗ To MAT 11:28–30 *cf.* **Gospel of Thomas, Logion 90.** — Jesus said, "Come to me, for my yoke is easy and my sovereignty is gentle, and you will find rest for yourselves." ◗ To MAT 11:29 *cf.* **Gospel according to the Hebrews** (in Clement of Alexandria, *Miscellanies II.9:45*). — As it also is written in the Gospel according to the Hebrews, "Those who seek will not rest until they find; and those who have found will marvel; and those who have marveled will reign; and those who have reigned will rest." ◗ To MAT 11:29 *cf.* **Gospel of Thomas, Logion 2.** — Jesus said, "Let those who seek not stop seeking until they find, and when they find they will be troubled, and when they have been troubled they will marvel and will reign over the All." *Ibid. V.14:96. Cf. Oxyrhynchus Papyrus 654, Logion 1.*

for him or his companions to eat, but only for the priests.	for any but the priests to eat, and he gave some to his companions."	for any but the priests to eat, and gave some to his companions?"
	27 Then he said to them, "The sabbath[D] was made for humankind, and not humankind for the sabbath;	5 Then he said to them,
5 Or have you not read in the law that on the sabbath the priests in the temple break the sabbath and yet are guiltless? 6 I tell you, something greater than the temple is here. 7 But if you had known what this means, 'I desire mercy and not sacrifice,' you would not have condemned the guiltless.		
8 For the Son of Man is lord of the sabbath."	28 so the Son of Man is lord even of the sabbath."	"The Son of Man is lord of the sabbath."[D]

§ 70 THE HEALING OF THE MAN WITH THE WITHERED HAND

MAT 12:9–14	MAR 3:1–6	LUK 6:6–11 +
9 He left that place and		6 On another sabbath
entered their synagogue;	1 Again he entered the synagogue,	he entered the synagogue and taught,
10 a man was there with a withered hand, and	and a man was there who had a withered hand.	and there was a man there whose right hand was withered.
they asked him, "Is it lawful to cure on the sabbath?"	2 They watched him to see whether he would cure him on the sabbath,	7 The scribes and the Pharisees watched him to see whether he would cure on the sabbath,
so that they might accuse him.	so that they might accuse him.	so that they might find an accusation against him.
		8 Even though he knew what they were thinking,
	3 And he said to the man who had the withered hand, "Come forward."	he said to the man who had the withered hand, "Come and stand here." He got up

✧ MAT 12:5 — NUM 28:9–10. ✧ MAT 12:7 = MAT 9:13 — HOS 6:6.

✦ [D] text: S A B C Θ λ ø ℜ vg sy[p] sa bo; omit verse 27: D it; omit verse 27b: W sy[s]. For LUK 6:5 D reads: On the same day, seeing someone working on the sabbath, Jesus said, "You, if indeed you know what you are doing, you are blessed; but if you do not, you are cursed and a transgressor of the law."

◗ To MAR 2:27–28 *cf.* **Gospel of Thomas, Logion 27b.** — Jesus said, "If you do not keep the sabbath as sabbath you will not see the Father." ◗ To MAT 12:10 *cf.* **Gospel of the Nazaraeans** (in Jerome, *Commentary on Matthew 12:13*). — In the Gospel which the Nazarenes and the Ebionites use, which we have recently translated from Hebrew to Greek, and which most people call the authentic Gospel of Matthew, the man who had the withered hand is described as a mason who begged for help in the following words: "I was a mason, earning a living with my hands; I beg you, Jesus, restore my health to me, so that I need not beg for my food in shame."

		and stood there.
11 He said to them, "Suppose one of you has only one sheep and it falls into a pit on the sabbath; will you not lay hold of it and lift it out? 12 How much more valuable is a human being than a sheep![1]		*△ 14:5 (§ 168, p. 131)* 5 *Then he said to them,* *"If one of you has* *a child or an ox that has fallen into* *a well,* *will you not immediately pull* *it out on a sabbath day?"*[1]
So it is lawful to do good on the sabbath."	4 Then he said to them, "Is it lawful to do good or to do harm on the sabbath, to save life or to kill?" But they were silent.[2] 5 He looked around at them with anger; he was grieved at their hardness of heart	9 Then Jesus said to them, "I ask you, is it lawful to do good or to do harm on the sabbath, to save life or to destroy it?"[2] 10 After looking around at all of them,
13 Then he said to the man, "Stretch out your hand." He stretched it out, and it was restored, as sound as the other.	and said to the man, "Stretch out your hand." He stretched it out, and his hand was restored.	he said to him, "Stretch out your hand." He did so, and his hand was restored.
14 But the Pharisees went out and conspired against him, how to destroy him.	6 The Pharisees went out and immediately conspired with the Herodians against him, how to destroy him.	11 But they were filled with fury and discussed with one another what they might do to Jesus. ▼ 6:12–16 (§ 72, p. 62)

§ 71 JESUS HEALS THE MULTITUDES

MAT 12:15–21 +	MAR 3:7–12	△ *LUK 6:17–19* *(§ 71, p. 60)* +
		17 *He came down with them and* *stood on a level place,*
15a When Jesus became aware of this, he departed. Many crowds followed him, *△ 4:25 (§ 16, p. 23)* 25 *And great crowds followed him* *from Galilee, the Decapolis,* *Jerusalem, Judea, and from* *beyond the Jordan.*	7 Jesus departed with his disciples to the sea, and a great multitude from Galilee followed him; 8 hearing all that he was doing, they came to him in great numbers from Judea, Jerusalem, Idumea, beyond the Jordan, and the region around Tyre and Sidon.	*with a great crowd of his disciples* *and* *a great multitude of people* *from all Judea, Jerusalem, and* *the coast of Tyre and Sidon.* 18 *They had come to hear him and*

[1] LUK 13:15–16 (§ 163, p. 128): 15 But the Lord answered him and said, "You hypocrites! Does not each of you on the sabbath untie his ox or his donkey from the manger, and lead it away to give it water? 16 And ought not this woman, a daughter of Abraham whom Satan bound for eighteen long years, be set free from this bondage on the sabbath day?"

[2] LUK 14:3 (§ 168, p. 131): And Jesus asked the lawyers and Pharisees, "Is it lawful to cure people on the sabbath, or not?"

12:15b and he cured all of them,

16 and he ordered them not to make
him known.

17 This was to fulfill what had been
spoken through the prophet Isaiah:
18 "Here is my servant, whom I
have chosen, my beloved, with
whom my soul is well pleased. I
will put my Spirit upon him, and he
will proclaim justice to the Gentiles. 19 He will not wrangle or cry
aloud, nor will anyone hear his
voice in the streets. 20 He will not
break a bruised reed or quench a
smoldering wick until he brings justice to victory. 21 And in his name
the Gentiles will hope."

▼ 12:22–24 (§ 85, p. 70)

9 He told his disciples to have a boat
ready for him because of the crowd,
so that they would not crush him;
10 for he had cured many, so that
all who had diseases
pressed upon him to touch him.[1]

11 Whenever the unclean spirits
saw him,[2] they fell down before
him and shouted,
"You are the Son of God!" 12 But
he sternly ordered them not to make
him known.

to be healed of their diseases; and those who were troubled with unclean spirits were cured.

19 And all in the crowd
were trying to touch him,[1]
for power came out from him and healed all of them.

Δ *4:41 (§ 14, p. 22)*

41 Demons also
came out of many,
shouting,
"You are the Son of God!" But
he rebuked them

and would not allow them to speak, because they knew that he was the Messiah.

---

[1] MAT 14:36b (§ 114, p. 92): and begged him [Jesus] that they might touch even the fringe of his cloak; and all who touched it were healed.

MAR 6:56 (§ 114, p. 92): And wherever he [Jesus] went, into villages or cities or farms, they laid the sick in the marketplaces, and begged him that they might touch even the fringe of his cloak; and all who touched it were healed.

[2] MAT 4:24 (§ 16, p. 23): So his [Jesus'] fame spread throughout all Syria, and they brought to him all the sick, those who were afflicted with various diseases and pains, demoniacs, epileptics, and paralytics, and he cured them.

✧ MAT 12:18–21 — ISA 42:1-4.

§ 72 THE CALL OF THE TWELVE

Δ *MAT 10:1–4* (*§ 58, p. 47*)	MAR 3:13–19*a*	LUK 6:12–16
	13 He went	12 Now during those days he went
Cf. 5:1 (§ 18, p. 24)	up the mountain	out to the mountain to pray; and he spent the night in prayer to God.
1 *Then Jesus summoned his twelve disciples*	and called to him those whom he wanted, and they came to him.	13 And when day came, he called his disciples
	14 And he appointed twelve,[E] whom he also named apostles,	and chose twelve of them, whom he also named apostles:
	to be with him, and to be sent out to proclaim the message,	
and gave them authority over unclean spirits, to cast them out, and to cure every disease and every sickness.	15 and to have authority to cast out demons.[1]	
2 *These are the names of the twelve apostles: first, Simon, also known as Peter,*	16 So he appointed the twelve: Simon[F] (to whom he gave the name Peter);	14 Simon, whom he named Peter,
and his brother Andrew;		and his brother Andrew, and
James son of Zebedee, and his brother John;	17 James son of Zebedee and John the brother of James (to whom he gave the name Boanerges, that is, Sons of Thunder);	James, and John, and
	18 and Andrew, and	
3 *Philip and Bartholomew; Thomas and Matthew the tax collector;*	Philip, and Bartholomew, and Matthew, and Thomas, and	Philip, and Bartholomew, 15 and Matthew, and Thomas, and
James son of Alphaeus, and Thaddaeus;[G]	James son of Alphaeus, and Thaddaeus,[H] and	James son of Alphaeus, and
4 *Simon the Cananaean,*	Simon the Cananaean,	Simon, who was called the Zealot,
		16 and Judas son of James,
and Judas Iscariot, the one who betrayed him.	19 and Judas Iscariot, who betrayed him.	and Judas Iscariot, who became a traitor.
	Then he went home;	
	▼ 3:19b–22 (§ 85, p. 70)	▲ 6:17–19 (§ 71, p. 60)

[1] MAR 6:7 (§ 109, p. 86): He [Jesus] called the twelve and began to send them out two by two, and gave them authority over the unclean spirits. | LUK 9:1–2 (§ 109, p. 86): 1 Then Jesus called the twelve together and gave them power and authority over all demons and to cure diseases, 2 and he sent them out to proclaim the kingdom of God and to heal.

✦ [E] text: S B C? W Θ sa bo; omit: *whom he also named apostles*: A D λ ℜ it vg sy[s] sy[p]. ✦ [F] text: S B C; omit: *So he appointed the twelve*: A D λ ø ℜ it vg sy[s] sy[p] sa bo. ✦ [G] text: S B ø it (some MSS.) vg sa bo; *Lebbaeus*: D; *Lebbaeus called Thaddaeus*: C? W Θ λ ℜ sy[p]; *Judas Zelotes*; it (some MSS.); add: *Judas the son of James* after "Cananaean" in verse 4: sy[s]. ✦ [H] text: S A B C Θ λ ø ℜ it (some MSS.) vg sy[s] sy[p] sa bo; *Lebbaeus*: D it (some MSS.).

• To LUK 6:14a and parallels, *cf.* JOH 1:42. — [ ] Jesus [ ] looked at him and said, "You are Simon son of John. You are to be called Cephas" (which is translated Peter).

The Sermon on the Plain

Luke 6:20–49

§ 73 THE BEATITUDES

Δ *MAT 5:3–4, 6, 11–12* (*§ 19, p. 25*)	MAR	LUK 6:20–23
 3 "Blessed are the poor in spirit, *for theirs is the kingdom of heaven.* *4 Blessed are those who mourn,* *for they will be comforted.* *[5] 6 Blessed are those who hunger and* *thirst for righteousness, for they will be filled.* *[7-10] 11 Blessed are you when people* *revile you and persecute you and* *utter all kinds of evil against you falsely* *on my account.* *12 Rejoice and be glad,* *for your reward is great in heaven, for* *in the same way they persecuted the prophets* *who were before you."*		20 Then he looked up at his disciples and said: "Blessed are you who are poor, for yours is the kingdom of God. 21 Blessed are you who are hungry now, for you will be filled. Blessed are you who weep now, for you will laugh. 22 Blessed are you when people hate you, and when they exclude you, revile you, and defame you on account of the Son of Man. 23 Rejoice in that day and leap for joy, for surely your reward is great in heaven; for that is what their ancestors did to the prophets."

§ 74 THE WOES

MAT	MAR	LUK 6:24–26
		24 "But woe to you who are rich, for you have received your consolation. 25 Woe to you who are full now, for you will be hungry. Woe to you who are laughing now, for you will mourn and weep. 26 Woe to you when all speak well of you, for that is what their ancestors did to the false prophets."

§ 75 ON LOVE OF ONE'S ENEMIES

Δ *MAT 5:39–42, 44–48* (*§ 26–27 p. 29*) *+*	MAR	LUK 6:27–36
Δ *5:44* *44 "But I say to you,* *Love your enemies and* *pray for those who persecute you,*		27 "But I say to you that listen, Love your enemies, do good to those who hate you, 28 bless those who curse you, pray for those who abuse you.
5:39 But I say to you, Do not resist an evildoer. *But if anyone strikes you on the right cheek, turn the other also;* *40 and if anyone wants to sue you and take your coat, give your cloak as well;* *41 and if anyone forces you to go one mile, go also the second mile.*		29 If anyone strikes you on the cheek, offer the other also; and from anyone who takes away your coat do not withhold even your shirt.
42 Give to everyone who begs from you, *and do not refuse anyone who wants to borrow from you."*		30 Give to everyone who begs from you; and if anyone takes away your goods, do not ask for them again.
Δ *7:12 (§ 39, p. 36)* *12 "In everything* *do to others as you would* *have them do to you;* *for this is the law and the prophets."*		31 Do to others as you would have them do to you.
Δ *5:46* *46 "For if you love those who love you, what reward do you have?* *Do not even the tax collectors do the same?* *47 And if you greet only your brothers and sisters, what more are you doing than others?* *Do not even the Gentiles do the same?*		32 If you love those who love you, what credit is that to you? For even sinners love those who love them. 33 If you do good to those who do good to you, what credit is that to you? For even sinners do the same. 34 If you lend to those from whom you hope to receive, what credit is that to you? Even sinners lend to sinners, to receive as much again. 35 But love your enemies, do good, and lend, expecting nothing in return.[I] Your reward will be great,
Δ *5:45* *45 so that you may* *be children of your Father in heaven; for he makes his sun rise on the evil and on the good, and sends rain on the righteous and on the unrighteous.*		and you will be children of the Most High; for he is kind to the ungrateful and the wicked.
Δ *5:48* *48 Be perfect,* *therefore, as your heavenly Father is perfect."*		36 Be merciful, just as your Father is merciful."

✦ [I] text: A B D Θ λ ø ℜ it vg sa bo; *despairing of no one*: S W sy[s] sy[p].

◗ To LUK 6:32 *cf.* **II Clement 13:4.** — God said, "It is no credit to you if you love those who love you; but it is a credit to you if you love your enemies and those who hate you."

§ 76 ON JUDGING

Δ *MAT 7:1–5* (*§ 36, p. 34*) +	MAR	LUK 6:37–42
1 *"Do not judge, so that you may not be judged.* 2 *For with the judgment you make* *you will be judged,*		37 "Do not judge, and you will not be judged;
		do not condemn, and you will not be condemned. Forgive, and you will be forgiven; 38 give, and it will be given to you. A good measure, pressed down, shaken together, running over, will be put into your lap;
and the measure you give *will be the measure you get."* [1]		for the measure you give will be the measure you get back." [1]
Δ *15:14* (*§ 115, p. 92*)		39 He also told them a parable:
14 *"Let them alone;* *they are blind guides of the blind.*		
And if one blind person guides another, *both will fall into a pit."*		"Can a blind person guide a blind person? Will not both fall into a pit?
Δ *10:24-25* (*§ 59, p. 51*)		
24 *"A disciple is not above the teacher,* *nor a slave above the master;*		40 A disciple is not above the teacher,
25 *it is enough for the disciple to be like the teacher, and the slave like the master."* [ ]		but everyone who is fully qualified will be like the teacher.
7:3 "Why do you see the speck in your neighbor's eye, but do not notice the log in your own eye? 4 *Or how can you say to your neighbor,* *'Let me take the speck out of your eye,'* *while* *the log is in your own eye?* 5 *You hypocrite, first take the log out of your own eye, and then you will see clearly to take the speck out of your neighbor's eye."*		41 Why do you see the speck in your neighbor's eye, but do not notice the log in your own eye? 42 Or how can you say to your neighbor, 'Friend, let me take out the speck in your eye,' when you yourself do not see the log in your own eye? You hypocrite, first take the log out of your own eye, and then you will see clearly to take the speck out of your neighbor's eye."

§ 77 THE TEST OF A GOOD PERSON

Δ *MAT 7:16–21* (*§ 41–42, p. 36*)	Δ *MAT 12:33–35* (*§ 86, p. 70*)	MAR	LUK 6:43–46
			43 "No good tree bears bad fruit, nor again does a bad tree bear good fruit;
	33 *"Either make the tree good, and its fruit good; or make the tree bad, and its fruit bad;*		
16 *"You will know them* *by their fruits.*	*for the tree is known* *by its fruit.*		44 for each tree is known by its own fruit.

---

[1] MAR 4:24 (§ 94, p. 77): And he [Jesus] said to them, "Pay attention to what you hear; the measure you give will be the measure you get, and still more will be given you."

- To LUK 6:40 *cf.* JOH 13:16; JOH 15:20. — [ ] "Servants are not greater than their master." [ ]

Are grapes gathered
from thorns,
or figs from thistles?
17 *In the same way, every good*
tree bears good fruit, but the
bad tree bears bad fruit.
18 *A good tree cannot bear bad*
fruit, nor can a bad tree bear
good fruit. 19 *Every tree that*
does not bear good fruit is cut
down and thrown into the fire.
20 *Thus you will know them by*
their fruits.

21 *Not everyone who says to me,*
'Lord, Lord,'
will enter the kingdom
of heaven, but only the one
who does the will of my Father
in heaven."

34 *You brood of vipers! How*
can you speak good things,
when you are evil? For out of
the abundance of the heart the
mouth speaks.

35 *The good person*
brings good things
out of a good treasure,
and the evil person
brings evil things
out of an evil treasure."

Figs are not gathered from
thorns, nor
are grapes picked
from a bramble bush.

45 The good person out of
the good treasure of the heart
produces good,
and the evil person out of
evil treasure
produces evil;
for it is out of the abundance of
the heart that the mouth speaks.
46 Why do you call me
'Lord, Lord,'
and do not do what I tell you?"

§ 78 HEARERS AND DOERS OF THE WORD

Δ *MAT 7:24–27* *(§ 43, p. 38)*

24 *"Everyone then*
who hears these words of mine and
acts on them
will be like a wise man who
built his house on rock.
25 *The rain fell, the floods came, and the winds*
blew and beat on that house, but it did not fall,

MAR

LUK 6:47–49

47 "I will show you what someone is like
who comes to me, hears my words, and
acts on them.
48 That one is like a man building a house, who
dug deeply and laid the foundation on rock;
when a flood arose, the river
burst against that house but could not shake it,

because it had been founded on rock.
26 *And everyone who hears these words of mine*
and does not act on them will be like a
foolish man who built his house
on sand.
27 *The rain fell, and the floods came, and the*
winds blew and beat against that house,
and it fell—and
great was its fall!"

because it had been well built.[J]
49 But the one who hears
and does not act is like a
man who built a house
on the ground without a foundation.

When the river burst against it,
immediately it fell, and
great was the ruin of that house."

§ 79 THE CENTURION'S SLAVE

MAT	MAR	LUK 7:1–10
Cf. 7:28a (§ 44, p. 38) *Cf.* 8:5–13 (§ 46, p. 39)		see below

1 After Jesus had finished all his sayings in the hearing of the people, he entered
Capernaum. 2 A centurion there had a slave whom he valued highly, and who was
ill and close to death. 3 When he heard about Jesus, he sent some Jewish elders
to him, asking him to come and heal his slave. 4 When they came to Jesus, they
appealed to him earnestly, saying, "He is worthy of having you do this for him,
5 for he loves our people, and it is he who built our synagogue for us." 6 And Jesus
went with them, but when he was not far from the house, the centurion sent friends
to say to him, "Lord, do not trouble yourself, for I am not worthy to have you
come under my roof; 7 therefore I did not presume to come to you. But only speak
the word, and let my servant be healed. 8 For I also am a man set under authority,
with soldiers under me; and I say to one, 'Go,' and he goes, and to another,
'Come,' and he comes, and to my slave, 'Do this,' and the slave does it."
9 When Jesus heard this he was amazed at him, and turning to the crowd that
followed him, he said, "I tell you, not even in Israel have I found such faith."
10 When those who had been sent returned to the house, they found the slave in
good health.

§ 80 THE WIDOW'S SON AT NAIN

MAT	MAR	LUK 7:11–17

11 Soon afterward[K] he went to a town called Nain, and his disciples and a large
crowd went with him. 12 As he approached the gate of the town, a man who had
died was being carried out. He was his mother's only son, and she was a widow;
and with her was a large crowd from the town. 13 When the Lord saw her, he had
compassion for her and said to her, "Do not weep." 14 Then he came forward and
touched the bier, and the bearers stood still. And he said, "Young man, I say to
you, rise!" 15 The dead man sat up and began to speak, and Jesus gave him to his

✧ LUK 7:15 — 1KI 17:23.

✦ [J] text: $P^{75?}$ S B W sa bo; *founded on rock*: A C D Θ λ ø 𝔐 it vg sy^{p}; omit phrase: $P^{45?}$ sy^{s}. ✦ [K] text: P^{75} A B Θ ø 𝔐 it (some MSS.) vg sy^{s} sa; *next day*: S C D W it (some MSS.) sy^{p} bo.

• To § 79 *cf.* JOH 4:46–54.

mother. 16 Fear seized all of them; and they glorified God, saying, "A great
prophet has risen among us!" and "God has looked favorably on his people!"
17 This word about him spread throughout Judea and all the surrounding country.

§ 81 JOHN'S QUESTION TO JESUS

MAT	MAR	LUK 7:18–23
Cf. 11:2–6 (§ 64, p. 55)		18 The disciples of John reported all these things to him. So John summoned two of his disciples 19 and sent them to the Lord to ask, "Are you the one who is to come, or are we to wait for another?" 20 When the men had come to him, they said, "John the Baptist has sent us to you to ask, 'Are you the one who is to come, or are we to wait for another?' " 21 Jesus had just then cured many people of diseases, plagues, and evil spirits, and had given sight to many who were blind. 22 And he answered them, "Go and tell John what you have seen and heard: the blind receive their sight, the lame walk, the lepers are cleansed, the deaf hear, the dead are raised, the poor have good news brought to them. 23 And blessed is anyone who takes no offense at me."

§ 82 JESUS' WORDS ABOUT JOHN

MAT	MAR	LUK 7:24–35
Cf. 11:7–19 (§ 65, p. 55)	*Cf.* 1:2 (§ 1, p. 11)	24 When John's messengers had gone, Jesus began to speak to the crowds about John: "What did you go out into the wilderness to look at? A reed shaken by the wind? 25 What then did you go out to see? Someone dressed in soft robes? Look, those who put on fine clothing and live in luxury are in royal palaces. 26 What then did you go out to see? A prophet? Yes, I tell you, and more than a prophet. 27 This is the one about whom it is written, 'See, I am sending my messenger ahead of you, who will prepare your way before you.' 28 I tell you, among those born of women no one is greater than John; yet the least in the kingdom of God is greater than he." 29 (And all the people who heard this, including the tax collectors, acknowledged the justice of God, because they had been baptized with John's baptism. 30 But by refusing to be baptized by him, the Pharisees and the lawyers rejected God's purpose for themselves.)[1] 31 "To what then will I compare the people of this generation, and what are they like? 32 They are like children sitting in the marketplace and calling to one another, 'We played the flute for you, and you did not dance; we wailed, and you did not weep.' 33 For John the Baptist has come eating no bread and drinking no wine, and you say, 'He has a demon'; 34 the Son of Man has come eating and drinking, and you say, 'Look, a glutton and a drunkard, a friend of tax collectors and sinners!' 35 Nevertheless, wisdom is vindicated by all her children."

---

[1] MAT 21:32 (§ 203, p. 158): "For John came to you in the way of righteousness and you did not believe him, but the tax collectors and the prostitutes believed him; and even after you saw it, you did not change your minds and believe him."

✧ LUK 7:22 = MAT 11:5 — ISA 29:18–19; 35:5–6; 61:1. ✧ LUK 7:27 = MAT 11:10 — MAL 3:1.

◗ To LUK 7:28 *cf.* **Gospel of Thomas, Logion 46.** — See note to MAT 11:11, p. 56.

§ 83 THE WOMAN WITH THE OINTMENT

MAT	MAR	LUK 7:36–50
Cf. 26:6–13	*Cf.* 14:3–9	36 One of the Pharisees asked Jesus to eat with him, and he went into the Pharisee's
(§ 232, p. 181)	(§ 232, p. 181)	house and took his place at the table. 37 And a woman in the city, who was a sinner,
		having learned that he was eating in the Pharisee's house, brought an alabaster jar
		of ointment. 38 She stood behind him at his feet, weeping, and began to bathe his
		feet with her tears and to dry them with her hair. Then she continued kissing his
		feet and anointing them with the ointment. 39 Now when the Pharisee who had
		invited him saw it, he said to himself, "If this man were a prophet, he would have
		known who and what kind of woman this is who is touching him—that she is a
		sinner." 40 Jesus spoke up and said to him, "Simon, I have something to say to
		you." "Teacher," he replied, "Speak." 41 "A certain creditor had two debtors;
		one owed five hundred denarii,[L] and the other fifty. 42 When they could not pay,
		he canceled the debts for both of them. Now which of them will love him more?"
		43 Simon answered, "I suppose the one for whom he canceled the greater debt."
		And Jesus said to him, "You have judged rightly." 44 Then turning toward the
		woman, he said to Simon, "Do you see this woman? I entered your house; you
		gave me no water for my feet, but she has bathed my feet with her tears and dried
		them with her hair. 45 You gave me no kiss, but from the time I came in she has
		not stopped kissing my feet. 46 You did not anoint my head with oil, but she has
		anointed my feet with ointment. 47 Therefore, I tell you, her sins, which were
		many, have been forgiven; hence she has shown great love. But the one to whom
	Cf. 5:34	little is forgiven, loves little." 48 Then he said to her, "Your sins are forgiven."
	(§ 107, p. 83)	49 But those who were at the table with him began to say among themselves, "Who
Cf. 9:22	*Cf.* 10:52	is this who even forgives sins?" 50 And he said to the woman, "Your faith has
(§ 55, p. 46)	(§ 193, p. 149)	saved you; go in peace."

§ 84 THE MINISTERING WOMEN

MAT	MAR	LUK 8:1–3
Cf. 4:23		1 Soon afterwards he went on through cities and villages, proclaiming and bringing
(§ 16, p. 23)		the good news of the kingdom of God. The twelve were with him, 2 as well as
Cf. 9:35	*Cf.* 16:9	some women who had been cured of evil spirits and infirmities: Mary, called
(§ 58, p. 47)	(p. 209)	Magdalene, from whom seven demons had gone out, 3 and Joanna, the wife of
Cf. 27:55	*Cf.* 15:41	Herod's steward Chuza, and Susanna, and many others, who provided for them[M]
(§ 250, p. 201)	(§ 250, p. 201)	out of their resources.
		Cf. 8:4-8 (§ 90, p. 74)

✧ LUK 7:50 — 1SM 1:17.

✦ [L] The denarius was a day's wage for a laborer. ✦ [M] text: B D W Θ ø 𝔑 it (some MSS.) vg (some MSS.) sy^{c} sy^{s} sy^{p}; *him*: S A λ it (some MSS.) vg (some MSS.) sa bo.

● To § 83 *cf.* JOH 12:1–8.

§ 85 ACCUSATIONS AGAINST JESUS

MAT 12:22–24	MAR 3:19b–22	Δ *LUK 11:14–16* *(§ 149, p. 117)*
Cf. 12:15–21 (§ 71, p. 61)	*Cf.* 3:13–19 (§ 72, p. 62) 19b Then he went home; 20 and the crowd came together again, so that they could not even eat. 21 When his family heard it, they went out to restrain him, for people were saying, "He has gone out of his mind."	
22 Then they brought to him a demoniac who was blind and mute; and he cured him, so that the one who had been mute could speak and see. 23 All the crowds were amazed[1] and said, "Can this be the Son of David?"		*14 Now he was casting out a demon that was mute; when the demon had gone out, the one who had been mute spoke, and the crowds were amazed.*[1]
24 But when the Pharisees heard it, they said, "It is only by Beelzebul, the ruler of the demons, that this fellow casts out the demons."[2]	22 And the scribes who came down from Jerusalem said, "He has Beelzebul, and by the ruler of the demons he casts out demons."[2]	*15 But some of them said, "He casts out demons by Beelzebul, the ruler of the demons."*[2]
		16 Others, to test him, kept demanding from him a sign from heaven.

§ 86 A HOUSE DIVIDED

MAT 12:25–37	MAR 3:23–30	Δ *LUK 11:17–23* *(§ 149, p. 117) +*
	23 And he called them to him,	
25 He knew what they were thinking and said to them,	and spoke to them in parables, "How can Satan cast out Satan?	*17 But he knew what they were thinking and said to them,*
"Every kingdom divided against itself is laid waste, and no city or house divided against itself will stand.	24 If a kingdom is divided against itself, that kingdom cannot stand. 25 And if a house is divided against itself, that house will not be able to stand.	*"Every kingdom divided against itself becomes a desert, and house falls on house.*
26 If Satan casts out Satan, he is divided against himself; how then will his kingdom stand?	26 And if Satan has risen up against himself and is divided, he cannot stand, but his end has come.	*18 If Satan also is divided against himself, how will his kingdom stand? — for you say that I cast out the demons by Beelzebul.*

[1] *Cf.* MAT 9:32–34 (§ 57, p. 46).
[2] MAT 9:34 (§ 57, p. 46): But the Pharisees said, "By the ruler of the demons he casts out the demons."

- To MAR 3:22 *cf.* JOH 7:20. — [ ] "You have a demon!" [ ] *Cf.* JOH 8:48, 52; 10:20.

27 If I cast out demons by Beelzebul, by whom do your own exorcists cast them out? Therefore they will be your judges. 28 But if it is by the Spirit of God that I cast out demons, then the kingdom of God has come to you.		*19 Now if I cast out the demons by Beelzebul, by whom do your exorcists cast them out? Therefore they will be your judges.* *20 But if it is by the finger of God that I cast out the demons, then the kingdom of God has come to you.*
29 Or how can one enter a strong man's house and plunder his property, without first tying up the strong man? Then indeed the house can be plundered.	27 But no one can enter a strong man's house and plunder his property without first tying up the strong man; then indeed the house can be plundered.	*21 When a strong man, fully armed, guards his castle, his property is safe. 22 But when one stronger than he attacks him and overpowers him, he takes away his armor in which he trusted and divides his plunder.*
30 Whoever is not with me is against me,[1] and whoever does not gather with me scatters.		*23 Whoever is not with me is against me,[1] and whoever does not gather with me scatters."*
31 Therefore I tell you, people will be forgiven for every sin and blasphemy, but blasphemy against the Spirit will not be forgiven.	28 Truly I tell you, people will be forgiven for their sins and whatever blasphemies they utter;	Δ *12:10 (§ 155, p. 122)*
32 Whoever speaks a word against the Son of Man will be forgiven, but whoever speaks against the Holy Spirit will not be forgiven, either in this age or in the age to come.	29 but whoever blasphemes against the Holy Spirit can never have[N] forgiveness, but is guilty of an eternal sin"— 30 for they had said, "He has an unclean spirit." ▼ 3:31–35 (§ 89, p. 73)	*10 "And everyone who speaks a word against the Son of Man will be forgiven; but whoever blasphemes against the Holy Spirit will not be forgiven."*
33 "Either make the tree good, and its fruit good; or make the tree bad, and its fruit bad; for the tree is known by its fruit.[2]		Δ *6:43–45 (§ 77, p. 65)* *43 "No good tree bears bad fruit, nor again does a bad tree bear good fruit; 44 for each tree is known by its own fruit.[2] Figs are not gathered from thorns, nor are grapes picked from a bramble bush.*
34 You brood of vipers! How can you speak good things, when you are evil? For out of the abundance of the heart the mouth speaks.		

[1] MAR 9:40 (§ 130, p. 107): "Whoever is not against us is for us." | LUK 9:50 (§ 130, p. 107): "for whoever is not against you is for you."

[2] MAT 7:16–20 (§ 41, p. 36): 16 "You will know them by their fruits. Are grapes gathered from thorns, or figs from thistles? 17 In the same way, every good tree bears good fruit, but the bad tree bears bad fruit. 18 A good tree cannot bear bad fruit, nor can a bad tree bear good fruit. 19 Every tree that does not bear good fruit is cut down and thrown into the fire. 20 Thus you will know them by their fruits."

✦ [N] text: S A B C ø ℜ vg sy[p] sa bo; *has not*: D W Θ λ it sy[s?].

35 The good person
brings good things
out of a good treasure, and

the evil person
brings evil things
out of an evil treasure.

36 I tell you, on the day of judgment
you will have to give an account for
every careless word you utter;
37 for by your words you will be
justified, and by your words you
will be condemned."

45 The good person

out of the good treasure of the heart
produces good, and
the evil person

out of evil treasure
produces evil;
for it is out of the abundance of the
heart that the mouth speaks."

§ 87 AGAINST SEEKING FOR SIGNS

MAT 12:38–42

38 Then some of the scribes and Pharisees said
to him, "Teacher, we wish to see a sign from
you."
39 But he answered them, "An evil and adulterous generation asks for a sign, but
no sign will be given to it except the sign of
the prophet Jonah.[1]
40 For just as Jonah
was three days and three nights in the belly of
the sea monster, so for three days and three
nights the
Son of Man will be in the heart of the earth.
41 The people of Nineveh will rise up at the
judgment with this generation and condemn it,
because they repented at the proclamation of
Jonah, and see, something greater than
Jonah is here!

MAR

Δ *LUK 11:29–30, 32* (*§ 152, p. 119*)

29 When the crowds were increasing,

he began to say, "This generation is an evil
generation; it asks for a sign, but
no sign will be given to it except the sign of
Jonah.[1]
30 For just as Jonah
became a sign to the people of Nineveh, so the

Son of Man will be to this generation.
32 The people of Nineveh will rise up at the
judgment with this generation and condemn it,
because they repented at the proclamation of
Jonah, and see, something greater than
Jonah is here!

---

[1] MAT 16:1–2a, 4a (§ 119, p. 96):
1 The Pharisees and Sad-
ducees came, and to test Jesus they asked him to show them a sign
from heaven.
2a He answered them, [3]
4a "An evil and adulterous generation asks
for a sign, but
no sign will be given to it except the sign of Jonah."

MAR 8:11–12 (§ 119, p. 96):
11 The Pharisees
came and began to argue with him [Jesus], asking him for a sign
from heaven, to test him.
12 And he sighed deeply in his spirit
and said, "Why does this generation ask
for a sign? Truly I tell you,
no sign will be given to this generation."

✧ MAT 12:40 — JON 1:17. ✧ MAT 12:41 = LUK 11:32 — JON 3:5.

▸ To MAT 12:40b *cf.* **Gospel of the Nazaraeans**. — The Jewish Gospel does not have: three days and three nights.

42 The queen of the South will rise up at the
judgment with
this generation and condemn
it, because she came from the ends of the
earth to listen to the wisdom of Solomon, and
see, something greater than Solomon is here!"

Δ 11:31
31 The queen of the South will rise at the
judgment with
the people of this generation and condemn
them, because she came from the ends of the
earth to listen to the wisdom of Solomon, and
see, something greater than Solomon is here!"

§ 88 THE RETURN OF THE UNCLEAN SPIRIT

MAT 12:43–45

43 "When the unclean spirit has gone out of a
person, it wanders through waterless regions
looking for a resting place, but it finds none.
44 Then it says, 'I will return to my house from
which I came.' When it comes, it finds it
empty, swept, and put in order. 45 Then it
goes and brings along seven other spirits more
evil than itself, and they enter and live there;
and the last state of that person is worse than
the first.
So will it be also with this evil generation."

MAR

Δ *LUK 11:24–26* *(§ 150, p. 119)*

24 "When the unclean spirit has gone out of a
person, it wanders through waterless regions
looking for a resting place, but not finding any,
it says, 'I will return to my house from
which I came.' 25 When it comes, it finds it
swept and put in order. 26 Then it
goes and brings seven other spirits more
evil than itself, and they enter and live there;
and the last state of that person is worse than
the first."

§ 89 JESUS' TRUE RELATIVES

MAT 12:46–50

46 While he was still speaking to the
crowds, his mother and his
brothers were standing outside, wanting to speak to him.[O]

47 Someone told him,
"Look, your mother and your
brothers are standing outside,
wanting to speak to you." 48 But to
the one who had told him this,

MAR 3:31–35

▲ 3:23–30 (§ 86, p. 70)
31 Then his mother and his
brothers came; and standing outside, they sent to him and
called him.

32 A crowd was sitting around him;
and they said to him,
"Your mother and your
brothers[P] and sisters are outside,
asking for you."

Δ *LUK 8:19–21* *(§ 104, p. 80)*

19 Then his mother and his
brothers came to him,

but they could not reach him be-
cause of the crowd.
20 And he was told,
"Your mother and your
brothers are standing outside,
wanting to see you."

⟡ MAT 12:42 = LUK 11:31 — 1KI 10:1*ff*.

✦ [O] text: C D W Θ λ ø ℜ it vg sy^{p} bo; omit verse 47: S B sy^{c} sy^{s} sa. ✦ [P] text: A D it (some MSS.); omit: *and sisters*: S B C W Θ λ ø ℜ it (some MSS.) vg sy^{s} sy^{p} bo.

▸ To MAT 12:47–50 *cf.* **Gospel of the Ebionites** (in Epiphanius, *Against Heresies, XXX.14:5*). — Moreover they deny that Jesus was a man, apparently because of the word which the Savior spoke when it was announced to him, "Look, your mother and your brothers are standing outside" — namely: "Who are my mother and brothers?" And stretching out his hand toward the disciples, Jesus said, "These who do the will of my Father are my brothers and mother and sisters."

Jesus replied, "Who is my mother, and who are my brothers?" 49 And pointing to his disciples, he said,	33 And he replied, "Who are my mother and my brothers?" 34 And looking at those who sat around him, he said,	21 *But he said to them,*
"Here are my mother and my broth- ers! 50 For whoever does the will of my Father in heaven is my brother and sister and mother."	"Here are my mother and my broth- ers! 35 Whoever does the will of God is my brother and sister and mother."	*"My mother and my broth- ers are those who hear the word of God and do it."*

§ 90 THE PARABLE OF THE SOWER

MAT 13:1–9	MAR 4:1–9	LUK 8:4–8
1 That same day Jesus went out of the house and sat beside the sea.	1 Again he began to teach beside the sea.	▲ 8:1–3 (§ 84, p. 69)
2 Such great crowds gathered	Such a very large crowd gathered	4 When a great crowd gathered and people from town after town came to him,
around him that he got into a boat and sat there, while the whole crowd stood on the beach.	around him that he got into a boat on the sea and sat there, while the whole crowd was beside the sea on the land.	*Cf.* 5:1–3 (§ 17, p. 24)
3 And he told them many things in parables, saying:	2 He began to teach them many things in parables, and in his teaching he said to them:	he said in a parable:
"Listen! A sower went out to sow. 4 And as he sowed, some seeds fell on the path, and the birds came and ate them up. 5 Other seeds fell on rocky ground, where they did not have much soil, and they sprang up quickly, since they had no depth of soil. 6 But when the sun rose, they were scorched; and since they had no root, they withered away.	3 "Listen! A sower went out to sow. 4 And as he sowed, some seed fell on the path, and the birds came and ate it up. 5 Other seed fell on rocky ground, where it did not have much soil, and it sprang up quickly, since it had no depth of soil. 6 And when the sun rose, it was scorched; and since it had no root, it withered away.	5 "A sower went out to sow his seed; and as he sowed, some fell on the path and was tram- pled on, and the birds of the air ate it up. 6 Some fell on the rock; and as it grew up, it withered for lack of moisture.
7 Other seeds fell among thorns, and the thorns grew up and choked them.	7 Other seed fell among thorns, and the thorns grew up and choked it, and it yielded no grain.	7 Some fell among thorns, and the thorns grew with it and choked it.
8 Other seeds fell on good soil and brought forth grain, some a hun- dredfold, some sixty, some thirty.	8 Other seed fell into good soil and brought forth grain, growing up and increasing and yielding thirty and sixty and a hundredfold."	8 Some fell into good soil, and when it grew, it produced a hundredfold."
9 Let anyone with ears[Q] listen!"	9 And he said, "Let anyone with ears to hear listen!"	As he said this, he called out, "Let anyone with ears to hear listen!"

✦ Q text: S B it (some MSS.) sy^{s}; add: *to hear*: C D W Θ λ φ 𝔐 it (some MSS.) vg sy^{c} sy^{p} sa bo.

● To MAT 12:50 and parallels, *cf.* JOH 15:14. — "You are my friends if you do what I command you."

§ 91 THE REASON FOR SPEAKING IN PARABLES

MAT 13:10–15	MAR 4:10–12	LUK 8:9–10
10 Then the disciples came and asked him, "Why do you speak to them in parables?"	10 When he was alone, those who were around him along with the twelve asked him about the parables.	9 Then his disciples asked him what this parable meant.
11 He answered, "To you it has been given to know the secrets of the kingdom of heaven, but to them it has not been given.	11 And he said to them, "To you has been given the secret of the kingdom of God,	10 He said, "To you it has been given to know the secrets of the kingdom of God;
12 For to those who have, more will be given, and they will have an abundance; but from those who have nothing, even what they have will be taken away.	*Cf.* 4:25 (§ 94, p. 77)	*Cf.* 8:18b (§ 94, p. 77)
13 The reason I speak to them in parables is that 'seeing they do not perceive, and hearing they do not listen, nor do they understand.'	but for those outside, everything comes in parables; 12 in order that 'they may indeed look, but not perceive, and may indeed listen, but not understand;	but to others I speak in parables, so that 'looking they may not perceive, and listening they may not understand.' "
14 With them indeed is fulfilled the prophecy of Isaiah that says: 'You will indeed listen, but never understand, and you will indeed look, but never perceive. 15 For this people's heart has grown dull, and their ears are hard of hearing, and they have shut their eyes; so that they might not look with their eyes, and listen with their ears, and understand with their heart and turn— and I would heal them.' "	so that they may not turn again and be forgiven.' "	

✧ MAT 13:13 and parallels — ISA 6:9–10. ✧ MAT 13:14–15 — ISA 6:9–10.

• To MAT 13:14–15 *cf.* JOH 12:40.

◗ To MAT 13:11 *cf.* Clement of Alexandria, *Miscellanies V.10:63, 7.* — Not grudgingly did the Lord declare in a certain gospel, "My secret is for me and the offspring of my house." ◗ To MAT 13:12 *cf.* **Gospel of Thomas, Logion 41.** — Jesus said, "All who have in their hand, to them shall be given; and all who do not have, from them shall be taken away, even the little they have."

§ 92 THE BLESSEDNESS OF THE DISCIPLES

MAT 13:16–17	MAR	Δ *LUK 10:23–24* (*§ 142, p. 114*)
		23 *Then turning to the disciples, Jesus said to them privately,*
16 "But blessed are your eyes, for they see, and your ears, for they hear.		*"Blessed are the eyes that see what you see!*
17 Truly I tell you, many prophets and righteous people longed to see what you see, but did not see it, and to hear what you hear, but did not hear it."		24 *For I tell you that many prophets and kings desired to see what you see, but did not see it, and to hear what you hear, but did not hear it."*

§ 93 THE INTERPRETATION OF THE PARABLE OF THE SOWER

MAT 13:18–23	MAR 4:13–20	LUK 8:11–15
18 "Hear then the parable of the sower.	13 And he said to them, "Do you not understand this parable?	11 "Now the parable is this:
19 When anyone hears the word of the kingdom and does not understand it,		
	Then how will you understand all the parables?	
	14 The sower sows the word.	The seed is the word of God.
the evil one comes and snatches away what is sown in the heart; this is what was sown on the path.	15 These are the ones on the path where the word is sown: when they hear, Satan immediately comes and takes away the word that is sown in them.	12 The ones on the path are those who have heard; then the devil comes and takes away the word from their hearts,
		so that they may not believe and be saved.
20 As for what was sown on rocky ground, this is the one who hears the word and immediately receives it with joy;	16 And these are the ones sown on rocky ground: when they hear the word, they immediately receive it with joy.	13 The ones on the rock are those who, when they hear the word, receive it with joy.
21 yet such a person has no root, but endures only for a while, and when trouble or persecution arises on account of the word, that person immediately falls away.[R]	17 But they have no root, and endure only for a while; then, when trouble or persecution arises on account of the word, immediately they fall away.[R]	But these have no root; they believe only for a while and in a time of testing fall away.
22 As for what was sown among thorns, this is the one who hears the word, but the cares of the world and the lure of wealth	18 And others are those sown among the thorns: these are the ones who hear the word, 19 but the cares of the world, and the lure of wealth, and the desire for other things	14 As for what fell among the thorns, these are the ones who hear; but as they go on their way, they are choked by the cares and riches and pleasures of life, and

✦ [R] Or, *stumble* (*stumbles*).

choke the word, and	come in and choke the word, and	
it yields nothing. 23 But	it yields nothing. 20 And these are	their fruit does not mature. 15 But
as for what was sown on good soil,	the ones sown on the good soil:	as for that in the good soil,
this is the one who		these are the ones who, when
hears the word and understands it,	they hear the word and accept it and	they hear the word, hold it fast
		in an honest and good heart, and
who indeed bears fruit and yields,	bear fruit,	bear fruit
in one case a hundredfold, in another sixty, and in another thirty."	thirty and sixty and a hundredfold."	with patient endurance."

§ 94 THE PURPOSE OF PARABLES

△ *MAT 13:12* (§ 91, p. 75)	**MAR 4:21–25**	**LUK 8:16–18**
	21 He said to them, "Is a lamp brought in[S] to be put under	16 "No one after lighting a lamp hides it under
	the bushel basket, or under the bed,	a jar, or puts it under a bed,
	and not on the lampstand?[1]	but puts it on a lampstand, so that those who enter may see the light.[1]
	22 For there is nothing hidden,	17 For nothing is hidden
	except to be disclosed;	that will not be disclosed,
	nor is anything secret,	nor is anything secret
	except to	that will not become known and
	come to light.[2]	come to light.[2]
	23 Let anyone with ears to hear listen!" 24 And he said to them,	
	"Pay attention to	18 Then pay attention to
	what you hear; the measure you give will be the measure you get,[3] and still more will be given you.	how you listen;
12 *"For to those who have, more will be given,*	25 For to those who have, more will be given;	for to those who have, more will be given;
and they will have an abundance;		
but from those who have nothing,	and from those who have nothing,	and from those who do not have,
even what they have will be taken away."[4]	even what they have will be taken away."[4]	even what they seem to have will be taken away."[4]

▼ 8:19–21 (§ 104, p. 80)

[1] MAT 5:15 (§ 20, p. 26): "No one after lighting a lamp puts it under the bushel basket, but on the lampstand, and it gives light to all in the house."
LUK 11:33 (§ 153, p. 120): "No one after lighting a lamp puts it in a cellar, but on the lampstand so that those who enter may see the light."

[2] MAT 10:26 (§ 60, p. 52): "So have no fear of them; for nothing is covered up that will not be uncovered, and nothing secret that will not become known."
LUK 12:2 (§ 155, p. 122): "Nothing is covered up that will not be uncovered, and nothing secret that will not become known."

[3] MAT 7:2 (§ 36, p. 34): "For with the judgment you make you will be judged, and the measure you give will be the measure you get."
LUK 6:38b (§ 76, p. 65): "for the measure you give will be the measure you get back."

[4] MAT 25:29 (§ 228, p. 178): "For to all those who have, more will be given, and they will have an abundance; but from those who have nothing, even what they have will be taken away."
LUK 19:26 (§ 195, p. 151): "I tell you, to all those who have, more will be given; but from those who have nothing, even what they have will be taken away."

✦ [S] text: S A B C Θ λ ℜ it (some MSS.) vg sy^{p}; *lighted*: D W ø it (some MSS.) sa bo.

§ 95 THE PARABLE OF THE SEED GROWING SECRETLY

MAT	MAR 4:26–29	LUK
	26 He also said, "The kingdom of God is as if someone would scatter seed on the ground, 27 and would sleep and rise night and day, and the seed would sprout and grow, he does not know how. 28 The earth produces of itself, first the stalk, then the head, then the full grain in the head. 29 But when the grain is ripe, at once he goes in with his sickle, because the harvest has come."	

§ 96 THE PARABLE OF THE WEEDS

MAT 13:24–30	MAR	LUK
24 He put before them another parable: "The kingdom of heaven may be compared to someone who sowed good seed in his field; 25 but while everybody was asleep, an enemy came and sowed weeds among the wheat, and then went away. 26 So when the plants came up and bore grain, then the weeds appeared as well. 27 And the slaves of the householder came and said to him, 'Master, did you not sow good seed in your field? Where, then, did these weeds come from?' 28 He answered, 'An enemy has done this.' The slaves said to him, 'Then do you want us to go and gather them?' 29 But he replied, 'No; for in gathering the weeds you would uproot the wheat along with them. 30 Let both of them grow together until the harvest; and at harvest time I will tell the reapers, Collect the weeds first and bind them in bundles to be burned, but gather the wheat into my barn.' "		

§ 97 THE PARABLE OF THE MUSTARD SEED

MAT 13:31–32	MAR 4:30–32	Δ *LUK 13:18–19 (§ 164, p. 129)*
31 He put before them another	30 He also said, "With what can we	*18 He said therefore, "What is the*
parable: "The kingdom of heaven	compare the kingdom of God,	*kingdom of God like? And*
	or what parable will we use for it?	*to what should I compare it?*
is like a mustard seed that some-	31 It is like a mustard seed, which,	*19 It is like a mustard seed that some-*
one took and sowed in his field;	when sown upon the ground,	*one took and sowed in the garden;*
32 it is the smallest of all the seeds,	is the smallest of all the seeds	
but	on earth; 32 yet when it is sown it	
when it has grown it is the greatest	grows up and becomes the greatest	*it grew and*
of shrubs and becomes a tree,	of all shrubs, and puts forth large	*became a tree, and*
	branches,	
so that the birds of the air come and	so that the birds of the air can	*the birds of the air*
make nests in its branches."	make nests in its shade."	*made nests in its branches."*

✧ MAR 4:29 — JOE 3:13. ✧ MAT 13:32 and parallels — DAN 4:21.

◗ To MAT 13:31–32 and parallels, *cf.* **Gospel of Thomas, Logion 20.** — The disciples said to Jesus, "Tell us what the kingdom of heaven is like." Jesus said to them, "It is like a mustard seed, smaller than all seeds. But when it falls on the tilled ground, it produces a large branch and becomes shelter for the birds of heaven."

§ 98 THE PARABLE OF THE YEAST

MAT 13:33	MAR	Δ LUK 13:20–21 (§ 164, p. 129)
33 He told them another parable: "The kingdom of heaven is like yeast that a woman took and mixed in with three measures of flour until all of it was leavened."		*20 And again he said, "To what should I compare the kingdom of God? 21 It is like yeast that a woman took and mixed in with three measures of flour until all of it was leavened."*

§ 99 JESUS' USE OF PARABLES

MAT 13:34–35	MAR 4:33–34	LUK
34 Jesus told the crowds all these things in parables; without a parable he told them nothing.	33 With many such parables he spoke the word to them, as they were able to hear it; 34 he did not speak to them except in parables, but he explained everything in private to his disciples.	
35 This was to fulfill what had been spoken through the prophet:[T] "I will open my mouth to speak in parables; I will proclaim what has been hidden from the foundation of the world."	▼ 4:35–41 (§ 105, p. 81)	

§ 100 THE INTERPRETATION OF THE PARABLE OF THE WEEDS

MAT 13:36–43	MAR	LUK
36 Then he left the crowds and went into the house. And his disciples approached him, saying, "Explain to us the parable of the weeds of the field." 37 He answered, "The one who sows the good seed is the Son of Man; 38 the field is the world, and the good seed are the children of the kingdom; the weeds are the children of the evil one, 39 and the enemy who sowed them is the devil; the harvest is the end of the age, and the reapers are angels. 40 Just as the weeds are collected and burned up with fire, so will it be at the end of the age. 41 The Son of Man will send his angels, and they will collect out of his kingdom all causes of sin and all evildoers, 42 and they will throw them into the furnace of fire, where there will be weeping and gnashing of teeth. 43 Then the righteous will shine like the sun in the kingdom of their Father. Let anyone with ears listen!"		

✧ MAT 13:35 — PSA 78:2. ✧ MAT 13:41 — ZEP 1:3. ✧ MAT 13:43 — DAN 12:3.

✦ [T] text: B C D W 𝔐 it vg sy[c] sy[s] sy[p] sa bo; *the prophet Isaiah*: S Θ λ φ.

§ 101 THE PARABLES OF THE HIDDEN TREASURE AND THE PEARL

MAT 13:44–46	MAR	LUK
44 "The kingdom of heaven is like treasure hidden in a field, which someone found and hid; then in his joy he goes and sells all that[U] he has and buys that field. 45 "Again, the kingdom of heaven is like a merchant in search of fine pearls; 46 on finding one pearl of great value, he went and sold all that he had and bought it."		

§ 102 THE PARABLE OF THE NET

MAT 13:47–50	MAR	LUK
47 "Again, the kingdom of heaven is like a net that was thrown into the sea and caught fish of every kind; 48 when it was full, they drew it ashore, sat down, and put the good into baskets but threw out the bad. 49 So it will be at the end of the age. The angels will come out and separate the evil from the righteous 50 and throw them into the furnace of fire, where there will be weeping and gnashing of teeth."		

§ 103 TREASURES NEW AND OLD

MAT 13:51–52	MAR	LUK
51 "Have you understood all this?" They answered, "Yes." 52 And he said to them, "Therefore every scribe who has been trained for the kingdom of heaven is like the master of a household who brings out of his treasure what is new and what is old." ▼ 13:53–58 (§ 108, p. 86)		

§ 104 JESUS' TRUE RELATIVES

MAT	MAR	LUK 8:19–21
Cf. 12:46–50 (§ 89, p. 73)	*Cf.* 3:31–35 (§ 89, p. 73)	19 Then his mother and his brothers came to him, but they could not reach him because of the crowd. 20 And he was told, "Your mother and your brothers are standing outside, wanting to see you." 21 But he said to them, "My mother and my brothers are those who hear the word of God and do it."

✦ [U] text: S C D W Θ λ φ 𝔐 it vg sy^{c} sy^{s} sy^{p} sa; *what*: B bo Origen.

● To LUK 8:21 *cf.* JOH 15:14. — "You are my friends if you do what I command you."

◗ To MAT 13:44 *cf.* **Gospel of Thomas, Logion 109**. — Jesus said, "The kingdom is like a man who had a treasure hidden in his field, and did not know it. And when he died he left it to his son, who also knew nothing about it, and accepted the field, and sold it. And the buyer went, and while he was plowing he found the treasure. And he began to lend at interest to whoever he wished." ◗ To MAT 13:45–46 *cf.* **Gospel of Thomas, Logion 76**. — Jesus said, "The kingdom of the Father is like a merchant who possessed merchandise and found a pearl. That merchant was prudent. He sold the merchandise and bought the pearl alone for himself. You, too, are to seek for the treasure that does not fail, that endures, where no moth comes near to devour and where no worm destroys."

§ 105 THE STILLING OF THE STORM

Δ *MAT 8:18, 23–27* (§ 49, p. 41)	**MAR 4:35–41**	**LUK 8:22–25**
	▲ 4:33–34 (§ 99, p. 79)	
18 *Now when Jesus*	35 On that day, when evening had come,	22 One day
		he got into a boat with his disciples,
saw great crowds around him, he gave orders to go over to the other side.	he said to them, "Let us go across to the other side."	and he said to them, "Let us go across to the other side of the lake." So they put out,
Δ *8:23-27 (§ 50, p. 41)*		
23 *And when he got into the boat, his disciples followed him.*	36 And leaving the crowd behind, they took him with them in the boat, just as he was. Other boats were with him.	23 and while they were sailing he fell asleep.
24 *A windstorm arose on the sea, so great that the boat was being swamped by the waves; but he was asleep.*	37 A great windstorm arose, and the waves beat into the boat, so that the boat was already being swamped. 38 But he was in the stern, asleep on the cushion;	A windstorm swept down on the lake, and the boat was filling with water, and they were in danger.
25 *And they went and woke him up, saying, "Lord, save us! We are perishing!"* 26 *And he said to them, "Why are you afraid, you of little faith?" Then he got up and rebuked the winds and the sea; and there was a dead calm.*	and they woke him up and said to him, "Teacher, do you not care that we are perishing?" 39 He woke up and rebuked the wind, and said to the sea, "Peace! Be still!" Then the wind ceased, and there was a dead calm.	24 They went to him and woke him up, shouting, "Master, Master, we are perishing!" And he woke up and rebuked the wind and the raging waves; they ceased, and there was a calm.
	40 He said to them, "Why are you afraid? Have you still no faith?"[V]	25 He said to them, "Where is your faith?"
27 *They were amazed, saying, "What sort of man is this, that even the winds and the sea obey him?"*	41 And they were filled with great awe and said to one another, "Who then is this, that even the wind and the sea obey him?"	They were afraid and amazed, and said to one another, "Who then is this, that he commands even the winds and the water, and they obey him?"

§ 106 THE GERASENE DEMONIAC

Δ *MAT 8:28–34* (§ 51, p. 42)	**MAR 5:1–20**	**LUK 8:26–39**
28 *When he came to the other side, to the country of the Gadarenes,*[W]	1 They came to the other side of the sea, to the country of the Gerasenes.[X]	26 Then they arrived at the country of the Gerasenes,[Y] which is opposite Galilee.
two demoniacs coming out of the tombs met	2 And when he had stepped out of the boat, immediately a man out of the tombs with an unclean spirit met	27 As he stepped out on land, a man of the city who had demons met

✦ [V] text: S B D Θ it vg sa bo; *Why are you so very afraid? Why have you no faith?*: A C 𝔎 sy^{p}; *Why are you so very afraid? Have you no faith?*: P$^{45?}$ λ ø. ✦ [W] text: S B C Θ sy^{s} sy^{p}; *Gerasenes*: it vg sa; *Gergesenes*: W λ ø 𝔎 bo. ✦ [X] text: S B D it vg sa; *Gadarenes*: A C ø 𝔎 sy^{p}; *Gergesenes*: Θ λ sy^{s} bo; *Gergustenes*: W. ✦ [Y] text: P^{75} B D it vg sa; *Gadarenes*: A W ø 𝔎 sy^{c} sy^{s} sy^{p}; *Gergesenes*: S Θ λ bo.

him. They were so fierce that no
one could pass that way.

29 Suddenly they shouted,
"What have you
to
do with us, Son of
God? Have you come here
to torment us before the time?"

30 Now a large herd of swine was
feeding at some distance from them.
31 The demons begged him, "If you
cast us out, send us into the
herd of swine." 32 And he
said to them, "Go!" So they
came out and
entered the swine; and
suddenly, the whole herd
rushed down the steep
bank into the sea and
perished in the water. 33 The
swineherds

ran off, and on going into the town,

---

him.

3 He lived among the tombs; and no
one could restrain him any more,
even with a chain; 4 for he had
often been restrained with shackles
and chains, but the chains he
wrenched apart, and the shackles
he broke in pieces; and no one had
the strength to subdue him.
5 Night and day among the tombs
and on the mountains he was always
howling and bruising himself with
stones. 6 When he saw Jesus from
a distance, he ran and bowed down
before him; 7 and he shouted at the
top of his voice, "What have you to
do with me, Jesus, Son of the Most
High God? I adjure you by God,
do not torment me." 8 For he had
said to him,
"Come out of the man, you unclean
spirit!"

9 Then Jesus[Z] asked him, "What is
your name?" He replied,
"My name is Legion; for
we are many."
10 He begged him earnestly not to
send them out of the country.
11 Now there on the hillside
a great herd of swine was
feeding; 12 and
the unclean spirits begged him,
"Send us into the
swine; let us enter them." 13 So he
gave them permission. And the
unclean spirits came out and
entered the swine; and
the herd, numbering about two
thousand, rushed down the steep
bank into the sea, and
were drowned in the sea. 14 The
swineherds

ran off and told it in the city and in

---

him. For a long time he had worn
no clothes, and he did
not live in a house but in the tombs.

28 When he saw Jesus,
he fell down
before him and shouted at the
top of his voice, "What have you to
do with me, Jesus, Son of the Most
High God? I beg you,
do not torment me" — 29 for Jesus
had commanded the unclean spirit
to come out of the man. (For
many times it had seized him; he
was kept under guard and bound
with chains and shackles, but he
would break the bonds and be
driven by the demon into the wilds.)
30 Jesus then asked him, "What is
your name?" He said,
"Legion"; for
many demons had entered him.
31 They begged him not to
order them to go back into the
abyss. 32 Now there on the hillside
a large herd of swine was
feeding; and
the demons begged Jesus

to let them enter these. So he
gave them permission. 33 Then the
demons came out of the man and
entered the swine, and
the herd
rushed down the steep
bank into the lake and
was drowned. 34 When the
swineherds saw what had happened, they
ran off and told it in the city and in

✦ [Z] Greek: *he.*

they told the whole story about what had happened to the demoniacs. 34 *Then the whole town came out to meet Jesus; and*	the country. Then people came to see what it was that had happened. 15 They came to Jesus and saw the demoniac sitting there, clothed and in his right mind, the very man who had had the legion; and they were afraid. 16 Those who had seen what had happened to the demoniac and	the country. 35 Then people came out to see what had happened, and when they came to Jesus, they found the man from whom the demons had gone sitting at the feet of Jesus, clothed and in his right mind. And they were afraid. 36 Those who had seen it told them how the one who had been possessed by demons had been healed.
	to the swine reported it.	
when they saw him, they	17 Then they	37 Then all the people of the surrounding country of the Gerasenes[B]
begged him to leave their neighborhood.	began to beg Jesus[A] to leave their neighborhood.	asked Jesus to leave them; for they were seized with great fear.
	18 As he was getting into the boat, the man who had been possessed by demons begged him that he might be with him. 19 But Jesus refused, and said to him, "Go home to your friends, and tell them how much the Lord has done for you, and what mercy he has shown you." 20 And he went away and began to proclaim in the Decapolis how much Jesus had done for him; and everyone was amazed.	So he got into the boat and returned. 38 The man from whom the demons had gone begged that he might be with him; but Jesus sent him away, saying, 39 "Return to your home, and declare how much God has done for you." So he went away, proclaiming throughout the city how much Jesus had done for him.

§ 107 JAIRUS' DAUGHTER AND A WOMAN'S FAITH

Δ *MAT 9:18–26 (§ 55, p. 46)*	MAR 5:21–43	LUK 8:40–56
18 *While he was saying these things*	21 When Jesus had crossed again in the boat to the other side,	40 Now when Jesus returned,
to them,	a great crowd gathered around him; and he was by the sea.	the crowd welcomed him, for they were all waiting for him.
suddenly	22 Then	41 Just then
a leader of the synagogue came in and	one of the leaders of the synagogue named Jairus came and,	there came a man named Jairus, a leader of the synagogue.
knelt before him, saying, "My daughter has just	when he saw him, fell at his feet 23 and begged him repeatedly, "My little daughter is at the point of	He fell at Jesus' feet and begged him to come to his house, 42 for he had an only daugh-

[A] Greek: *him.* ✦ [B] text: P^{75} B C D it vg sa; *Gergesenes*: S Θ λ ϕ bo; *Gadarenes*: A W 𝔑 sy^{c} sy^{s} sy^{p}.

died; but come and lay your hand
on her, and she will
live.” 19 And Jesus
got up and followed him, with his
disciples.
20 Then suddenly a woman who had
been suffering from hemorrhages
for twelve years
came up behind him
and touched the fringe of his cloak,
21 for she said to herself,
“If I only touch his cloak, I will be
made well.”
22 Jesus turned, and seeing her
he said, “Take heart, daughter;
your faith has made you well.”
And instantly the woman was made
well.

death. Come and lay your hands
on her, so that she may
be made well, and live.” 24 So he
went with him. And a large crowd
followed him and pressed in on him.
25 Now there was a woman who had
been suffering from hemorrhages
for twelve years. 26 She
had endured much under many
physicians, and had spent all that
she had; and she was no better, but
rather grew worse. 27 She had
heard about Jesus, and
came up behind him in the crowd
and touched his cloak,
28 for she said,
“If I but touch his clothes, I will be
made well.” 29 Immediately her
hemorrhage stopped; and she felt
in her body that she was healed of
her disease. 30 Immediately aware
that power had gone forth from him,
Jesus turned about in the crowd and
said, “Who touched my clothes?”
31 And his disciples said to him,
“You see the crowd
pressing in on you; how can you
say, ‘Who touched me?’ ” 32 He
looked all around to see who had
done it.
33 But the woman, knowing what
had happened to her, came
in fear and trembling, fell down
before him, and told
him the whole truth.
34 He said to her, “Daughter,
your faith has made you well; go in
peace, and be healed of your disease.”
35 While he was still speaking,
some people came from the leader’s

ter, about twelve years old, who
was dying.
As he
went, the crowds
pressed in on him.
43 Now there was a woman who had
been suffering from hemorrhages
for twelve years;[C] and though she
had spent all she had on
physicians,
no one could cure her.
44 She came up behind him and
touched the fringe of his clothes,
and immediately her
hemorrhage stopped.
45 Then Jesus
asked, “Who touched me?”
When all denied it, Peter[D] said,
“Master, the crowds
surround you and press in on you.”
46 But Jesus said, “Someone
touched me; for I noticed that
power had gone out from me.”
47 When the woman saw that she
could not remain hidden, she came
trembling; and falling down before
him, she declared
in the presence of all the people
why she had touched him, and how
she had been immediately healed.
48 He said to her, “Daughter,
your faith has made you well; go in
peace.”
49 While he was still speaking,
someone came from the leader’s

✦ [C] text: S A C W Θ λ ø ℜ it vg sy[c] sy[p] bo; omit: *though she had spent all she had on physicians*: P[75] B D sy[s] sa.
✦ [D] text: P[75] B sy[c] sy[s] sa; add: *and those who were with him*: S A C D W Θ λ ø ℜ it vg sy[p] bo.

	house to say, "Your daughter is dead. Why trouble the teacher any further?" 36 But overhearing[E] what they said, Jesus said to the leader of the synagogue,	house to say, "Your daughter is dead; do not trouble the teacher any longer." 50 When Jesus heard this, he replied,
	"Do not fear, only believe."	"Do not fear. Only believe, and she will be saved."
	37 He allowed no one to follow him except Peter, James, and John, the brother of James.	51 When he came to the house, he did not allow anyone to enter with him, except Peter, John, and James, and the child's father and mother.
23 When Jesus came to the leader's house and saw the flute players and the crowd making a commotion,	38 When they came to the house of the leader of the synagogue, he saw a commotion, people weeping and wailing loudly.	52 They were all weeping and wailing for her; but
24 he said, "Go away; for the girl is not dead but sleeping."	39 When he had entered, he said to them, "Why do you make a commotion and weep? The child is not dead but sleeping."	he said, "Do not weep; for she is not dead but sleeping."
And they laughed at him.	40 And they laughed at him.	53 And they laughed at him, knowing that she was dead.
25 But when the crowd had been put outside,	Then he put them all outside, and took the child's father and mother and those who were	
he went in and	with him, and went in where the child was.	
took her by the hand,	41 He took her by the hand and said to her, "Talitha cum," which means, "Little girl, get up!"	54 But he took her by the hand and called out, "Child, get up!"
and the girl got up.	42 And immediately the girl got up and began to walk about (she was twelve years of age).	55 Her spirit returned, and she got up at once.
	At this they were overcome with amazement.	Then he directed them to give her something to eat. 56 Her parents were astounded; but
26 And the report of this spread throughout that district.	43 He strictly ordered them that no one should know this, and told them to give her something to eat.	he ordered them to tell no one what had happened.

✦ [E] Or, *ignoring*; text: S B W; *hearing*: A C D Θ λ ø ℜ it vg sa bo.

§ 108 JESUS IS REJECTED AT NAZARETH

MAT 13:53–58

▲ 13:51–52 (§ 103, p. 80)
53 When Jesus had finished these parables,
he left that place. 54 He came to his hometown
and
began to teach the people in their synagogue,
so that they were astounded and
said, "Where did this man get this
wisdom and
these deeds of power?
55 Is not this the carpenter's son?
Is not his mother called Mary? And
are not his brothers James and Joseph and Simon and Judas? 56 And are not all his sisters
with us? Where then did this man get all this?"
57 And they took offense[F] at him. But Jesus
said to them, "Prophets are not without honor
except in their own country and
in their own house." 58 And he
did not do many deeds of power there,
because of their unbelief.

MAR 6:1–6a

1 He left that place and came to his hometown,
and his disciples followed him. 2 On the sabbath he began to teach in the synagogue,
and many who heard him were astounded.
They said, "Where did this man get all this?
What is this wisdom that has been given to him?
What deeds of power are being done by his
hands! 3 Is not this the carpenter,
the son of Mary and
brother of James and Joses and Judas and Simon, and are not his sisters
here with us?"
And they took offense[F] at him. 4 Then Jesus
said to them, "Prophets are not without honor,
except in their hometown, and among their
own kin, and in their own house." 5 And he
could do no deed of power there,
except that he laid his hands on a few sick
people and cured them.
6a And he was amazed at their unbelief.

LUK

Cf. 4:16–30 (§ 10, p. 18)

Cf. 4:22 (§ 10, p. 18)

Cf. 4:24 (§ 10, p. 18)

§ 109 THE SENDING OUT OF THE TWELVE

Δ *MAT 9:35; 10:1, 9–11, 14 (§ 58, p. 47)*

9:35 Then Jesus went about all the cities and villages, teaching in their synagogues, and proclaiming the good news of the kingdom, and curing every disease and every sickness.
10:1 Then Jesus summoned his twelve disciples
and gave them authority

MAR 6:6b–13

6b Then he went about among the
villages teaching.
7 He
called the twelve and
began to send them out two by two,
and gave them authority

LUK 9:1–6

Cf. 10:1–12 (§ 139, p. 112)
1 Then Jesus
called the twelve together
and gave them power and authority

✦ [F] Or, *stumbled.*

• To MAT 13:54 *cf.* JOH 7:15. — The Jews were astonished at it, saying, "How does this man have such learning, when he has never been taught?" • To MAT 13:55 *cf.* JOH 6:42. — They were saying, "Is not this Jesus, the son of Joseph, whose father and mother we know? How can he now say, 'I have come down from heaven'?" • To MAT 13:57 *cf.* JOH 4:44. — ...for Jesus himself had testified that a prophet has no honor in the prophet's own country. • To MAT 13:58 *cf.* JOH 7:5. — For not even his brothers believed in him.

◗ To MAT 13:57 *cf.* **Gospel of Thomas, Logion 31.** — Jesus said, "No prophets are acceptable in their own village; no physicians heal those who know them."

over unclean spirits, to cast them out, and to cure every disease and every sickness.	over the unclean spirits.[1]	over all demons and to cure diseases,
		2 and he sent them out to proclaim the kingdom of God and to heal.[1]
[2-8] 9 *"Take no gold, or silver, or copper in your belts,* 10 *no bag for your journey, or two tunics, or sandals, or a staff; for laborers deserve their food.*	8 He ordered them to take nothing for their journey except a staff; no bread, no bag, no money in their belts; 9 but to wear sandals and not to put on two tunics.	3 He said to them, "Take nothing for your journey, no staff, nor bag, nor bread, nor money— not even an extra tunic.
	10 He said to them,	
11 *Whatever town or village you enter, find out who in it is worthy, and stay there until you leave.*	"Wherever you enter a house, stay there until you leave the place.	4 Whatever house you enter, stay there, and leave from there.
[12-13] 14 *If anyone will not welcome you or listen to your words, shake off the dust from your feet as you leave that house or town."*	11 If any place will not welcome you and they refuse to hear you, as you leave, shake off the dust that is on your feet as a testimony against them."	5 Wherever they do not welcome you, as you are leaving that town shake the dust off your feet as a testimony against them."
	12 So they went out and proclaimed that all should repent.	6 They departed and went through the villages, bringing the good news and
	13 They cast out many demons, and anointed with oil many who were sick and cured them.	curing diseases everywhere.

§ 110 HEROD THINKS JESUS IS JOHN, RAISED

MAT 14:1–2	MAR 6:14–16	LUK 9:7–9
1 At that time Herod the ruler heard reports about Jesus;	14 King Herod heard of it, for Jesus'[G] name had become known.	7 Now Herod the ruler heard about all that had taken place, and
		he was perplexed, because
2 and he said to his servants, "This is John the Baptist; he has been raised from the dead, and for this reason these powers are at work in him."	Some[H] were saying, "John the baptizer has been raised from the dead; and for this reason these powers are at work in him."	it was said by some that John had been raised from the dead,
	15 But others said, "It is Elijah." And others said, "It is a prophet, like one of the prophets of	8 by some that Elijah had appeared, and by others that one of the ancient prophets had arisen.

[1] MAR 3:14–15 (§ 72, p. 62): 14 And he [Jesus] appointed twelve, whom he also named apostles, to be with him, and to be sent out to proclaim the message, 15 and to have authority to cast out demons.

✦ [G] Greek: *his*. ✦ [H] text: B D W it (some MSS.); *he said*: S A C Θ λ ø 𝔐 it (some MSS.) vg sy^s sy^p sa bo.

	old." 16 But when Herod heard of it, he said, "John, whom I beheaded, has been raised."	9 Herod said, "John I beheaded; but who is this about whom I hear such things?" And he tried to see him.

§ 111 THE DEATH OF JOHN

MAT 14:3–12	MAR 6:17–29	LUK
3 For Herod had arrested John, bound him, and put him in prison on account of Herodias, his brother Philip's wife,[I]	17 For Herod himself had sent men who arrested John, bound him, and put him in prison on account of Herodias, his brother Philip's wife, because Herod had married her.	
4 because John had been telling him, "It is not lawful for you to have her."[1]	18 For John had been telling Herod, "It is not lawful for you to have your brother's wife."[1]	
5 Though Herod wanted to put him to death, he feared the crowd, because they regarded him as a prophet.		
	19 And Herodias had a grudge against him, and wanted to kill him. But she could not, 20 for Herod feared John, knowing that he was a righteous and holy man, and he protected him. When he heard him, he was greatly perplexed;	
6 But when Herod's birthday came,	and yet he liked to listen to him. 21 But an opportunity came when Herod on his birthday gave a banquet for his courtiers and officers and for the leaders of Galilee.	
the daughter of Herodias danced before the company, and she pleased Herod 7 so much that he promised on oath to grant her whatever she might ask.	22 When his daughter Herodias came in and danced, she pleased Herod and his guests; and the king said to the girl, "Ask me for whatever you wish, and I will give it." 23 And he solemnly swore to her, "Whatever you ask me, I will give you, even half of my kingdom."	
8 Prompted by her mother,	24 She went out and said to her mother, "What should I ask for?" She replied, "The head of John the baptizer."	
she said, "Give me the head of John the Baptist here on a platter." 9 The king was grieved, yet out of regard for his oaths and for the guests,	25 Immediately she rushed back to the king and requested, "I want you to give me at once the head of John the Baptist on a platter." 26 The king was deeply grieved; yet out of regard for his oaths and for the guests, he did not want to refuse her. 27 Immediately	

[1] LUK 3:19–20 (§ 5, p. 13): 19 But Herod the ruler, who had been rebuked by him because of Herodias, his brother's wife, and because of all the evil things that Herod had done, 20 added to them all by shutting up John in prison.

✧ MAR 6:18 — LEV 18:16; 20:21.

✦ [I] text: S B C W Θ λ ø ℜ it (some MSS.) sy[c] sy[s] sy[p] sa bo; *his brother's wife*: D it (some MSS.) vg.

he commanded it to be given; 10 he sent and had	the king sent a soldier of the guard with orders to bring John's head.
John beheaded in the prison.	He went and beheaded him in the prison,
11 The head was brought on a platter and given to the girl, who brought it to her mother. 12 His disciples came and took the body and buried it; then they went and told Jesus.	28 brought his head on a platter, and gave it to the girl. Then the girl gave it to her mother. 29 When his disciples heard about it, they came and took his body, and laid it in a tomb.

§ 112 THE RETURN OF THE TWELVE, AND THE FEEDING OF THE FIVE THOUSAND

Cf. MAT 15:32–39 = MAR 8:1–10 (§ 118, p. 95)

MAT 14:13–21	MAR 6:30–44	LUK 9:10–17
	30 The apostles gathered around Jesus, and told him all that they had done and taught.	10 On their return the apostles told Jesus all they had done.[1]
	31 He said to them, "Come away to a deserted place all by yourselves and rest a while." For many were coming and going, and they had no leisure even to eat.	
13 Now when Jesus heard this,		
		He took them with him and
he withdrew from there in a boat to a deserted place by himself.	32 And they went away in the boat to a deserted place by themselves.	withdrew privately to a city called Bethsaida.
	33 Now many saw them going and recognized them, and	
But when the crowds heard it, they followed him on foot from the towns.	they hurried there on foot from all the towns and arrived ahead of them.	11 When the crowds found out about it, they followed him; and he welcomed
14 When he went ashore, he saw a great crowd; and he had compassion for them and	34 As he went ashore, he saw a great crowd; and he had compassion for them, because they were like sheep without a shepherd;[2] and he began to teach them many things.	them, and spoke to them about the kingdom of God,
cured their sick.		and healed those who needed to be cured.
15 When it was evening,	35 When it grew late,	12 The day was drawing to a close,

[1] LUK 10:17 (§ 140, p. 113): The seventy returned with joy, saying, "Lord, in your name even the demons submit to us!"
[2] MAT 9:36 (§ 58, p. 47): When he [Jesus] saw the crowds, he had compassion for them, because they were harassed and helpless, like sheep without a shepherd.

✧ MAR 6:34 — NUM 27:17; 1KI 22:17.

• To § 112 *cf.* JOH 6:1–13.

the disciples came to him and
said, "This is a deserted place, and
the hour is now late;
send the crowds away so that they
may go into the
villages
and buy food for themselves."
16 Jesus said
to them, "They need not go away;
you give them something to eat."
17 They replied, "We have nothing
here but five loaves and two fish."
18 And he said, "Bring them here to
me." 19 Then he ordered the
crowds to sit down on
the grass.
Taking the five loaves and the two
fish, he looked up to heaven, and
blessed and broke the loaves, and
gave them to the disciples, and the
disciples gave them to the crowds.
20 And all ate and were filled; and
they took up what was left over of
the broken pieces, twelve baskets
full.
21 And those who ate were about
five thousand men, besides women
and children.

his disciples came to him and
said, "This is a deserted place, and
the hour is now very late;
36 send them away so that they
may go into the
surrounding country and villages
and buy something for themselves
to eat." 37 But he answered
them,
"You give them something to eat."
They said to him, "Are we to go
and buy two hundred denarii[J] worth
of bread, and give it to them to
eat?" 38 And he said to them,
"How many loaves have you? Go
and see." When they had found
out, they said,
"Five, and two fish."
39 Then he ordered them to
get all the people to sit down in
groups on the green grass. 40 So
they sat down in groups of
hundreds and of fifties.
41 Taking the five loaves and the two
fish, he looked up to heaven, and
blessed and broke the loaves, and
gave them to his disciples to set
before the people; and he divided
the two fish among them all.
42 And all ate and were filled; 43 and
they took up
twelve baskets
full of broken pieces and of the fish.
44 Those who had eaten the loaves
numbered five thousand men.

and the twelve came to him and
said,
"Send the crowd away, so that they
may go into the
surrounding villages and country-
side, to lodge
and get provisions; for we are here
in a deserted place." 13 But he said
to them,
"You give them something to eat."
They said, "We have no more than
five loaves and two fish—unless we
are to go and buy food for all these
people." 14 For there were
about five thousand men.
And he said to his disciples,
"Make them sit down in
groups of
about fifty each."
15 They did so and made them all sit
down. 16 And
taking the five loaves and the two
fish, he looked up to heaven, and
blessed and broke them, and
gave them to the disciples to set
before the crowd.
17 And all ate and were filled.
What was left over was gathered up,
twelve baskets
of broken pieces.

▼ 9:18–22 (§ 122, p. 99)

✦ [J] The denarius was a day's wage for a laborer.

§ 113 THE WALKING ON THE WATER

MAT 14:22–33

22 Immediately he made the disciples get into the
boat and go on ahead to the other side,
while he dismissed the crowds. 23 And
after he had dismissed the crowds, he went up
the mountain by himself to pray. When
evening came,
he was there alone, 24 but by this time the boat,
battered by the waves, was far from the land,[K]
for the wind was against them. 25 And
early in the morning he came
walking toward them on the sea.
26 But when the disciples saw him walking on
the sea, they were terrified, saying, "It is a
ghost!" And they cried out in fear.
27 But immediately Jesus spoke to
them and said, "Take heart, it is I; do not be
afraid." 28 Peter answered him, "Lord, if it is
you, command me to come to you on the
water." 29 He said, "Come." So Peter got
out of the boat, started walking on the water,
and came toward Jesus. 30 But when he noticed the strong wind,[M] he became frightened,
and beginning to sink, he cried out, "Lord,
save me!" 31 Jesus immediately reached out
his hand and caught him, saying to him, "You
of little faith, why did you doubt?"
32 When they got into the boat, the
wind ceased. 33 And those in the boat worshiped him, saying, "Truly you are the Son of
God."

MAR 6:45–52

45 Immediately he made his disciples get into the
boat and go on ahead to the other side, to
Bethsaida, while he dismissed the crowd.
46 After saying farewell to them, he went up on
the mountain to pray. 47 When
evening came, the boat was out on the sea, and
he was alone on the land.
48 When he saw that they were straining at the
oars against an adverse wind,
he came towards them early in the morning,
walking on the sea. He intended to pass them
by. 49 But when they saw him walking on
the sea, they thought it was a
ghost and cried out; 50 for they all saw him[L] and
were terrified. But immediately he spoke to
them and said, "Take heart, it is I; do not be
afraid."
51 Then he got into the boat with them and the
wind ceased.
And they were utterly astounded, 52 for they did
not understand about the loaves, but their
hearts were hardened.

LUK

✦ [K] text: B Θ ø sy^c sy^p sa bo; omit: *far distant from the land,* and insert, *was out on the sea*: S C D W λ ℜ it vg.
✦ [L] text: $P^{45?}$ S A B W λ ø ℜ it (some MSS.) vg sy^s sy^p sa bo; omit: *for they saw him,* and read *all* before *cried out* in verse 49: D Θ it (some MSS.). ✦ [M] text: C D Θ λ ø ℜ it vg sy^c sy^s sy^p; omit: *strong*: S B sa bo; *very strong wind*: W.

• To § 113 *cf.* JOH 6:15–21.

§ 114 HEALINGS AT GENNESARET

MAT 14:34–36	MAR 6:53–56	LUK
34 When they had crossed over, they came to land at Gennesaret.	53 When they had crossed over, they came to land at Gennesaret and moored the boat. 54 When they got out of the boat,	
35 After the people of that place recognized him, they sent word throughout the region and brought all who were sick to him,	people at once recognized him, 55 and rushed about that whole region and began to bring the sick on mats to wherever they heard he was. 56 And wherever he went, into villages or cities or farms, they laid the sick in the marketplaces,	
36 and begged him that they might touch even the fringe of his cloak; and all who touched it were healed.[1]	and begged him that they might touch even the fringe of his cloak; and all who touched it were healed.[1]	

§ 115 WHAT DEFILES A PERSON

MAT 15:1–20	MAR 7:1–23	LUK
1 Then Pharisees and scribes came to Jesus from Jerusalem	1 Now when the Pharisees and some of the scribes who had come from Jerusalem gathered around him, 2 they noticed that some of his disciples were eating with defiled hands, that is, without washing them. 3 (For the Pharisees, and all the Jews, do not eat unless they thoroughly wash[N] their hands, thus observing the tradition of the elders; 4 and they do not eat anything from the market unless they wash it;[O] and there are also many other traditions that they observe, the washing of cups, pots, and bronze[P] kettles.)	
and said, 2 "Why do your disciples break the tradition of the elders? For they do not wash their hands before they eat." 3 He answered them, "And why do you break	5 So the Pharisees and the scribes asked him, "Why do your disciples not live[Q] according to the tradition of the elders, but eat with defiled hands?"	

[1] MAT 4:24 (§ 16, p. 23): So his [Jesus'] fame spread throughout all Syria, and they brought to him all the sick, those who were afflicted with various diseases and pains, demoniacs, epileptics, and paralytics, and he cured them.	MAR 3:10 (§ 71, p. 60): for he [Jesus] had cured many, so that all who had diseases pressed upon him to touch him. *Cf.* MAR 1:32–33 (§ 14, p. 22).	LUK 6:18b–19 (§ 71, p. 60): 18b and those who were troubled with unclean spirits were cured. 19 And all in the crowd were trying to touch him [Jesus], for power came out from him and healed all of them. *Cf.* LUK 4:40–41 (§ 14, p. 22).

✦ [N] text: A B D Θ λ ø ℜ it; *frequently wash*: S W vg sy^{p} bo; no adverb: sy^{s} sa. ✦ [O] text: S B sa; *unless they purify themselves*: A D Θ λ ø ℜ it vg sy^{s} sy^{p} bo. ✦ [P] text: P$^{45?}$ S B bo; add: *and beds*: A D W Θ λ ø ℜ it vg sy^{p} sa; omit: *and bronze kettles and beds*: sy^{s}. ✦ [Q] Greek: *walk*.

the commandment of God for the sake of your
tradition? 4 For God said, 'Honor your father
and your mother,' and, 'Whoever speaks evil
of father or mother must surely die.' 5 But you
say that whoever tells father or mother, 'Whatever support you might have had from me is
given to God,'[R] then that person need not
honor the father. 6 So, for the sake of your
tradition, you make void the word[S] of God.
7 You hypocrites! Isaiah prophesied rightly
about you when he said:

8 'This people honors me with their lips,
but their hearts are far from me;
9 in vain do they worship me,
teaching human precepts as doctrines.' "

Cf. 15:3–6

10 Then he called the crowd to him and said to
them, "Listen and
understand: 11 it is not what goes into the mouth
that defiles a person, but
it is what comes out of the mouth that defiles."
12 Then the disciples approached and said to
him, "Do you know that the Pharisees took
offense when they heard what you said?"
13 He answered, "Every plant that my heavenly
Father has not planted will be uprooted. 14 Let
them alone; they are blind guides of the blind.
And if one blind person guides another, both

Cf. 7:9–13

6 He said to them, "Isaiah prophesied rightly
about you hypocrites, as it is written,

'This people honors me with their lips,
but their hearts are far from me;
7 in vain do they worship me,
teaching human precepts as doctrines.'

8 You abandon the commandment of God and
hold to human tradition." 9 Then he said to
them, "You have a fine way of rejecting the
commandment of God in order to keep your
tradition! 10 For Moses said, 'Honor your father and your mother'; and, 'Whoever speaks
evil of father or mother must surely die.' 11 But
you say that if anyone tells father or mother,
'Whatever support you might have had from me
is Corban' (that is, an offering to God)—
12 then you no longer permit doing anything for
a father or mother, 13 thus making void the word
of God through your tradition that you have
handed on. And you do many things like this."
14 Then he called the crowd again and said to
them, "Listen to me, all of you, and
understand: 15 there is nothing outside
a person that by going in can defile, but
the things that come out are what defile."[T]
[16]

✧ MAT 15:4 = MAR 7:10 — EXO 20:12; DEU 5:16; EXO 21:17; LEV 20:9. ✧ MAT 15:8–9 = MAR 7:6–7 — ISA 29:13.

✦ [R] Or, *an offering*. ✦ [S] text: B D Θ it (some MSS.) sy^{c} sy^{s} sy^{p} sa bo Origen; *law*: S C ø; *commandment*: W λ ℜ it (some MSS.) vg. ✦ [T] text: S B bo (some MSS.); add verse 16: *"Let anyone with ears to hear listen"*: A D W Θ λ ø ℜ it vg sy^{s} sy^{p} sa bo (some MSS.).

◗ To MAT 15:5 *cf.* **Gospel of the Nazaraeans 12**. — The Jewish Gospel has: Corban is what you should gain from us.

◗ To MAT 15:11 *cf.* **Gospel of Thomas, Logion 14**. — "For what goes into your mouth will not defile you, but what comes out of your mouth, that is what will defile you."

MAT	MAR	LUK
will fall into a pit." [1]		
	17 When he had left the crowd and entered	
15 But Peter said to him, "Explain this parable to us." 16 Then he said, "Are you also still without understanding? 17 Do you not see that whatever goes into the mouth enters the stomach,	the house, his disciples asked him about the parable. 18 He said to them, "Then do you also fail to understand? Do you not see that whatever goes into a person from outside cannot defile, 19 since it enters, not the heart but the stomach,	
and goes out into the sewer?	and goes out into the sewer?" (Thus he de- clared all foods clean.) 20 And he said,	
18 But what comes out of the mouth proceeds from the heart, and this is what defiles. 19 For out of the heart come evil intentions, murder, adultery, fornication, theft, false witness, slander. 20 These are what defile a person, but to eat with unwashed hands does not defile."	"It is what comes out of a person that defiles. 21 For it is from within, from the human heart, that evil intentions come: fornication, theft, murder, 22 adultery, avarice, wickedness, deceit, licentiousness, envy, slander, pride, folly. 23 All these evil things come from within, and they defile a person."	

§ 116 THE SYROPHOENICIAN WOMAN

MAT 15:21–28	MAR 7:24–30	LUK
21 Jesus left that place and went away to the district of Tyre and Sidon.	24 From there he set out and went away to the region of Tyre.[U] He entered a house and did not want anyone to know he was there. Yet he could not escape notice,	
22 Just then a Canaanite woman from that region came out and started shouting, "Have mercy on me, Lord, Son of David; my daughter is tormented by a demon." 23 But he did not an- swer her at all. And his disciples came and urged him, saying, "Send her away, for she keeps shouting after us." 24 He answered, "I was sent only to the lost sheep of the house of Israel." 25 But she came and knelt before him,	25 but a woman whose little daughter had an unclean spirit immediately heard about him, and she came and bowed down at his feet.	
saying, "Lord, help me."	26 Now the woman was a Gentile, of Syro- phoenician origin. She begged him to cast the demon out of her daughter.	
26 He answered,	27 He said to her, "Let the children be fed first, for	
"It is not fair to take the children's food and throw it to the dogs." 27 She said, "Yes, Lord, yet even the dogs eat the crumbs that fall from their masters' table."	it is not fair to take the children's food and throw it to the dogs." 28 But she answered him, "Sir, even the dogs under the table eat the children's crumbs."	

[1] LUK 6:39 (§ 76, p. 65): He [Jesus] also told them a parable: "Can a blind person guide a blind person? Will not both fall into a pit?"

✦ [U] text: S A B λ ø 𝔐 it (some MSS.) vg sy^{p} sa bo; omit: *and Sidon*: D W Θ it (some MSS.) sy^{s}.

28 Then Jesus answered her, "Woman, great is your faith! Let it be done for you as you wish."	29 Then he said to her, "For saying that, you may go— the demon has left your daughter."	
And her daughter was healed instantly.	30 So she went home, found the child lying on the bed, and the demon gone.	

§ 117 THE HEALING OF MANY SICK PEOPLE (MAT) AND OF THE DEAF PERSON WITH A SPEECH IMPEDIMENT (MAR)

MAT 15:29–31	MAR 7:31–37	LUK
29 After Jesus had left that place, he passed along the Sea of Galilee, and	31 Then he returned from the region of Tyre, and went by way of Sidon towards the Sea of Galilee, in the region of the Decapolis.	
he went up the mountain, where he sat down. 30 Great crowds came to him, bringing with them the lame, the maimed, the blind, the mute, and many others. They put them at his feet, and he cured them,		
	32 They brought to him a deaf man who had an impediment in his speech; and they begged him to lay his hand on him. 33 He took him aside in private, away from the crowd, and put his fingers into his ears, and he spat and touched his tongue. 34 Then looking up to heaven, he sighed and said to him, "Ephphatha," that is, "Be opened." 35 And immediately his ears were opened, his tongue was released, and he spoke plainly. 36 Then Jesus ordered them to tell no one; but the more he ordered them, the more zealously they proclaimed it.	
31 so that the crowd was amazed when they saw the mute speaking, the maimed whole, the lame walking, and the blind seeing. And they praised the God of Israel.	37 They were astounded beyond measure, saying, "He has done everything well; he even makes the deaf to hear and the mute to speak."	

§ 118 THE FEEDING OF THE FOUR THOUSAND

Cf. MAT 14:13–21 = MAR 6:30–44 = LUK 9:10–17 (§ 112, p. 89)

MAT 15:32–39	MAR 8:1–10	LUK
	1 In those days when there was again a great crowd without anything to eat,	
32 Then Jesus called his disciples to him and said, "I have compassion for the crowd, because they have been with me now for three days and have nothing to eat; and I do not want to send them away hungry, for they	he called his disciples and said to them, 2 "I have compassion for the crowd, because they have been with me now for three days and have nothing to eat. 3 If I send them away hungry to their homes, they	

might faint on the way."	will faint on the way—and some of them have come from a great distance."
33 The disciples said to him, "Where are we to get enough bread in the desert to feed so great a crowd?" 34 Jesus asked them, "How many loaves have you?" They said, "Seven, and a few small fish." 35 Then ordering the crowd to sit down on the ground, 36 he took the seven loaves and the fish; and after giving thanks he broke them and gave them to the disciples, and	4 His disciples replied, "How can one feed these people with bread here in the desert?" 5 He asked them, "How many loaves do you have?" They said, "Seven." 6 Then he ordered the crowd to sit down on the ground; and he took the seven loaves, and after giving thanks he broke them and gave them to his disciples to distribute; and
the disciples gave them to the crowds.	they distributed them to the crowd. 7 They had also a few small fish; and after blessing them, he ordered that these too should be distributed.
37 And all of them ate and were filled; and they took up the broken pieces left over, seven bas- kets full. 38 Those who had eaten were four thousand men, besides women and children. 39 After sending away the crowds, he got into the boat and went to the region of Magadan.	8 They ate and were filled; and they took up the broken pieces left over, seven bas- kets full. 9 Now there were about four thousand people. And he sent them away. 10 And immediately he got into the boat with his disciples and went to the district of Dalmanutha.[V]

§ 119 THE PHARISEES SEEK A SIGN

MAT 16:1–4	Δ *MAT 12:38–39 (§ 87, p. 72)*	MAR 8:11–13	Δ *LUK 11:29 (§ 152, p. 119) +*
1 The Pharisees and Sad- ducees came, and	*38 Then some of the scribes and Pharisees*	11 The Pharisees came and began to argue with him,	*29a When the crowds were increasing, he began to say,* Δ *11:16 (§ 149, p. 118)*
to test Jesus they asked him to show them a sign from heaven.	 *said to him, "Teacher, we wish to see a sign from you."*	 asking him for a sign from heaven, to test him.	*16 Others, to test him, kept demanding from him a sign from heaven.*
2 He answered them,[W] * "When it is evening, you say, 'It will be fair weather, for the sky is red.' 3 And in the morn- ing, 'It will be stormy today, for the sky is red	*39 But he answered them,*	12 And he sighed deeply in his spirit and said,	Δ *12:54–56 (§ 160, p. 127)* *54 He also said to the crowds, "When you see a cloud rising in the west, you immediately say, 'It is going to rain'; and so it happens. 55 And when you see the south wind*

✦ [V] text: S A B C ℜ vg sy^{p} sa bo; *Dalmounai*: W; *Melegada*: D; *Magdala*: Θ λ ø; *Magedan*: it sy^{s}. ✦ [W] text: C D W Θ λ ℜ it vg sy^{p} bo (some MSS.); the following words to the end of verse 3 are omitted: S B ø sy^{c} sy^{s} sa bo (some MSS.).

● To MAT 16:1 *cf.* JOH 6:30. — So they said to him, "What sign are you going to give us then, so that we may see it and believe you? What work are you performing?"

◗ To MAT 16:2 *cf.* **Gospel of the Nazaraeans**. — What is marked with an asterisk (i.e., from "When it is evening" to the end of verse 3) is not found in other manuscripts, and is not found in the Jewish Gospel.

and threatening.'			*blowing, you say, 'There will be scorching heat'; and it happens.* 56 *You hypocrites! You know*
You know how to interpret the appearance of the sky, but you cannot interpret the signs of the times.			*how to interpret the appearance of earth and sky, but why do you not know how to interpret the present time?"*
		"Why does this	11:29b *"This generation is an evil generation;*
4 An evil and adulterous generation asks for a sign, but no sign will be given to it except the sign of Jonah."	*"An evil and adulterous generation asks for a sign, but no sign will be given to it except the sign of the prophet Jonah."*	generation ask for a sign? Truly I tell you, no sign will be given to this generation."	*it asks for a sign, but no sign will be given to it except the sign of Jonah."*
Then he left them and went away.		13 And he left them, and getting into the boat again, he went across to the other side.	

§ 120 THE YEAST OF THE PHARISEES AND OF HEROD

MAT 16:5–12	MAR 8:14–21	Δ *LUK 12:1 (§ 154, p. 121)*
5 When the disciples reached the other side,	14 Now	1 *Meanwhile,*
		when the crowd gathered by the thousands, so that they trampled on one another,
they had forgotten to bring any bread.	the disciples had forgotten to bring any bread; and they had only one loaf with them in the boat.	
6 Jesus said to them, "Watch out, and beware of the yeast of the Pharisees and Sadducees."	15 And he cautioned them, saying, "Watch out—beware of the yeast of the Pharisees and the yeast of Herod."[X]	*he began to speak first to his disciples, "Beware of the yeast of the Pharisees,*
		that is, their hypocrisy."
7 They said to one another, "It is because we have brought no bread."	16 They said to one another, "It is because we have no bread."	
8 And becoming aware of it, Jesus said, "You of little faith, why are you talking about having no bread? 9 Do you still not perceive?	17 And becoming aware of it, Jesus said to them, "Why are you talking about having no bread? Do you still not perceive or understand? Are your	

✦ [X] text: S A B C D 𝔎 it vg sy[s] sy[p] bo; *the Herodians*: P[45] W Θ λ ø sa.

• To MAT 16:9 *cf.* MAT 14:19–21.

MAT

Do you not remember
the five loaves for the five
thousand, and how many baskets
you gathered?
10 Or the seven loaves for the four
thousand, and how many baskets
you gathered?
11 How could you fail to perceive
that I was not speaking about bread?
Beware of the yeast of the Pharisees
and Sadducees!" 12 Then they understood that he had not told them
to beware of the yeast of bread, but
of the teaching of the Pharisees and
Sadducees.

MAR

hearts hardened? 18 Do you have
eyes, and fail to see? Do you
have ears, and fail to hear? And
do you not remember? 19 When I
broke the five loaves for the five
thousand, how many baskets full
of broken pieces did you collect?"
They said to him, "Twelve."
20 "And the seven for the four
thousand, how many baskets full
of broken pieces did you collect?"
And they said to him, "Seven."
21 Then he said to them,
"Do you not yet understand?"

§ 121 THE BLIND MAN OF BETHSAIDA

MAT	MAR 8:22–26	LUK

MAR 8:22–26

22 They came to Bethsaida. Some people brought a blind man to him and begged
him to touch him. 23 He took the blind man by the hand and led him out of the
village; and when he had put saliva on his eyes and laid his hands on him, he asked
him, "Can you see anything?" 24 And the man looked up and said, "I can see
people, but they look like trees, walking." 25 Then Jesus laid his hands on his
eyes again; and he looked intently and his sight was restored, and he saw everything clearly. 26 Then he sent him away to his home, saying, "Do not even go into
the village."[Y]

◇ MAR 8:18 — JER 5:21; EZE 12:2.

✦ [Y] text: S B W λ sy[s] sa bo; add: *or tell anyone in the village*: A C 𝔐 sy[p]; *saying, "Go into your house and tell no one in the village"*: D; *saying, "Go into your house and if you enter the village tell no one"*: it vg.

● To § 121 *cf.* JOH 9:1–7.

§ 122 THE CONFESSION AT CAESAREA PHILIPPI AND THE FIRST PREDICTION OF THE PASSION

MAT 16:13–23	MAR 8:27–33	LUK 9:18–22
		▲ 9:10–17 (§ 112, p. 89)
		18 Once when Jesus was praying alone, with only the disciples near
13 Now when Jesus came into the district of Caesarea Philippi,	27 Jesus went on with his disciples to the villages of Caesarea Philippi; and on the way	
he asked his disciples, "Who do people say that the Son of Man is?"[Z]	he asked his disciples, "Who do people say that I am?"	him,[A] he asked them, "Who do the crowds say that I am?"
14 And they said, "Some say John the Baptist, but others Elijah, and still others Jeremiah or one of the prophets."	28 And they answered him, "John the Baptist; and others, Elijah; and still others, one of the prophets."	19 They answered, "John the Baptist; but others, Elijah; and still others, that one of the ancient prophets has arisen."
15 He said to them, "But who do you say that I am?" 16 Simon Peter answered, "You are the Messiah, the Son of the living God."	29 He asked them, "But who do you say that I am?" Peter answered him, "You are the Messiah."	20 He said to them, "But who do you say that I am?" Peter answered, "The Messiah of God."
17 And Jesus answered him, "Blessed are you, Simon son of Jonah! For flesh and blood has not revealed this to you, but my Father in heaven. 18 And I tell you, you are Peter,[B] and on this rock[C] I will build my church, and the gates of Hades will not prevail against it. 19 I will give you the keys of the kingdom of heaven, and whatever you bind on earth will be bound in heaven, and whatever you loose on earth will be loosed in heaven."[1]		
20 Then he sternly ordered the disciples not to tell anyone that he was the Messiah.	30 And he sternly ordered them not to tell anyone about him.	21 He sternly ordered and commanded them not to tell anyone,
21 From that time on, Jesus[D] began to show his disciples that he	31 Then he began to teach them that the Son of Man	22 saying, "The Son of Man

[1] MAT 18:18 (§ 134, p. 109): "Truly I tell you, whatever you bind on earth will be bound in heaven, and whatever you loose on earth will be loosed in heaven." *Cf.* JOH 20:23.

✦ [Z] text: S B vg sa bo; *Who do people say that I, the Son of Man, am?*: C D W Θ λ φ 𝔐 it sy[c] sy[s] sy[p] Irenaeus. ✦ [A] *the disciples met him and* (between commas): B. ✦ [B] Greek: *Petros.* ✦ [C] Greek: *Petra.* ✦ [D] text: C D W Θ λ φ 𝔐 it vg sy[c] sy[p] sa; add: *Christ*: S B bo; omit both names: Irenaeus, Origen.

• To MAT 16:16 *cf.* JOH 6:68–69. — 68 Simon Peter answered him, "Lord, to whom can we go? You have the words of eternal life. 69 We have come to believe and know that you are the Holy One of God." • To MAT 16:19 *cf.* JOH 20:22–23. — 22 When he had said this, he breathed on them and said to them, "Receive the Holy Spirit. 23 If you forgive the sins of any, they are forgiven them; if you retain the sins of any, they are retained."

◗ To MAT 16:17 *cf.* **Gospel of the Nazaraeans.** — The Jewish Gospel has: "son of John" (for "Bar-Jona").

must go to Jerusalem and undergo great suffering at the hands of the elders and chief priests and scribes, and be killed, and on the third day be raised.	must undergo great suffering, and be rejected by the elders, the chief priests, and the scribes, and be killed, and after three days rise again. 32 He said all this quite openly.	must undergo great suffering, and be rejected by the elders, chief priests, and scribes, and be killed, and on the third day be raised."
22 And Peter took him aside and began to rebuke him, saying, "God forbid it, Lord! This must never happen to you." 23 But he turned	And Peter took him aside and began to rebuke him.	
	33 But turning and looking at his disciples,	
and said to Peter, "Get behind me, Satan! You are a stumbling block to me;	he rebuked Peter and said, "Get behind me, Satan!	
for you are setting your mind not on divine things but on human things."	For you are setting your mind not on divine things but on human things."	

§ 123 THE CONDITIONS OF DISCIPLESHIP

MAT 16:24–28	MAR 8:34—9:1	LUK 9:23–27
24 Then Jesus told his disciples,	34 He called the crowd with his disciples, and said to them,	23 Then he said to them all,
"If any want to become my followers, let them deny themselves and take up their cross and follow me. 25 For those who want to save their life will lose it, and those who lose their life for my sake	"If any want to become my followers, let them deny themselves and take up their cross and follow me. 35 For those who want to save their life will lose it, and those who lose their life for my sake, and for the sake of the gospel,	"If any want to become my followers, let them deny themselves and take up their cross daily and follow me. 24 For those who want to save their life will lose it, and those who lose their life for my sake
will find it.[1] 26 For what will it profit them if they gain the whole world but forfeit their life? Or what will they give in return for their life?	will save it.[1+E] 36 For what will it profit them to gain the whole world and forfeit their life? 37 Indeed, what can they give in return for their life?	will save it.[1] 25 What does it profit them if they gain the whole world, but lose or forfeit themselves?
	38 Those who are ashamed of me and of my words in this adulterous and sinful generation,	26 Those who are ashamed of me and of my words,
27 For the Son	of them the Son	of them the Son

[1] MAT 10:38–39 (§ 62, p. 53): 38 "and whoever does not take up the cross and follow me is not worthy of me. 39 Those who find their life will lose it, and those who lose their life for my sake will find it."

LUK 14:27 (§ 171, p. 133): "Whoever does not carry the cross and follow me cannot be my disciple."
LUK 17:33 (§ 184, p. 140): "Those who try to make their life secure will lose it, but those who lose their life will keep it."

✧ MAT 16:27 — PSA 62:12.

✦ [E] text: S A B C W Θ λ ø 𝔐 it (some MSS.) vg sy[p] sa bo; *lose their life for the sake of the gospel*: P[45] D it (some MSS.) sy[s].

• To MAT 16:25 and parallels, *cf.* JOH 12:25. — "Those who love their life lose it, and those who hate their life in this world will keep it for eternal life."

of Man is to come with his angels in the glory of his Father, and	of Man will also be ashamed[1] when he comes in the glory of his Father with the holy angels."	of Man will be ashamed when he comes in his glory and the glory of the Father and of the holy angels.
then he will repay everyone for what has been done.		
	9:1 And he said to them,	
28 Truly I tell you, there are some standing here who will not taste death before they see the Son of Man coming in his kingdom."	"Truly I tell you, there are some standing here who will not taste death until they see that the kingdom of God has come with power."	27 But truly I tell you, there are some standing here who will not taste death before they see the kingdom of God."

§ 124 THE TRANSFIGURATION

MAT 17:1–8	MAR 9:2–8	LUK 9:28–36
1 Six days later, Jesus took with him Peter and James and his brother John and led them up a high mountain, by themselves.	2 Six days later, Jesus took with him Peter and James and John, and led them up a high mountain apart, by themselves.	28 Now about eight days after these sayings Jesus took with him Peter and John and James, and went up on the mountain to pray.
2 And he was transfigured before them, and his face shone like the sun, and his clothes became dazzling white.	And he was transfigured before them, 3 and his clothes became dazzling white,[F] such as no one on earth could bleach them.	29 And while he was praying, the appearance of his face changed, and his clothes became dazzling white.
3 Suddenly there appeared to them Moses and Elijah, talking with him.	4 And there appeared to them Elijah with Moses, who were talking with Jesus.	30 Suddenly they saw two men, Moses and Elijah, talking to him. 31 They appeared in glory and were speaking of his departure, which he was about to accomplish at Jerusalem. 32 Now Peter and his companions were weighed down with sleep; but since they had stayed awake, they saw his glory and the two men who stood with him. 33 Just as they were leaving him,
4 Then Peter said to Jesus, "Lord, it is good for us to be here; if you wish, I will make three dwellings here, one for you, one	5 Then Peter said to Jesus, "Rabbi, it is good for us to be here; let us make three dwellings, one for you, one	Peter said to Jesus, "Master, it is good for us to be here; let us make three dwellings, one for you, one

[1] MAT 10:33 (§ 60, p. 52): "but whoever denies me before others, I also will deny before my Father in heaven." | LUK 12:9 (§ 155, p. 122): "but whoever denies me before others will be denied before the angels of God."

✦ [F] text: P^{45} S B C W Θ λ sa; *white as snow*: A D ø 𝔐 it vg sy^s sy^p bo.

• To MAT 17:5 and parallels, *cf*. MAT 3:17. • To LUK 9:32 *cf*. JOH 1:14b. — and we have seen his glory, the glory as of a father's only son, full of grace and truth.

for Moses, and one for Elijah."	for Moses, and one for Elijah." 6 He did not know what to say, for they were terrified.	for Moses, and one for Elijah" — not knowing what he said.
5 While he was still speaking, suddenly a bright cloud overshadowed them,	7 Then a cloud overshadowed them,	34 While he was saying this, a cloud came and overshadowed them; and they were terrified as they entered the cloud.
and from the cloud a voice said, "This is my Son,[G] the Beloved; with him I am well pleased; listen to him!"	and from the cloud there came a voice, "This is my Son,[G] the Beloved; listen to him!"	35 Then from the cloud came a voice that said, "This is my Son, my Chosen;[H] listen to him!"
6 When the disciples heard this, they fell to the ground and were overcome by fear. 7 But Jesus came and touched them, saying, "Get up and do not be afraid."		36 When the voice had spoken,
8 And when they looked up, they saw no one	8 Suddenly when they looked around, they saw no one with them any more,	
except Jesus himself alone.	but only Jesus.	Jesus was found alone. And they kept silent and in those days told no one any of the things they had seen.

§ 125 THE COMING OF ELIJAH

MAT 17:9–13	MAR 9:9–13	LUK
9 As they were coming down the mountain, Jesus ordered them, "Tell no one about the vision until after the Son of Man has been raised from the dead."	9 As they were coming down the mountain, he ordered them to tell no one about what they had seen, until after the Son of Man had risen from the dead. 10 So they kept the matter to themselves, questioning what this rising from the dead could mean.	*Cf.* 9:37 (§ 126, p. 103)
10 And the disciples asked him, "Why, then, do the scribes say that Elijah must come first?" 11 He replied, "Elijah is indeed coming and will restore all things;	11 Then they asked him, "Why do the scribes say that Elijah must come first?" 12 He said to them, "Elijah is indeed coming first to restore all things. How then is it written about the Son of Man, that he is to go through many sufferings and be treated with contempt?	
Cf. 12 b		
12 but I tell you that Elijah has already come, and they did not recognize him, but they did to him whatever they pleased. So also the Son of Man is about to suffer at their	13 But I tell you that Elijah has come, and they did to him whatever they pleased, as it is written about him."	

✧ MAT 17:10–11 = MAR 9:11–12 — MAL 4:5–6. ✧ MAT 17:12 = MAR 9:13 — 1KI 19:2, 10. ✧ MAR 9:12b — PSA 22:6; ISA 53:3.

✦ [G] Or, *my beloved Son.* ✦ [H] text: P^{45} P^{75} S B Θ λ it (some MSS.) sy^s sa bo; *my Beloved*: A C W ø ℜ it (some MSS.) vg sy^c sy^p; *my Beloved, with whom I am well pleased*: D.

hands." 13 Then the disciples understood that he was speaking to them about John the Baptist.

§ 126 THE HEALING OF THE BOY WITH A SPIRIT

MAT 17:14–21	MAR 9:14–29	LUK 9:37–43a +
Cf. 17:9 (§ 125, p. 102)	*Cf.* 9:9 (§ 125, p. 102)	37 On the next day, when they had come down from the mountain,
14 When they came to the crowd,	14 When they came to the disciples, they saw a great crowd around them, and some scribes arguing with them. 15 When the whole crowd saw him, they were immediately overcome with awe, and they ran forward to greet him. 16 He asked them, "What are you arguing about with them?"	a great crowd met him.
a man came to him, knelt before him, 15 and said, "Lord, have mercy on my son, for he is	17 Someone from the crowd answered him, "Teacher, I brought you my son; he has	38 Just then a man from the crowd shouted, "Teacher, I beg you to look at my son; he is
		my only child. 39 Suddenly
an epileptic and he suffers terribly;	a spirit that makes him unable to speak; 18 and whenever it seizes him, it dashes him down; and	a spirit seizes him, and all at once he shrieks. It convulses him
he often falls	*Cf.* 9:22	
into the fire and often into the water.	he foams and grinds his teeth and becomes rigid;	until he foams at the mouth;
		it mauls him and will scarcely leave him.
16 And I brought him to your disciples, but they could not cure him."	and I asked your disciples to cast it out, but they could not do so."	40 I begged your disciples to cast it out, but they could not."
17 Jesus answered, "You faithless and perverse generation, how much longer must I be with you? How much longer must I put up with you? Bring him here to me."	19 He answered them, "You faithless generation, how much longer must I be among you? How much longer must I put up with you? Bring him to me."	41 Jesus answered, "You faithless and perverse generation, how much longer must I be with you and bear with you? Bring your son here."
	20 And they brought the boy to him.	
	When the spirit saw him, immediately it convulsed the boy, and he fell on the ground and rolled about, foaming at the mouth. 21 Jesus[I] asked the father, "How long has	42 While he was coming, the demon dashed him to the ground in convulsions.

✦ [I] Greek: *he.*

• To MAT 17:17 *cf.* JOH 14:9. — Jesus said to him, "Have I been with you all this time, Philip, and you still do not know me? Whoever has seen me has seen the Father. How can you say, 'Show us the Father'?"

Cf. 17:15	this been happening to him?" And he said, "From childhood. 22 It has often cast him into the fire and into the water, to destroy him; but if you are able to do anything, have pity on us and help us." 23 Jesus said to him, "If you are able!—All things can be done for the one who believes." 24 Immediately the fa- ther of the child cried out,[J] "I believe; help my unbelief!"	
	25 When Jesus saw that a crowd came running together,	But
18 And Jesus rebuked the demon, and it came out of him, and	he rebuked the unclean spirit,	Jesus rebuked the unclean spirit,
	saying to it, "You spirit that keeps this boy from speaking and hearing, I command you, come out of him, and never enter him again!" 26 Af- ter crying out and convulsing him terribly, it came out, and the boy was like a corpse, so that most of them said, "He is dead." 27 But Jesus took him by the hand	
the boy was cured instantly.	and lifted him up, and he was able to stand.	healed the boy, and gave him back to his father. 43 And all were astounded at the greatness of God.
19 Then the disciples came to Jesus privately and said, "Why could we not cast it out?" 20 He said to them,	28 When he had entered the house, his disciples asked him privately, "Why could we not cast it out?" 29 He said to them,	*Δ 17:6 (§180, p. 139)* 6 *The Lord replied,*
"Because of your little faith. For truly I tell you, if you have faith the size of a mustard seed, you will say to this mountain, 'Move from here to there,' and it will move; and nothing will be impossible for you."[1 + K]		*"If you had faith the size of a mustard seed, you could say to this mulberry tree, 'Be uprooted and planted in the sea,' and it would obey you."*
	"This kind can come out only through prayer."[L]	

[1] MAT 21:21 (§ 201, p. 156): Jesus answered them, "Truly I tell you, if you have faith and do not doubt, not only will you do what has been done to the fig tree, but even if you say to this mountain, 'Be lifted up and thrown into the sea,' it will be done."	MAR 11:22–23 (§ 201, p. 156): 22 Jesus answered them, "Have faith in God. 23 Truly I tell you, if you say to this mountain, 'Be taken up and thrown into the sea,' and if you do not doubt in your heart, but believe that what you say will come to pass, it will be done for you."

✦ [J] text: P^{45} S A B C W sy^{s} sa bo; add: *with tears*: D Θ λ ø ℜ it vg sy^{p}. ✦ [K] text: S B Θ sy^{c} sy^{s} sa bo; add verse 21: *But this kind does not come out except by prayer and fasting*: C D W λ ø ℜ it vg sy^{p} Origen. *Cf.* MAR 9:29. ✦ [L] text: S B Clement; add: *and fasting*: $P^{45?}$ A C D W Θ λ ø ℜ it vg sy^{s} sy^{p} sa bo.

§ 127 THE SECOND PREDICTION OF THE PASSION

MAT 17:22–23	MAR 9:30–32	LUK 9:43b–45
22 As they were gathering[M] in Galilee,	30 They went on from there and passed through Galilee.	
		43b While everyone was amazed at all that he was doing,
	He did not want anyone to know it; 31 for he was teaching his disciples,	
Jesus said to them,	saying to them,	he said to his disciples, 44 "Let these words sink into your ears:
"The Son of Man is going to be betrayed into human hands, 23 and they will kill him, and on the third day he will be raised."	"The Son of Man is to be betrayed into human hands, and they will kill him, and three days after being killed, he will rise again."	The Son of Man is going to be betrayed into human hands."
	32 But they did not understand what he was saying	45 But they did not understand this saying; its meaning was concealed from them, so that they could not perceive it.
	and were afraid to ask him.	And they were afraid to ask him about this saying.
And they were greatly distressed.		

§ 128 THE TEMPLE TAX

MAT 17:24–27	MAR	LUK
24 When they reached Capernaum, the collectors of the temple tax came to Peter and said, "Does your teacher not pay the temple tax?" 25 He said, "Yes, he does." And when he came home, Jesus spoke of it first, asking, "What do you think, Simon? From whom do kings of the earth take toll or tribute? From their children or from others?" 26 When Peter said, "From others," Jesus said to him, "Then the children are free. 27 However, so that we do not give offense to them, go to the sea and cast a hook; take the first fish that comes up; and when you open its mouth, you will find a coin; take that and give it to them for you and me."		

✧ MAT 17:24 — EXO 30:13.

✦ [M] text: S B λ it vg; *living*: C D W Θ ø ℜ sy[c] sy[s] sy[p] sa bo.

• To MAR 9:30 *cf.* JOH 7:1. — After this Jesus went about in Galilee. He did not wish to go about in Judea because the Jews were looking for an opportunity to kill him.

§ 129 THE DISPUTE ABOUT GREATNESS

MAT 18:1–5	MAR 9:33–37 +	LUK 9:46–48 +
	33 Then they came to Capernaum; and when he was in the house he asked them, "What were you arguing about on the way?" 34 But they were silent, for on the way	
1 At that time the disciples came to Jesus and asked, "Who is the greatest in the kingdom of heaven?"[1]	they had argued with one another who was the greatest.	46 An argument arose among them as to which one of them was the greatest.
		47 But Jesus, aware of their inner thoughts,
	35 He sat down, called the twelve, and said to them, "Whoever wants to be first must be last of all and servant of all."[1]	*Cf.* 9:48b[1]
2 He called a child, whom he put among them,	36 Then he took a little child and put it among them; and taking it in his arms,	took a little child and put it by his side,
3 and said,	he said to them,	48a and said to them,
	Δ *10:15 (§ 188, p. 144)*	Δ *18:17 (§ 188, p. 144)*
"Truly I tell you, unless you change and become like children, you will never enter the kingdom of heaven.	15 *"Truly I tell you, whoever does not receive the kingdom of God as a little child will never enter it."*	17 *"Truly I tell you, whoever does not receive the kingdom of God as a little child will never enter it."*
4 Whoever becomes humble like this child is the greatest in the kingdom of heaven.[2]		
5 Whoever welcomes one such	37 "Whoever welcomes one such	9:48b "Whoever welcomes this

[1] MAT 20:26–27 (§ 192, p. 148): 26 "It will not be so among you; but whoever wishes to be great among you must be your servant, 27 and whoever wishes to be first among you must be your slave." MAT 23:11 (§ 210, p. 165): "The greatest among you will be your servant."	MAR 10:43–44 (§ 192, p. 148): 43 "But it is not so among you; but whoever wishes to become great among you must be your servant, 44 and whoever wishes to be first among you must be slave of all."	LUK 22:26 (§ 237b, p. 185): "But not so with you; rather the greatest among you must become like the youngest, and the leader like one who serves."
[2] MAT 23:12 (§ 210, p. 165): "All who exalt themselves will be humbled, and all who humble themselves will be exalted."		LUK 14:11 (§ 169, p. 132): "For all who exalt themselves will be humbled, and those who humble themselves will be exalted." LUK 18:14b (§ 186, p. 142): "for all who exalt themselves will be humbled, but all who humble themselves will be exalted."

• To MAT 18:3 *cf.* JOH 3:3, 5. — 3 Jesus answered him, "Very truly, I tell you, no one can see the kingdom of God without being born from above." [4] 5 Jesus answered, "Very truly, I tell you, no one can enter the kingdom of God without being born of water and Spirit." • To MAR 9:37; LUK 9:48 *cf.* JOH 12:44–45; 13:20. — 44 Then Jesus cried aloud: "Whoever believes in me believes not in me but in him who sent me. 45 And whoever sees me sees him who sent me." 13:20 "Very truly, I tell you, whoever receives one whom I send receives me; and whoever receives me receives him who sent me."

▸ To MAT 18:3 *cf.* **Acts of Philip 34.** — "Unless you change your 'down' to 'up' (and 'up' to 'down' and 'right' to 'left') and 'left' to 'right', you will not enter my kingdom (of heaven)."

child in my name welcomes me."[1]	child in my name welcomes me, and whoever welcomes me welcomes not me but the one who sent me."[1] *Cf.* 9:35b	child in my name welcomes me, and whoever welcomes me welcomes the one who sent me;[1] for the least among all of you is the greatest."

§ 130 ANOTHER EXORCIST

MAT	MAR 9:38–41	LUK 9:49–50
	38 John said to him, "Teacher, we saw someone casting out demons in your name, and we tried to stop him, because he was not following us."[N] 39 But Jesus said, "Do not stop him; for no one who does a deed of power in my name will be able soon afterward to speak evil of me.	49 John answered, "Master, we saw someone casting out demons in your name, and we tried to stop him, because he does not follow with us." 50 But Jesus said to him, "Do not stop him;
	40 Whoever is not against us is for us.[2] 41 For truly I tell you, whoever gives you a cup of water to drink because you bear the name of Christ will by no means lose the reward."[3]	for whoever is not against you is for you."[2] *Cf.* 9:51–56 (§ 137, p. 111)

§ 131 ON TEMPTATIONS

MAT 18:6–9	MAR 9:42–48	Δ *LUK 17:1–2 (§ 178, p. 138)*
6 "If any of you put a stumbling block before one of these little ones who believe in me, it would be better for you if a great millstone were fastened around your neck and you were drowned in the depth of the sea. 7 Woe to the world because of stumbling blocks!	42 "If any of you put a stumbling block before one of these little ones who believe in me, it would be better for you if a great millstone were hung around your neck and you were thrown into the sea.	
Occasions for stumbling are		*1 Jesus said to his disciples, "Occasions for stumbling are*

[1] MAT 10:40 (§ 63, p. 54): "Whoever welcomes you welcomes me, and whoever welcomes me welcomes the one who sent me." *Cf.* LUK 10:16 (§ 139, p. 112).

[2] MAT 12:30 (§ 86, p. 70) = LUK 11:23 (§ 149, p. 117): "Whoever is not with me is against me, and whoever does not gather with me scatters."

[3] MAT 10:42b (§ 63, p. 54): "and whoever gives even a cup of cold water to one of these little ones in the name of a disciple—truly I tell you, none of these will lose their reward."

✦ [N] text: S B C Θ sy[s] sy[p] sa bo; *in your name, who does not follow* (was not following: W) *us, and we forbade him:* D W λ ø it vg; *in your name, who does not follow us, and we forbade him because he does not follow us*: A 𝔐.

▸ To MAR 9:40; LUK 9:50 *cf. Oxyrhynchus Papyrus 1224, fol. 2 recto, col. 1.* — "For the one who is not against you is for you. The one who today is far away will tomorrow be near you."

MAT 18:8–9	MAR 9:43–50	LUK 17:1–2
bound to come, but woe to the one by whom the stumbling block comes!		*bound to come, but woe to anyone by whom they come!*
8 "If your hand or your foot causes you to stumble, cut it off and throw it away; it is better for you to enter life maimed or lame than to have two hands or two feet and to be thrown into the eternal fire.	43 If your hand causes you to stumble, cut it off; it is better for you to enter life maimed than to have two hands and to go to hell, [O] to the unquenchable fire. [P]	
	[44] 45 And if your foot causes you to stumble, cut it off; it is better for you to enter life lame than to have two feet and to be thrown into hell. [O+P]	
9 And if your eye causes you to stumble, tear it out and throw it away; it is better for you to enter life with one eye than to have two eyes and to be thrown into the hell [O] of fire." [1]	[46] 47 And if your eye causes you to stumble, tear it out; it is better for you to enter the kingdom of God with one eye than to have two eyes and to be thrown into hell, [1+O] 48 where their worm never dies, and the fire is never quenched."	
		2 It would be better for you if a millstone were hung around your neck and you were thrown into the sea than for you to cause one of these little ones to stumble."

§ 132 CONCERNING SALT

Δ *MAT 5:13* *(§ 20, p. 26)*	**MAR 9:49–50**	Δ *LUK 14:34–35* *(§ 171, p. 133)*
13 *"You are the salt of the earth; but if salt has lost its taste, how can its saltiness be restored? It is no longer good for anything, but is thrown out and trampled under foot."*	49 "For everyone will be salted with fire. [Q] 50 Salt is good; but if salt has lost its saltiness, how can you season it?	34 *"Salt is good; but if salt has lost its taste, how can its saltiness be restored?* 35 *It is fit neither for the soil nor for the manure pile; they throw it away. Let anyone with ears to hear listen!"*
	Have salt in yourselves, and be at peace with one another."	
	▾ 10:1–12 (§ 187, p. 143)	

[1] MAT 5:29–30 (§ 23, p. 28): 29 "If your right eye causes you to sin, tear it out and throw it away; it is better for you to lose one of your members than for your whole body to be thrown into hell. 30 And if your right hand causes you to sin, cut it off and throw it away; it is better for you to lose one of your members than for your whole body to go into hell."

✧ MAR 9:48 — ISA 66:24. ✧ MAR 9:49 — LEV 2:13.

✦ [O] Greek: *Gehenna.* ✦ [P] Verses 44, 46 — identical with verse 48 — omitted, S B C W λ sy[s] sa bo; added, A D Θ ø ℜ it vg sy[p]. ✦ [Q] text: S B W λ ø sy[s] sa bo; *For every one will be salted (consumed:* Θ*) with fire, and every sacrifice will be salted with salt:* A C Θ ℜ vg sy[p]; *For every sacrifice will be salted with salt:* D it.

§ 133 THE PARABLE OF THE LOST SHEEP

MAT 18:10–14	MAR	Δ *LUK 15:3–7* (*§ 172, p. 134*)
10 "Take care that you do not despise one of these little ones; for, I tell you, in heaven their angels continually see the face of my Father in heaven.[R]		
[11] 12 What do you think? If a shepherd has a hundred sheep, and one of them has gone astray, does he not leave the ninety-nine on the mountains and go in search of the one that went astray? 13 And if he finds it, truly I tell you, he rejoices over it more than over the ninety-nine that never went astray. 14 So it is not the will of your[S] Father in heaven that one of these little ones should be lost."		*3 So he told them this parable:* *4 "Which one of you, having a hundred sheep* *and losing one of them, does not* *leave the ninety-nine in the wilderness and go* *after the one that is lost until he finds it?* *5 When he has found it, he lays it on his shoulders and rejoices.*
		6 And when he comes home, he calls together his friends and neighbors, saying to them, 'Rejoice with me, for I have found my sheep that was lost.' 7 Just so, I tell you, there will be more joy in heaven over one sinner who repents than over ninety-nine righteous persons who need no repentance."

§ 134 ON REPROVING ANOTHER BELIEVER

MAT 18:15–20	MAR	Δ *LUK 17:3* (*§ 179, p. 138*)
15 "If another member of the church sins against you, go and point out the fault when the two of you are alone. If the member listens to you, you have regained that one.		*3 "Be on your guard! If another disciple sins,* *you must rebuke the offender, and* *if there is repentance,* *you must forgive."*
16 But if you are not listened to, take one or two others along with you, so that every word may be confirmed by the evidence of two or three witnesses. 17 If the member refuses to listen to them, tell it to the church; and if the offender refuses to listen even to the church, let such a one be to you as a Gentile and a tax collector.		

✧ MAT 18:16 — DEU 19:15.

✦ [R] text: S B Θ λ ø sy^{s} sa bo; add verse 11: *for the Son of Man came to save the lost*: D W 𝔐 it vg sy^{c} sy^{p}. *Cf.* LUK 19:10.
✦ [S] text: S W λ 𝔐 it vg sy^{c} sy^{p}; *my*: B Θ ø sy^{s} sa bo; *our*: D.

▸ To MAT 18:12–13; LUK 15:3–7 *cf.* **Gospel of Thomas, Logion 107.** — Jesus said, "The kingdom is like a shepherd who had a hundred sheep. One of them, that was the largest, went astray. The shepherd left behind the ninety-nine, and sought for the one until he found it. When he had tired himself out, he said to the sheep, 'I love you more than the ninety-nine.' "

18 Truly I tell you, whatever you bind on earth will be bound in heaven, and whatever you loose on earth will be loosed in heaven.[1]
19 Again, truly I tell you, if two of you agree on earth about anything you ask, it will be done for you by my Father in heaven. 20 For where two or three are gathered in my name, I am there among them."

§ 135 ON FORGIVENESS

MAT 18:21–22	MAR	Δ *LUK 17:4* (§ 179, p. 138)
21 Then Peter came and said to him, "Lord, if another member of the church sins against me, how often should I forgive? As many as seven times?" 22 Jesus said to him, "Not seven times, but, I tell you, seventy-seven times." [T]		*4 "And if the same person sins against you seven times a day, and turns back to you seven times and says, 'I repent,' you must forgive."*

§ 136 THE PARABLE OF THE UNMERCIFUL SERVANT

MAT 18:23–35	MAR	LUK
23 "For this reason the kingdom of heaven may be compared to a king who wished to settle accounts with his slaves. 24 When he began the reckoning, one who owed him ten thousand talents [U] was brought to him; 25 and, as he could not pay, his lord ordered him to be sold, together with his wife and children and all his possessions, and payment to be made. 26 So the slave fell on his knees before him, saying, 'Have patience with me, and I will pay you everything.' 27 And out of pity for him, the lord of that slave released him and forgave him the debt. 28 But that same		

[1] MAT 16:19 (§ 122, p. 99): "I will give you the keys of the kingdom of heaven, and whatever you bind on earth will be bound in heaven, and whatever you loose on earth will be loosed in heaven."

✦ [T] Or, *seventy times seven.* ✦ [U] This talent was worth a great deal of money.

● To MAT 18:18 *cf.* JOH 20:23. — "If you forgive the sins of any, they are forgiven them; if you retain the sins of any, they are retained."

◗ To MAT 18:20 *cf. Oxyrhynchus Papyrus 1, Logion 5.* — Jesus said, "Where there are two, they are not without God; and where there is one alone, I say, I am there. Raise the stone, and there you will find me; split the wood, and there I am."

◗ To MAT 18:20 *cf.* **Gospel of Thomas, Logia 30 and 77b.** — 30 Jesus said, "Where there are three gods, they are gods; where there are two or one, I am with him." 77b "Cleave a piece of wood, and there I am; lift up the stone and you will find me there."

◗ To MAT 18:21–22; LUK 17:3–4 *cf.* **Gospel of the Nazaraeans** (in Jerome, *Against Pelagius, III.2*). — He says, "If your sister or brother has sinned by a word, and repented, receive them seven times a day." Simon, Jesus' disciple, asked him, "Seven times a day?" The Lord answered, "Yes, I tell you, as much as seventy times seven times! For in the prophets also, after they were anointed by the Holy Spirit, a word of sin (sinful speech?) was found."

◗ To MAT 18:22 *cf.* **Gospel of the Nazaraeans.** — The Jewish gospel has, immediately after "seventy times seven": For in the prophets also, after they were anointed by the Holy Spirit, a word of sin (sinful speech?) was found in them.

slave, as he went out, came upon one of his fellow slaves who owed him a hundred
denarii;[V] and seizing him by the throat, he said, ‘Pay what you owe.’ 29 Then his
fellow slave fell down and pleaded with him, ‘Have patience with me, and I will pay
you.’ 30 But he refused; then he went and threw him into prison until he would pay
the debt. 31 When his fellow slaves saw what had happened, they were greatly
distressed, and they went and reported to their lord all that had taken place. 32 Then
his lord summoned him and said to him, ‘You wicked slave! I forgave you all that
debt because you pleaded with me. 33 Should you not have had mercy on your fellow
slave, as I had mercy on you?’ 34 And in anger his lord handed him over to be tortured
until he would pay his entire debt. 35 So my heavenly Father will also do to every one
of you, if you do not forgive your brother or sister from your heart.”[1]

▼ *Cf.* 19:1–12 (§ 187, p. 143)

LUKE'S SPECIAL SECTION

Luke 9:51—18:14

§ 137 THE SAMARITAN VILLAGERS

MAT	MAR	LUK 9:51–56
		▲ 9:49–50 (§ 130, p. 107) 51 When the days drew near for him to be taken up, he set his face to go to Jerusalem. 52 And he sent messengers ahead of him. On their way they entered a village of the Samaritans to make ready for him; 53 but they did not receive him, because his face was set toward Jerusalem. 54 When his disciples James and John saw it, they said, “Lord, do you want us to command fire to come down from heaven and consume them?”[W] 55 But he turned and rebuked them.[X] 56 Then they went on to another village.

§ 138 WOULD-BE FOLLOWERS OF JESUS

Δ *MAT 8:19–22* (*§ 49, p. 41*)	MAR	LUK 9:57–62
19 A scribe then approached and *said, “Teacher, I will follow you wherever you*		57 As they were going along the road, someone said to him, “I will follow you wherever you

[1] MAT 6:15 (§ 30, p. 31): “but if you do not forgive others, neither will your Father forgive your trespasses.”

✧ LUK 9:54 — 2KI 1:10, 12.

✦ [V] The denarius was a day's wage for a laborer. ✦ [W] text: P^{45} P^{75} S B it (some MSS.) vg sy^c sy^s sa bo; add: *as Elijah did*: A C D W Θ λ φ ℜ it (some MSS.) sy^p. ✦ [X] text: P^{45} P^{75} S A B C W sy^s sa bo; add: *and he said, “You do not know what spirit you are of”*: D; *and he said, “You do not know what spirit you are of, for the Son of Man has not come to destroy the lives of human beings but to save them”*: Θ λ φ ℜ it vg sy^c sy^p. *Cf.* LUK 19:10.

go.” 20 And Jesus said to him, “Foxes have
holes, and birds of the air have nests; but the
Son of Man has nowhere to lay his head.”

21 Another of his disciples said to him,
“Lord, first let me go and bury my father.”
22 But Jesus said to him, “Follow me, and
let the dead bury their own dead.”

go.” 58 And Jesus said to him, “Foxes have
holes, and birds of the air have nests; but the
Son of Man has nowhere to lay his head.”
59 To another he said, “Follow me.”
But he said,
“Lord, first let me go and bury my father.”
60 But Jesus said to him,
“Let the dead bury their own dead;
but as for you, go and proclaim the kingdom of
God.” 61 Another said, “I will follow you,
Lord; but let me first say farewell to those at
my home.” 62 Jesus said to him, “No one who
puts a hand to the plow and looks back is fit for
the kingdom of God.”

§ 139 THE SENDING OUT OF THE SEVENTY

Δ *MAT 9:37–38, 10:7–16* (§ 58, p. 47)

37 Then he said to his disciples, “The harvest is
plentiful, but the laborers are few; 38 therefore
ask the Lord of the harvest to send out laborers
into his harvest.”

Δ *10:16, 9, 10a, 11–13, 10b, 8, 14–15* (§ 58, p. 48)

16a “See, I am sending you out
like sheep into the midst of wolves; so be wise
as serpents and innocent as doves. 9 Take no
gold, or silver, or copper in your belts,
10a no bag for your journey, or two tunics, or
sandals, or a staff;
11 Whatever town or village you enter,
find out who in it is worthy, and stay there until
you leave. 12 As you enter the house, greet it.
13 If the house is worthy,
let your peace come upon it; but if it is not
worthy, let your peace return to you.

10b for laborers deserve their food.
7 As you go, proclaim the good news, ‘The
kingdom of heaven has come near.’

MAR

Cf. 6:6b-13 (§ 109, p. 86)

LUK 10:1–16

1 After this the Lord appointed seventy [Y] others
and sent them on ahead of him in pairs to every
town and place where he himself intended to go.
2 He said to them, “The harvest is
plentiful, but the laborers are few; therefore
ask the Lord of the harvest to send out laborers
into his harvest.

Cf. 9:1–6 (§ 109, p. 86)

3 Go on your way. See, I am sending you out
like lambs into the midst of wolves.
4 Carry no
purse,
no bag,
no sandals; and greet no one on the road.
5 Whatever house you enter,

first say, ‘Peace to this house!’
6 And if anyone is there who shares in peace,
your peace will rest on that person; but if not,
it will return to you. 7 Remain in the same
house, eating and drinking whatever they provide, for the laborer deserves to be paid.

Do not move about from house to house.
8 Whenever you enter a town and its people

✦ [Y] text: S A C W Θ λ φ 𝔑 it (some MSS.) sy^{p} bo; *seventy-two*: P^{75} B D it (some MSS.) vg sy^{c} sy^{s} sa.

• To LUK 10:2 *cf.* JOH 4:35. — “Do you not say, ‘Four months more, then comes the harvest’? But I tell you, look around you, and see how the fields are ripe for harvesting.” • To LUK 10:7 *cf.* MAT 10:10, p. 49.

8 Cure the sick, raise the dead, cleanse the
lepers, cast out demons. You received with-
out payment; give without payment.

14 If anyone will not welcome you or listen to

your words, shake off the dust from your feet as
you leave that house or town.
15 Truly I tell you,
it will be more tolerable for the land of Sodom
and Gomorrah on the day of judgment
than for that town."
Δ *11:21–23 (§ 66, p. 57)*
21 "Woe to you, Chorazin! Woe to you, Beth-
saida! For if the deeds of power done in you
had been done in Tyre and Sidon, they would
have repented long ago in sackcloth and
ashes. 22 But I tell you, on the day of judgment
it will be more tolerable for Tyre and
Sidon than for you. 23 And you, Capernaum,
will you be exalted to heaven? No, you will
be brought down to Hades. For if the deeds of
power done in you had been done in Sodom, it
would have remained until this day.
Δ *10:40 (§ 63, p. 54)*
40 "Whoever welcomes you welcomes me,
and
whoever welcomes me welcomes the one who
sent me." [1]

welcome you, eat what is set before you;
9 cure the sick who are there,

and say to them, 'The kingdom of God has
come near to you.' 10 But whenever you enter
a town and they do not welcome you,

go out into its streets and say, 11 'Even the dust
of your town that clings to our feet, we wipe
off in protest against you. Yet know this: the
kingdom of God has come near.' 12 I tell you,
on that day it will be more tolerable for Sodom

than for that town.

13 Woe to you, Chorazin! Woe to you, Bethsaida! For if the deeds of power done in you
had been done in Tyre and Sidon, they would
have repented long ago, sitting in sackcloth and
ashes. 14 But at the judgment
it will be more tolerable for Tyre and
Sidon than for you. 15 And you, Capernaum,
will you be exalted to heaven? No, you will
be brought down to Hades.

16 Whoever listens to you listens to me,
and whoever rejects you rejects me, and
whoever rejects me rejects the one who
sent me." [1]

§ 140 THE RETURN OF THE SEVENTY

MAT	MAR	LUK 10:17–20
	Cf. 16:17–18 (p. 210)	17 The seventy[Z] returned with joy, saying, "Lord, in your name even the demons submit to us!"[2] 18 He said to them, "I watched Satan fall from heaven like a flash of lightning. 19 See, I have given you authority to tread on snakes and scorpions, and over all the power of the enemy; and nothing will hurt you. 20 Nevertheless,

[1] *Cf.* MAT 18:5 = MAR 9:37 = LUK 9:48 (§ 129, p. 106). [2] *Cf.* MAR 6:30 = LUK 9:10 (§ 112, p. 89).

✦ [Z] text: S A C W Θ λ ø ℜ it (some MSS.) sy^{c} sy^{s} sy^{p} bo; *seventy-two*: P^{75} B D it (some MSS.) vg sa.

• To LUK 10:16; MAT 10:40 *cf.* JOH 5:23b. — "Anyone who does not honor the Son does not honor the Father who sent him." *Cf.* JOH 15:23. — "Whoever hates me hates my Father also." *Cf.* JOH 12:48. • To LUK 10:18 *cf.* JOH 12:31. — "Now is the judgment of this world; now the ruler of this world will be driven out."

do not rejoice at this, that the spirits submit to you, but rejoice that your names are written in heaven."

§ 141 JESUS' GRATITUDE TO THE FATHER

∆ *MAT 11:25–27* (*§ 67, p. 57*)	MAR	LUK 10:21–22
25 *At that time Jesus said, "I thank you, Father, Lord of heaven and earth, because you have hidden these things from the wise and the intelligent and have revealed them to infants;* 26 *yes, Father, for such was your gracious will.*[A] 27 *All things have been handed over to me by my Father; and no one knows the Son except the Father, and no one knows the Father except the Son and anyone to whom the Son chooses to reveal him."*		21 At that same hour Jesus rejoiced in the Holy Spirit and said, "I thank you, Father, Lord of heaven and earth, because you have hidden these things from the wise and the intelligent and have revealed them to infants; yes, Father, for such was your gracious will.[A] 22 All things have been handed over to me by my Father; and no one knows who the Son is except the Father, or who the Father is except the Son and anyone to whom the Son chooses to reveal him."

§ 142 THE BLESSEDNESS OF THE DISCIPLES

∆ *MAT 13:16–17* (*§ 92, p. 76*)	MAR	LUK 10:23–24
16 *"But blessed are your eyes, for they see, and your ears, for they hear.* 17 *Truly I tell you, many prophets and righteous people longed to see what you see, but did not see it, and to hear what you hear, but did not hear it."*		23 Then turning to the disciples, Jesus said to them privately, "Blessed are the eyes that see what you see! 24 For I tell you that many prophets and kings desired to see what you see, but did not see it, and to hear what you hear, but did not hear it."

§ 143 THE LAWYER'S QUESTION

∆ *MAT 22:34–40* (*§ 208, p. 163*)	∆ *MAR 12:28–31* (*§ 208, p. 163*)	LUK 10:25–28
34 *When the Pharisees*	28 *One of the scribes came near and heard them disputing with one another, and*	25 Just then

---

✦ [A] Or, *for so it was well-pleasing in your sight.*

● To LUK 10:22; MAT 11:27 *cf.* JOH 10:15b. — "just as the Father knows me and I know the Father." *Cf.* JOH 17:2.

▸ To LUK 10:21 *cf.* **Gospel of Thomas, Logion 4.** — Jesus said, "An old person will not hesitate to ask a little child of seven days about the place of life, and the person will live." ▸ To LUK 10:22. — "no one knew . . ." in Marcion, Justin, Tatian, Eusebius, Clement, but not in any manuscripts. ▸ To LUK 10:24 *cf.* **Gospel of Thomas, Logion 38.** — Jesus said, "Many times you have desired to hear these words which I say to you, and you have no one else to hear them from. There will be days when you will seek me and you will not find me."

heard that he had silenced the Sadducees, they gathered together, *35 and one of them, a lawyer,* *asked him a question to test him.* *36 "Teacher, which commandment in the law is the greatest?"*	*seeing that he answered them well,* *he asked him,* *"Which commandment is the first of all?"*	a lawyer stood up to test Jesus. "Teacher,"
		he said, "what must I do to inherit eternal life?" 26 He said to him, "What is written in the law? What do you read there?" 27 He answered,
37 He said to him,	*29 Jesus answered, "The first is, 'Hear, O Israel: the Lord our God, the Lord is one;*	
"'You shall love the Lord your God with all your heart, and with all your soul, *and with all your mind.' 38 This is the greatest and first commandment.*	*30 you shall love the Lord your God with all your heart, and with all your soul,* *and with all your mind, and with all your strength.'*	"You shall love the Lord your God with all your heart, and with all your soul, and with all your strength, and with all your mind;
39 And a second is like it: 'You shall love your neighbor as yourself.' *40 On these two commandments hang all the law and the prophets."*	*31 The second is this, 'You shall love your neighbor as yourself.' There is no other commandment greater than these."*	and your neighbor as yourself."
		28 And he said to him, "You have given the right answer; do this, and you will live."

§ 144 THE PARABLE OF THE GOOD SAMARITAN

MAT	MAR	LUK 10:29–37
		29 But wanting to justify himself, he asked Jesus, "And who is my neighbor?" 30 Jesus replied, "A man was going down from Jerusalem to Jericho, and fell into the hands of robbers, who stripped him, beat him, and went away, leaving him half dead. 31 Now by chance a priest was going down that road; and when he saw him, he passed by on the other side. 32 So likewise a Levite, when he came to the place and saw him, passed by on the other side. 33 But a Samaritan while traveling came near him; and when he saw him, he was moved with pity. 34 He went to him and bandaged his wounds, having poured oil and wine on them. Then he put him on his own animal, brought him to an inn, and took care of him. 35 The next day

✧ LUK 10:27 — DEU 6:5; LEV 19:18. ✧ LUK 10:28 — LEV 18:5.

◗ To LUK 10:27 *cf.* **Didache 1:2.** — This is the way of life: "First, you shall love the God who made you; second, your neighbor as yourself; and whatever you would not have done to you, do not to another." ◗ To LUK 10:27 *cf.* **Gospel of Thomas, Logion 25.** — Jesus said, "Love your brother or sister as your soul; guard them as the apple of your eye."

he took out two denarii,[B] gave them to the innkeeper, and said, 'Take care of him;
and when I come back, I will repay you whatever more you spend.' 36 Which of
these three, do you think, was a neighbor to the man who fell into the hands of the
robbers?" 37 He said, "The one who showed him mercy." Jesus said to him, "Go
and do likewise."

§ 145 MARTHA AND MARY

MAT

MAR

LUK 10:38–42

38 Now as they went on their way, he entered a certain village, where a woman
named Martha welcomed him into her home. 39 She had a sister named Mary, who
sat at the Lord's feet and listened to what he was saying. 40 But Martha was
distracted by her many tasks; so she came to him and asked, "Lord, do you not
care that my sister has left me to do all the work by myself? Tell her then to help
me." 41 But the Lord answered her, "Martha, Martha, you are worried and distracted by many things; 42 there is need[C] of only one thing. Mary has chosen the
better part, which will not be taken away from her."

§ 146 THE LORD'S PRAYER

Δ *MAT 6:9–13* *(§ 30, p. 31)*

9 *"Pray then in this way:*
Our Father in heaven,
hallowed be your name.
10 *Your kingdom come.*
Your will be done,
on earth as it is in heaven.
11 *Give us this day our daily bread.*[E]
12 *And forgive us our debts,*
as we also have forgiven
our debtors.
13 *And do not bring us to the time of trial,*
but rescue us from the evil one."[F]

MAR

LUK 11:1–4

1 He was praying in a certain place, and after he
had finished, one of his disciples said to him,
"Lord, teach us to pray, as John taught his
disciples." 2 He said to them,
"When you pray, say:
Father,[D]
hallowed be your name.
Your kingdom come.
3 Give us each day our daily bread.[E]
4 And forgive us our sins,
for we ourselves forgive
everyone indebted to us.
And do not bring us to the time of trial."

✦ [B] The denarius was a day's wage for a laborer. ✦ [C] text: P^{45} P^{75} A C W Θ ø ℜ vg sy^{c} sy^{p} sa; *few things are necessary, or only one*: P^{3} S B λ bo; omit: *you are worried...one thing*: it sy^{s}. ✦ [D] text: P^{75} S B λ vg sy^{s} Marcion, Origen; *Our Father in heaven*: A C D W Θ ø ℜ it sy^{c} sy^{p} sa bo. *Cf.* MAT 6:9. ✦ [E] Or, *our bread for the morrow.* ✦ [F] text: S B D λ it vg bo; add: *For the kingdom and the power and the glory are yours forever. Amen*: W Θ ø ℜ sy^{p}; add: *For the power and the glory are yours forever. Amen*: sa (**Didache:** omit: *Amen*); add: *For the kingdom and the glory are yours forever. Amen*: sy^{c}.

• To § 145 *cf.* JOH 11:1*ff.* — Now a certain man was ill, Lazarus of Bethany, the village of Mary and her sister Martha.

§ 147 THE FRIEND AT MIDNIGHT

MAT	MAR	LUK 11:5–8
		5 And he said to them, "Suppose one of you has a friend, and you go to him at midnight and say to him, 'Friend, lend me three loaves of bread; 6 for a friend of mine has arrived, and I have nothing to set before him.' 7 And he answers from within, 'Do not bother me; the door has already been locked, and my children are with me in bed; I cannot get up and give you anything.' 8 I tell you, even though he will not get up and give him anything because he is his friend, at least because of his persistence he will get up and give him whatever he needs."

§ 148 THE ANSWER TO PRAYER

Δ *MAT 7:7–11* *(§ 38, p. 35)*	MAR	LUK 11:9–13
7 "Ask, and it will be given you; search, and you will find; knock, and the door will be opened for you. 8 For everyone who asks receives, and everyone who searches finds, and for everyone who knocks, the door will be opened. 9 Is there anyone among you who, if your child asks for bread, will give a stone? 10 Or if the child asks for a fish, will give a snake? 11 If you then, who are evil, know how to give good gifts to your children, how much more will your Father in heaven give good things to those who ask him!"		9 "So I say to you, Ask, and it will be given you; search, and you will find; knock, and the door will be opened for you. 10 For everyone who asks receives, and everyone who searches finds, and for everyone who knocks, the door will be opened. 11 Is there anyone among you who, if your child asks for[G] a fish, will give a snake instead of a fish? 12 Or if the child asks for an egg, will give a scorpion? 13 If you then, who are evil, know how to give good gifts to your children, how much more will the heavenly Father give the Holy Spirit to those who ask him!"

§ 149 THE BEELZEBUL CONTROVERSY

Δ *MAT 12:22–30* *(§ 85, p. 70)*	Δ *MAR 3:22–27* *(§ 85, p. 70)*	LUK 11:14–23
22 Then they brought to him a demoniac who was blind and mute; and he cured him, so that the one who had been mute could speak and see. 23 All the crowds were amazed and said, "Can this be the Son of David?"		14 Now he was casting out a demon that was mute; when the demon had gone out, the one who had been mute spoke, and the crowds were amazed.
24 But when the Pharisees heard it, they said, "It is only by Beelzebul, the ruler of the demons, that this fellow casts out	*22 And the scribes who came down from Jerusalem said, "He has Beelzebul, and by the ruler of the demons he casts out*	15 But some of them said, "He casts out demons by Beelzebul, the ruler of the

✦ G text: P^{45} P^{75} B sy^{s} sa; add: *bread, will give a stone; or if your child asks for*: S A C D W Θ λ ø ℜ it vg sy^{c} sy^{p} bo.

the demons."[1]	*demons."*[1]	demons."[1]
		16 Others, to test him, kept demanding from him a sign from heaven.[2]
25 *He knew what they were thinking and said to them,*	23 *And he called them to him, and spoke to them in parables, "How can Satan cast out Satan?*	17 But he knew what they were thinking and said to them,
"Every kingdom divided against itself is laid waste,	24 *If a kingdom is divided against itself, that kingdom cannot stand.*	"Every kingdom divided against itself becomes a desert,
and no city or house divided against itself will stand.	25 *And if a house is divided against itself, that house will not be able to stand.*	and house falls on house.
26 *If Satan casts out Satan, he is divided against himself; how then will his kingdom stand?*	26 *And if Satan has risen up against himself and is divided, he cannot stand, but his end has come.*	18 If Satan also is divided against himself, how will his kingdom stand?—for you say that I cast out the demons by Beelzebul.
27 *If I cast out demons by Beelzebul, by whom do your own exorcists cast them out? Therefore they will be your judges.*		19 Now if I cast out the demons by Beelzebul, by whom do your exorcists cast them out? Therefore they will be your judges.
28 *But if it is by the Spirit of God that I cast out demons, then the kingdom of God has come to you.*		20 But if it is by the finger of God that I cast out the demons, then the kingdom of God has come to you.
29 *Or how can one enter a strong man's house and plunder his property, without first tying up the strong man? Then indeed the house can be plundered.*	27 *But no one can enter a strong man's house and plunder his property without first tying up the strong man; then indeed the house can be plundered."*	
		21 When a strong man, fully armed, guards his castle, his property is safe. 22 But when one stronger than he attacks him and overpowers him, he takes away his armor in which he trusted and divides his plunder.
30 *Whoever is not with me is against me, and whoever does not gather with me scatters."*	*Cf.* 9:40 = LUK 9:50 (§ 130, p. 107)	23 Whoever is not with me is against me, and whoever does not gather with me scatters."

[1] MAT 9:32–34 (§ 57, p. 46): 32 After they had gone away, a demoniac who was mute was brought to him [Jesus]. 33 And when the demon had been cast out, the one who had been mute spoke; and the crowds were amazed and said, "Never has anything like this been seen in Israel." 34 But the Pharisees said, "By the ruler of the demons he casts out the demons."

[2] *Cf.* MAT 12:38 (§ 87, p. 72) and MAT 16:1 = MAR 8:11 (§ 119, p. 96); see below LUK 11:29 (§ 151, p. 119).

§ 150 THE RETURN OF THE UNCLEAN SPIRIT

Δ *MAT 12:43–45* (*§ 88, p. 73*)	MAR	LUK 11:24–26
43 "When the unclean spirit has gone out of a person, it wanders through waterless regions looking for a resting place, but it finds none. 44 Then it says, 'I will return to my house from which I came.' When it comes, it finds it empty, swept, and put in order. 45 Then it goes and brings along seven other spirits more evil than itself, and they enter and live there; and the last state of that person is worse than the first. So will it be also with this evil generation."		24 "When the unclean spirit has gone out of a person, it wanders through waterless regions looking for a resting place, but not finding any, it says, 'I will return to my house from which I came.' 25 When it comes, it finds it swept and put in order. 26 Then it goes and brings seven other spirits more evil than itself, and they enter and live there; and the last state of that person is worse than the first."

§ 151 TRUE BLESSEDNESS

MAT	MAR	LUK 11:27–28
		27 While he was saying this, a woman in the crowd raised her voice and said to him, "Blessed is the womb that bore you and the breasts that nursed you!" 28 But he said, "Blessed rather are those who hear the word of God and obey it!"

§ 152 THE SIGN OF JONAH

Δ *MAT 12:38–42* (*§ 87, p. 72*)	MAR	LUK 11:29–32
38 Then some of the scribes and Pharisees said to him, "Teacher, we wish to see a sign from you." 39 But he answered them, "An evil and adulterous generation asks for a sign, but no sign will be given to it except the sign of the prophet Jonah.[1] 40 For just as Jonah		29 When the crowds were increasing, *Cf.* 11:16 (§ 149, p. 118) he began to say, "This generation is an evil generation; it asks for a sign, but no sign will be given to it except the sign of Jonah.[1] 30 For just as Jonah became a sign to the people of Nineveh, so the Son of Man will be to this generation.

---

[1] MAT 16:1–2, 4 (§ 119, p. 96): 1 The Pharisees and Sadducees came, and to test Jesus they asked him to show them a sign from heaven.
2 He answered them, "When it is evening, you say, 'It will be fair weather, for the sky is red.'
[3] 4 An evil and adulterous generation asks for a sign, but no sign will be given to it except the sign of Jonah." Then he left them and went away.

MAR 8:11–12 (§ 119, p. 96): 11 The Pharisees came and began to argue with him [Jesus], asking him for a sign from heaven, to test him. 12 And he sighed deeply in his spirit and said,
"Why does this generation ask for a sign? Truly I tell you, no sign will be given to this generation."

▸ To LUK 11:27–28 *cf.* **Gospel of Thomas, Logion 79.** — A woman from the crowd said to Jesus, "Blessed is the womb that bore you and the breasts that nourished you." Jesus said to her, "Blessed are those who have heard the word of the Father and have kept it in truth. For there will be days when you will say, 'Blessed is the womb that has not conceived and the breasts that have not nursed.'"

was three days and three nights in the belly of
the sea monster, so for three days and three
nights the Son of Man will be in the heart of the
earth. 42 *The queen of the South will rise up at*
the judgment with this generation
and condemn it, because she came from the
ends of the earth to listen to the wisdom of
Solomon, and see, something greater than
Solomon is here! 41 *The people of Nineveh*
will rise up at the judgment with this generation
and condemn it, because they repented at the
proclamation of Jonah, and see, something
greater than Jonah is here!"

31 The queen of the South will rise at
the judgment with the people of this generation
and condemn them, because she came from the
ends of the earth to listen to the wisdom of
Solomon, and see, something greater than
Solomon is here! 32 The people of Nineveh
will rise up at the judgment with this generation
and condemn it, because they repented at the
proclamation of Jonah, and see, something
greater than Jonah is here!"

§ 153 THE LIGHT OF THE BODY

Δ MAT 5:15 (§ 20, p. 26) +

15 *"No one after lighting a lamp puts it*
under the bushel basket, but on the lampstand,
and it gives light to all in the house." [1]

Δ 6:22–23 (§ 33, p. 33)

22 *"The eye is the lamp of the body. So, if your*
eye is healthy, your whole body will be full of
light; 23 *but if your eye is unhealthy, your*
whole body will be full of darkness. If then
the light in you is darkness,
how great is the darkness!"

MAR

LUK 11:33–36

33 "No one after lighting a lamp puts it
in a cellar, but on the lampstand
so that those who enter may see the light. [1]

34 Your eye is the lamp of your body. If your
eye is healthy, your whole body is full of
light; but if it is not healthy, your
body is full of darkness. 35 Therefore consider
whether the light in you is not darkness.

36 If then your whole body is full of light, with
no part of it in darkness, it will be as full of light
as when a lamp gives you light with its rays."

§ 154 DISCOURSE AGAINST THE PHARISEES

Δ MAT 23:25–26, 23, 6–7, 27, 4, 29–31, 34–36 (§ 210, p. 165)

25 *"Woe to you, scribes and Pharisees, hypo-*
crites! For you clean the outside of the cup
and of the plate, but inside they are full of

MAR

LUK 11:37—12:1

37 While he was speaking, a Pharisee invited
him to dine with him; so he went in and took
his place at the table. 38 The Pharisee was
amazed to see that he did not first wash before
dinner. [2] 39 Then the Lord said to him, "Now
you Pharisees clean the outside of the cup and
of the dish, but inside you are full of

---

[1] *Cf.* MAR 4:21 = LUK 8:16 (§ 94, p. 77). [2] *Cf.* MAT 15:1*ff.* = MAR 7:1*ff.* (§ 115, p. 92).

✧ LUK 11:31 — 1KI 10:1*ff.* ✧ LUK 11:32 — JON 3:5.

greed and self-indulgence.
26 You blind Pharisee!
First clean the inside of the cup, so that the
outside also may become clean.

23 "Woe to you, scribes and Pharisees,
hypocrites! For you tithe mint, dill,
and cummin, and have neglected the
weightier matters of the law: justice and mercy
and faith. It is these you ought to have
practiced without neglecting the others."
6 "They love to have
the place of honor at banquets and
the best seats in the synagogues, 7 and to be
greeted with respect in the marketplaces,[1] and
to have people call them rabbi."
27 "Woe to you, scribes and Pharisees, hypo-
crites! For you are like whitewashed tombs,

which on the outside look beautiful, but inside
they are full of the bones of the dead and of all
kinds of filth."

4 "They tie up heavy burdens, hard to bear,[H]
and lay them on the shoulders of others; but
they themselves are unwilling to lift a finger to
move them."
29 "Woe to you, scribes and Pharisees, hypo-
crites! For you build the tombs of the
prophets
and decorate the graves of the righteous, 30 and
you say, 'If we had lived in the days of our
ancestors, we would not have taken part with
them in shedding the blood of the prophets.'
31 Thus you testify against yourselves that you
are descendants of those who murdered
the prophets."

greed and wickedness.
40 You fools!

Did not the one who made the outside make the
inside also? 41 So give for alms those things
that are within; and see, everything will be
clean for you. 42 "But woe to you Pharisees!
For you tithe mint and rue and herbs of all kinds,
and neglect
justice and
the love of God; it is these you ought to have
practiced, without neglecting the others.
43 Woe to you Pharisees! For you love to have

the seat of honor in the synagogues and to be
greeted with respect in the marketplaces.[1]

44 Woe to you!
For you are like unmarked graves, and people
walk over them without realizing it."

45 One of the lawyers answered him, "Teacher,
when you say these things, you insult us too."
46 And he said, "Woe also to you lawyers! For
you load people with burdens hard to bear,
and
you yourselves do not lift a finger to
ease them.
47 Woe to you!
For you build the tombs of the
prophets whom your ancestors killed.

48 So you are witnesses and approve of the deeds
of your ancestors; for they killed
them, and you build their tombs.

---

[1] MAR 12:38–39 (§ 210, p. 165): 38 As he [Jesus] taught, he said, "Beware of the scribes, who like to walk around in long robes, and to be greeted with respect in the marketplaces,
39 and to have the best seats in the synagogues and places of honor at banquets!"

LUK 20:46 (§ 210, p. 165): "Beware of the scribes, who like to walk around in long robes, and love to be greeted with respect in the marketplaces, and to have the best seats in the synagogues and places of honor at banquets."

✧ LUK 11:42 = MAT 23:23 — MIC 6:8.

✦ [H] text: B W Θ ø ℜ it (some MSS.) vg sa; omit: *hard to bear*: S λ it (some MSS.) sy[c] sy[s] sy[p] bo; *not hard to bear*: D.

34 "Therefore I
send you prophets, sages, and scribes, some
of whom you will kill and crucify, and some you
will flog in your synagogues and pursue from
town to town,
35 so that upon you may come all
the righteous blood shed
on earth,
from the blood of righteous Abel to the blood of
Zechariah son of Barachiah, whom you
murdered between the sanctuary and the altar.
36 Truly I tell you, all this will come upon this
generation." 13 "But woe to you, scribes and
Pharisees, hypocrites!
For you lock people out of the kingdom of
heaven. For you do not go in yourselves, and
when others are going in, you stop them."

Cf. 16:6, 12 (§ 120, p. 97)

Cf. 8:15 (§ 120, p. 97)

49 "Therefore also the Wisdom of God said, 'I
will send them prophets and apostles, some
of whom they will kill and persecute,'
50 so that this generation may be charged with
the blood of all the prophets shed
since the foundation of the world,
51 from the blood of Abel to the blood of
Zechariah, who
perished between the altar and the sanctuary.
Yes, I tell you, it will be charged against this
generation. 52 Woe to you lawyers!
For you have taken away the key of knowledge;
you did not enter yourselves, and
you hindered those who were entering."
53 When he went outside, the scribes and the
Pharisees began to be very hostile toward him
and to cross-examine him about many things,
54 lying in wait for him, to catch him in something he might say. 12:1 Meanwhile, when the
crowd gathered by the thousands, so that they
trampled on one another, he began to speak
first to his disciples, "Beware of the yeast of
the Pharisees, that is, their hypocrisy."

§ 155 EXHORTATION TO FEARLESS CONFESSION

Δ *MAT 10:26–33* *(§ 60, p. 52)*	MAR	LUK 12:2–12
26 "So have no fear of them; for nothing is covered up that will not be uncovered, and		2 "Nothing is covered up that will not be uncovered, and

◇ LUK 11:50-51 = MAT 23:35 — GEN 4:8; 2CH 24:20-21.

◗ To LUK 11:49 *cf.* Origen, *Homily on Jeremiah 14:5.* — In the gospel it is written, "And wisdom will send forth its children." ◗ To LUK 11:49 *cf.* Tertullian, *Against Marcion IV.31.* — And here it begins: "And I have sent to you all my servants the prophets." ◗ To LUK 11:52 = MAT 23:13 *cf.* **Gospel of Thomas, Logia 39 and 102.** — 39 Jesus said, "The Pharisees and scribes have received the keys of knowledge and have hidden them. They themselves did not enter, and they did not allow those to enter who wished to. But you, become as wise as serpents and as innocent as doves." 102 Jesus said, "Woe to the Pharisees, for they are like a dog sleeping in the eating trough of oxen, which neither eats nor allows the oxen to eat." ◗ To LUK 11:52 = MAT 23:13 *cf.* *Oxyrhynchus Papyrus 655:2.* — Jesus said, "The Pharisees and scribes have received the keys of knowledge and have hidden them. They have neither entered nor permitted others to enter. You, however, be as wise as serpents and as innocent as doves." ◗ To LUK 12:2 *cf.* *Oxyrhynchus Papyrus 654, Logion 4.* — Jesus said, "Everything that is not before you, and what is hidden from you will be revealed. For there is nothing hidden that will not be revealed; nor buried, that will not be raised." ◗ To LUK 12:2 *cf.* **Gospel of Thomas, Logion 5.** — Jesus said, "Know what is in your sight, and what is hidden from you will be revealed to you. For there is nothing hidden that will not be revealed."

nothing secret that will not become known.[1]
27 *What I say to you in the dark,*
tell in the light; and what you
hear whispered,
proclaim from the housetops.
28 *Do not fear those who kill the body*
but cannot kill the soul;
rather
fear him who
can destroy both soul and body in hell.[I]

29 *Are not two sparrows sold for a penny?*
Yet not one of them
will fall to the ground apart from your Father.
30 *And even the hairs of your head are all*
counted. 31 *So do not be afraid; you are of*
more value than many sparrows.
32 *"Everyone therefore who acknowledges me*
before others, I also will
acknowledge before my Father in heaven;
33 *but whoever denies me before others, I also*
will deny before my Father in heaven."[2]
Δ *12:32 (§ 86, p. 70)*
32 *"Whoever speaks a word against the*
Son of Man will be forgiven, but whoever
speaks against the Holy Spirit will not be

nothing secret that will not become known.[1]
3 Therefore whatever you have said in the dark
will be heard in the light, and what you
have whispered behind closed doors will be
proclaimed from the housetops. 4 I tell you,
my friends, do not fear those who kill the body,
and after that can do nothing more.
5 But I will warn you whom to fear:
fear him who, after
he has killed, has authority to cast into hell.[I]
Yes, I tell you, fear him!
6 Are not five sparrows sold for two pennies?
Yet not one of them
is forgotten in God's sight.
7 But even the hairs of your head are all
counted. Do not be afraid; you are of
more value than many sparrows. 8 And I tell
you, everyone who acknowledges me
before others, the Son of Man also will
acknowledge before the angels of God;
9 but whoever denies me before others
will be denied before the angels of God.[2]

10 And everyone who speaks a word against the
Son of Man will be forgiven; but whoever
blasphemes against the Holy Spirit will not be

---

[1] MAR 4:22 (§ 94, p. 77): "For there is nothing hidden, except to be disclosed; nor is anything secret, except to come to light."

LUK 8:17 (§ 94, p. 77): "For nothing is hidden that will not be disclosed, nor is anything secret that will not become known and come to light."

[2] MAR 8:38 (§ 123, p. 100): "Those who are ashamed of me and of my words in this adulterous and sinful generation, of them the Son of Man will also be ashamed when he comes in the glory of his Father with the holy angels."

LUK 9:26 (§ 123, p. 100): "Those who are ashamed of me and of my words, of them the Son of Man will be ashamed when he comes in his glory and the glory of the Father and of the holy angels."

✦ [I] Greek: *Gehenna.*

◗ To LUK 12:10 c*f.* **Gospel of Thomas, Logion 44.** — Jesus said, "Whoever blasphemes against the Father will be forgiven, and whoever blasphemes against the Son will be forgiven, but whoever blasphemes against the Holy Spirit will not be forgiven, either on earth or in heaven."

forgiven,
either in this age or in the age to come." [1]
Δ *10:19–20 (§ 59, p. 51)*
19 *"When they hand you over,*
do not worry
about how you are to speak or what
you are to say;
for what you are to say will be given to you at
that time;
20 *for it is not you who speak, but the Spirit of*
your Father speaking through you." [2]

forgiven. [1]

11 When they bring you before the synagogues,
the rulers, and the authorities, do not worry
about how you are to defend yourselves or what
you are to say;
12 for the Holy Spirit will teach you at that very
hour what you ought to say." [2]

§ 156 THE PARABLE OF THE RICH FOOL

MAT	MAR	LUK 12:13–21
		13 Someone in the crowd said to him, "Teacher, tell my brother to divide the family inheritance with me." 14 But he said to him, "Friend, who set me to be a judge or arbitrator over you?" 15 And he said to them, "Take care! Be on your guard against all kinds of greed; for one's life does not consist in the abundance of possessions." 16 Then he told them a parable: "The land of a rich man produced abundantly. 17 And he thought to himself, 'What should I do, for I have no place to store my crops?' 18 Then he said, 'I will do this: I will pull down my barns and build larger ones, and there I will store all my grain and my goods. 19 And I will say to my soul, 'Soul, you have ample goods laid up for many years; relax, eat, drink, be merry.' 20 But God said to him, 'You fool! This very night your life is being demanded of you. And the things you have prepared, whose will they be?' 21 So it is with those who store up treasures for themselves but are not rich toward God."

[1] MAR 3:28–30 (§ 86, p. 70): 28 "Truly I tell you, people will be forgiven for their sins and whatever blasphemies they utter; 29 but whoever blasphemes against the Holy Spirit can never have forgiveness, but is guilty of an eternal sin" — 30 for they had said, "He has an unclean spirit."

[2] MAR 13:11 (§ 215, p. 170): "When they bring you to trial and hand you over, do not worry beforehand about what you are to say; but say whatever is given you at that time, for it is not you who speak, but the Holy Spirit."

LUK 21:14–15 (§ 215, p. 170): 14 "So make up your minds not to prepare your defense in advance; 15 for I will give you words and a wisdom that none of your opponents will be able to withstand or contradict."

• To LUK 12:12 *cf.* JOH 14:26b. — "But the Advocate, the Holy Spirit, whom the Father will send in my name, will teach you everything, and remind you of all that I have said to you."

◗ To LUK 12:13–14 *cf.* **Gospel of Thomas, Logion 72.** — Someone said to Jesus, "Tell my brothers and sisters to divide my father's possessions with me." Jesus answered, "Tell me, who made me a divider?" Then Jesus turned to the disciples and said, "I am not a divider, am I?" ◗ To LUK 12:16–21 *cf.* **Gospel of Thomas, Logion 63.** — Jesus said, "There was a rich person who had a lot of money and said, 'I will use my money so that I may sow and reap and plant and fill my storehouses with fruit, so that I won't need anything.' This was what the person thought. But that night the person died. Those who have ears, let them hear."

§ 157 ON ANXIETY

Δ *MAT 6:25–33* (*§ 35, p. 33*)

*25 "Therefore I tell you, do not worry about
your life, what you will eat or what you will
drink,[J] or about your body, what you will
wear. Is not life more than food, and the
body more than clothing? 26 Look at the
birds of the air; they neither sow nor reap
nor gather into barns, and yet your heavenly
Father feeds them. Are you not of more value
than they? 27 And can any of you
by worrying add a single hour to your span of
life?[K]
28 And why do you worry about clothing?*

*Consider the lilies of the field, how they grow;
they neither toil nor spin, 29 yet I tell you, even
Solomon in all his glory was not clothed like
one of these. 30 But if God so clothes the grass
of the field, which is alive today and tomorrow
is thrown into the oven, will he not much more
clothe you—you of little faith? 31 Therefore do
not worry, saying, 'What will we eat?' or
'What will we drink?' or 'What will we
wear?' 32 For it is the Gentiles who
strive for all these things; and indeed your
heavenly Father knows that you need
all these things. 33 But strive first for
the kingdom of God and his righteousness, and
all these things will be given to you as well."*

Δ *6:19–21* (*§ 32, p. 32*)
*19 "Do not store up for yourselves
treasures on earth,
where moth and rust[N] consume and where
thieves break in and steal; 20 but store up for
yourselves treasures in heaven, where
neither moth nor rust[N] consumes and where
thieves do not break in and steal. 21 For where
your treasure is, there your heart will be also."*

MAR

LUK 12:22–34

22 He said to his disciples,
"Therefore I tell you, do not worry about
your life, what you will eat,
or about your body, what you will
wear. 23 For life is more than food, and the
body more than clothing. 24 Consider the
ravens: they neither sow nor reap,
they have neither storehouse nor barn, and yet
God feeds them. Of how much more value
are you than the birds! 25 And can any of you
by worrying add a single hour to your span of
life?[K]

26 If then you are not able to do so small a thing
as that, why do you worry about the rest?
27 Consider the lilies, how they grow:
they neither toil nor spin;[L] yet I tell you, even
Solomon in all his glory was not clothed like
one of these. 28 But if God so clothes the grass
of the field, which is alive today and tomorrow
is thrown into the oven, how much more
will he clothe you—you of little faith! 29 And
do not keep striving for what you are to eat and
what you are to drink, and do not keep worrying. 30 For it is the nations of the world that
strive after all these things, and your
Father knows that you need
them. 31 Instead, strive for
his[M] kingdom, and
these things will be given to you as well.
32 Do not be afraid, little flock, for it is your
Father's good pleasure to give you the kingdom.
33 Sell your possessions, and give alms.
Make purses for yourselves that do not wear
out,

an unfailing treasure in heaven, where
no thief comes near and no moth destroys.
34 For where
your treasure is, there your heart will be also."

✦ [J] text: B W ø it (some MSS.) sa (some MSS.) bo; *what you will eat and what you will drink*: Θ ℜ sy^{p}; omit: *or what you will drink:* S λ it (some MSS.) vg sy^{c} sa (some MSS.). ✦ [K] Or, *add a cubit to your stature.* ✦ [L] text: P^{45} P^{75} S A B W Θ λ ø ℜ it (some MSS.) vg sy^{p} sa bo; *lilies, how they neither spin nor weave*: D sy^{c} sy^{s}; *how they grow; they neither toil nor spin nor weave*: it (some MSS.). ✦ [M] text: S B D sa bo; *God's*: P^{45} A W Θ λ ø ℜ it vg sy^{c} sy^{s} sy^{p}; *the kingdom*: P^{75}.
✦ [N] Or, *eating.*

▸ To LUK 12:31 *cf.* Clement of Alexandria, *Miscellanies I.24:158.* — "Ask for great things, and God will add the little things."

§ 158 WATCHFULNESS AND FAITHFULNESS

Δ *MAT 24:43–51* (*§ 225–226, p. 176*)	**MAR**	**LUK 12:35–46**
C*f.* 25:1–13 (§ 227, p. 177)		35 "Be dressed for action and have your lamps lit; 36 be like those who are waiting for their master to return from the wedding banquet, so that they may open the door for him as soon as he comes and knocks. 37 Blessed are those slaves whom the master finds alert when he comes; truly I tell you, he will fasten his belt and have them sit down to eat, and he will come and serve them. 38 If he comes during the middle of the night, or near dawn, and finds them so, blessed are those slaves.
43 "But understand this: if the owner of the house had known in what part of the night the thief was coming, he would have stayed awake and would not have let his house be broken into. 44 Therefore you also must be ready, for the Son of Man is coming at an unexpected hour.[1]		39 "But know this: if the owner of the house had known at what hour the thief was coming, he[O] would not have let his house be broken into. 40 You also must be ready, for the Son of Man is coming at an unexpected hour."[1]
		41 Peter said, "Lord, are you telling this parable for us or for everyone?" 42 And the Lord said,
45 "Who then is the faithful and wise slave, whom his master has put in charge of his household, to give the other slaves their allowance of food at the proper time? 46 Blessed is that slave whom his master will find at work when he arrives. 47 Truly I tell you, he will put that one in charge of all his possessions. 48 But if that wicked slave says to himself, 'My master is delayed,' 49 and he begins to beat his fellow slaves, and eats and drinks with drunkards, 50 the master of that slave will come on a day when he does not expect him and at an hour that he does not know. 51 He will cut him in pieces[P] *and put him with the hypocrites, where there will be weeping and gnashing of teeth."*		"Who then is the faithful and prudent manager whom his master will put in charge of his slaves, to give them their allowance of food at the proper time? 43 Blessed is that slave whom his master will find at work when he arrives. 44 Truly I tell you, he will put that one in charge of all his possessions. 45 But if that slave says to himself, 'My master is delayed in coming,' and if he begins to beat the other slaves, men and women, and to eat and drink and get drunk, 46 the master of that slave will come on a day when he does not expect him and at an hour that he does not know, and will cut him in pieces,[P] and put him with the unfaithful."

[1] MAR 13:35–36 (§ 222, p. 175): 35 "Therefore, keep awake—for you do not know when the master of the house will come, in the evening, or at midnight, or at cockcrow, or at dawn, 36 or else he may find you asleep when he comes suddenly."

✦ [O] text: P^{75} S D sy[c] sy[s] sa; add: *would have watched and*: A B W Θ λ ø 𝔐 it vg sy[p] bo. ✦ [P] Or, *cut him off.*

• To LUK 12:37 c*f.* JOH 13:4–5. — 4 [Jesus] got up from the table, took off his outer robe, and tied a towel around himself. 5 Then he poured water into a basin and began to wash the disciples' feet and to wipe them with the towel that was tied around him.

◗ To LUK 12:39 c*f.* **Gospel of Thomas, Logion 103.** — Jesus said, "Blessed are those who know in which part of the night the robbers will come, so that they will get up, get ready, and arm themselves before the robbers arrive."

§ 159 THE SLAVE'S WAGES

MAT	MAR	LUK 12:47–48
		Cf. LUK 17:7–10 (§ 181, p. 139) 47 "That slave who knew what his master wanted, but did not prepare himself or do what was wanted, will receive a severe beating. 48 But the one who did not know and did what deserved a beating will receive a light beating. From everyone to whom much has been given, much will be required; and from the one to whom much has been entrusted, even more will be demanded."

§ 160 JESUS THE CAUSE OF DIVISION

△ *MAT 10:34–36* (*§ 61, p. 53*) +	MAR	LUK 12:49–56
		49 "I came to bring fire to the earth, and how I wish it were already kindled! 50 I have a baptism with which to be baptized, and what stress I am under until it is completed![1]
34 *"Do not think that I have come to bring peace to the earth; I have not come to bring peace, but a sword.*		51 Do you think that I have come to bring peace to the earth? No, I tell you, but rather division! 52 From now on five in one household will be divided, three against two and two against three; 53 they will be divided:
35 *For I have come to set a man against his father, and a daughter against her mother, and a daughter-in-law against her mother-in-law;* 36 *and one's foes will be members of one's own household."*		father against son and son against father, mother against daughter and daughter against mother, mother-in-law against her daughter-in-law and daughter-in-law against mother-in-law."
△ *16:2–3* (*§ 119, p. 96*) 2 *He answered them,*[Q] *"When it is evening, you say, 'It will be fair weather, for the sky is red.'* 3 *And in the morning, 'It will be stormy today, for the sky is red and*		54 He also said to the crowds, "When you see a cloud rising in the west, you immediately say, 'It is going to rain'; and so it happens. 55 And when you see the south wind blowing, you say, 'There will be scorching heat';

[1] MAR 10:38b (§ 192, p. 149): "Are you able to drink the cup that I drink, or be baptized with the baptism that I am baptized with?"

✧ LUK 12:53 = MAT 10:35 — MIC 7:6.

✦ [Q] text: C D W Θ λ 𝔐 it vg sy[p] bo (some MSS.); omit from here to end of verse 3: S B ø sy[c] sy[s] sa bo (some MSS.).

• To LUK 12:50 *cf.* JOH 12:27. — "Now my soul is troubled. And what should I say — 'Father, save me from this hour'? No, it is for this reason that I have come to this hour."

◗ To LUK 12:49 *cf.* Didymus on PSA 89:7; Origen, *Homily on Jeremiah 3:3.* — So the Savior said, "One who is near me is near the fire, and one who is far from me is far from the kingdom." ◗ To LUK 12:49 *cf.* **Gospel of Thomas, Logion 10.** — Jesus said, "I have cast fire upon the world, and see, I guard it until the world is on fire." ◗ To LUK 12:51–53 *cf.* **Gospel of Thomas, Logion 16.** — Jesus said, "People possibly think that I have come to throw peace upon the world, and they do not know that I have come to throw divisions upon the earth — fire, the sword, and war. For there will be five in a house: three will be against two and two against three, the parent against the child and the child against the parent, and they will stand deserted."

threatening.'
You know how to interpret the appearance of
the sky, but you cannot
interpret the signs of the times."

and it happens. 56 You hypocrites!
You know how to interpret the appearance of
earth and sky, but why do you not know how to
interpret the present time?"

§ 161 SETTLING WITH ONE'S ACCUSER

Δ *MAT 5:25–26* (*§ 22, p. 27*)

25 "Come to terms quickly with your accuser
while you are on the way to court with him,

or your accuser may hand you over to the judge,
and the judge to the guard, and
you will be thrown into prison.
26 Truly I tell you, you will never get out until
you have paid the last penny."

MAR

LUK 12:57–59

57 "And why do you not judge for yourselves
what is right?
58 Thus, when you go with your accuser
before a magistrate, on the way
make an effort to settle the case,
or you may be dragged before the judge,
and the judge hand you over to the officer, and
the officer throw you in prison.
59 I tell you, you will never get out until you
have paid the very last penny."

§ 162 REPENTANCE OR DESTRUCTION

MAT

MAR

LUK 13:1–9

1 At that very time there were some present who told him about the Galileans whose
blood Pilate had mingled with their sacrifices. 2 He asked them, "Do you think
that because these Galileans suffered in this way they were worse sinners than all
other Galileans? 3 No, I tell you; but unless you repent, you will all perish as
they did. 4 Or those eighteen who were killed when the tower of Siloam fell on
them—do you think that they were worse offenders than all the others living in
Jerusalem? 5 No, I tell you; but unless you repent, you will all perish just as they
did." 6 Then he told this parable: "A man had a fig tree planted in his vineyard;
and he came looking for fruit on it and found none. 7 So he said to the gardener,
'See here! For three years I have come looking for fruit on this fig tree, and still
I find none. Cut it down! Why should it be wasting the soil?' 8 He replied, 'Sir,
let it alone for one more year, until I dig around it and put manure on it. 9 If it
bears fruit next year, well and good; but if not, you can cut it down.' "

§ 163 THE HEALING OF THE CRIPPLED WOMAN

MAT

MAR

LUK 13:10–17

Cf. LUK 14:1–6 (§ 168, p. 131)

10 Now he was teaching in one of the synagogues on the sabbath. 11 And just then
there appeared a woman with a spirit that had crippled her for eighteen years. She
was bent over and was quite unable to stand up straight. 12 When Jesus saw her,

he called her over and said, "Woman, you are set free from your ailment."
13 When he laid his hands on her, immediately she stood up straight and began
praising God. 14 But the leader of the synagogue, indignant because Jesus had
cured on the sabbath, kept saying to the crowd, "There are six days on which work
ought to be done; come on those days and be cured, and not on the sabbath day."
15 But the Lord answered him and said, "You hypocrites! Does not each of you
on the sabbath untie his ox or his donkey from the manger, and lead it away to give
it water? 16 And ought not this woman, a daughter of Abraham whom Satan bound
for eighteen long years, be set free from this bondage on the sabbath day?"[1]
17 When he said this, all his opponents were put to shame; and the entire crowd
was rejoicing at all the wonderful things that he was doing.

§ 164 THE PARABLES OF THE MUSTARD SEED AND THE YEAST

Δ *MAT 13:31–33 (§ 97-98, p. 78)*	Δ *MAR 4:30–32 (§ 97, p. 78)*	**LUK 13:18–21**
31 He put before them another parable: "The kingdom of heaven	*30 He also said, "With what can we compare the kingdom of God, or what parable will we use for it?*	18 He said therefore, "What is the kingdom of God like? And to what should I compare it? 19 It
is like a mustard seed that someone took and sowed in his field; 32 it is the smallest of all the seeds,	*31 It is like a mustard seed, which, when sown upon the ground, is the smallest of all the seeds on earth;*	is like a mustard seed that someone took and sowed in the garden;
but when it has grown it is the greatest of shrubs and becomes a tree,	*32 yet when it is sown it grows up and becomes the greatest of all shrubs, and puts forth large branches,*	it grew and became a tree,
so that the birds of the air come and make nests in its branches."	*so that the birds of the air can make nests in its shade."*	and the birds of the air made nests in its branches."
33 He told them another parable:		20 And again he said, "To what should I compare the kingdom of God?
"The kingdom of heaven is like yeast that a woman took and mixed in with three measures of flour until all of it was leavened."		21 It is like yeast that a woman took and mixed in with three measures of flour until all of it was leavened."

[1] MAT 12:11–12 (§ 70, p. 59): 11 He said to them, "Suppose one of you has only one sheep and it falls into a pit on the sabbath, will you not lay hold of it and lift it out? 12 How much more valuable is a human being than a sheep! So it is lawful to do good on the sabbath."

LUK 14:5 (§ 168, p. 131): Then he said to them, "If one of you has a child or an ox that has fallen into a well, will you not immediately pull it out on a sabbath day?"

✧ LUK 13:14 — EXO 20:9; DEU 5:13. ✧ LUK 13:19 = MAT 13:32 = MAR 4:32 — DAN 4:21.

▸ To LUK 13:20 *cf.* **Gospel of Thomas, Logion 96.** — Jesus said, "The kingdom of the Father is like a woman who took a little yeast and mixed it in with dough and made large loaves of it. Those who have ears let them hear."

§ 165 THE NARROW DOOR

Δ *MAT 7:13–14 (§ 40, p. 36) +*

13 *"Enter through the narrow gate;*

for the gate is wide and the road is
easy[R] *that leads to destruction,*
and there are many who take it.
14 *For the gate is narrow and the*
road is hard that leads to life, and
there are few who find it."

Δ *25:10b–12 (§ 227, p. 177)*
10b *"and the door was shut.*
11 *Later the other bridesmaids came*
also, saying, 'Lord, lord,
open to us.' 12 *But he replied,*
'Truly I tell you, I do not know
you.' "

Δ *7:22–23 (§ 42, p. 37)*
22 *"On that day many will say to me,*
'Lord, Lord, did we not prophesy
in your name, and cast out demons
in your name, and do many deeds
of power in your name?'
23 *Then I will declare to them, 'I*
never knew you;
go away from me,
you evildoers.' "

Δ *8:11–12 (§ 46, p. 39)*
11 *"I tell you, many will come from*
east and west and will eat with
Abraham and Isaac and Jacob in
the kingdom of
heaven, 12 *while the heirs of the*
kingdom will be thrown into the
outer darkness, where there will be
weeping and gnashing of teeth."

Δ *MAR 10:31 (§ 189, p. 145)*

LUK 13:22–30

22 Jesus went through one town and
village after another, teaching as
he made his way to Jerusalem.
23 Someone asked him, "Lord,
will only a few be saved?" He said
to them, 24 "Strive to
enter through the narrow door;
for many, I tell you, will try to enter and will not be able.

25 When once the owner of the house
has got up and shut the door, and
you begin to stand outside and to
knock at the door, saying, 'Lord,
open to us,' then in reply he will
say to you, 'I do not know
where you come from.' 26 Then
you will begin to say, 'We ate and
drank with you, and you taught in
our streets.'

27 But he will say, 'I
do not know where you come from;
go away from me,
all you evildoers!'
28 There will be weeping and gnashing of teeth when you see

Abraham and Isaac and Jacob and
all the prophets in the kingdom of
God, and you yourselves
thrown
out.

29 Then people will come from east

✧ LUK 13:27 = MAT 7:23 — PSA 6:8. ✧ LUK 13:29 = MAT 8:11 — PSA 107:3.

✦ [R] text: B C W Θ λ φ 𝔐 it (some MSS.) vg sy[c] sy[p] sa bo; *for the road is wide and easy*: S it (some MSS.) Clement, Origen.

		and west, from north and south, and will eat in the kingdom of God.
Δ *19:30 (§ 189, p. 145)* 30 *"But many who are first will be* *last, and the last will be first."* Δ *20:16 (§ 190, p. 147)* 16 *"So the last will be* *first, and the first will be* *last."*	31 *"But many who are first will be* *last, and the last will be first."*	30 Indeed, some are last who will be first, and some are first who will be last."

§ 166 THE DEPARTURE FROM GALILEE

MAT	MAR	LUK 13:31–33
		31 At that very hour some Pharisees came and said to him, "Get away from here, for Herod wants to kill you." 32 He said to them, "Go and tell that fox for me, 'Listen, I am casting out demons and performing cures today and tomorrow, and on the third day I finish my work. 33 Yet today, tomorrow, and the next day I must be on my way, because it is impossible for a prophet to be killed outside of Jerusalem.' "

§ 167 THE LAMENT OVER JERUSALEM

Δ *MAT 23:37–39 (§ 211, p. 168)*	MAR	LUK 13:34–35
37 *"Jerusalem, Jerusalem, the city that kills* *the prophets and stones those who are sent to* *it! How often have I desired to gather your* *children together as a hen gathers her brood* *under her wings, and you were not willing!* 38 *See, your house is left to you, desolate.*[S] 39 *For I tell you, you will not see me again until* *you say, 'Blessed is the one who* *comes in the name of the Lord.' "*		34 "Jerusalem, Jerusalem, the city that kills the prophets and stones those who are sent to it! How often have I desired to gather your children together as a hen gathers her brood under her wings, and you were not willing! 35 See, your house is left to you. And I tell you, you will not see me until the time comes when you say, 'Blessed is the one who comes in the name of the Lord.' "

§ 168 THE HEALING OF A MAN WITH DROPSY[1]

MAT	MAR	LUK 14:1–6
		1 On one occasion when Jesus was going to the house of a leader of the Pharisees to eat a meal on the sabbath, they were watching him closely. 2 Just then, in front

[1] *Cf.* MAT 12:9–14 = MAR 3:1–6 = LUK 6:6–11 (§ 70, p. 59). *Cf.* LUK 13:10–17 (§ 163, p. 128).

✧ LUK 13:34 = MAT 23:37 — ISA 31:5. ✧ LUK 13:35 = MAT 23:38 — PSA 118:26.

✦ [S] text: S C D W Θ λ ø ℜ it vg sy[p] bo (some MSS.); *cf.* JER 22:5; omit: *desolate*: B sy[s] sa bo (some MSS.). *Cf.* LUK 13:35, add: *desolate*: D Θ ø ℜ it vg sy[c] sy[p].

of him, there was a man who had dropsy. 3 And Jesus asked the lawyers and
Pharisees, "Is it lawful to cure people on the sabbath, or not?" 4 But they were
silent. So Jesus took him and healed him, and sent him away. 5 Then he said to
them, "If one of you has a child[T] or an ox that has fallen into a well, will you not
immediately pull it out on a sabbath day?" 6 And they could not reply to this.

§ 169 TEACHING ON HUMILITY

MAT	MAR	LUK 14:7–14

7 When he noticed how the guests chose the places of honor, he told them a parable.
8 "When you are invited by someone to a wedding banquet, do not sit down at the
place of honor, in case someone more distinguished than you has been invited by
your host;[U] 9 and the host who invited both of you may come and say to you, 'Give
this person your place,' and then in disgrace you would start to take the lowest
place. 10 But when you are invited, go and sit down at the lowest place, so that
when your host comes, he may say to you, 'Friend, move up higher'; then you
will be honored in the presence of all who sit at the table with you. 11 For all who
exalt themselves will be humbled, and those who humble themselves will be
exalted."[1] 12 He said also to the one who had invited him, "When you give a
luncheon or a dinner, do not invite your friends or your brothers or your relatives
or rich neighbors, in case they may invite you in return, and you would be repaid.
13 But when you give a banquet, invite the poor, the crippled, the lame, and the
blind. 14 And you will be blessed, because they cannot repay you, for you will be
repaid at the resurrection of the righteous."

§ 170 THE PARABLE OF THE GREAT DINNER

Δ *MAT 22:1–10* (*§ 205, p. 160*)	MAR	LUK 14:15–24
		15 One of the dinner guests, on hearing this, said to him, "Blessed is anyone who will eat bread in the kingdom of God!" 16 Then Jesus said to him,
1 Once more Jesus spoke to them in parables, saying: 2 "The kingdom of heaven may be compared to a king who gave a wedding banquet for his son.		"Someone gave a great dinner and invited many.
3 He sent his slaves to call those who had been invited to the wedding banquet,		17 At the time for the dinner he sent his slave to say to those who had been invited,

[1] *Cf.* MAT 18:4 (§ 129, p. 106); MAT 23:12 (§ 210, p. 165); LUK 18:14 (§ 186, p. 142).

✦ [T] text: P[45] P[75] A B W ℜ (some MSS.) sa; *an ass or an ox*: S λ ø ℜ (some MSS.) it vg bo; *a child or an ox or an ass*: sy[c]; *an ass, a child or an ox*: Θ; *an ox or an ass*: sy[s]; *a sheep or an ox*: D. ✦ [U] *Cf.* the addition that some MSS. (D it vg sy[c]) make at MAT 20:28 — "But seek to increase from the insignificant, and to be less than the greatest. And when you enter and are asked to dine, do not sit in the prominent places, lest someone more honored than you should come in, and the host should come and say to you, 'Move further down,' and you be humiliated. But if you sit down in the less conspicuous place and someone less important than you arrives, the host will say, 'Come up higher'; and this will be (more) advantageous for you."

but they would not come.

4 Again he sent other slaves, saying, 'Tell
those who have been invited: Look, I have pre-
pared my dinner, my oxen and my fat calves
have been slaughtered, and everything is
ready; come to the wedding banquet.' 5 But
they made light of it and went away, one to his
farm, another to his business, 6 while the rest
seized his slaves, mistreated them, and killed
them. 7 The king was enraged. He sent his
troops, destroyed those murderers, and
burned their city. 8 Then he said to his slaves,
'The wedding is ready, but those invited were
not worthy. 9 Go therefore into the main
streets, and invite everyone you find to the wed-
ding banquet.' 10 Those slaves went out into
the streets and gathered all whom they found,
both good and bad;

so the wedding hall was filled with guests."

'Come; for everything is ready now.'
18 But they all alike began to make excuses.
The first said to him, 'I have bought a piece of
land, and I must go out and see it; please accept my regrets.' 19 Another said, 'I have
bought five yoke of oxen, and I am going to try
them out; please accept my regrets.' 20 Another said, 'I have just been married, and
therefore I cannot come.' 21 So the slave returned and reported this to his master.

Then the owner of the house became angry and

said to his slave,

'Go out at once into the streets and lanes of the
town and bring in the poor, the crippled, the
blind, and the lame.'

22 And the slave said, 'Sir, what you ordered
has been done, and there is still room.'
23 Then the master said to the slave, 'Go out into
the roads and lanes, and compel people to come
in, so that my house may be filled. 24 For I tell
you[V], none of those who were invited will taste
my dinner.' "

§ 171 THE COST OF DISCIPLESHIP

Δ *MAT 10:37–38* (*§ 62, p. 53*)	MAR	LUK 14:25–35
37 "Whoever loves father or mother more than me is not worthy of me; and whoever loves son or		25 Now large crowds were traveling with him; and he turned and said to them, 26 "Whoever comes to me and does not hate father and mother, wife and children, brothers and sisters, yes, and even life itself, cannot be my disciple.

✦ [V] The Greek word for *you* here is plural.

◗ To LUK 14:26–27 = MAT 10:37–38 *cf.* **Gospel of Thomas, Logia 55 and 101.** — See note to MAT 10:37–38, (§ 62, p. 53).

daughter more than me is not worthy of me;
38 *and whoever does not take up the cross and*
follow me is not worthy of me." [1]

Cf. 5:13 (§ 20, p. 26)

Cf. 9:50
(§ 132, p. 108)

27 Whoever does not carry the cross and
follow me cannot be my disciple[1]. 28 For
which of you, intending to build a tower, does
not first sit down and estimate the cost, to see
whether he has enough to complete it? 29 Otherwise, when he has laid a foundation and is not
able to finish, all who see it will begin to ridi-
cule him, 30 saying, 'This fellow began to build
and was not able to finish.' 31 Or what king,
going out to wage war against another king,
will not sit down first and consider whether he
is able with ten thousand to oppose the one who
comes against him with twenty thousand? 32 If
he cannot, then, while the other is still far
away, he sends a delegation and asks for the
terms of peace. 33 So therefore, none of you
can become my disciple if you do not give up
all your possessions. 34 "Salt is good; but if
salt has lost its taste, how can its saltiness be
restored? 35 It is fit neither for the soil nor for
the manure pile; they throw it away. Let anyone with ears to hear listen!"

§ 172 THE PARABLES OF THE LOST SHEEP AND THE LOST COIN

Δ *MAT 18:12–14* (*§ 133, p. 109*)

Cf. 9:10–11 (§ 53, p. 44)

12 *"What do you think?*
If a shepherd has a hundred sheep,
and one of them has gone astray, does he not
leave the ninety-nine on the mountains and go
in search of the one that went astray? 13 *And*
if he finds it, truly I tell you,

he rejoices over it more than over the ninety-
nine that never went astray. 14 *So it is not the*

MAR

Cf. 2:15–16
(§ 53, p. 44)

LUK 15:1–10

Cf. 5:29–30 (§ 53, p. 44)

1 Now all the tax collectors and sinners were
coming near to listen to him. 2 And the Pharisees and the scribes were grumbling and saying,
"This fellow welcomes sinners and eats with
them." 3 So he told them this parable:
4 "Which one of you, having a hundred sheep
and losing one of them, does not
leave the ninety-nine in the wilderness and go
after the one that is lost until he finds it?
5 When he has found it, he lays it on his shoulders and rejoices. 6 And when he comes home,
he calls together his friends and neighbors, saying to them, 'Rejoice with me,

[1] MAT 16:24b (§ 123, p. 100): "If any want to become my followers, let them deny themselves and take up their cross and follow me."

MAR 8:34b (§ 123, p. 100): "If any want to become my followers, let them deny themselves and take up their cross and follow me."

LUK 9:23b (§ 123, p. 100): "If any want to become my followers, let them deny themselves and take up their cross daily and follow me."

will of your[W] *Father in heaven that one of these little ones should be lost."*

for I have found my sheep that was lost.' 7 Just
so, I tell you, there will be more joy in heaven
over one sinner who repents than over ninety-
nine righteous persons who need no repentance.
8 Or what woman having ten silver coins,[X] if
she loses one of them, does not light a lamp,
sweep the house, and search carefully until she
finds it? 9 When she has found it, she calls
together her friends and neighbors, saying,
'Rejoice with me, for I have found the coin that
I had lost.' 10 Just so, I tell you, there is joy
in the presence of the angels of God over one
sinner who repents."

§ 173 THE PARABLE OF THE PRODIGAL SON AND HIS BROTHER

MAT	MAR	LUK 15:11–32

11 Then Jesus said, "There was a man who had two sons. 12 The younger of them
said to his father, 'Father, give me the share of the property that will belong to
me.' So he divided his property between them. 13 A few days later the younger
son gathered all he had and traveled to a distant country, and there he squandered
his property in dissolute living. 14 When he had spent everything, a severe famine
took place throughout that country, and he began to be in need. 15 So he went and
hired himself out to one of the citizens of that country, who sent him to his fields
to feed the pigs. 16 He would gladly have filled himself with[Y] the pods that the
pigs were eating; and no one gave him anything. 17 But when he came to himself
he said, 'How many of my father's hired hands have bread enough and to spare,
but here I am dying of hunger! 18 I will get up and go to my father, and I will say
to him, "Father, I have sinned against heaven and before you; 19 I am no longer
worthy to be called your son; treat me like one of your hired hands." ' 20 So he
set off and went to his father. But while he was still far off, his father saw him
and was filled with compassion; he ran and put his arms around him and kissed
him. 21 Then the son said to him, 'Father, I have sinned against heaven and before
you; I am no longer worthy to be called your son.'[Z] 22 But the father said to his
slaves, 'Quickly, bring out a robe—the best one—and put it on him; put a ring on
his finger and sandals on his feet. 23 And get the fatted calf and kill it, and let us
eat and celebrate; 24 for this son of mine was dead and is alive again; he was lost
and is found!' And they began to celebrate.
25 "Now his elder son was in the field; and when he came and approached the house,
he heard music and dancing. 26 He called one of the slaves and asked what was
going on. 27 He replied, 'Your brother has come, and your father has killed the
fatted calf, because he has got him back safe and sound.' 28 Then he became angry

✦ [W] text: S W λ ℜ it vg sy^{c} sy^{p}; *my:* B Θ ø sy^{s} sa bo; *our:* D. ✦ [X] The drachma, rendered here by *silver coin,* was about a day's wage for a laborer. ✦ [Y] text: P^{75} S B D λ ø sy^{c} sa; *filled his belly with:* A Θ ℜ it vg sy^{s} sy^{p} bo; *filled his belly and fed on:* W. ✦ [Z] text: P^{75} A W Θ λ ø ℜ it vg sy^{c} sy^{s} sy^{p} sa bo; add: *treat me as one of your hired servants:* S B D.

and refused to go in. His father came out and began to plead with him. 29 But he
answered his father, 'Listen! For all these years I have been working like a slave
for you, and I have never disobeyed your command; yet you have never given me
even a young goat so that I might celebrate with my friends. 30 But when this son
of yours came back, who has devoured your property with prostitutes, you killed
the fatted calf for him!' 31 Then the father said to him, 'Son, you are always with
me, and all that is mine is yours. 32 But we had to celebrate and rejoice, because
this brother of yours was dead and has come to life; he was lost and has been
found.' "

§ 174 THE UNJUST MANAGER

MAT	MAR	LUK 16:1–13

1 Then Jesus said to the disciples, "There was a rich man who had a manager, and
charges were brought to him that this man was squandering his property. 2 So he
summoned him and said to him, 'What is this that I hear about you? Give me an
accounting of your management, because you cannot be my manager any longer.'
3 Then the manager said to himself, 'What will I do, now that my master is taking
the position away from me? I am not strong enough to dig, and I am ashamed to
beg. 4 I have decided what to do so that, when I am dismissed as manager, people
may welcome me into their homes.' 5 So, summoning his master's debtors one
by one, he asked the first, 'How much do you owe my master?' 6 He answered,
'A hundred jugs of olive oil.' He said to him, 'Take your bill, sit down quickly,
and make it fifty.' 7 Then he asked another, 'And how much do you owe?' He
replied, 'A hundred containers of wheat.' He said to him, 'Take your bill and
make it eighty.' 8 And his master commended the dishonest manager because he
had acted shrewdly; for the children of this age are more shrewd in dealing with
their own generation than are the children of light. 9 And I tell you, make friends
for yourselves by means of dishonest wealth[A] so that when it is gone, they may
welcome you into the eternal homes.
10 "Whoever is faithful in a very little is faithful also in much; and whoever is
dishonest in a very little is dishonest also in much. 11 If then you have not been
faithful with the dishonest wealth,[A] who will entrust to you the true riches? 12 And
if you have not been faithful with what belongs to another, who will give you what
is your own? 13 No slave can serve two masters; for a slave will either hate the
one and love the other, or be devoted to the one and despise the other. You cannot
serve God and wealth."[A+1]

[1] MAT 6:24 (§ 34, p. 33): "No one can serve two masters; for a slave will either hate the one and love the other, or be devoted to the one and despise the other. You cannot serve God and wealth."

✦ [A] Greek: *mammon.*

▸ To LUK 16:10–11 *cf.* **II Clement 8:5.** — For the Lord says in the Gospel, "If you have not taken care of what is small, who will give you what is great? For I tell you, that the one who is faithful in a very little, is also faithful in much." ▸ To LUK 16:10–11 *cf.* Irenaeus, *Against Heresies II.34:3.* — Therefore the Lord said to those who were ungrateful, "If you have not been faithful in a little, who will give you what is great?"

§ 175 THE HYPOCRISY OF THE PHARISEES

MAT	MAR	LUK 16:14–15
		14 The Pharisees, who were lovers of money, heard all this, and they ridiculed him. 15 So he said to them, "You are those who justify yourselves in the sight of others; but God knows your hearts; for what is prized by human beings is an abomination in the sight of God."

§ 176 ABOUT THE LAW AND ABOUT DIVORCE

∆ *MAT 11:12–13 (§ 65, p. 55) +*	MAR	LUK 16:16–18
12 *"From the days of John the Baptist until now the kingdom of heaven has suffered violence,*[B] *and the violent take it by force.* 13 *For all the prophets and the law prophesied until John came;"*		16 "The law and the prophets were in effect until John came; since then the good news of the kingdom of God is proclaimed, and everyone tries to enter it by force.
∆ *5:18 (§ 21, p. 26)* 18 *"For truly I tell you, until heaven and earth pass away, not one letter, not one stroke of a letter, will pass from the law until all is accomplished."*		17 But it is easier for heaven and earth to pass away, than for one stroke of a letter in the law to be dropped.
∆ *5:32 (§ 24, p. 28)* 32 *"But I say to you that anyone who divorces his wife, except on the ground of unchastity, causes her to commit adultery; and whoever marries a divorced woman commits adultery."*[1]		18 "Anyone who divorces his wife and marries another commits adultery, and whoever marries a woman divorced from her husband commits adultery."[1]

§ 177 THE RICH MAN AND LAZARUS

MAT	MAR	LUK 16:19–31
		19 "There was a rich man who was dressed in purple and fine linen and who feasted sumptuously every day. 20 And at his gate lay a poor man named Lazarus, covered with sores, 21 who longed to satisfy his hunger with what fell from the rich man's table; even the dogs would come and lick his sores. 22 The poor man died and was carried away by the angels to be with Abraham. The rich man also died and was buried. 23 In Hades, where he was being tormented, he looked up and saw Abra- ham far away with Lazarus by his side. 24 He called out, 'Father Abraham, have mercy on me, and send Lazarus to dip the tip of his finger in water and cool my tongue; for I am in agony in these flames.' 25 But Abraham said, 'Child, remem- ber that during your lifetime you received your good things, and Lazarus in like

[1] *Cf.* MAT 19:9 = MAR 10:11–12 (§ 187, p. 143).

✦ [B] Or, *has been coming violently.*

manner evil things; but now he is comforted here, and you are in agony.
26 Besides all this, between you and us a great chasm has been fixed, so that those
who might want to pass from here to you cannot do so, and no one can cross from
there to us.' 27 He said, 'Then, father, I beg you to send him to my father's house
—28 for I have five brothers—that he may warn them, so that they will not also
come into this place of torment.' 29 Abraham replied, 'They have Moses and the
prophets; they should listen to them.' 30 He said, 'No, father Abraham; but if
someone goes to them from the dead, they will repent.' 31 He said to him, 'If they
do not listen to Moses and the prophets, neither will they be convinced even if
someone rises from the dead.' "

§ 178 ON CAUSING SIN

Δ *MAT 18:6–7* *(§ 131, p. 107)*	Δ *MAR 9:42* *(§ 131, p. 107)*	**LUK 17:1–2**
		1 Jesus said to his disciples,
6 *"If any of you put a stumbling block before one of these little ones who believe in me, it would be better for you if a great millstone were fastened around your neck and you were drowned in the depth of the sea.* 7 *Woe to the world because of stumbling blocks! Occasions for stumbling are bound to come, but woe to the one by whom the stumbling block comes!"*	42 *"If any of you put a stumbling block before one of these little ones who believe in me, it would be better for you if a great millstone were hung around your neck and you were thrown into the sea."*	"Occasions for stumbling are bound to come, but woe to anyone by whom they come! 2 It would be better for you if a millstone were hung around your neck and you were thrown into the sea than for you to cause one of these little ones to stumble."

§ 179 ON FORGIVENESS

Δ *MAT 18:15* *(§ 134, p. 109) +*	**MAR**	**LUK 17:3–4**
15 *"If another member of the church sins against you, go and point out the fault when the two of you are alone. If the member listens to you, you have regained that one."*		3 "Be on your guard! If another disciple sins, you must rebuke the offender, and if there is repentance, you must forgive.
Δ *18:21–22 (§ 135, p. 110)* 21 *Then Peter came and said to him, "Lord, if another member of the church sins against me, how often should I forgive? As many as seven times?"* 22 *Jesus said to him, "Not*		4 And if the same person sins against you seven times a day, and

seven times, but, I tell you, seventy-seven times." [C]		turns back to you seven times and says, 'I re- pent,' you must forgive."

§ 180 ON FAITH

Δ *MAT 17:20* (*§ 126, p. 103*)	MAR	LUK 17:5–6
20 *He said to them, "Because of your little faith.* *For truly I tell you, if you have faith the size of* *a mustard seed, you will say to this mountain,* *'Move from here to there,' and* *it will move; and nothing will be impossible* *for you."* [1]		5 The apostles said to the Lord, "Increase our faith!" 6 The Lord replied, "If you had faith the size of a mustard seed, you could say to this mulberry tree, 'Be uprooted and planted in the sea,' and it would obey you." [1]

§ 181 THE SLAVE'S WAGES

MAT	MAR	LUK 17:7–10
		7 "Who among you would say to your slave who has just come in from plowing or tending sheep in the field, 'Come here at once and take your place at the table'? 8 Would you not rather say to him, 'Prepare supper for me, put on your apron and serve me while I eat and drink; later you may eat and drink'? 9 Do you thank the slave for doing what was commanded? 10 So you also, when you have done all that you were ordered to do, say, 'We are worthless slaves; we have done only what we ought to have done!' "

§ 182 THE HEALING OF TEN LEPERS

MAT	MAR	LUK 17:11–19
		11 On the way to Jerusalem Jesus was going through the region between Samaria and Galilee. 12 As he entered a village, ten lepers approached him. Keeping their distance, 13 they called out, saying, "Jesus, Master, have mercy on us!" 14 When he saw them, he said to them, "Go and show yourselves to the priests."

[1] MAT 21:21b (§ 201, p. 156): "Truly I tell you, if you have faith and do not doubt, not only will you do what has been done to the fig tree, but even if you say to this mountain, 'Be lifted up and thrown into the sea,' it will be done."	MAR 11:22–23b (§ 201, p. 156): 22 "Have faith in God. 23 Truly I tell you, if you say to this mountain, 'Be taken up and thrown into the sea,' and if you do not doubt in your heart, but believe that what you say will come to pass, it will be done for you."

✦ [C] Or, *seventy times seven.*

And as they went, they were made clean. 15 Then one of them, when he saw that
he was healed, turned back, praising God with a loud voice. 16 He prostrated
himself at Jesus' feet and thanked him. And he was a Samaritan. 17 Then Jesus
asked, "Were not ten made clean? But the other nine, where are they? 18 Was
none of them found to return and give praise to God except this foreigner?" 19 Then
he said to him, "Get up and go on your way; your faith has made you well."

§ 183 ON THE KINGDOM OF GOD

MAT	MAR	LUK 17:20–21
		20 Once Jesus was asked by the Pharisees when the kingdom of God was coming, and he answered, "The kingdom of God is not coming with things that can be observed; 21 nor will they say, 'Look, here it is!' or 'There it is!' For, in fact, the kingdom of God is among you."[D+1]

§ 184 THE DAY OF THE SON OF MAN

Δ *MAT 24:26–28* (§ 218, p. 173) +

26 "So, if they say to you, 'Look! He is in the wilderness,' do not go out. If they say, 'Look! He is in the inner rooms,' do not believe it. 27 For as the lightning comes from the east and flashes as far as the west, so will be the coming of the Son of Man."

Δ *24:37–39* (§ 224, p. 176)

37 "For as the days of Noah were, so will be the coming of the Son of

MAR

LUK 17:22–37

22 Then he said to the disciples, "The days are
coming when you will long to see one of the
days of the Son of Man, and you will not see it.
23 They will say to you, 'Look there!' or
'Look here!' Do not go, do not set off in
pursuit.
24 For as the lightning flashes and lights up the
sky from one side to the other, so will
the Son of Man be in his day.[E] 25 But first he
must endure much suffering and be rejected by
this generation. 26 Just as it was in the days of
Noah, so too it will be in the days of the Son of

---

[1] MAT 24:23 (§ 217, p. 173): "Then if anyone says to you, 'Look! Here is the Messiah!' or 'There he is!' — do not believe it."

MAR 13:21 (§ 217, p. 173): "And if anyone says to you at that time, 'Look! Here is the Messiah!' or 'Look! There he is!' — do not believe it."

✧ LUK 17:26–27 = MAT 24:38 — GEN 7:7

✦ [D] Or, *within you.* ✦ [E] text: S A W Θ λ ø ℜ it (some MSS.) vg sy[c] sy[s] sy[p] bo; omit: *in his day*: P[75] B D it (some MSS.) sa.

◗ To LUK 17:21 *cf. Oxyrhynchus Papyrus 654, Logion 2.* — "and the kingdom of heaven is in the midst of you, and all who know themselves will find it" ◗ To LUK 17:21 *cf.* **Gospel of Thomas, Logia 3 and 113.** — 3 Jesus said, "If those who lead you say to you, 'Look! the kingdom is in heaven,' then the birds of heaven will precede you. If they say to you, 'It is in the sea,' then the fish will precede you. But the kingdom is within you and it is outside of you. If you will know yourselves, then you will be known, and you will realize that you are the children of the living Father. But if you do not know yourselves, then you dwell in poverty and you are poverty." 113 Jesus' disciples said to him, "When will the kingdom come?" Jesus answered, "It will not come by waiting for it. People will not say, 'Look! Here it is!' or 'There it is!' But the kingdom of the Father is spread out upon the earth and people do not see it."

Man. 38 *For as in those days before the flood*
they were eating and drinking, marrying
and giving in marriage, until the day Noah
entered the ark, 39 *and they knew nothing until*
the flood came and swept them all away,

so too will be the coming of the Son of Man."

Δ *10:39 (§ 62, p. 53)*
39 *"Those who find their life will*
lose it, and those who lose their life for my sake
will find it."
Δ *24:40–41 (§ 224, p. 176)*
40 *"Then*
two will be in the field; one will be taken and
one will be left. 41 *Two women*
will be grinding meal together; one will be
taken and one will be left."

24:28 *"Wherever the corpse is, there the vultures*
will gather."

Man.
27 They were eating and drinking, and marrying
and being given in marriage, until the day Noah
entered the ark, and
the flood came and destroyed all of them.
28 Likewise, just as it was in the days of Lot:
they were eating and drinking, buying and selling, planting and building, 29 but on the day
that Lot left Sodom, it rained fire and sulfur
from heaven and destroyed all of them 30 —it
will be like that on the day that the Son of Man
is revealed. 31 On that day, anyone on the
housetop who has belongings in the house must
not come down to take them away; and likewise anyone in the field must not turn back.[1]
32 Remember Lot's wife.
33 Those who try to make their life secure will
lose it, but those who lose their life
will keep it.[2]

34 I tell you, on that night there will be
two in one bed; one will be taken and
the other left. 35 There will be two women
grinding meal together; one will be
taken and the other left."[F] [36] 37 Then they
asked him, "Where, Lord?" He said to them,
"Where the corpse is, there the vultures
will gather."

§ 185 THE PARABLE OF THE WIDOW AND THE UNJUST JUDGE

MAT	MAR	LUK 18:1–8
		1 Then Jesus told them a parable about their need to pray always and not to lose heart. 2 He said, "In a certain city there was a judge who neither feared God nor

[1] MAT 24:17–18 (§ 216, p. 172): 17 "the one on the housetop must not go down to take what is in the house; 18 the one in the field must not turn back to get a coat."	MAR 13:15–16 (§ 216, p. 172): 15 "the one on the housetop must not go down or enter the house to take anything away; 16 the one in the field must not turn back to get a coat."	
[2] MAT 16:25 (§ 123, p. 100): "For those who want to save their life will lose it, and those who lose their life for my sake will find it."	MAR 8:35 (§ 123, p. 100): "For those who want to save their life will lose it, and those who lose their life for my sake, and for the sake of the gospel, will save it."	LUK 9:24 (§ 123, p. 100): "For those who want to save their life will lose it, and those who lose their life for my sake will save it."

✦ [F] text: P^{75} S A B W Θ λ 𝔐 sa bo; add verse 36: *Two men will be in the field; one will be taken and the other left*: D ø it vg sy^c sy^s sy^p.

◗ To LUK 17:32–33 *cf.* Clement of Alexandria, *Excerpts from Theodotus 2:2.* — Because of this the Savior said, "Be saved, you and your soul."

had respect for people. 3 In that city there was a widow who kept coming to him
and saying, 'Grant me justice against my opponent.' 4 For a while he refused; but
later he said to himself, 'Though I have no fear of God and no respect for anyone,
5 yet because this widow keeps bothering me, I will grant her justice, so that she
may not wear me out by continually coming.' " 6 And the Lord said, "Listen to
what the unjust judge says. 7 And will not God grant justice to his chosen ones
who cry to him day and night? Will he delay long in helping them? 8 I tell you,
he will quickly grant justice to them. And yet, when the Son of Man comes, will
he find faith on earth?"

§ 186 THE PARABLE OF THE PHARISEE AND THE TAX COLLECTOR

MAT	MAR	LUK 18:9–14

9 He also told this parable to some who trusted in themselves that they were
righteous and regarded others with contempt: 10 "Two men went up to the temple
to pray, one a Pharisee and the other a tax collector. 11 The Pharisee, standing by
himself, was praying thus, 'God, I thank you that I am not like other people:
thieves, rogues, adulterers, or even like this tax collector. 12 I fast twice a week;
I give a tenth of all my income.' 13 But the tax collector, standing far off, would
not even look up to heaven, but was beating his breast and saying, 'God, be
merciful to me, a sinner!' 14 I tell you, this man went down to his home justified
rather than the other; for all who exalt themselves will be humbled, but all who
humble themselves will be exalted."[1]

▲ *Cf.* 18:15–17 (§ 188, p. 144)

---

[1] *Cf.* MAT 18:4 (§ 129, p. 106); MAT 23:12 (§ 210, p. 165); and LUK 14:11 (§ 169, p. 132).

THE JUDEAN SECTION

Matthew 19—27; Mark 10—15; Luke 18:15—23:26

The Journey to Jerusalem

Matthew 19—20; Mark 10; Luke 18:15—19:27

§ 187 MARRIAGE AND DIVORCE

MAT 19:1–12

▲ 18:23–35 (§ 136, p. 110)

1 When Jesus had finished saying these things,
he left Galilee and went to the region of
Judea beyond the Jordan. 2 Large crowds
followed him, and
he cured them there.
3 Some Pharisees came to him, and to test him
they asked, "Is it lawful for a man to divorce
his wife for any cause?"

Cf. 19:7–8

4 He answered, "Have you not read
that the one who made them at the beginning
'made them male and female,' 5 and said, 'For
this reason a man shall leave his father and
mother and be joined to his wife, and the two
shall become one flesh'? 6 So they are no
longer two, but one flesh. Therefore what
God has joined together, let no one separate."
7 They said to him, "Why then did Moses command us to give a certificate of dismissal and to
divorce her?" 8 He said to them, "It was because you were so hard-hearted that Moses
allowed you to divorce your wives, but from
the beginning it was not so.

MAR 10:1–12

▲ 9:49–50 (§ 132, p. 108)

1 He left that place and went to the region of
Judea and beyond the Jordan. And crowds
again gathered around him; and,
as was his custom, he again taught them.
2 Some Pharisees came, and to test him
they asked, "Is it lawful for a man to divorce
his wife?" 3 He answered them,
"What did Moses command you?" 4 They
said, "Moses allowed a man to write a certificate of dismissal and to divorce her." 5 But
Jesus said to them, "Because of your hardness
of heart he wrote this commandment for you.

6 But from the beginning of creation, 'God
made them male and female.' 7 'For
this reason a man shall leave his father and
mother and be joined to his wife,[G] 8 and the two
shall become one flesh.' So they are no
longer two, but one flesh. 9 Therefore what
God has joined together, let no one separate."

Cf. 10:3–5

10 Then in the house the disciples asked him
again about this matter.

LUK

✧ MAT 19:4 = MAR 10:6 — GEN 1:27. ✧ MAT 19:5 = MAR 10:7–8 — GEN 2:24. ✧ MAT 19:7 = MAR 10:4 — DEU 24:1.

✦ [G] text: A C D W Θ λ φ 𝔐 it vg sy^{p} sa bo; omit: *and be joined to his wife*: S B sy^{s}.

● To MAT 19:4 = MAR 10:6 *cf.* 1CO 7:10–11. — 10 To the married I give this command — not I but the Lord — that the wife should not separate from her husband 11 (but if she does separate, let her remain unmarried or else be reconciled to her husband), and that the husband should not divorce his wife.

MAT 19:9–12

9 And I say to you, whoever divorces his wife,
except for unchastity,[H] and marries another
commits adultery."[I+1]

10 His disciples said to him, "If such is the case
of a man with his wife, it is better not to marry."
11 But he said to them, "Not everyone can accept this teaching, but only those to whom it is
given. 12 For there are eunuchs who have been
so from birth, and there are eunuchs who have
been made eunuchs by others, and there are
eunuchs who have made themselves eunuchs
for the sake of the kingdom of heaven. Let
anyone accept this who can."

MAR 10:11–12

11 He said to them, "Whoever divorces his wife
and marries another
commits adultery against her; 12 and if she divorces her husband and marries another, she
commits adultery."[I]

§ 188 JESUS BLESSES THE CHILDREN

MAT 19:13–15 +

13 Then little children were being
brought to him in order that he
might lay his hands on them and
pray. The disciples spoke sternly
to those who brought them; 14 but
Jesus
said, "Let the little

MAR 10:13–16

13 People were bringing little children to him in order that he
might touch them; and
the disciples spoke sternly
to them. 14 But
when Jesus saw this, he was indignant and said to them, "Let the little

LUK 18:15–17

▲ 18:9–14 (§ 186, p. 142)

15 People were bringing even infants
to him that he
might touch them; and when
the disciples saw it, they sternly
ordered them not to do it. 16 But
Jesus called for them and
said, "Let the little

---

[1] MAT 5:32 (§ 24, p. 28): "But I say to you that anyone who divorces his wife, except on the ground of unchastity, causes her to commit adultery; and whoever marries a divorced woman commits adultery."

LUK 16:18 (§ 176, p. 137): "Anyone who divorces his wife and marries another commits adultery, and whoever marries a woman divorced from her husband commits adultery."

✦ [H] text: S W Θ ℜ vg sy^{s} sy^{p}; *except on the ground of unchastity, and marries another, commits adultery* (*against her:* sy^{c}): D ø it sy^{c} sa; *except on the ground of unchastity, makes her commit adultery*: P$^{25?}$ B λ bo; *except for unchastity, and marries another, makes her commit adultery*: C. ✦ [I] text: S D it (some MSS.) sy^{c} sy^{s} sa; add: *And whoever marries a divorced woman commits adultery*: P^{25} B C W Θ λ ø ℜ it (some MSS.) vg sy^{p} bo. C*f*. MAT 5:32.

◗ To MAT 19:12 c*f*. **Gospel of the Egyptians.** (As quoted by Clement of Alexandria in his *Miscellanies*) — [A] The Lord said to Salome when she inquired, "How long shall death prevail?", "As long as you women bear children." *Miscellanies III.6:45, 3.* — [B] Salome said, "How long will people continue to die?" The Lord answered, "So long as women bear children." *Ibid. III.9:64, 1.* [C] on MAT 5:17: "I came to destroy the works of the female." *Ibid. III.9:63, 2.* [D] When she said, "I have done well, then, in not bearing children," the Lord answered, "Eat every plant, but do not eat the bitter ones." *Ibid. III.9:66, 2.* [E] When Salome inquired when the things concerning which she asked should be known, the Lord said, "When you have trampled on the garment of shame, and when the two become one, and the male with the female neither male nor female." *Ibid. III.13:92, 2.* C*f*. **II Clement 12:2, 5.** ◗ To MAT 19:12 c*f*. **Gospel of Thomas, Logion 22.** — Jesus saw the children who were being suckled, and said to the disciples, "These children who are being suckled are like those who enter the kingdom." The disciples said to Jesus, "Shall we then, being children, enter the kingdom?" Jesus answered, "When you make the two one, and when you make the inner as the outer and the outer as the inner and the above as the below, and when you make the male and the female into a single one, so that the male will not be male and the female will not be female, when you make eyes in the place of an eye, and a hand in the place of a hand, and a foot in the place of a foot, and an image in the place of an image, then you will enter the kingdom."

children come to me, and do not stop them; for it is to such as these that the kingdom of heaven belongs."	children come to me; do not stop them; for it is to such as these that the kingdom of God belongs.	children come to me, and do not stop them; for it is to such as these that the kingdom of God belongs.
Δ *18:3 (§ 129, p. 106)* 3 *"Truly I tell you, unless you change and become like children, you will never enter the kingdom of heaven."* 19:15 And he laid his hands on them and went on his way.	15 Truly I tell you, whoever does not receive the kingdom of God as a little child will never enter it." 16 And he took them up in his arms, laid his hands on them, and blessed them.	17 Truly I tell you, whoever does not receive the kingdom of God as a little child will never enter it."

§ 189 THE RICH YOUNG MAN

MAT 19:16–30	MAR 10:17–31	LUK 18:18–30 +
	17 As he was setting out on a journey,	
16 Then someone came to him and said, "Teacher, what good deed must I do to have eternal life?" 17 And he said to him, "Why do you ask me about what is good? There is only one who is good. If you wish to enter into life, keep the commandments." 18 He said to him, "Which ones?" And Jesus said,	a man ran up and knelt before him, and asked him, "Good Teacher, what must I do to inherit eternal life?" 18 Jesus said to him, "Why do you call me good? No one is good but God alone. 19 You know the commandments:	18 A certain ruler asked him, "Good Teacher, what must I do to inherit eternal life?" 19 Jesus said to him, "Why do you call me good? No one is good but God alone. 20 You know the commandments:
"You shall not murder;	'You shall not murder;	
You shall not commit adultery;	You shall not commit adultery;	'You shall not commit adultery;
		You shall not murder;
You shall not steal;	You shall not steal;	You shall not steal;
You shall not bear false witness;	You shall not bear false witness;	You shall not bear false witness;
	You shall not defraud;	
19 Honor your father and mother; also, You shall love your neighbor as yourself."	Honor your father and mother.' "	Honor your father and mother.' "
20 The young man said to him, "I have kept	20 He said to him, "Teacher, I have kept	21 He replied, "I have kept

◇ MAT 19:18–19a = MAR 10:19 — EXO 20:12–16; DEU 5:16–20. ◇ MAT 19:19b — LEV 19:18.

● To MAR 10:15 and parallels, *cf.* JOH 3:3, 5.

◗ To MAT 19:16–24 *cf.* **Gospel of the Nazaraeans** (in Origen, *Commentary on Matthew 15:14* in the Latin version). —The second of the rich people said to Jesus, "Teacher, what good thing can I do and live?" Jesus answered, "Fulfill the law and the prophets." The person answered, "I have." Jesus said, "Go, sell all that you have and distribute to the poor; and come, follow me." But the rich man began to scratch his head, for it did not please him. And the Lord said to him. "How can you say, I have fulfilled the law and the prophets, when it is written in the law: You shall love your neighbor as yourself; and look, many of your neighbors, children of Abraham and Sarah, are covered with filth, dying of hunger, and your house is full of many good things, none of which is given to them?" And Jesus turned and said to Simon, the disciple, who was sitting nearby, "Simon, son of Jonah, it is easier for a camel to go through the eye of a needle than for a rich person to enter the kingdom of heaven." ◗ To MAR 10:18; LUK 18:19 *cf.* **Gospel of the Naassenes** (in Hippolytus, *Refutation of All Heresies*, V.7:26)—"Why do you call me good? One there is who is good—my Father who is in heaven—who makes his sun to rise on the just and on the unjust, and sends rain on the pure and on sinners." *Cf.* MAT 5:45.

all these; what do I still lack?"
21 Jesus
said to him, "If you wish to be perfect, go, sell your possessions, and give the money to the
poor, and you will have treasure in heaven; then come, follow me."
22 When the young man heard this word, he went away
grieving, for he
had many possessions.
23 Then Jesus
said to his disciples, "Truly I tell you, it will be hard for a rich
person to enter the kingdom of heaven.
24 Again I tell you,
it is easier for a camel to go through the eye of a needle than for someone who is rich to enter the kingdom of God."
25 When the disciples heard this, they were greatly astounded and said, "Then who
can be saved?"
26 But Jesus
looked at them and said,
"For mortals it is impossible,
but for God all things
are possible."
27 Then Peter said in reply, "Look, we have left everything and followed you. What then will we have?"
28 Jesus said to them, "Truly I tell you, at the renewal of all things, when the Son of Man is seated on the throne of his glory, you who have followed me
will also sit on twelve thrones, judging the twelve tribes of Israel.
29 And everyone who has left houses or brothers or sisters or father or mother or children or

all these since my youth."
21 Jesus, looking at him, loved him and said, "You lack one thing;
go, sell what you own,
and give the money to the
poor, and you will have treasure in heaven; then come, follow me."
22 When he heard this,
he was shocked and went away
grieving, for he
had many possessions.
23 Then Jesus looked around and said to his disciples, "How
hard it will be for those who have wealth to enter the kingdom of
God!"
24 And the disciples were perplexed at these words. But Jesus said to them again, "Children, how hard it is[J] to enter the kingdom
of God!
25 It is easier for a camel to go through the eye of a needle than for someone who is rich to enter the kingdom of God."
26 They were greatly astounded and said to one another,[K] "Then who
can be saved?"
27 Jesus
looked at them and said,
"For mortals it is impossible,
but not for God; for God all things
are possible."
28 Peter began to say to him, "Look, we have left everything and followed you."
29 Jesus said,
"Truly I tell you,
there is no one who has left house or brothers or sisters or mother or father or children or

all these since my youth."
22 When Jesus heard this, he
said to him, "There is still one thing lacking. Sell all that you own
and distribute the money to the
poor, and you will have treasure in heaven; then come, follow me."
23 But when he heard this,
he became sad;
for he
was very rich.
24 Jesus looked at him and
said, "How
hard it is for those who have wealth to enter the kingdom of
God!
25 Indeed, it is easier for a camel to go through the eye of a needle than for someone who is rich to enter the kingdom of God."
26 Those who heard it
said, "Then who
can be saved?"
27 He
replied,
"What is impossible for mortals
is possible for God."
28 Then Peter said,
"Look, we have left our homes and followed you."
29 And he said to them,
"Truly I tell you,

Δ *22:28–30 (§ 237, p. 186)*
28 "You are those who have stood by me in my trials;
29 and I confer on you, just as my Father has conferred on me, a kingdom,
30 so that you may eat and drink at my table in my kingdom, and you will sit on thrones judging the twelve tribes of Israel."

18:29b there is no one who has left house or wife or brothers or parents or children,

✦ [J] text: S B sa; add: *for those who trust in riches*: A C D Θ λ ø 𝔐 it vg sy^s sy^p bo; add: *for a rich person*: W. ✦ [K] text: A D W Θ λ ø 𝔐 it vg sy^c sy^s sy^p; *to him*: S B C sa bo.

fields, for my name's sake,	fields, for my sake and for the sake of the good news,	for the sake of the kingdom of God,
will receive a hundredfold,[L]	30 who will not receive a hundredfold now in this age— houses, brothers and sisters, mothers and children, and fields with persecutions—and in the	30 who will not get back very much more in this age, and in the
and will inherit eternal life.	age to come eternal life.	age to come eternal life."
Cf. 20:16 (§ 190, p. 147)		Δ *13:30 (§ 165, p. 130)*
30 But many who are first will be last, and the last will be first."	31 But many who are first will be last, and the last will be first."	*30 Indeed, some are last who will be first, and some are first who will be last."*

§ 190 THE PARABLE OF THE LABORERS IN THE VINEYARD

MAT 20:1–16	MAR	LUK

1 "For the kingdom of heaven is like a landowner who went out early in the morning
to hire laborers for his vineyard. 2 After agreeing with the laborers for the usual
daily wage,[M] he sent them into his vineyard. 3 When he went out about nine
o'clock, he saw others standing idle in the marketplace; 4 and he said to them,
'You also go into the vineyard, and I will pay you whatever is right.' So they
went. 5 When he went out again about noon and about three o'clock, he did the
same. 6 And about five o'clock he went out and found others standing around;
and he said to them, 'Why are you standing here idle all day?' 7 They said to him,
'Because no one has hired us.' He said to them, 'You also go into the vineyard.'
8 When evening came, the owner of the vineyard said to his manager, 'Call the
laborers and give them their pay, beginning with the last and then going to the first.'
9 When those hired about five o'clock came, each of them received the usual daily
wage. 10 Now when the first came, they thought they would receive more; but
each of them also received the usual daily wage. 11 And when they received it,
they grumbled against the landowner, 12 saying, 'These last worked only one hour,
and you have made them equal to us who have borne the burden of the day and the
scorching heat.' 13 But he replied to one of them, 'Friend, I am doing you no
wrong; did you not agree with me for the usual daily wage? 14 Take what belongs
to you and go; I choose to give to this last the same as I give to you. 15 Am I not
allowed to do what I choose with what belongs to me? Or are you envious because
I am generous?'[N] 16 So the last will be first, and the first will be last."

Cf. 19:30 (§ 189, p. 145)

✦ [L] text: S C D W Θ λ φ 𝔐 it vg sy[c] sy[s] sy[p] bo; *manifold*: B sa. ✦ [M] Greek: *a denarius.* ✦ [N] Or: *is your eye evil because I am good?*

◗ To MAT 19:30 and parallels, *cf.* *Oxyrhynchus Papyrus 654, Logion 3.* — "for many that are first will be last, and the last first, and few will find it." ◗ To MAT 19:30 and parallels, *cf.* **Barnabas 6:13.** — The Lord said, "See, I make the last things like the first."

§ 191 THE THIRD PREDICTION OF THE PASSION

MAT 20:17–19	MAR 10:32–34	LUK 18:31–34
17 While Jesus was going up to Jerusalem,	32 They were on the road, going up to Jerusalem, and Jesus was walking ahead of them; they were amazed, and those who followed were afraid.	
he took the twelve disciples aside by themselves, and said to them on the way,	He took the twelve aside again and began to tell them what was to happen to him,	31 Then he took the twelve aside and said to them,
18 “See, we are going up to Jerusalem,	33 saying, “See, we are going up to Jerusalem,	“See, we are going up to Jerusalem, and everything that is written about the Son of Man by the prophets will be accomplished.
and the Son of Man will be handed over to the chief priests and scribes, and they will condemn him to death;	and the Son of Man will be handed over to the chief priests and the scribes, and they will condemn him to death;	
19 then they will hand him over to the Gentiles	then they will hand him over to the Gentiles;	32 For he will be handed over to the Gentiles;
to be mocked	34 they will mock him, and spit upon him,	and he will be mocked and insulted and spat upon.
and flogged	and flog him,	33 After they have flogged him,
and crucified; and on the third day he will be raised.”	and kill him; and after three days he will rise again.”	they will kill him, and on the third day he will rise again.” 34 But they understood nothing about all these things; in fact, what he said was hidden from them, and they did not grasp what was said.

§ 192 JESUS AND THE SONS OF ZEBEDEE

MAT 20:20–28	MAR 10:35–45	Δ *LUK 22:24–27* (*§ 237b, p. 185*)
20 Then the mother of the sons of Zebedee came to him with her sons, and kneeling before him, she asked a favor of him.	35 James and John, the sons of Zebedee, came forward to him and said to him, “Teacher, we want you to do for us whatever we ask of you.”	
21 And he said to her, “What do you want?”	36 And he said to them, “What is it you want me to do for you?”	
She said to him, “Declare that these two sons of mine will sit, one at your right hand and one at your left, in your kingdom.”	37 And they said to him, “Grant us to sit, one at your right hand and one at your left, in your glory.”	
22 But Jesus answered, “You do not know what you are	38 But Jesus said to them, “You do not know what you are	

▸ To MAT 20:22 *cf.* **Gospel of the Naassenes** (in Hippolytus, *Refutation of All Heresies, V.8:11*). — “But” Jesus says, “even if you drink the cup which I drink, you will not be able to enter where I go.”

asking. Are you able to drink the
cup that I am about to drink?"
They said to him, "We are
able." 23 He said to them,
"You will indeed drink my cup,
but to sit at my right hand and at my
left, this is not mine to grant, but it
is for those for whom it has been
prepared by my Father." 24 When
the ten heard it, they were
angry with the two brothers. 25 But
Jesus called them to him and said,
"You know that the rulers of the
Gentiles
lord it over them,
and their great ones are tyrants over
them.
26 It will not be so among you; but
whoever wishes to be great
among you must
be your servant,
27 and whoever wishes to be first
among you must be your slave;[1]
28 just as the Son of Man came not
to be served but to serve, and to
give his life a ransom for many."

asking. Are you able to drink the
cup that I drink, or be baptized with
the baptism that I am baptized
with?" 39 They replied, "We are
able." Then Jesus said to them,
"The cup that I drink you will drink;
and with the baptism with which I
am baptized, you will be baptized;
40 but to sit at my right hand or at my
left is not mine to grant, but it
is for those for whom it has been
prepared." 41 When
the ten heard this, they began to be
angry with James and John. 42 So
Jesus called them and said to them,
"You know that among the
Gentiles those whom they recog-
nize as their rulers lord it over them,
and their great ones are tyrants over
them.
43 But it is not so among you; but
whoever wishes to become great
among you must
be your servant,
44 and whoever wishes to be first
among you must be slave of all.[1]
45 For the Son of Man came not
to be served but to serve, and to
give his life a ransom for many."

Cf. 12:50 (§ 160, p. 127)

24 A dispute also arose among them
as to which one of them was to be
regarded as the greatest.
25 But
he said to them,
"The kings of the
Gentiles
lord it over them;
and those in authority over
them are called benefactors.
26 But not so with you; rather
the greatest
among you must
become like the youngest,
and the leader
like one who serves.[1]
27 For who is greater, the one who
is at the table or the one who
serves? Is it not the one at the
table? But I am among you as one
who serves."

§ 193 THE HEALING OF BARTIMAEUS

MAT 20:29–34

Cf. 9:27–31 (§ 56, p. 46)
29 As they were
leaving Jericho, a large crowd followed him. 30 There were
two blind men sitting by the

MAR 10:46–52

46 They came to Jericho. As he and
his disciples and
a large crowd were leaving Jericho,
Bartimaeus son of Timaeus,
a blind beggar, was sitting by the

LUK 18:35–43

35 As he approached Jericho,
a blind man was sitting by the

---

[1] *Cf.* MAR 9:35 = LUK 9:48b (§ 129, p. 106) and MAT 23:11 (§ 210, p. 165).

MAT 20:31–34	MAR 10:47–52	LUK 18:36–43
roadside. When they	roadside. 47 When he	roadside begging. 36 When he heard a crowd going by, he asked what was happening. 37 They told
heard that Jesus was passing by, they shouted,[O] "Lord, have mercy on us, Son of David!"	heard that it was Jesus of Nazareth, he began to shout out and say, "Jesus, Son of David, have mercy	him, "Jesus of Nazareth is passing by." 38 Then he shouted, "Jesus, Son of David, have mercy
31 The crowd sternly ordered them to be quiet; but they shouted even more loudly,	on me!" 48 Many sternly ordered him to be quiet, but he cried out even more loudly, "Son of David,	on me!" 39 Those who were in front sternly ordered him to be quiet; but he shouted even more loudly, "Son of David,
"Have mercy on us, Lord, Son of David!" 32 Jesus stood still and called them, saying,	have mercy on me!" 49 Jesus stood still and said, "Call him here."	have mercy on me!" 40 Jesus stood still and ordered the man to be brought to him;
	And they called the blind man, saying to him, "Take heart; get up, he is calling you." 50 So throwing off his cloak, he sprang up and came to Jesus. 51 Then Jesus said to him,	and when he came near, he asked him,
"What do you want me to do for you?" 33 They said to him, "Lord, let our eyes be opened."	"What do you want me to do for you?" The blind man said to him, "My teacher,[P] let me see again."	41 "What do you want me to do for you?" He said, "Lord, let me see again."
34 Moved with compassion, Jesus touched their eyes.	52 Jesus said to him, "Go; your faith has made you well."	42 Jesus said to him, "Receive your sight; your faith has saved you."
Immediately they regained their sight and followed him.	Immediately he regained his sight and followed him on the way.	43 Immediately he regained his sight and followed him, glorifying God; and all the people, when they saw it, praised God.
▼ 21:1–9 (§ 196, p. 153)	▼ 11:1–10 (§ 196, p. 153)	

§ 194 ZACCHAEUS

MAT	MAR	LUK 19:1–10
		1 He entered Jericho and was passing through it. 2 A man was there named Zacchaeus; he was a chief tax collector and was rich. 3 He was trying to see who Jesus was, but on account of the crowd he could not, because he was short in stature. 4 So he ran ahead and climbed a sycamore tree to see him, because he was going to pass that way. 5 When Jesus came to the place, he looked up and said to him, "Zacchaeus, hurry and come down; for I must stay at your house today." 6 So he hurried down and was happy to welcome him. 7 All who saw it began to grumble and said, "He has gone to be the guest of one who is a sinner." 8 Zacchaeus stood there and said to the Lord, "Look, half of my possessions, Lord, I will give to the poor; and if I have defrauded anyone of anything, I will pay back four times as much." 9 Then Jesus said to him, "Today salvation has come to this house, because he too is a son of Abraham. 10 For the Son of Man came to seek out and to save the lost."

✧ LUK 19:10 — EZE 34:16.

✦ [O] text: P[45?] B C W λ 𝔑 it (some MSS.) vg sy[p] sa; *Have mercy on us:* D it (some MSS.) sy[c]; *Have mercy on us, Jesus* (*Cf.* MAR 10:47; LUK 18:38.): S Θ ø it (some MSS.); *Lord, have mercy on us, Jesus:* bo. ✦ [P] Or, *Rabbi.*

§ 195 THE PARABLE OF THE POUNDS

Δ MAT 25:14–30 (§ 228, p. 178)

14 "For it is as if a man, going on a journey,

summoned his slaves and entrusted his
property to them; 15 to one he gave five talents,[Q]
to another two, to another one, to each ac-
cording to his ability. Then he went away.
16 The one who had received the five talents went
off at once and traded with them, and made five
more talents. 17 In the same way, the one who
had the two talents made two more talents. 18
But the one who had received the one talent
went off and dug a hole in the ground and hid
his master's money.

19 After a long time the master of those slaves
came

and settled accounts with them.
20 Then the one who had received the five talents
came forward, bringing five more talents, say-
ing, 'Master, you handed over to me five
talents; see, I have made five more talents.'
21 His master said to him, 'Well done, good
and trustworthy slave; you have been
trustworthy in a few things,
I will put you in charge of many things; enter
into the joy of your master.'
22 And the one with the two talents also came
forward, saying, 'Master, you handed over to
me two talents; see, I have made two more
talents.' 23 His master said to him, 'Well
done, good and trustworthy slave; you have
been trustworthy in a few things,
I will put you in charge of many things; enter
into the joy of your master.' 24 Then the one
who had received the one talent also came
forward, saying, 'Master, I knew that you
were a harsh man, reaping where you did not
sow, and gathering where you did not scatter

MAR

LUK 19:11–27

11 As they were listening to this, he went on to
tell a parable, because he was near Jerusalem,
and because they supposed that the kingdom of
God was to appear immediately. 12 So he said,
"A nobleman went to a distant country to get
royal power for himself and then return. 13 He
summoned ten of his slaves, and gave them
ten pounds,[R] and said to them,

'Do business with these until I come back.'

14 But the citizens of his country hated him and
sent a delegation after him, saying, 'We do not
want this man to rule over us.'
15 When he
returned, having received royal power, he ordered these slaves, to whom he had given the
money, to be summoned so that he might find
out what they had gained by trading. 16 The
first came forward and said,
'Lord,
your pound has made ten more pounds.'
17 He said to him, 'Well done, good
slave! Because you have been
trustworthy in a very small thing,
take charge of ten cities.'

18 Then the second came,
saying, 'Lord,
your pound has made five
pounds.' 19 He said to him,

'And you, rule over five cities.'
20 Then the other
came,
saying, 'Lord,

✦ [Q] This talent was worth a great deal of money. ✦ [R] The mina, rendered here by *pound*, was about three months' wages for a laborer.

seed; 25 *so I was afraid, and I went and hid*
your talent in the ground.
Here you have what is yours.'

26 *But his master replied,*
'You wicked and lazy slave! You knew, did
you,
that I reap where
I did not sow, and gather where I did not
scatter? 27 *Then you ought to have invested my*
money with the bankers, and on my return
I would have received what was my own with
interest. 28 *So take*
the talent from him, and give it to the one
with the ten talents.
29 *For to all*
those who have, more will be given, and they
will have an abundance; but from those who
have nothing, even what they have will be
taken away.[1] 30 *As for this worthless slave,*
throw him into the outer darkness, where there
will be weeping and gnashing of teeth.' "

here is your pound. I wrapped it up in a piece
of cloth, 21 for I was afraid of you, because you
are a harsh man; you take what you did not
deposit, and reap what you did not sow.'
22 He said to him, 'I will judge you by your own
words, you wicked slave! You knew, did
you, that I was a harsh man,
taking what I did not deposit and reaping what
I did not sow?
23 Why then did you not put my
money into the bank? Then when I returned,
I could have collected it with
interest.' 24 He said to the bystanders, 'Take
the pound from him and give it to the one
who has ten pounds.' 25 (And they said to him,
'Lord, he has ten pounds!') 26 'I tell you, to all
those who have, more will be given;
but from those who
have nothing, even what they have will be
taken away. 27 But as for these enemies of
mine who did not want me to be king over them
—bring them here and
slaughter them in my presence.' "

[1] *Cf.* MAT 13:12 (§ 91, p. 75) = MAR 4:25 = LUK 8:18 (§ 94, p. 77).

◗ To LUK 19:26 *cf.* **Gospel of Thomas, Logion 41.** — Jesus said, "All who have in their hand, to them shall be given; and all who do not have, from them shall be taken away, even the little they have."

The Days in Jerusalem

Matthew 21—25; Mark 11—13; Luke 19:28—21:38

§ 196 THE ENTRY INTO JERUSALEM

MAT 21:1–9	MAR 11:1–10	LUK 19:28–38
▲ 20:29–34 (§ 193, p. 149)	▲ 10:46–53 (§ 193, p. 149)	28 After he had said this,
1 When they had come near Jerusalem and had reached Bethphage, at the Mount of Olives, Jesus sent two disciples, 2 saying to them, "Go into the village ahead of you, and immediately you will find a donkey tied, and a colt with her; untie them and bring them to me. 3 If anyone says anything to you, just say this, 'The Lord needs them.' And he will send them immediately." 4 This took place to fulfill what had been spoken through the prophet, saying, 5 "Tell the daughter of Zion, Look, your king is coming to you, humble, and mounted on a donkey, and on a colt, the foal of a donkey."	1 When they were approaching Jerusalem, at Bethphage and Bethany, near the Mount of Olives, he sent two of his disciples 2 and said to them, "Go into the village ahead of you, and immediately as you enter it, you will find tied there a colt that has never been ridden; untie it and bring it. 3 If anyone says to you, 'Why are you doing this?' just say this, 'The Lord needs it and will send it back here immediately.' "	he went on ahead, going up to Jerusalem. 29 When he had come near Bethphage and Bethany, at the place called the Mount of Olives, he sent two of the disciples, 30 saying, "Go into the village ahead of you, and as you enter it you will find tied there a colt that has never been ridden. Untie it and bring it here. 31 If anyone asks you, 'Why are you untying it?' just say this, 'The Lord needs it.' "
6 The disciples went and did as Jesus had directed them;	4 They went away and found a colt tied near a door, outside in the street. As they were untying it, 5 some of the bystanders said to them, "What are you doing, untying the colt?" 6 They told them what Jesus had said; and they allowed them to take it. 7 Then	32 So those who were sent departed and found it as he had told them. 33 As they were untying the colt, its owners asked them, "Why are you untying the colt?" 34 They said, "The Lord needs it." 35 Then
7 they brought the donkey and the colt, and put their cloaks on them,[S] and he sat on them. 8 A very large crowd spread their cloaks on the road, and others cut branches from the trees	they brought the colt to Jesus and threw their cloaks on it; and he sat on it. 8 Many people spread their cloaks on the road, and others	they brought it to Jesus; and after throwing their cloaks on the colt, they set Jesus on it. 36 As he rode along, people kept spreading their cloaks on the road. 37 As

✧ MAT 21:5 — ISA 62:11; ZEC 9:9.

✦ [S] text: S B C W λ 𝔐 vg sa bo; *on it*: D Θ ø it; *on the colt*: sy^{p}; phrase omitted: sy^{c}.

• To § 196 *cf.* JOH 12:12–19.

		he was now approaching the path down from the Mount of Olives,
and spread them on the road.	spread leafy branches that they had cut in the fields.	
9 The crowds that went ahead of him	9 Then those who went ahead	the whole multitude of the disciples began to praise God joyfully with a loud voice for all the deeds of power that they had seen,
and that followed were shouting, "Hosanna to the Son of David! Blessed is the one who comes in the name of the Lord!	and those who followed were shouting, "Hosanna! Blessed is the one who comes in the name of the Lord!	38 saying, "Blessed is the king who comes in the name of the Lord!
	10 Blessed is the coming kingdom of	Peace in heaven, and
Hosanna in the highest heaven!"	our ancestor David! Hosanna in the highest heaven!"	glory in the highest heaven!"

§ 197 PREDICTION OF THE DESTRUCTION OF JERUSALEM

MAT	MAR	LUK 19:39–44
		39 Some of the Pharisees in the crowd said to him, "Teacher, order your disciples to stop." 40 He answered, "I tell you, if these were silent, the stones would shout out." 41 As he came near and saw the city, he wept over it, 42 saying, "If you, even you, had only recognized on this day the things that make for peace! But now they are hidden from your eyes. 43 Indeed, the days will come upon you, when your enemies will set up ramparts around you and surround you, and hem you in on every side. 44 They will crush you to the ground, you and your children within you, and they will not leave within you one stone upon another; because you did not recognize the time of your visitation from God."

§ 198 JESUS CLEANSES THE TEMPLE

MAT 21:10–17	MAR 11:11	LUK 19:45–46
10 When he entered Jerusalem, the whole city was in turmoil, asking, "Who is this?" 11 The crowds were saying, "This is the prophet Jesus from Nazareth in Galilee."	11 Then he entered Jerusalem	
12 Then Jesus entered the temple[T] and drove out all who	and went into the temple; *Cf.* 11:15–19 (§ 200, p. 156)	45 Then he entered the temple and began to drive out those who

◇ MAT 21:9 = MAR 11:9–10 = LUK 19:38 — PSA 118:26. ◇ LUK 19:44 — PSA 137:9.

✦ [T] text: S B Θ ø sa bo; add: *of God:* C D W λ 𝔐 it vg sy[c] sy[p].

▸ To MAT 21:12 *cf.* **Gospel of the Nazaraeans,** quoted in a marginal note of a thirteenth century manuscript of the *Aurora,* by Peter of Riga. — In the Gospel books which the Nazarenes use it is written: From his eyes went forth rays which terrified them and put them to flight.

were selling and buying in the temple, and he overturned the tables of the money changers and the seats of those who sold doves.		were selling things there;
13 He said to them, “It is written, ‘My house shall be called a house of prayer’; but you are making it a den of robbers.”		46 and he said, “It is written, ‘My house shall be a house of prayer’; but you have made it a den of robbers.”
14 The blind and the lame came to him in the temple, and he cured them. 15 But when the chief priests and the scribes saw the amazing things that he did, and heard the children crying out in the temple, “Hosanna to the Son of David,” they became angry 16 and said to him, “Do you hear what these are saying?” Jesus said to them, “Yes; have you never read, ‘Out of the mouths of infants and nursing babies you have prepared praise for yourself’?”		
	and when he had looked around at everything, as it was already late,	
17 He left them, went out of the city to Bethany, and spent the night there.	he went out to Bethany with the twelve.	

§ 199 THE CURSING OF THE FIG TREE

MAT 21:18–19	MAR 11:12–14	LUK
18 In the morning, when he returned to the city, he was hungry. 19 And seeing a fig tree by the side of the road, he went to	12 On the following day, when they came from Bethany, he was hungry. 13 Seeing in the distance a fig tree in leaf, he went to see whether perhaps he would find anything on it.	
it and found nothing at all on it but leaves.	When he came to it, he found nothing but leaves, for it was not the season for figs.	
Then he said to it, “May no fruit ever come from you again!” And the fig tree withered at once.	14 He said to it, “May no one ever eat fruit from you again.” And his disciples heard it.	

✧ MAT 21:13 = MAR 11:17 = LUK 19:46 — ISA 56:7; JER 7:11. ✧ MAT 21:16 — PSA 8:2.

§ 200 THE CLEANSING OF THE TEMPLE

Δ *MAT 21:12–13* (*§ 198, p. 154*)	MAR 11:15–19	LUK 19:45–48
	15 Then they came to Jerusalem.	
12 *Then Jesus entered the temple*[U] *and drove out all who* *were selling and* *buying in the temple, and he over-* *turned the tables of the money* *changers and the seats of those who* *sold doves.*	And he entered the temple and began to drive out those who were selling and those who were buying in the temple, and he over- turned the tables of the money changers and the seats of those who sold doves; 16 and he would not al- low anyone to carry anything through the temple.	45 Then he entered the temple and began to drive out those who were selling things there;
13 *He said to them,* *"It is written, 'My house shall* *be called a house of prayer';* *but you are making* *it a den of robbers."*	17 He was teaching and saying, "Is it not written, 'My house shall be called a house of prayer for all the nations'? But you have made it a den of robbers."	46 and he said, "It is written, 'My house shall be a house of prayer'; but you have made it a den of robbers." 47 Every day he was teaching in the temple.
	18 And when the chief priests and the scribes heard it, they kept looking for a way to kill him; for they were afraid of him,	The chief priests, the scribes, and the leaders of the peo- ple kept looking for a way to kill him; 48 but they did not find anything they could do,
Cf. 22:33 (§ 207, p. 163)	because the whole crowd was spellbound by his teaching. 19 And when evening came, Jesus and his disciples[V] went out of the city.	for all the people were spellbound by what they heard. Cf. 21:37 (§ 230, p. 180)

§ 201 THE LESSON FROM THE WITHERED FIG TREE

MAT 21:20–22 +	MAR 11:20–25 [26]	LUK
	20 In the morning as they passed by, they saw the fig tree withered away to its roots. 21 Then	
20 When the disciples saw it, they were amazed, saying, "How did the fig tree wither at once?" 21 Jesus answered them,	Peter remembered and said to him, "Rabbi, look! The fig tree that you cursed has withered." 22 Jesus answered them, "Have	

✦ [U] text: S B Θ ø sa bo; add: *of God*: C D W λ ℜ it vg sy^{c} sy^{p}. ✦ [V] text: A B W it (some MSS.) sy^{p}; *he*: S C D Θ λ ø ℜ it (some MSS.) vg sy^{s} sa bo.

• To § 200 *cf.* JOH 2:13–17. • To MAT 21:21–22 = MAR 11:23–24 *cf.* JOH 14:13–14. — 13 "I will do whatever you ask in my name, so that the Father may be glorified in the Son. 14 If in my name you ask me for anything, I will do it." *Cf.* JOH 16:23. — "On that day you will ask nothing of me. Very truly, I tell you, if you ask anything of the Father in my name, he will give it to you."

◗ To MAT 21:21 *cf.* **Gospel of Thomas, Logion 48.** — Jesus said, "If two make peace with one another in this house, they will say to the mountain, 'Be moved,' and it will be moved."

"Truly I tell you, if you have faith and do not
doubt, not only will you do what has been done
to the fig tree, but even if you say to this
mountain, 'Be lifted up and thrown into the
sea,'
it will be done.[1]
22 Whatever you ask for in prayer with faith,
you will receive."
Δ 6:14 (§ 30, p. 31)
14 *"For if you forgive others their trespasses,*
your heavenly Father will also forgive
you;"

faith in God. 23 Truly I tell you,
if you say to this
mountain, 'Be taken up and thrown into the
sea,' and if you do not doubt in your heart, but
believe that what you say will come to pass,
it will be done for you.[1] 24 So I tell you,
whatever you ask for in prayer, believe that
you have received[W] it, and it will be yours.
25 Whenever you stand praying,
forgive, if you have anything against anyone;
so that your Father in heaven may also forgive
you your trespasses."[X]

§ 202 THE QUESTION ABOUT JESUS' AUTHORITY

MAT 21:23–27

23 When he entered the temple,
the chief priests and
the elders of the people came to
him as he was teaching, and said,
"By what authority are you doing
these things, and who gave
you this authority?"
24 Jesus said to them, "I will also
ask you one question; if you tell me
the answer, then I will also tell you
by what authority I do these things.
25 Did the baptism of John come
from heaven, or was it of human
origin?" And they
argued with one another,
"If we say, 'From heaven,'
he will say to us, 'Why then did
you not believe him?' 26 But if
we say, 'Of human origin,'
we are afraid of the crowd; for

MAR 11:27–33

27 Again they came to Jerusalem.
As he was walking in the temple,
the chief priests,
the scribes, and the elders came to
him 28 and said,
"By what authority are you doing
these things? Who gave
you this authority to do them?"
29 Jesus said to them, "I will
ask you one question; answer me,
and I will tell you
by what authority I do these things.
30 Did the baptism of John come
from heaven, or was it of human
origin? Answer me." 31 They
argued with one another,
"If we say, 'From heaven,'
he will say, 'Why then did
you not believe him?' 32 But shall
we say, 'Of human origin'?"—
they were afraid of the crowd, for

LUK 20:1–8

1 One day, as he was teaching the
people in the temple and telling the
good news, the chief priests and
the scribes came with the elders
2 and said to him, "Tell us,
by what authority are you doing
these things? Who is it who gave
you this authority?"
3 He answered them, "I will also
ask you a question, and you tell me:
4 Did the baptism of John come
from heaven, or was it of human
origin?" 5 They
discussed it with one another,
saying, "If we say, 'From heaven,'
he will say, 'Why did
you not believe him?' 6 But if
we say, 'Of human origin,'
all the people will stone us; for

[1] MAT 17:20 (§ 126, p. 103): He [Jesus] said to them, "Because of your little faith. For truly I tell you, if you have faith the size of a mustard seed, you will say to this mountain, 'Move from here to there,' and it will move; and nothing will be impossible for you."

LUK 17:6 (§ 180, p. 139): The Lord replied, "If you had faith the size of a mustard seed, you could say to this mulberry tree, 'Be uprooted and planted in the sea,' and it would obey you."

✦ [W] text: S B C; *are receiving*: A ø 𝔑 sy[s] sy[p]; *will receive: D* Θ λ it vg. ✦ [X] text: S B W sy[s] sa bo; add verse 26: *But if you do not forgive, neither will your Father who is in heaven forgive your trespasses*: A C D Θ λ ø 𝔑 it vg sy[p] Cyprian.

• To MAT 21:23 and parallels, *cf.* JOH 2:18. — The Jews then said to him, "What sign can you show us for doing this?"

all regard John as a prophet.” 27 So they answered Jesus, “We do not know.” And he said to them, “Neither will I tell you by what authority I am doing these things.”	all regarded John as truly a prophet. 33 So they answered Jesus, “We do not know.” And Jesus said to them, “Neither will I tell you by what authority I am doing these things.”	they are convinced that John was a prophet.” 7 So they answered that they did not know where it came from. 8 Then Jesus said to them, “Neither will I tell you by what authority I am doing these things.”

§ 203 THE PARABLE OF THE TWO SONS

MAT 21:28–32	MAR	LUK
28 “What do you think? A man had two sons; he went to the first and said, ‘Son, go and work in the vineyard today.’ 29 He answered, ‘I will not’; but later he changed his mind and went. 30 The father went to the second and said the same; and he answered, ‘I go, sir’; but he did not go. 31 Which of the two did the will of his father?” They said, “The first.” Jesus said to them, “Truly I tell you, the tax collectors and the prostitutes are going into the kingdom of God ahead of you. 32 For John came to you in the way of righteousness and you did not believe him, but the tax collectors and the prostitutes believed him; and even after you saw it, you did not change your minds and believe him.”[Y] [1]		

§ 204 THE PARABLE OF THE WICKED TENANTS

MAT 21:33–46	MAR 12:1–12	LUK 20:9–19
33 “Listen to another parable. There was a landowner who planted a vineyard, put a fence around it, dug a wine press in it, and built a watchtower. Then he leased it to tenants and went to another country. 34 When the harvest time had come, he sent his slaves to the tenants to collect his produce. 35 But the tenants seized his slaves and beat one, killed another, and	1 Then he began to speak to them in parables. “A man planted a vineyard, put a fence around it, dug a pit for the wine press, and built a watchtower; then he leased it to tenants and went to another country. 2 When the season came, he sent a slave to the tenants to collect from them his share of the produce of the vine- yard. 3 But they seized him, and beat him, and sent him away	9 He began to tell the people this parable: “A man planted a vineyard, and leased it to tenants, and went to another country for a long time. 10 When the season came, he sent a slave to the tenants in order that they might give him his share of the produce of the vine- yard; but the tenants beat him and sent him away

[1] LUK 7:29–30 (§ 82, p. 68): 29 (And all the people who heard this, including the tax collectors, acknowledged the justice of God, because they had been baptized with John’s baptism. 30 But by refusing to be baptized by him [Jesus], the Pharisees and the lawyers rejected God’s purpose for themselves.)

✧ MAT 21:33 = MAR 12:1 = LUK 20:9 — ISA 5:2.

✦ [Y] text: S B C W Θ λ ø 𝔐 it vg sa bo; *even when you did not see it, you afterward repented*; sy[c] sy[p]; *when you saw it you afterward repented*: D sy[s].

stoned another. 36 Again he	empty-handed. 4 And again he	empty-handed. 11 Next he
sent other slaves,	sent another slave to them; this one	sent another slave; that one also
more than the first; and		
they treated them in the same way.	they beat over the head and insulted.	they beat and insulted
		and sent away empty-handed.
	5 Then he sent another, and that one	12 And he sent still a third; this one
	they killed. And so it was with	also they wounded and threw out.
	many others; some they beat, and	
	others they killed. 6 He had still	
	one other, a beloved son.	
		13 Then the owner of the vineyard
		said, 'What shall I do?
37 Finally he sent his son to them,	Finally he sent him to them,	I will send my beloved son;
saying, 'They will respect my son.'	saying, 'They will respect my son.'	perhaps they will respect him.'
38 But when the tenants saw the son,	7 But those tenants	14 But when the tenants saw him,
they said to themselves,	said to one another,	they discussed it among themselves
'This is the heir; come, let us	'This is the heir; come, let us	and said, 'This is the heir; let us
kill him and get his inheritance.'	kill him, and the inheritance will	kill him so that the inheritance may
39 So they seized him,	be ours.' 8 So they seized him, killed	be ours.' 15 So they
threw him out of the vineyard, and	him, and threw him out of the vine-	threw him out of the vineyard and
killed him. 40 Now when the	yard. 9 What then will the	killed him. What then will the
owner of the vineyard comes,	owner of the vineyard	owner of the vineyard
what will he do to those tenants?"	do?	do to them?
41 They said to him, "He will put	He will	16 He will
those wretches to a miserable death,	come and destroy the tenants	come and destroy those tenants
and lease the vineyard to other ten-	and give the vineyard to others.	and give the vineyard to others."
ants who will give him the produce		
at the harvest time."		
		When they heard this, they said,
		"Heaven forbid!"
42 Jesus said to them,		17 But he looked at them and said,
"Have you never read in the scrip-	10 Have you not read this scripture:	"What then does this text mean:
tures: 'The stone that the builders	'The stone that the builders	'The stone that the builders
rejected has become the corner-	rejected has become the corner-	rejected has become the corner-
stone; this was the Lord's doing,	stone; 11 this was the Lord's doing,	stone'?
and it is amazing in our eyes'?	and it is amazing in our eyes'?"	
43 Therefore I tell you, the kingdom		
of God will be taken away from you		
and given to a people that produces		
the fruits of the kingdom.		
44 The one who falls on this stone		18 Everyone who falls on that stone
will be broken to pieces; and it will		will be broken to pieces; and it will
crush anyone on whom it falls."[Z]		crush anyone on whom it falls."
45 When the chief priests and the	12 When they	19 When the scribes and chief priests
Pharisees heard his parables, they		
realized that he was speaking about	realized that he had told this parable	realized that he had told this parable
them. 46 They wanted to	against them, they wanted to	against them, they wanted to

---

✧ MAT 21:42 = MAR 12:10–11 = LUK 20:17 — PSA 118:22-23.

✦ [Z] text: S B C W Θ λ ø 𝔐 it (some MSS.) vg sy^c sy^p sa bo (*Cf.* LUK 20:18.); omit verse 44: D it (some MSS.) sy^s. (*Cf.* LUK 20:18.)

arrest him,
but they feared the crowds,
because they regarded him as a
prophet.
Cf. 22:22 (§ 206, p. 162)

arrest him,
but they feared the crowd.

So they left him and went away.

lay hands on him at that very hour,
but they feared the people.

§ 205 THE PARABLE OF THE WEDDING BANQUET

MAT 22:1–14

1 Once more Jesus spoke to them in parables,
saying: 2 "The kingdom of heaven may be
compared to a king who gave a wedding banquet for his son. 3 He sent his slaves to call
those who had been invited to the wedding
banquet, but they would not come. 4 Again he
sent other slaves, saying, 'Tell those who have
been invited: Look, I have prepared my dinner, my oxen and my fat calves have been
slaughtered, and everything is ready; come to
the wedding banquet.' 5 But they
made light of it and went away,
one to his farm,

another to his business,

6 while the rest seized his slaves, mistreated
them, and killed them.
7 The king was enraged. He sent his troops,
destroyed those murderers, and burned their
city. 8 Then he said to his slaves, 'The wedding is ready, but those invited were not
worthy. 9 Go therefore into the main streets,
and invite everyone you find to the wedding
banquet.' 10 Those slaves went out into the
streets and gathered all whom they found, both
good and bad; so the wedding hall was filled
with guests. 11 But when the king came in to
see the guests, he noticed a man there who was
not wearing a wedding robe, 12 and he said to
him, 'Friend, how did you get in here without
a wedding robe?' And he was speechless.
13 Then the king said to the attendants, 'Bind
him hand and foot, and throw him into the outer
darkness, where there will be weeping and

MAR

Δ *LUK 14:16–24* *(§ 170, p. 132)*

16 Then Jesus said to him,

"Someone gave a great dinner and invited
many.

17 At the time for the dinner he
sent his slave to say to those who had
been invited, 'Come; for

everything is ready now.'
18 But they all alike
began to make excuses. The first said to him,
'I have bought a piece of land, and I must go
out and see it; please accept my regrets.'
19 Another said, 'I have bought five yoke of
oxen, and I am going to try them out; please
accept my regrets.' 20 Another said, 'I have
just been married, and therefore I cannot
come.' 21 So the slave returned and reported
this to his master.

Then the owner of the house became angry

and said to his slave,

'Go out at once into the streets and lanes of the
town and bring in the poor, the crippled, the
blind, and the lame.'

gnashing of teeth.'		
		22 *And the slave said, 'Sir, what you ordered has been done, and there is still room.'* 23 *Then the master said to the slave, 'Go out into the roads and lanes, and compel people to come in, so that my house may be filled.*
14 For many are called, but few are chosen."		24 *For I tell you,*[A] *none of those who were invited will taste my dinner.' "*

§ 206 THE QUESTION OF PAYING TAXES TO CAESAR

MAT 22:15–22	MAR 12:13–17	LUK 20:20–26
15 Then the Pharisees went and plotted to entrap him in what he said.	13 Then they sent to him some Pharisees and some Herodians to trap him in what he said.	20 So they watched him and sent spies who pretended to be honest, in order to trap him by what he said, so as to hand him over to the jurisdiction and authority of the governor.
16 So they sent their disciples to him, along with the Herodians,	14 And they came	21 So they
saying, "Teacher, we know that you are sincere, and teach the way of God in accordance with truth, and show deference to no one; for you do not regard people with partiality.	and said to him, "Teacher, we know that you are sincere, and show deference to no one; for you do not regard people with partiality, but teach the way of God in accordance with truth.	asked him, "Teacher, we know that you are right in what you say and teach, and you show deference to no one, but teach the way of God in accordance with truth.
17 Tell us, then, what you think. Is it lawful to pay taxes to the emperor, or not?"	Is it lawful to pay taxes to the emperor, or not? 15 Should we pay them, or should we not?"	22 Is it lawful for us to pay taxes to the emperor, or not?"
18 But Jesus, aware of their malice, said, "Why are you	But knowing their hypocrisy, he said to them, "Why are you	23 But he perceived their craftiness and said to them,

✦ [A] The Greek word for *you* here is plural.

● To MAT 22:16 and parallels, *cf.* JOH 3:2. — He came to Jesus by night and said to him, "Rabbi, we know that you are a teacher who has come from God; for no one can do these signs that you do apart from the presence of God."

◗ To MAT 22:14 *cf.* **Gospel of Thomas, Logion 23.** — Jesus said, "I will choose you, one out of a thousand, and two out of ten thousand, and they will stand as a single one." ◗ To MAT 22:15*ff.* *cf.* *Egerton Papyrus 2.* — And coming to Jesus to test him, they said, "Teacher Jesus, we know that you are from God, for what you do testifies to you beyond all the prophets. Tell us, then, is it lawful to give to kings what pertains to their rule? Shall we pay them or not?" And Jesus, knowing their thoughts and being moved with indignation, said to them, "Why do you call me teacher with your mouth and do not hear what I say? Well did Isaiah prophecy of you, when he said: 'This people honors me with their lips, but their heart is far from me; in vain do they worship me, teaching as doctrines the precepts of human beings.'" (*Cf.* MAT 15:78 = MAR 7:6–7 (§ 115, p. 92).

◗ To MAT 22:17*ff.* and parallels, *cf.* **Gospel of Thomas, Logion 100.** — They showed Jesus a gold (coin) and said to him, "Caesar's officers demand taxes from us." Jesus said to them, "Give to Caesar what belongs to Caesar, give to God what belongs to God, and give to me what is mine."

putting me to the test, you hypocrites? 19 Show me the coin used
for the tax." And they brought
him a denarius. 20 Then he said to
them, "Whose head is this, and
whose title?" 21 They
answered, "The emperor's."
Then he said to them, "Give therefore to the emperor the things that
are the emperor's, and to God the
things that are God's."
22 When they heard this, they were
amazed; and
they left him and went away.

putting me to the test?
Bring me a denarius and let me see
it." 16 And they brought
one. Then he said to
them, "Whose head is this, and
whose title?" They
answered, "The emperor's."
17 Jesus said to them, "Give
to the emperor the things that
are the emperor's, and to God the
things that are God's." And
they were
utterly amazed at him.

Cf. 12:12 (§ 204, p. 158)

24 "Show me a denarius.
Whose head and
whose title does it bear?" They
said, "The emperor's."
25 He said to them, "Then give
to the emperor the things that
are the emperor's, and to God the
things that are God's." 26 And they
were not able in the presence of the
people to trap him by what he said;
and being
amazed by his answer,
they became silent.

§ 207 THE QUESTION ABOUT THE RESURRECTION

MAT 22:23–33

23 The same day some Sadducees
came to him, saying there is no
resurrection; and they
asked him a question, saying,
24 "Teacher, Moses said,
'If a man dies
childless, his brother
shall marry the widow, and raise up
children for his brother.' 25 Now
there were seven brothers among
us; the first married, and died
childless, leaving the widow to his
brother. 26 The second did the
same,
so also the third, down to the
seventh.
27 Last of all, the woman herself
died. 28 In the resurrection, then,
whose wife of the seven will
she be? For all of them had
married her." 29 Jesus answered
them,

MAR 12:18–27

18 Some Sadducees,
who say there is no
resurrection, came to him and
asked him a question, saying,
19 "Teacher, Moses wrote for us that
'if a man's brother dies, leaving a
wife but no child, the man[B]
shall marry the widow and raise up
children for his brother.'
20 There were seven brothers;
the first married and, when he died,
left no children;
21 and the second married her and
died, leaving no children;
and the third likewise; 22 none of
the seven left children.
Last of all the woman herself
died. 23 In the resurrection[C]
whose wife will
she be? For the seven had
married her." 24 Jesus said to
them,

LUK 20:27–40

27 Some Sadducees,
those who say there is no
resurrection, came to him 28 and
asked him a question,
"Teacher, Moses wrote for us that
'if a man's brother dies, leaving a
wife but no children, the man[B]
shall marry the widow and raise up
children for his brother. 29 Now
there were seven brothers;
the first married, and died
childless;
30 then the second
31 and the third married her, and so
in the same way all seven died
childless. 32 Finally the woman
also died. 33 In the resurrection,
therefore, whose wife will
the woman be? For the seven had
married her." 34 Jesus said to
them, "Those who belong to this
age marry and are given in marriage; 35 but those who are
considered worthy of a place in that
age

✧ MAT 22:24 = MAR 12:19 = LUK 20:28 — DEU 25:5–6; GEN 38:8.

✦ [B] Greek: *his brother*. ✦ [C] text: S B C D W sy^{p} sa bo; add: *when they rise*: A Θ λ ø 𝔑 it vg sy^{s}.

“You are wrong, because you know neither the scriptures nor the power of God. 30 For in the resurrection they neither marry nor are given in marriage,	“Is not this the reason you are wrong, that you know neither the scriptures nor the power of God? 25 For when they rise from the dead, they neither marry nor are given in marriage,	and in the resurrection from the dead neither marry nor are given in marriage. 36 Indeed they cannot die anymore, because
but are like angels[D] in heaven.	but are like angels in heaven.	they are like angels and are children of God, being children of the resur- rection. 37 And the fact that the
31 And as for the resurrection of the dead, have you not read what was said to you by God,	26 And as for the dead being raised, have you not read in the book of Moses, in the story about the bush, how God said	dead are raised Moses himself showed, in the story about the bush, where he
32 ‘I am the God of Abraham, the God of Isaac, and the God of Jacob’? He is God not of the dead, but of the liv- ing.”	to him, ‘I am the God of Abraham, the God of Isaac, and the God of Jacob’? 27 He is God not of the dead, but of the liv- ing; you are quite wrong.”	speaks of the Lord as the God of Abraham, the God of Isaac, and the God of Jacob. 38 Now he is God not of the dead, but of the liv- ing; for to him all of them are alive.”
33 And when the crowd heard it, they were astounded at his teaching.	*Cf.* 11:18b (§ 200, p. 156)	
	Cf. 12:32a (§ 208, p. 163)	39 Then some of the scribes an- swered, “Teacher, you have
Cf. 22:46 (§ 209, p. 164)	*Cf.* 12:34b (§ 208, p. 163)	spoken well.” 40 For they no longer dared to ask him another question.

§ 208 THE GREAT COMMANDMENT

MAT 22:34–40	MAR 12:28–34	Δ *LUK 10:25–28 (§ 143, p. 114)*
34 When the Pharisees heard that he had silenced the Sadducees, they gathered together, 35 and one of	28 One of the scribes came near and heard them disputing with one an- other, and seeing that he answered them well,	
them, a lawyer, asked him a ques- tion to test him. 36 “Teacher, which commandment in the law is the greatest?” 37 He said to him,	he asked him, “Which commandment is the first of all?” 29 Jesus answered, “The first is, ‘Hear, O Israel: the Lord our God, the Lord is one;	*25 Just then a lawyer stood up to test Jesus. “Teacher,” he said, “what must I do to inherit eternal life?” 26 He said to him, “What is written in the law? What do you read there?” 27 He answered,*
“ ‘You shall love the Lord your God with all your heart, and with all your soul, and with all your mind.’	30 you shall love the Lord your God with all your heart, and with all your soul, and with all your mind,	*“You shall love the Lord your God with all your heart, and with all your soul, and with all your*

✧ MAT 22:32 = MAR 12:26 = LUK 20:37 — EXO 3:6. ✧ MAR 12:29 — DEU 6:4. ✧ MAT 22:37 = MAR 12:30 = LUK 10:27 — DEU 6:5.

✦ [D] text: B D Θ λ it (some MSS.) sy^c sy^s sa Origen; add: *of God*: S W ø ℜ it (some MSS.) vg sy^p bo.

38 This is the greatest and first commandment. 39 And a second is like it: 'You shall love your neighbor as yourself.' 40 On these two commandments hang all the law and the prophets."	and with all your strength.' 31 The second is this, 'You shall love your neighbor as yourself.' There is no other commandment greater than these."	*strength, and with all your mind;* *and your neighbor as yourself."*
		28 *And he said to him, "You have given the right answer; do this, and you will live."* C*f.* 20:39 (§ 207, p. 163)
C*f.* 22:46 (§ 209, p. 165)	32 Then the scribe said to him, "You are right, Teacher; you have truly said that 'he is one, and besides him there is no other'; 33 and 'to love him with all the heart, and with all the understanding, and with all the strength,' and 'to love one's neighbor as oneself,'—this is much more important than all whole burnt offerings and sacrifices." 34 When Jesus saw that he answered wisely, he said to him, "You are not far from the kingdom of God." After that no one dared to ask him any question.	C*f.* 20:40 (§ 207, p. 163)

§ 209 ABOUT DAVID'S SON

MAT 22:41–46	MAR 12:35–37a	LUK 20:41–44
41 Now while the Pharisees were gathered together, Jesus asked them this question: 42 "What do you think of the Messiah? Whose son is he?" They said to him, "The son of David." 43 He said to them, "How is it then that	35 While Jesus was teaching in the temple, he said, "How can the scribes say that the Messiah is the son of David?	41 Then he said to them, "How can they say that the Messiah is David's son?
David by the Spirit[E] calls him Lord, saying,	36 David himself, by the Holy Spirit, declared,	42 For David himself says in the book of Psalms,
44 'The Lord said to my Lord, "Sit at my right hand, until I put your enemies	'The Lord said to my Lord, "Sit at my right hand, until I put your enemies	'The Lord said to my Lord, "Sit at my right hand, 43 until I make your enemies

---

✧ MAT 22:39 = MAR 12:31 = LUK 10:27b — LEV 19:18. ✧ MAR 12:33 — 1SM 15:22. ✧ MAT 22:44 = MAR 12:36 = LUK 20:42–43 — PSA 110:1.

✦ [E] Or, *David in spirit.*

◗ To MAT 22:39 c*f.* **Gospel of Thomas, Logion 25.** — Jesus said, "Love your brother or sister as your soul, and guard them as the apple of your eye."

under your feet" '?
45 If David thus calls him Lord,
how can he be his son?" 46 No one
was able to give him an answer, nor
from that day did anyone dare to ask
him any more questions.

under your feet." '
37 David himself calls him Lord;
so how can he be his son?"

Cf. 12:34 (§ 208, p. 163)

your footstool." '
44 David thus calls him Lord;
so how can he be his son?"

Cf. 20:40 (§ 207, p. 162)

§ 210 JESUS DENOUNCES SCRIBES AND PHARISEES

MAT 23:1–36

1 Then Jesus said to the crowds and
to his disciples, 2 "The scribes and
the Pharisees sit on Moses' seat;
3 therefore, do whatever they teach
you and follow it; but do not do as
they do, for they do not practice
what they teach.

4 They tie up
heavy burdens, hard to bear,[F] and
lay them on the shoulders of others;
but they themselves are unwilling to
lift a finger to move them. 5 They
do all their deeds to be seen by
others; for they make their phylac-
teries broad and their fringes long.
6 They love to have the place of
honor at banquets and

the best seats in the synagogues,

7 and to be greeted with respect in
the marketplaces,[1] and to have
people call them rabbi. 8 But you
are not to be called rabbi, for you
have one teacher, and you are all

MAR 12:37b–40

37b And the large crowd was listening to him with delight. 38 As he
taught, he said,

"Beware of the scribes, who
like to walk around in long robes,
and to be greeted with respect
in the marketplaces, 39 and to have
the best seats in the synagogues
and places of honor at banquets![1]

LUK 20:45–47 +

45 In the hearing of all the people

he said
to the disciples,

∆ *11:46 (§ 154, p. 120)*
46 And he said, "Woe also to you
lawyers! For you load people
with burdens hard to bear, and

you yourselves do not
lift a finger to ease them."

46 "Beware of the scribes, who
like to walk around in long robes,
and love to be greeted with respect
in the marketplaces, and to have
the best seats in the synagogues
and places of honor at banquets."[1]

---

[1] LUK 11:43 (§ 154, p. 120): "Woe to you Pharisees! For you love to have the seat of honor in the synagogues and to be greeted with respect in the marketplaces."

✧ MAT 23:5 — NUM 15:38–39.

✦ [F] text: B W Θ ø ℜ it (some MSS.) vg sa; omit: *hard to bear*: S λ it (some MSS.) sy^c sy^s sy^p bo; *not hard to bear*: D.

Matthew

students.
9 And call no one your father on earth, for you have one Father—the one in heaven.
10 Nor are you to be called instructors, for you have one instructor, the Messiah.
11 The greatest among you will be your servant.[1]
12 All who exalt themselves will be humbled, and all who humble themselves will be exalted.
13 But woe to you, scribes and Pharisees, hypocrites!
For you lock people out of the kingdom of heaven. For you do not go in yourselves, and when others are going in, you stop them."[G]

15 "Woe to you, scribes and Pharisees, hypocrites! For you cross sea and land to make a single convert, and you make the new convert twice as much a child of hell[H] as yourselves.
16 Woe to you, blind guides, who say, 'Whoever swears by the sanctuary is bound by nothing, but whoever swears by the gold of the sanctuary is bound by the oath,'
17 You blind fools! For which is greater, the gold or the sanctuary that has made the gold sacred?
18 And you say, 'Whoever swears by the altar is bound by nothing, but whoever swears by the gift that is on the altar is bound by the oath.'
19 How blind you are! For which is greater, the gift or the altar that makes the gift sacred?
20 So whoever swears by the altar, swears by it and by everything on it;

Mark

Cf. 9:35 (§ 129, p. 106)

40 They devour widows' houses and for the sake of appearance say long prayers. They will receive the greater condemnation."

Luke

Cf. 9:48b (§ 129, p. 106)
Cf. MAT 18:4 (§ 129, p. 106)
Cf. 14:11 (§ 169, p. 132)
Cf. 18:14 (§ 186, p. 142)
Δ *11:52 (§ 154, p. 120)*

52 "Woe to you lawyers!

For you have taken away the key of knowledge; you did not enter yourselves, and you hindered those who were entering."

20:47 They devour widows' houses and for the sake of appearance say long prayers. They will receive the greater condemnation."

---

[1] *Cf.* MAT 20:26–27 = MAR 10:43–44 (§ 192, p. 148) = LUK 22:26 (§ 237b, p. 185).

✦ [G] text: S B D Θ λ it (some MSS.) vg (some MSS.) sy[s] sa bo Origen; add verse 14 (sometimes found after verse 12) — *Woe to you, scribes and Pharisees, hypocrites! For you devour widows' houses and for the sake of appearance you make long prayers; therefore you will receive the greater condemnation* = MAR 12:40; LUK 20:47: W ø ℜ it (some MSS.) vg (some MSS.) sy[c] sy[p].
✦ [H] Greek: *Gehenna.*

◗ To MAT 23:13 = LUK 11:52 *cf.* **Gospel of Thomas, Logion 39.** — Jesus said, "The Pharisees and the scribes have received the keys of knowledge and have hidden them. They themselves did not enter, and they did not allow to enter those who wished to. But you, become as wise as serpents and as innocent as doves."

21 and whoever swears by the sanctuary, swears by it and by the one
who dwells in it; 22 and whoever
swears by heaven, swears by the
throne of God and by the one who
is seated upon it. 23 Woe to you,
scribes and Pharisees, hypocrites!
For you tithe mint, dill, and
cummin, and have neglected
the weightier matters of the law:
justice and mercy and faith. It is
these you ought to have practiced
without neglecting the others.
24 You blind guides! You strain out
a gnat but swallow a camel!
25 "Woe to you, scribes and Pharisees, hypocrites!

For you clean the
outside of the cup and of the plate,
but inside they are full of greed and
self-indulgence.
26 You blind Pharisee! First clean
the inside of the cup, so that the
outside also

may become clean.
27 "Woe to you, scribes and Pharisees, hypocrites! For you are like
whitewashed tombs,

which on the outside look beautiful,
but inside they are full of bones
of the dead and of all kinds of filth.
28 So you also on the outside look
righteous to others, but inside you
are full of hypocrisy and lawlessness. 29 Woe to you, scribes and
Pharisees, hypocrites! For you
build the tombs of the prophets

and decorate the graves of the righteous, 30 and you say, 'If we had
lived in the days of our ancestors,
we would not have taken part with

Δ *11:39–42, 44, 47–51 (§ 154, p. 120)*

42 "But woe to you
Pharisees!
For you tithe mint and rue and
herbs of all kinds, and neglect
justice and the love of God;
it is
these you ought to have practiced,
without neglecting the others."

39 Then the Lord said to him,
"Now you Pharisees clean the
outside of the cup and of the dish,
but inside you are full of greed and
wickedness.
40 You fools!

Did not the one who made the out-
side make the inside also? 41 So
give for alms those things that are
within; and see,
everything will be clean for you."
44 Woe to you!
For you are like
unmarked graves, and people walk
over them without realizing it."

47 Woe to you!
For you
build the tombs of the prophets
whom your ancestors killed.

▸ To MAT 23:27 *cf.* **Gospel of the Naassenes** (in Hippolytus, *Refutation of All Heresies, V.8:23*). — "You are whitewashed tombs filled with the bones of the dead," that is, no life is within you.

them in shedding the blood of the
prophets.' 31 Thus you testify
against yourselves that you are
descendants of those who murdered
the prophets.
32 Fill up, then, the measure of
your ancestors. 33 You snakes,
you brood of vipers! How can you
escape being sentenced to hell? [I]
34 Therefore
I send you prophets, sages, and
scribes, some of whom you will
kill and crucify, and some you will
flog in your synagogues and pursue
from town to town, 35 so that
upon you may come
all the righteous blood
shed on
earth, from the blood of righteous
Abel to the blood of Zechariah son
of Barachiah, whom you murdered
between the sanctuary and the altar.
36 Truly I tell you, all this will come
upon this generation."

Cf. MAT 3:7b (§ 2, p. 12)

48 So you are witnesses and
approve of the deeds
of your ancestors; for they killed
them, and you build their tombs.

Cf. 3:7b (§ 2, p. 12)

49 Therefore also the Wisdom of God
said, 'I will send them prophets
and apostles, some of whom they
will kill and persecute,'
50 so that
this generation may be charged
with the blood of all the prophets
shed since the foundation of the
world, 51 from the blood of
Abel to the blood of Zechariah,
who perished
between the altar and the sanctu-
ary. Yes, I tell you, it will be
charged against this generation.

§ 211 THE LAMENT OVER JERUSALEM

MAT 23:37–39

37 "Jerusalem, Jerusalem, the city that kills
the prophets and stones those who are sent to
it! How often have I desired to gather your
children together as a hen gathers her brood
under her wings, and you were not willing!
38 See, your house is left to you, desolate. [J]
39 For I tell you, you will not see me again until
you say, 'Blessed is the
one who comes in the name of the Lord.' "

MAR

Δ *LUK 13:34–35* *(§ 167, p. 131)*

34 "Jerusalem, Jerusalem, the city that kills
the prophets and stones those who are sent to
it! How often have I desired to gather your
children together as a hen gathers her brood
under her wings, and you were not willing!
35 See, your house is left to you.
And I tell you, you will not see me until
the time comes when you say, 'Blessed is the
one who comes in the name of the Lord.' "

✧ MAT 23:35 = LUK 11:50–51 — GEN 4:8; 2CH 24:20–21; ZEC 1:1. ✧ MAT 23:37 = LUK 13:34 — ISA 31:5.
✧ MAT 23:39 = LUK 13:35 — PSA 118:26.

✦ [I] Greek: *Gehenna*. ✦ [J] text: S C D W Θ λ φ 𝔐 it vg sy^p bo (some MSS.); *cf.* JER 22:5; omit: *desolate*: B sy^s sa bo (some MSS.).

◗ To MAT 23:35 *cf.* **Gospel of the Nazaraeans** (in Jerome, *Commentary on Matthew 23:35*). — In the gospel which the Nazarenes use, for "son of Barachiah" we find written, "son of Jehoiada." ◗ To MAT 23:35 *cf.* Peter of Laodicea, *Commentary on Matthew 23:35*, ed. Heinrici, V. 267. — And Zechariah the son of Jehoiada said, "For he was of two names."

§ 212 THE WIDOW'S GIFT

MAT	MAR 12:41–44	LUK 21:1–4
	Cf. 12:38–40 (§ 210, p. 165)	▲ 20:45–47 (§ 210, p. 165)
	41 He sat down opposite the treasury, and	1 He looked up and
	watched the crowd putting money into the	saw rich people putting their gifts into the
	treasury. Many rich people put in large sums.	treasury;
	42 A poor widow came and put in two small	2 he also saw a poor widow put in two small
	copper coins, which are worth a penny.	copper coins.
	43 Then he called his disciples and said to them,	3 He said,
	"Truly I tell you, this poor widow has put in	"Truly I tell you, this poor widow has put in
	more than all those who are contributing to the	more than all of them;
	treasury. 44 For all of them have contributed	4 for all of them have contributed
	out of their abundance; but she out of her pov-	out of their abundance, but she out of her pov-
	erty has put in everything she had, all she had	erty has put in all she had
	to live on."	to live on."

§ 213 PREDICTION OF THE DESTRUCTION OF THE TEMPLE

MAT 24:1–3	MAR 13:1–4	LUK 21:5–7
1 As Jesus came out of the temple	1 As he came out of the temple,	5 When some
and was going away, his disciples	one of his disciples	were speaking about the temple,
came to point out to him the	said to him, "Look, Teacher,	how it was adorned with beautiful
	what large stones and what large	stones and gifts dedicated to God,
buildings of the temple. 2 Then	buildings!" 2 Then	
he asked them, "You see all these,	Jesus asked him, "Do you see these	he said, 6 "As for these
do you not? Truly I tell you,	great buildings?	things that you see, the days will
not one stone will be left	Not one stone will be left	come when not one stone will be left
here upon another; all will be	here upon another; all will be	upon another; all will be
thrown down." 3 When he was	thrown down."[J] 3 When he was	thrown down."
sitting on the Mount of Olives,	sitting on the Mount of Olives	
the disciples	opposite the temple, Peter, James,	
came to him	John, and Andrew asked him	7 They asked him,
privately, saying, "Tell us, when	privately, 4 "Tell us, when	"Teacher, when
will this be, and what will be the	will this be, and what will be the	will this be, and what will be the
sign of your coming	sign that all these things	sign that this
	are about to be accomplished?"	is about to take place?"
and of the end of the age?"		

✦ [J] text: S A B λ ø 𝔐 vg sa bo; add: *and after three days another will be raised up without hands*: D W it Cyprian. *Cf.* MAR 14:58; JOH 2:19.

The Synoptic Apocalypse

Matthew 24:4–36; Mark 13:5–37; Luke 21:8–36

§ 214 THE SIGNS OF THE END OF THE AGE

MAT 24:4–8	MAR 13:5–8	LUK 21:8–11
4 Jesus answered them, "Beware that no one leads you astray. 5 For many will come in my name, saying, 'I am the Messiah!' and they will lead	5 Then Jesus began to say to them, "Beware that no one leads you astray. 6 Many will come in my name and say, 'I am he!' and they will lead	8 And he said, "Beware that you are not led astray; for many will come in my name and say, 'I am he!' and, 'The time is near!' Do not go after them.[1]
many astray.[1] 6 And you will hear of wars and rumors of wars; see that you are not alarmed; for this must take place, but the end is not yet.	many astray.[1] 7 When you hear of wars and rumors of wars, do not be alarmed; this must take place, but the end is still to come.	9 When you hear of wars and insurrections, do not be terrified; for these things must take place first, but the end will not follow immediately."
7 For nation will rise against nation, and kingdom against kingdom, and there will be famines and earthquakes in various places:	8 For nation will rise against nation, and kingdom against kingdom; there will be earthquakes in various places; there will be famines.	10 Then he said to them, "Nation will rise against nation, and kingdom against kingdom; 11 there will be great earthquakes, and in various places famines and plagues; and there will be dreadful portents and great signs from heaven."
8 all this is but the beginning of the birth pangs."	This is but the beginning of the birth pangs."	

§ 215 THE COMING OF PERSECUTION

MAT 24:9–14 +	MAR 13:9–13	LUK 21:12–19
9 "Then they will hand you over to be tortured"		
Δ *10:17–21 (§ 59, p. 51)* *17 Beware of them, for they will hand you over to councils and flog you in their synagogues;*	9 "As for yourselves, beware; for they will hand you over to councils; and you will be beaten in synagogues;	12 "But before all this occurs, they will arrest you and persecute you; they will hand you over to synagogues and prisons,
18 and you will be dragged before governors and kings because of	and you will stand before governors and kings because of	and you will be brought before kings and governors because of

[1] *Cf.* MAT 24:23–26 = MAR 13:21–22 (§ 217, p. 173) = LUK 17:23 (§ 184, p. 140).

✧ MAT 24:6 = MAR 13:7 = LUK 21:9 — DAN 2:28–29, 45. ✧ MAT 24:7 = MAR 13:8 = LUK 21:10 — ISA 19:2; 2CH 15:6.

me, as a testimony to them and the
Gentiles.

C*f.* 24:14

19 *When they*
hand you over, do not worry
about how you are to speak or what
you are to say; for what you are to
say will be given to you at that time;
20 *for it is not you who speak, but*
the Spirit of your Father speaking
through you.[1] 21 *Brother will*
betray brother to death, and a
father his child, and children will
rise against parents and have them
put to death;
24:9b "and will put you to death,
and you will be hated by all
nations because of my name.[2]
10 Then many will fall away,[K] and
they will betray one another and
hate one another. 11 And many
false prophets will arise and lead
many astray. 12 And because of the
increase of lawlessness, the love of
many will grow cold. 13 But the
one who endures to the end will
be saved.[4] 14 And this good news
of the kingdom will be proclaimed
throughout the world, as a testimony to all the nations; and then
the end will come."

me, as a testimony to them.
10 And the good news must first be
proclaimed to all nations.
11 When they bring you to trial and
hand you over, do not worry
beforehand about what
you are to say; but
say whatever is given you at that time,
for it is not you who speak, but
the Holy Spirit.[1]
12 Brother will
betray brother to death, and a
father his child, and children will
rise against parents and have them
put to death;
13 and you will be hated by all
because of my name.[2]
But the
one who endures to the end will
be saved."[4]

C*f.* 13:10

my name.
13 This will give you an opportunity
to testify.
14 So make up your minds not
to prepare your defense in advance;
15 for I will give you words and a
wisdom that none of your opponents will be able to withstand or
contradict.[1]
16 You will be
betrayed even by parents and brothers,
by relatives and friends; and
they will put some of you to death;
17 You will be hated by all
because of my name.[2] 18 But not a
hair of your head will perish.[3]
19 By your endurance you will
gain your souls."[4]

---

[1] LUK 12:11–12 (§ 155, p. 122): 11 "When they bring you before the synagogues, the rulers, and the authorities, do not worry about how you are to defend yourselves or what you are to say; 12 for the Holy Spirit will teach you at that very hour what you ought to say."

[2] MAT 10:22a (§ 59, p. 51): "and you will be hated by all because of my name."

[3] MAT 10:30 (§ 60, p. 52): "And even the hairs of your head are all counted." | LUK 12:7 (§ 155, p. 122): "But even the hairs of your head are all counted."

[4] MAT 10:22b (§ 59, p. 51): "But the one who endures to the end will be saved."

✧ MAR 13:12 = MAT 10:21 — MIC 7:6.

✦ [K] Or, *stumble.*

• To MAT 10:19–20 = MAR 13:11 = LUK 21:14 *cf.* JOH 14:26. — "But the Advocate, the Holy Spirit, whom the Father will send in my name, will teach you everything, and remind you of all that I have said to you." • To MAT 24:9b = MAR 13:13 = LUK 21:17 *cf.* JOH 15:21. — "But they will do all these things to you on account of my name, because they do not know him who sent me." C*f.* JOH 16:2. — "They will put you out of the synagogues. Indeed, an hour is coming when those who kill you will think that by doing so they are offering worship to God."

§ 216 THE DESOLATING SACRILEGE

MAT 24:15–22	MAR 13:14–20	LUK 21:20–24
15 “So when you see	14 “But when you see	20 “When you see
the desolating sacrilege standing in the holy place,	the desolating sacrilege set up where it ought not to be	Jerusalem surrounded by armies,
as was spoken of by the prophet Daniel		then know that its desolation has come near.
(let the reader understand), 16 then those in Judea must flee to the mountains; 17 the one on the housetop must not go down to take what is in the house; 18 the one in the field must not turn back to get a coat.[1]	(let the reader understand), then those in Judea must flee to the mountains; 15 the one on the housetop must not go down or enter the house to take anything away; 16 the one in the field must not turn back to get a coat.[1]	21 Then those in Judea must flee to the mountains, and
		those inside the city must leave it, and those out in the country must not enter it;[1] 22 for these are days of vengeance, as a fulfillment of all that is written.
19 Woe to those who are pregnant and to those who are nursing infants in those days!	17 Woe to those who are pregnant and to those who are nursing infants in those days!	23 Woe to those who are pregnant and to those who are nursing infants in those days!
20 Pray that your flight may not be in winter or on a sabbath. 21 For at that time there will be great suffering, such as has not been from the beginning of the world until now, no, and never will be. 22 And if those days had not been cut short, no one would be saved; but for the sake of the elect those days will be cut short.”	18 Pray that it may not be in winter. 19 For in those days there will be suffering, such as has not been from the beginning of the creation that God created until now, no, and never will be. 20 And if the Lord had not cut short those days, no one would be saved; but for the sake of the elect, whom he chose, he has cut short those days.”	
		For there will be great distress on the earth and wrath against this people; 24 they will fall by the edge of the sword and be taken away as captives among all nations; and Jerusalem will be trampled on by the Gentiles, until the times of the Gentiles are fulfilled.”

[1] LUK 17:31 (§ 184, p. 140): “On that day, anyone on the housetop who has belongings in the house must not come down to take them away; and likewise anyone in the field must not turn back.”

✧ MAT 24:15 = MAR 13:14 — DAN 9:27, 11:31, 12:11; 1 Maccabees 1:54. ✧ MAT 24:16 = MAR 13:14b — EZE 7:16. ✧ MAT 24:21 = MAR 13:19 — DAN 12:1. ✧ LUK 21:22 — DEU 32:35. ✧ LUK 21:24 — ZEC 12:3.

§ 217 FALSE MESSIAHS WILL ARISE

MAT 24:23–25	MAR 13:21–23	LUK
23 "Then if anyone says to you, 'Look! Here is the Messiah!' or 'There he is!'—do not believe it. 24 For false messiahs and false prophets will appear and produce great signs and omens, to lead astray, if possible, even the elect. 25 Take note, I have told you beforehand."	21 "And if anyone says to you at that time, 'Look! Here is the Messiah!' or 'Look! There he is!'—do not believe it. 22 False messiahs and false prophets will appear and produce signs and omens, to lead astray, if possible, the elect. 23 But be alert; I have already told you everything."	*Cf.* 17:21, 23 (§ 183–184, p. 140)

§ 218 THE DAY OF THE SON OF MAN

MAT 24:26–28	MAR	Δ *LUK 17:23–24, 37* (*§ 184, p. 140*)
26 "So, if they say to you, 'Look! He is in the wilderness,' do not go out. If they say, 'Look! He is in the inner rooms,' do not believe it. 27 For as the lightning comes from the east and flashes as far as the west, so will be the coming of the Son of Man. 28 "Wherever the corpse is, there the vultures will gather."		*23 "They will say to you, 'Look there!' or 'Look here!' Do not go,* *do not set off in pursuit.* *24 For as the lightning flashes and lights up the sky from one side to the other, so will the Son of Man be in his day."* [L] *37 Then they asked him, "Where, Lord?" He said to them, "Where the corpse is, there the vultures will gather."*

§ 219 THE COMING OF THE SON OF MAN

MAT 24:29–31	MAR 13:24–27	LUK 21:25–28
29 "Immediately after the suffering of those days the sun will be darkened, and the moon will not give its light; the stars will fall from heaven,	24 "But in those days, after that suffering, the sun will be darkened, and the moon will not give its light, 25 and the stars will be falling from heaven,	25 "There will be signs in the sun, the moon, and the stars, and on the earth distress among na- tions confused by the roaring of the sea and the waves. 26 People will faint from fear and foreboding of what is coming upon the world, for

---

✧ MAT 24:24 = MAR 13:22 — DEU 13:2. ✧ MAT 24:29 = MAR 13:24–25 = LUK 21:25–26 — PSA 65:7; ISA 13:10; 34:4.

✦ [L] text: S A W Θ λ ø 𝔐 it (some MSS.) vg sy^c sy^s sy^p bo; omit: *in his day*: P^{75} B D it (some MSS.) sa.

▸ To MAT 24:23 *cf.* **Gospel of Thomas, Logion 113.** — Jesus' disciples asked him, "When will the kingdom come?" Jesus said, "It will not come by waiting for it. People will not say, 'Here it is,' or 'There it is,' but the kingdom of the Father is spread upon the earth and people do not see it."

and the powers of heaven will be shaken. 30 Then the sign of the Son of Man will appear in heaven, and then all the tribes of the earth will mourn, and	and the powers in the heavens will be shaken. 26 Then	the powers of the heavens will be shaken. 27 Then
they will see 'the Son of Man coming on the clouds of heaven' with power and great glory. 31 And he will send out his angels with a loud trumpet call, and they will gather his elect from the four winds, from	they will see 'the Son of Man coming in clouds' with great power and glory. 27 Then he will send out the angels, and gather his elect from the four winds, from the ends of the earth	they will see 'the Son of Man coming in a cloud' with power and great glory.
one end of heaven to the other."	to the ends of heaven."	
		28 Now when these things begin to take place, stand up and raise your heads, because your redemption is drawing near."

§ 220 THE LESSON OF THE FIG TREE

MAT 24:32–33	MAR 13:28–29	LUK 21:29–31
		29 Then he told them a parable:
32 "From the fig tree learn its lesson: as soon as its branch becomes tender and puts forth its leaves, you know that summer is near.	28 "From the fig tree learn its lesson: as soon as its branch becomes tender and puts forth its leaves, you know that summer is near.	"Look at the fig tree and all the trees; 30 as soon as they sprout leaves you can see for yourselves and know that summer is already near.
33 So also, when you see all these things, you know that he is near, at the very gates."	29 So also, when you see these things taking place, you know that he is near, at the very gates."	31 So also, when you see these things taking place, you know that the kingdom of God is near."

§ 221 THE DAY AND HOUR ARE UNKNOWN EXCEPT TO GOD

MAT 24:34–36	MAR 13:30–32	LUK 21:32–33
34 "Truly I tell you, this generation will not pass away until all these things have taken place.[1]	30 "Truly I tell you, this generation will not pass away until all these things have taken place.[1]	32 "Truly I tell you, this generation will not pass away until all things have taken place.[1]

[1] *Cf.* MAT 16:28 = MAR 9:1 = LUK 9:27 (§ 123, p. 100).

✧ MAT 24:30 — ZEC 12:12–14. ✧ MAT 24:30 = MAR 13:26 = LUK 21:27 — DAN 7:13. ✧ MAT 24:31 = MAR 13:27 — DEU 30:4; ISA 27:13; ZEC 2:6.

• To MAT 24:30 *cf.* REV 1:7. • To MAT 24:30–31 and parallels, *cf.* 1TH 4:15–16. — 15 For this we declare to you by the word of the Lord, that we who are alive, who are left until the coming of the Lord, will by no means precede those who have died. 16 For the Lord himself, with a cry of command, with the archangel's call and with the sound of God's trumpet, will descend from heaven, and the dead in Christ will rise first.

35 Heaven and earth will pass away, but my words will not pass away.[1] 36 But about that day and hour no one knows, neither the angels of heaven, nor the Son,[M] but only the Father."	31 Heaven and earth will pass away, but my words will not pass away.[1] 32 But about that day or hour no one knows, neither the angels in heaven, nor the Son, but only the Father."	33 Heaven and earth will pass away, but my words will not pass away."[1]

§ 222 THE NECESSITY OF WATCHFULNESS

Δ *MAT 25:14–15b (§ 228, p. 178) +*	MAR 13:33–37	Δ *LUK 19:12–13 (§ 195, p. 151) +*
	33 "Beware, keep alert;[N] for you do not know when the time will	12 *So he said,*
14 *"For it is as if a man, going on a journey,*	come. 34 It is like a man going on a journey, when he leaves home	*"A nobleman went to a distant country to get royal power[O] for himself and then return.*
summoned his slaves and entrusted his property to them; 15 *to each according to his ability. Then he went away."*	and puts his slaves in charge, each with his work, and	13 *He summoned ten of his slaves, and gave them ten pounds,"*
Δ *24:42 (§ 225, p. 176)* 42 *"Keep awake therefore, for you do not know on what day your Lord is coming."*	commands the doorkeeper to be on the watch. 35 Therefore, keep awake—for you do not know when the master of the house will come, in the evening, or at midnight, or at cockcrow, or at dawn, 36 or else he may find you asleep when he comes	
Δ *25:13 (§ 227, p. 177)* 13 *"Keep awake therefore, for you know neither the day nor the hour."*	suddenly. 37 And what I say to you I say to all: Keep awake."	
	▾ 14:1–2 (§ 231, p. 181)	Δ *12:38 (§ 158, p. 126)* 38 *"If he comes during the middle of the night, or near dawn, and finds them so, blessed are those slaves."*

§ 223 LUKE'S ENDING TO THE DISCOURSE

MAT	MAR	LUK 21:34-36
		34 "Be on guard so that your hearts are not weighed down with dissipation and drunkenness and the worries of this life, and that day catch you unexpectedly,

[1] *Cf.* MAT 5:17 (§ 21, p. 26) = LUK 16:17 (§ 176, p. 137).

✧ LUK 21:34 — ISA 24:17.

✦ [M] text: S B D Θ ø it Irenaeus; omit: *nor the Son*: W λ ℜ vg sy[s] sy[p] sa bo Didymus. ✦ [N] text: B D it (some MSS.); add: *and pray*: S A C W Θ λ ø ℜ it (some MSS.) vg sy[s] sy[p] sa bo. ✦ [O] Greek: *a kingdom*.

		35 like a trap. For it will come upon all who live on the face of the whole earth. 36 Be alert at all times, praying that you may have the strength to escape all these things that will take place, and to stand before the Son of Man."

§ 224 THE SUDDENNESS OF THE COMING OF THE SON OF MAN

MAT 24:37–41	MAR	Δ *LUK 17:26–27, 30, 34–35 (§ 184, p. 140)*
37 "For as the days of Noah were, so will be the coming of the Son of Man. 38 For as in those days before the flood they were eating and drinking, marrying and giving in marriage, until the day Noah entered the ark, 39 and they knew nothing until the flood came and swept them all away, so too will be the coming of the Son of Man. 40 Then two will be in the field; one will be taken and one will be left. 41 Two women will be grinding meal together; one will be taken and one will be left."		*26 "Just as it was in the days of Noah, so too it will be in the days of the Son of Man. 27 They were eating and drinking, and marrying and being given in marriage, until the day Noah entered the ark, and the flood came and destroyed all of them. 30 —it will be like that on the day that the Son of Man is revealed. 34 I tell you, on that night there will be two in one bed; one will be taken and the other left. 35 There will be two women grinding meal together; one will be taken and the other left."*

§ 225 THE WATCHFUL HOUSE OWNER

MAT 24:42–44	MAR	Δ *LUK 12:39–40 (§ 158, p. 126)*
42 "Keep awake therefore, for you do not know on what day your Lord is coming.[1] 43 But understand this: if the owner of the house had known in what part of the night the thief was coming, he would have stayed awake and would not have let his house be broken into. 44 Therefore you also must be ready, for the Son of Man is coming at an unexpected hour."		 *39 "But know this: if the owner of the house had known at what hour the thief was coming, he[P] would not have let his house be broken into. 40 You also must be ready, for the Son of Man is coming at an unexpected hour."*

---

[1] *Cf.* MAR 13:33, 35 (§ 222, p. 175).

✧ MAT 24:38 = LUK 17:26–27 — GEN 7:7.

✦ [P] text: P^{75} S D sy^{c} sy^{s} sa; add: *would have watched and*: A B W Θ λ ø ℜ it vg sy^{p} bo.

● To MAT 24:42–43 *cf.* 1TH 5:2. — For you yourselves know very well that the day of the Lord will come like a thief in the night. *Cf.* REV 16:15. — "See, I am coming like a thief!"

◗ To MAT 24:42–43 *cf.* Epiphanius, *Ancoratus 21:2.* — For he (the Son) said, "That day will come like a thief in the night." *Cf.* Didymus, *On the Trinity, III.22.*

§ 226 THE FAITHFUL AND WISE SLAVE

MAT 24:45–51

45 "Who then is the faithful and wise
slave, whom his master has put in charge of
his household, to give the other slaves their
allowance of food at the proper time?
46 Blessed is that slave whom his master will
find at work when he arrives. 47 Truly I tell
you, he will put that one in charge of all his
possessions. 48 But if that wicked slave says to
himself, 'My master is delayed,'
49 and he begins to beat his fellow slaves, and
eats and drinks with drunkards,
50 the master of that slave will come on
a day when he does not expect him and at an
hour that he does not know. 51 He will cut him
in pieces[Q] and put him with the hypocrites,
where there will be weeping and gnashing of
teeth."

MAR

Δ *LUK 12:42–46* (*§ 158, p. 126*)

42 "Who then is the faithful and prudent
manager whom his master will put in charge of
his slaves, to give them their
allowance of food at the proper time?
43 Blessed is that slave whom his master will
find at work when he arrives. 44 Truly I tell
you, he will put that one in charge of all his
possessions. 45 But if that slave says to
himself, 'My master is delayed in coming,'
and if he begins to beat the other slaves, men
and women, and to eat and drink and get
drunk, 46 the master of that slave will come on
a day when he does not expect him and at an
hour that he does not know, and will cut him
in pieces,[Q] and put him with the unfaithful."

§ 227 THE PARABLE OF THE TEN BRIDESMAIDS[1]

MAT 25:1–13

1 "Then the kingdom of heaven will be like this. Ten bridesmaids took their lamps
and went to meet the bridegroom.[R] 2 Five of them were foolish, and five were
wise. 3 When the foolish took their lamps, they took no oil with them; 4 but the
wise took flasks of oil with their lamps. 5 As the bridegroom was delayed, all of
them became drowsy and slept. 6 But at midnight there was a shout, 'Look!
Here is the bridegroom! Come out to meet him.' 7 Then all those bridesmaids
got up and trimmed their lamps. 8 The foolish said to the wise, 'Give us some of
your oil, for our lamps are going out.' 9 But the wise replied, 'No! there will
not be enough for you and for us; you had better go to the dealers and buy some
for yourselves.' 10 And while they went to buy it, the bridegroom came, and those
who were ready went with him into the wedding banquet; and the door was shut.
11 Later the other bridesmaids came also, saying, 'Lord, lord, open to us.' 12 But
he replied, 'Truly I tell you, I do not know you.'[2] 13 Keep awake therefore, for
you know neither the day nor the hour."

MAR

Cf. 13:35–37
(§ 222, p. 175)

LUK

[1] LUK 12:35–36 (§ 158, p. 126): 35 "Be dressed for action and have your lamps lit; 36 be like those who are waiting for their master to return from the wedding banquet, so that they may open the door for him as soon as he comes and knocks."

[2] LUK 13:25 (§ 165, p. 130): "When once the owner of the house has got up and shut the door, and you begin to stand outside and to knock at the door, saying, 'Lord, open to us,' then in reply he will say to you, 'I do not know where you come from.' "

✦ [Q] Or, *cut him off.* ✦ [R] text: S B C W ø 𝔐 sa bo; add: *and the bride*: D Θ λ it vg sy^{s} sy^{p}.

§ 228 THE PARABLE OF THE TALENTS

MAT 25:14–30

14 "For it is as if a man, going on a
journey,
summoned his
slaves and entrusted his property to them; 15 to
one he gave five talents,[S] to another two, to
another one, to each according to his ability.
Then he went away. 16 The one who had received the five talents went off at once and
traded with them, and made five more talents.
17 In the same way, the one who had the two
talents made two more talents. 18 But the one
who had received the one talent went off and
dug a hole in the ground and hid his master's
money.

19 After a long time the master of those slaves
came

and settled accounts with them.
20 Then the one who had received the five talents
came forward, bringing five more talents,
saying, 'Master, you handed over to me five
talents; see, I have made five more talents.'
21 His master said to him, 'Well done, good and
trustworthy slave; you have been trustworthy
in a few things, I will put you in charge of
many things; enter into the joy of your master.'
22 And the one with the two talents also came
forward, saying, 'Master, you handed over to
me two talents; see, I have made two more
talents.' 23 His master said to him, 'Well done,
good and trustworthy slave; you have been
trustworthy in a few things,
I will put you in charge of many things; enter
into the joy of your master.'

MAR

Cf. MAR 13:34
(§ 222, p. 175)

Δ LUK 19:12–27 (§ 195, p. 151)

12 So he said, "A nobleman went to a
distant country to get royal power for himself
and then return. 13 He summoned ten of his
slaves, and gave them ten pounds,[T] and said

to them, 'Do business with these until I come
back.' 14 But the citizens of his country hated
him and sent a delegation after him, saying,
'We do not want this man to rule over us.'
15 When he
returned, having received royal power, he or-
dered these slaves, to whom he had given the
money, to be summoned so that he
might find out what they had gained by trading.
16 The first
came forward and
said, 'Lord,
your pound has made ten more pounds.'
17 He said to him, 'Well done, good
slave! Because you have been trustworthy
in a very small thing, take charge of
ten cities.'
18 Then the second came,
saying, 'Lord,
your pound has made five
pounds.' 19 He said to him,

'And you, rule over five cities.'

✦ [S] This talent was worth a great deal of money. ✦ [T] The mina, rendered here by *pound*, was about three months' wages for a laborer.

◗ To MAT 25:14–30 *cf.* Clement of Alexandria, *Miscellanies I.28:177,* and frequently elsewhere. — "Be skillful bankers, rejecting some things but retaining what is good." ◗ To MAT 25:22*ff.* *cf.* **Gospel of the Nazaraeans** (in Eusebius, *Theophany on Matthew 25:14–15*). — But the Gospel (written) in Hebrew letters which has reached our hands turns the threat not against the person who had hid (the talent), but against the one who had lived dissolutely — for it told of three servants: one who wasted his master's possessions with harlots and flute-girls, one who multiplied the gains, and one who hid the talent; and accordingly, one was accepted, one was only rebuked, and one was shut up in prison.

24 Then the one who had received the one talent
also came forward, saying, 'Master, I knew
that you were a harsh man, reaping where you
did not sow, and gathering where you did not
scatter seed; 25 so I was afraid, and I went and
hid your talent in the ground.
Here you have what is yours.'
26 But his master replied,
'You wicked and lazy slave! You knew, did
you, that I
reap where I did not sow, and gather where I
did not scatter? 27 Then you ought to have
invested my money with the bankers, and
on my return I would have received
what was my own with interest. 28 So
take the talent from him, and give it to the one
with the ten talents.
29 For to all
those who have, more will be given, and they
will have an abundance; but from those who
have nothing, even what they have will be
taken away.[1] 30 As for this worthless slave,
throw him into the outer darkness, where there
will be weeping and gnashing of teeth.' "

20 Then the other
came, saying, 'Lord,
here is your pound. I wrapped it up in a piece
of cloth, 21 for I was afraid of you, because you
are a harsh man; you take what you did not
deposit, and reap what you did not sow.'
22 He said to him, 'I will judge you by your own
words, you wicked slave! You knew, did you,
that I was a harsh man, taking what I did not
deposit and reaping what I did not sow?
23 Why then did you not
put my money into the bank? Then
when I returned, I could have collected
it with interest.' 24 He said to the bystanders,
'Take the pound from him and give it to the one
who has ten pounds.' 25 (And they said to him,
Lord, he has ten pounds!') 26 I tell you, to all
those who have, more will be given;
but from those who
have nothing, even what they have will be
taken away.[1] 27 But as for these enemies of mine
who did not want me to be king over them—
bring them here and slaughter them in my
presence.' "

§ 229 THE LAST JUDGMENT

MAT 25:31–46	MAR	LUK
31 "When the Son of Man comes in his glory, and all the angels with him, then he will sit on the throne of his glory. 32 All the nations will be gathered before him, and he will separate people one from another as a shepherd separates the sheep from the goats, 33 and he will put the sheep at his right hand and the goats at the left. 34 Then the king will say to those at his right hand, 'Come, you that are blessed by my Father, inherit the kingdom prepared for you from the foundation of the world; 35 for I was hungry and you gave me food, I was thirsty and you gave me something to drink, I was a stranger and you welcomed me, 36 I was naked and you gave me		

[1] *Cf.* MAT 13:12 (§ 91, p. 75), = MAR 4:25 = LUK 8:18 (§ 94, p. 77).

◗ To MAT 25:29 *cf.* **Gospel of Thomas, Logion 41.** — Jesus said, "All who have in their hands, to them will be given; and all who do not have, from them will be taken away, even the little they have." ◗ To MAT 25:31 *cf.* Origen, *Commentary on Matthew 13:2.* — And Jesus said, "Because of the sick they were sick, and because of the hungry they were hungry, and because of the thirsty they were thirsty."

clothing, I was sick and you took care of me, I was in prison and you visited me.'
37 Then the righteous will answer him, 'Lord, when was it that we saw you hungry
and gave you food, or thirsty and gave you something to drink? 38 And when was
it that we saw you a stranger and welcomed you, or naked and gave you clothing?
39 And when was it that we saw you sick or in prison and visited you?' 40 And the
king will answer them, 'Truly I tell you, just as you did it to one of the least of
these who are members of my family, you did it to me.' 41 Then he will say to
those at his left hand, 'You that are accursed, depart from me into the eternal fire
prepared for the devil and his angels; 42 for I was hungry and you gave me no food,
I was thirsty and you gave me nothing to drink, 43 I was a stranger and you did not
welcome me, naked and you did not give me clothing, sick and in prison and you
did not visit me.' 44 Then they also will answer, 'Lord, when was it that we saw
you hungry or thirsty or a stranger or naked or sick or in prison, and did not take
care of you?' 45 Then he will answer them, 'Truly I tell you, just as you did not
do it to one of the least of these, you did not do it to me.' 46 And these will go
away into eternal punishment, but the righteous into eternal life."

§ 230 A SUMMARY OF THE DAYS SPENT IN JERUSALEM

MAT	MAR	LUK 21:37–38
		▲ 34–36 (§ 223, p. 175)
Cf. 21:17 (§ 198, p. 155)	*Cf.* 11:19 (§ 200, p. 156)	37 Every day he was teaching in the temple, and at night he would go out and spend the night on the Mount of Olives, as it was called. 38 And all the people would get up early in the morning to listen to him in the temple.

• To MAT 25:46 *cf.* JOH 5:28b–29. — 28 "the hour is coming when all who are in their graves will hear his voice 29 and will come out — those who have done good, to the resurrection of life, and those who have done evil, to the resurrection of condemnation."

◗ To MAT 25:40 *cf.* Clement of Alexandria, *Miscellanies I.19:94, 5.* — "For," he said, "you have seen your brother or sister; you have seen your God." *Cf. Ibid. II.15:70, 5.* ◗ To MAT 25:40 *cf.* Tertullian, *On Prayer 26.* — He said, "You have seen your brother or sister; you have seen your God."

The Passion Narrative
Matthew 26—27; Mark 14—15; Luke 22—23

§ 231 THE CONSPIRACY AGAINST JESUS

MAT 26:1–5	MAR 14:1–2	LUK 22:1–2
1 When Jesus had finished saying all these things, he said to his disciples,	▲ 13:33–37 (§ 222, p. 175)	
2 “You know that after two days the Passover is coming, and the Son of Man will be handed over to be crucified.”	1 It was two days before the Passover and the festival of Unleavened Bread.	1 Now the festival of Unleavened Bread, which is called the Passover, was near.
3 Then the chief priests and the elders of the people gathered in the palace of the high priest, who was called Caiaphas, 4 and they conspired to arrest	The chief priests and the scribes	2 The chief priests and the scribes
Jesus by stealth and kill him.	were looking for a way to arrest Jesus by stealth and kill him;	were looking for a way to put Jesus to death,
5 But they said, “Not during the festival, or there may be a riot among the people.”	2 for they said, “Not during the festival, or there may be a riot among the people.”	for they were afraid of the people.

§ 232 THE ANOINTING AT BETHANY

MAT 26:6–13	MAR 14:3–9	LUK
6 Now while Jesus was at Bethany in the house of Simon the leper,	3 While he was at Bethany in the house of Simon the leper, as he sat at the table,	*Cf.* 7:36–50 (§ 83, p. 69)
7 a woman came to him with an alabaster jar of very costly ointment,	a woman came with an alabaster jar of very costly ointment of nard,	
and she poured it on his head as he sat at the table.	and she broke open the jar and poured the ointment on his head.	
8 But when the disciples saw it, they were angry and said, “Why this waste?	4 But some were there who said to one another in anger, “Why was the ointment wasted in this way?	
9 For this ointment could have been sold for a large sum, and the money given to the poor.”	5 For this ointment could have been sold for more than three hundred denarii,[U] and the money given to the poor.” And they scolded her.	
10 But Jesus, aware of this, said to them, “Why do you trouble the woman? She has performed a good service for me.	6 But Jesus said, “Let her alone; why do you trouble her? She has performed a good service for me.	
11 For you always have the poor with you,	7 For you always have the poor with you, and you can show kindness to them whenever you wish;	

✦ [U] The denarius was a day’s wage for a laborer.

• To § 231 *cf.* JOH 11:47–53. • To § 232 *cf.* JOH 12:1–8.

but you will not always have me. 12 By pour-	but you will not always have me.
ing this ointment on my body she has prepared	8 She has done what she could; she has anointed
me for burial. 13 Truly I tell	my body beforehand for its burial. 9 Truly I tell
you, wherever this good news is proclaimed in	you, wherever the good news is proclaimed in
the whole world, what she has done will be told	the whole world, what she has done will be told
in remembrance of her."	in remembrance of her."

§ 233 JUDAS AGREES TO BETRAY JESUS

MAT 26:14–16	MAR 14:10–11	LUK 22:3–6
14 Then one of the twelve, who was	10 Then	3 Then Satan entered into
called Judas Iscariot,	Judas Iscariot, who was one	Judas called Iscariot, who was one
went to	of the twelve, went to	of the twelve; 4 he went away
the chief priests 15 and said, "What	the chief priests	and conferred with the chief priests
will you give me		and officers of the temple police
if I betray him to	in order to betray him to	about how he might betray him to
you?" They	them. 11 When they heard it, they	them. 5 They
	were greatly pleased, and	were greatly pleased and
paid him thirty pieces of silver.	promised to give him money. So	agreed to give him money. 6 So
16 And from that moment he began	he began	he consented and began
to look for an opportunity to	to look for an opportunity to	to look for an opportunity to
betray him.	betray him.	betray him to them when no crowd
		was present.

§ 234 PREPARATION FOR THE PASSOVER

MAT 26:17–19	MAR 14:12–16	LUK 22:7–13
17 On the first day of Unleavened	12 On the first day of Unleavened	7 Then came the day of Unleavened
Bread	Bread, when the Passover lamb	Bread, on which the Passover lamb
	is sacrificed,	had to be sacrificed. 8 So Jesus[V]
		sent Peter and John, saying, "Go
		and prepare the Passover meal for
		us that we may eat it."
the disciples came to Jesus, saying,	his disciples said to him,	9 They asked him,
"Where do you want us to	"Where do you want us to	"Where do you want us to
make the preparations for	go and make the preparations for	make preparations for it?"
you to eat the Passover?" 18 He	you to eat the Passover?" 13 So he	10 "Listen," he
said,	sent two of his disciples, saying	said

✧ MAT 26:15 — ZEC 11:12

✦ [V] Greek: *he.*

▸ To MAT 26:17 (LUK 22:9, 15) *cf.* **Gospel of the Ebionites** (in Epiphanius, *Against Heresies, XXX.22:4*). — But leaving the proper sequence of the words and perverting the meaning..., they make the disciples say: "Where will you have us prepare for you to eat the passover?" And he (Jesus) asks, "Have I earnestly desired to eat this passover meat (flesh?) with you?"

"Go into the
city to a certain man, and
say
to him, 'The
Teacher says, My time is near; I
will keep the Passover at your house
with my disciples.' "
19 So the disciples did as Jesus had
directed them,
and
they prepared the Passover meal.

to them, "Go into the
city, and a man carrying a jar of
water will meet you; follow him,
14 and wherever he enters, say
to the owner of the house, 'The
Teacher asks, Where is my
guest room where I may eat the
Passover with my disciples?'
15 He will show you a large room
upstairs, furnished and ready.
Make preparations for us there."
16 So the disciples set out and went
to the city, and found everything as
he had told them; and
they prepared the Passover meal.

to them, "when you have entered
the city, a man carrying a jar of
water will meet you; follow him
into the house he enters 11 and say
to the owner of the house, 'The
teacher asks you, "Where is the
guest room, where I may eat the
Passover with my disciples?" '
12 He will show you a large room
upstairs, already furnished.
Make preparations for us there."
13 So they went
and found everything as
he had told them; and
they prepared the Passover meal.

The Last Supper

Matthew 26:20–29; Mark 14:17–25; Luke 22:14–38

§ 235 THE TRAITOR

MAT 26:20–25

20 When it was evening, he took his
place with the twelve;[W]
21 and while they were eating, he
said, "Truly I tell you, one of you
will betray me."
22 And they became greatly distressed and began to say to him one
after another, "Surely not I,
Lord?" 23 He answered, "The
one who has dipped his hand
into the bowl with me will betray
me. 24 The Son of Man goes as it
is written of him, but woe to
that one by whom the Son of Man
is betrayed! It would have been
better for that one not to have been
born." 25 Judas, who betrayed

MAR 14:17–21

17 When it was evening, he came
with the twelve.
18 And when they had taken their
places and were eating, Jesus
said, "Truly I tell you, one of you
will betray me, one who is eating
with me." 19 They began to be distressed and to say to him one
after another, "Surely, not I?"
20 He said to them, "It is one of the
twelve, one who is dipping bread
into the bowl with me.
21 For the Son of Man goes as it
is written of him, but woe to
that one by whom the Son of Man
is betrayed! It would have been
better for that one not to have been
born."

LUK 22:14, 21–23

14 When the hour came, he took his
place at the table, and the apostles
with him.

Δ *22:21–23 (§ 237a, p. 185)*
21 "But see, the one who
betrays me is
with me,
and his hand is on the table.
22 For the Son of Man is going as it
has been determined, but woe to
that one by whom he
is betrayed!"

✧ MAR 14:18 — PSA 41:9.

✦ W text: $P^{37?}$ $P^{45?}$ B D λ ø ℜ sy^{s}; add: *disciples*: S A W Θ it vg sy^{p} sa bo.

him, said, "Surely not I, Rabbi?" He replied, "You have said so."		
		23 *Then they began to ask one another, which one of them it could be who would do this.*

§ 236 THE INSTITUTION OF THE LORD'S SUPPER

MAT 26:26–29	MAR 14:22–25	LUK 22:15–20
Cf. 26:29	*Cf.* 14:25	15 He said to them, "I have eagerly desired to eat this Passover with you before I suffer; 16 for I tell you, I will not eat it[X] until it is fulfilled in the kingdom of God." 17 Then he took a cup, and after giving thanks he said, "Take this and divide it among yourselves; 18 for I tell you that from now on I will not drink of the fruit of the vine until the kingdom of God comes."
26 While they were eating, Jesus took a loaf of bread, and after blessing it he broke it, gave it to the disciples, and said, "Take, eat; this is my body."	22 While they were eating, he took a loaf of bread, and after blessing it he broke it, gave it to them, and said, "Take; this is my body."	19 Then he took a loaf of bread, and when he had given thanks, he broke it and gave it to them, saying, "This is my body, which is given for you. Do this in remembrance of me." 20 And
27 Then he took a cup, and after giving thanks he gave it to them, saying, "Drink from it, all of you; 28 for this is my blood of the[Y] covenant, which is poured out	23 Then he took a cup, and after giving thanks he gave it to them, and all of them drank from it. 24 He said to them, "This is my blood of the[Z] covenant, which is poured out	he did the same with the cup after supper, saying, "This cup that is poured out

✧ MAT 26:28 = MAR 14:24 = LUK 22:20 — EXO 24:8; JER 31:31; ZEC 9:11.

✦ [X] text: $P^{75?}$ S A B Θ λ sa bo; *never eat it again*: C D W ø 𝔎 it vg sy^c sy^s sy^p. ✦ [Y] text: P^{37} S B Θ; add: *new*: A C D W λ ø 𝔎 it vg sy^s sy^p sa bo. ✦ [Z] text S B C D W Θ bo; add: *new*: A λ ø 𝔎 it vg sy^s sy^p sa.

● To § 236 *cf.* JOH 13:21–30.

◗ To MAT 26:27–28 *cf.* Justin, *Apology I.66:3.* — For the apostles, in the writings which were composed by them, called gospels, have thus delivered what was demanded of them: that Jesus took bread, gave thanks, and said, "Do this in remembrance of me; this is my body." And likewise taking the cup, and having given thanks, Jesus said, "This is my blood." ◗ To MAT 26:27–28 and parallels, *cf.* **Didache 9:1–5.** — 1 Concerning the Eucharist, celebrate it in this way: 2 First, concerning the cup: "We give thanks to you, our Father, for the Holy Vine of David your child, which you made known to us through Jesus your child; to you be glory forever." 3 And concerning the broken bread: "We give thanks to you, our Father, for the life and knowledge which you made known to us through Jesus your child; to you be glory forever. 4 As this broken bread was scattered upon the mountains, but was brought together and became one, so let your church be gathered together from the ends of the earth into your kingdom, for yours is the glory and the power, through Jesus Christ, forever." 5 But let none eat or drink of your eucharist except those who have been baptized in the Lord's name. For concerning this also the Lord said, "Give not what is holy to the dogs."

for many for the forgiveness of sins.[1]	for many.[1]	for you is the new covenant in my blood."[A+1]
29 I tell you, I will never again drink of this fruit of the vine until that day when I drink it new with you in my Father's kingdom."	25 Truly I tell you, I will never again drink of the fruit of the vine until that day when I drink it new in the kingdom of God."	*Cf.* 22:16, 18

§ 237 LAST WORDS
Luke 22:21–38

a) The Betrayal Foretold

MAT	MAR	LUK 22:21–23
Cf. 26:21–25 (§ 235, p. 183)	*Cf.* 14:18–21 (§ 235, p. 183)	21 "But see, the one who betrays me is with me, and his hand is on the table. 22 For the Son of Man is going as it has been determined, but woe to that one by whom he is betrayed!" 23 Then they began to ask one another, which one of them it could be who would do this.

b) Greatness in the Kingdom of God

Δ *MAT 20:25–28* (§ 192, p. 148) +	Δ *MAR 10:42–45* (§ 192, p. 148)	LUK 22:24–30
		24 A dispute also arose among them as to which one of them was to be regarded as the greatest.
25 But Jesus called them to him and said, "You know that the rulers of the Gentiles	*42 So Jesus called them and said to them, "You know that among the Gentiles those whom they recognize as their rulers*	25 But he said to them, "The kings of the Gentiles
lord it over them, and their great ones are tyrants over them. 26 It will not be so among you; but whoever wishes to be great among you must be your servant, 27 and whoever wishes to be first among you must be your slave; 28 just as the Son of Man came not to be served but to serve, and to	*lord it over them, and their great ones are tyrants over them. 43 But it is not so among you; but whoever wishes to become great among you must be your servant, 44 and whoever wishes to be first among you must be slave of all. 45 For the Son of Man came not to be served but to serve, and to*	lord it over them; and those in author- ity over them are called benefactors. 26 But not so with you; rather the greatest among you must become like the youngest, and the leader like one who serves. *Cf.* 9:48b = MAR 9:35, (§ 129, p. 106)

[1] 1CO 11:23–25. — 23 For I received from the Lord what I also handed on to you, that the Lord Jesus on the night when he was betrayed took a loaf of bread, 24 and when he had given thanks, he broke it and said, "This is my body that is for you. Do this in remembrance of me." 25 In the same way he took the cup also, after supper, saying, "This cup is the new covenant in my blood. Do this, as often as you drink it, in remembrance of me."

✦ [A] text: P^{75} S A B C W Θ λ ø 𝔑 it (some MSS.) vg sa bo; omit: *that is poured out for you* through verse 20: D it (some MSS.); verses 19, 17, 18: sy^{c}; verses 19, 20: sy^{p}; verses 19, 20a (*after supper*), 17, 20b (*This blood of mine is the new covenant*): sy^{s}.

give his life a ransom for many.”	*give his life a ransom for many.”*	
		27 For who is greater, the one who is at the table or the one who serves? Is it not the one at the table? But I am among you as one who serves.
Δ *19:28 (§ 189, p. 145)* 28 *Jesus said to them, “Truly I tell you, at the renewal of all things, when the Son of Man is seated on the throne of his glory, you who have followed me*		28 You are those who have stood by me in my trials; 29 and I confer on you, just as my Father has conferred on me, a kingdom, 30 so that you may eat and drink at my table in my kingdom,
will also sit on twelve thrones, judging the twelve tribes of Israel.”		and you will sit on thrones judging the twelve tribes of Israel.”

c) Peter’s Denial Predicted

MAT	MAR	LUK 22:31–34
Cf. 26:30–35 (§ 238, p. 187)	*Cf.* 14:26–31 (§ 238, p. 187)	31 “Simon, Simon, listen! Satan has demanded to sift all of you like wheat, 32 but I have prayed for you[B] that your own faith may not fail; and you, when once you have turned back, strengthen your brothers.” 33 And he said to him, “Lord, I am ready to go with you to prison and to death!” 34 Jesus said, “I tell you, Peter, the cock will not crow this day, until you have denied three times that you know me.”

d) Purse, Bag, and Sword

MAT	MAR	LUK 22:35–38
		35 He said to them, “When I sent you out without a purse, bag, or sandals, did you lack anything?” They said, “No, not a thing.” 36 He said to them, “But now, the one who has a purse must take it, and likewise a bag. And the one who has no sword must sell his cloak and buy one. 37 For I tell you, this scripture must be

✧ LUK 22:37 — ISA 53:12.

✦ [B] The Greek word for *you* in verse 32 is singular.

• To LUK 22:27 and parallels, *cf.* JOH 13:4-5, 12–14. — 4 [Jesus] got up from the table, took off his outer robe, and tied a towel around himself. 5 Then he poured water into a basin and began to wash the disciples’ feet and to wipe them with the towel that was tied around him. [6-11] 12 After he had washed their feet, had put on his robe, and had returned to the table, he said to them, “Do you know what I have done to you? 13 You call me Teacher and Lord — and you are right, for that is what I am. 14 So if I, your Lord and Teacher, have washed your feet, you also ought to wash one another’s feet.” • To LUK 22:31–34 *cf.* JOH 13:36–38. — 36 Simon Peter said to him, “Lord, where are you going?” Jesus answered, “Where I am going, you cannot follow me now; but you will follow afterward.” 37 Peter said to him, “Lord, why can I not follow you now? I will lay down my life for you.” 38 Jesus answered, “Will you lay down your life for me? Very truly, I tell you, before the cock crows, you will have denied me three times.”

fulfilled in me, 'And he was counted among the lawless'; and indeed what is written about me is being fulfilled." 38 They said, "Lord, look, here are two swords." He replied, "It is enough."

§ 238 PETER'S DENIAL PREDICTED

MAT 26:30–35	MAR 14:26–31	LUK 22:39 +
30 When they had sung the hymn, they went out to the Mount of Olives. 31 Then Jesus said to them, "You will all become deserters because of me this night; for it is written, 'I will strike the shepherd, and the sheep of the flock will be scattered.' 32 But after I am raised up, I will go ahead of you to Galilee."	26 When they had sung the hymn, they went out to the Mount of Olives. 27 And Jesus said to them, "You will all become deserters; for it is written, 'I will strike the shepherd, and the sheep will be scattered.' 28 But after I am raised up, I will go before you to Galilee."[C]	39 He came out and went, as was his custom, to the Mount of Olives; and the disciples followed him.
		Δ *22:31–34 (§ 237c, p. 186)* *31 "Simon, Simon, listen! Satan has demanded to sift all of you like wheat, 32 but I have prayed for you that your own faith may not fail; and you, when once you have turned back, strengthen your brothers."*
33 Peter said to him, "Though all become deserters because of you, I will never desert you." 34 Jesus said to him, "Truly I tell you, this very night, before the cock crows, you will deny me three times."	29 Peter said to him, "Even though all become deserters, I will not." 30 Jesus said to him, "Truly I tell you, this day, this very night, before the cock crows twice,[D] you will deny me three times."	*33 And he said to him, "Lord, I am ready to go with you to prison and to death!" 34 Jesus said, "I tell you, Peter, the cock will not crow this day, until you have denied three times that you know me."*
35 Peter said to him, "Even though I must die with you, I will not deny you." And so said all the disciples.	31 But he said vehemently, "Even though I must die with you, I will not deny you." And all of them said the same.	

✧ MAT 26:31 = MAR 14:27 — ZEC 13:7.

✦ [C] Verse 28 omitted in the Fayum Fragment. ✦ [D] text: A B Θ λ φ 𝔐 vg sy[s] sy[p] sa bo; omit: *twice*: S C D W it.

• To MAT 26:30 and parallels, *cf.* JOH 18:1. — After Jesus had spoken these words, he went out with his disciples across the Kidron valley to a place where there was a garden, which he and his disciples entered. • To MAT 26:31 and parallels, *cf.* JOH 16:32. — "The hour is coming, indeed it has come, when you will be scattered, each one to his home, and you will leave me alone. Yet I am not alone because the Father is with me." • To MAT 26:33 and parallels, *cf.* JOH 13:36–38. — 36 Simon Peter said to him, "Lord, where are you going?" Jesus answered, "Where I am going, you cannot follow me now; but you will follow afterward." 37 Peter said to him, "Lord, why can I not follow you now? I will lay down my life for you." 38 Jesus answered, "Will you lay down your life for me? Very truly, I tell you, before the cock crows, you will have denied me three times."

◗ To MAR 14:27–30 *cf.* Fayum Fragment. — while leading them out Jesus said, "This night you will all fall away, as it is written, 'I will strike the shepherd, and the sheep will be scattered.' " When Peter said, "Even though all, not I," Jesus answered, "Before the cock crows twice, you will this day deny me three times."

§ 239 JESUS IN GETHSEMANE

MAT 26:36–46	MAR 14:32–42	LUK 22:40–46
36 Then Jesus went with them to a place called Gethsemane; and he said to his disciples, "Sit here while I go over there and pray."	32 They went to a place called Gethsemane; and he said to his disciples, "Sit here while I pray."	40 When he reached the place, he said to them, "Pray that you may not come into the time of trial."
37 He took with him Peter and the two sons of Zebedee, and began to be grieved and agitated. 38 Then he said to them, "I am deeply grieved, even to death; remain here, and stay awake with me."	33 He took with him Peter and James and John, and began to be distressed and agitated. 34 And he said to them, "I am deeply grieved, even to death; remain here, and keep awake."	
39 And going a little farther, he threw himself on the ground and prayed, "My Father, if it is possible, let this cup pass from me; yet not what I want but what you want."	35 And going a little farther, he threw himself on the ground and prayed that, if it were possible, the hour might pass from him. 36 He said, "Abba, Father, for you all things are possible; remove this cup from me; yet, not what I want, but what you want."	41 Then he withdrew from them about a stone's throw, knelt down, and prayed, 42 "Father, if you are willing, remove this cup from me; yet, not my will but yours be done."[E]
		43 [Then an angel from heaven appeared to him and gave him strength. 44 In his anguish he prayed more earnestly, and his sweat became like great drops of blood falling down on the ground.]
40 Then he came to the disciples and found them sleeping; and he said to Peter, "So, could you not stay awake with me one hour? 41 Stay awake and pray that you may not come into the time of trial; the spirit indeed is willing, but the flesh is weak."	37 He came and found them sleeping; and he said to Peter, "Simon, are you asleep? Could you not keep awake one hour? 38 Keep awake and pray that you may not come into the time of trial; the spirit indeed is willing, but the flesh is weak."	45 When he got up from prayer, he came to the disciples and found them sleeping because of grief, 46 and he said to them, "Why are you sleeping? Get up and pray that you may not come into the time of trial."
42 Again he went away for the second time and prayed, "My Father, if this cannot pass unless I drink it, your will be done." 43 Again he came and found them sleeping, for their eyes were heavy.	39 And again he went away and prayed, saying the same words. 40 And once more he came and found them sleeping, for their eyes were very heavy; and	

✧ MAT 26:38 = MAR 14:34 — PSA 42:5–6, 11; 43:5.

✦ [E] text: S D Θ λ 𝔐 it vg sy^c sy^p Justin, Irenaeus, Hippolytus; omit verses 43-44: P^{75} A B W sy^s sa bo Marcion, Clement, Origen.

• To MAT 26:36 and parallels, *cf.* JOH 18:1. • To MAT 26:38 = MAR 14:34 *cf.* JOH 12:27. — "Now my soul is troubled. And what should I say — 'Father, save me from this hour'? No, it is for this reason that I have come to this hour."
• To MAT 26:39b and parallels, *cf.* JOH 18:11. — Jesus said to Peter, "...Am I not to drink the cup that the Father has given me?"

	they did not know what to say to him.	
44 So leaving them again, he went away and prayed for the third time, saying the same words. 45 Then he came to the disciples and said to them, “Are you still sleeping and taking your rest? See, the hour is at hand, and the Son of Man is betrayed into the hands of sinners. 46 Get up, let us be going. See, my betrayer is at hand.”	41 He came a third time and said to them, “Are you still sleeping and taking your rest? Enough! The hour has come; the Son of Man is betrayed into the hands of sinners. 42 Get up, let us be going. See, my betrayer is at hand.”	

§ 240 JESUS TAKEN CAPTIVE

MAT 26:47–56	MAR 14:43–52	LUK 22:47–53
47 While he was still speaking, Judas, one of the twelve, arrived; with him was a large crowd with swords and clubs, from the chief priests and the elders of the people.	43 Immediately, while he was still speaking, Judas, one of the twelve, arrived; and with him there was a crowd with swords and clubs, from the chief priests, the scribes, and the elders.	47 While he was still speaking, suddenly a crowd came, and the one called Judas, one of the twelve, was leading them. *Cf.* 22:52
48 Now the betrayer had given them a sign, saying, “The one I will kiss is the man; arrest him.”	44 Now the betrayer had given them a sign, saying, “The one I will kiss is the man; arrest him and lead him away under guard.”	
49 At once he came up to Jesus and said, “Greetings, Rabbi!” and kissed him. 50 Jesus said to him, “Friend, do what you are here to do.”	45 So when he came, he went up to him at once and said, “Rabbi!” and kissed him.	He approached Jesus to kiss him; 48 but Jesus said to him, “Judas, is it with a kiss that you are betraying the Son of Man?”
Then they came and laid hands on Jesus and arrested him.	46 Then they laid hands on him and arrested him.	
51 Suddenly, one of those with Jesus put his hand on his sword, drew it, and struck the slave of the high priest, cutting off his ear. 52 Then Jesus said to him,	47 But one of those who stood near drew his sword and struck the slave of the high priest, cutting off his ear.	49 When those who were around him saw what was coming, they asked, “Lord, should we strike with the sword?” 50 Then one of them struck the slave of the high priest and cut off his right ear. 51 But Jesus said, “No more of this!” And he touched his ear and healed him.
“Put your sword back into its place; for all who take the sword will perish by the sword. 53 Do you think		

• To MAT 26:46 = MAR 14:42 *cf.* JOH 14:31b. — “Rise, let us be on our way.” • To § 240 *cf.* JOH 18:2–11.

that I cannot appeal to my Father,
and he will at once send me more
than twelve legions of angels?
54 But how then would the scriptures
be fulfilled, which say it must hap-
pen in this way?" 55 At that hour
Jesus said to the crowds,
"Have you come
out with swords and clubs to arrest
me as though I were a bandit?
Day after day I sat in
the temple teaching, and you did
not arrest me. 56 But
all this has taken place, so that the
scriptures of the prophets may be
fulfilled." Then all the disciples
deserted him and fled.

48 Then Jesus said to them,
Cf. 14:43
"Have you come
out with swords and clubs to arrest
me as though I were a bandit?
49 Day after day I was with you in
the temple teaching, and you did
not arrest me. But
let the
scriptures be
fulfilled." 50 All of them
deserted him and fled. 51 A certain
young man was following him,
wearing nothing but a linen cloth.
They caught hold of him, 52 but he
left the linen cloth and ran off naked.

52 Then Jesus said to the chief
priests, the officers of the temple
police, and the elders who had
come for him, "Have you come
out with swords and clubs
as if I were a bandit? 53 When
I was with you day after day in
the temple, you did
not lay hands on me. But
this is your hour, and the power of
darkness!"

§ 241 JESUS BEFORE THE COUNCIL. PETER'S DENIAL

MAT 26:57–75

57 Those who had arrested Jesus
took him to
Caiaphas the high priest, in whose
house the scribes and the elders
had gathered. 58 But Peter was
following him at a distance,
as far as the courtyard of the high
priest; and going inside, he sat
with the guards in order to see how

MAR 14:53–72

53 They
took Jesus to
the high priest; and all the chief
priests, the elders, and the scribes
were assembled. 54 Peter had
followed him at a distance,
right into the courtyard of the high
priest; and he was sitting
with the guards,

LUK 22:54–71

54 Then they seized him and
led him away, bringing him[F] into
the high priest's
house.
But Peter was
following at a distance. 55 When
they had kindled a fire in the middle
of the courtyard
and sat down
together, Peter sat among them.

✦ [F] text: S A B W ø ℜ sa bo; omit: *bringing him*: D Θ λ it vg sy[c] sy[s].

• To MAT 26:55b and parallels, *cf.* JOH 18:20. — Jesus answered, "I have spoken openly to the world; I have always taught in synagogues and in the temple, where all the Jews come together. I have said nothing in secret." • To MAT 26:57 and parallels, *cf.* JOH 18:12–14. — 12 So the soldiers, their officer, and the Jewish police arrested Jesus and bound him. 13 First they took him to Annas, who was the father-in-law of Caiaphas, the high priest that year. 14 Caiaphas was the one who had advised the Jews that it was better to have one person die for the people. • To MAT 26:58 and parallels, *cf.* JOH 18:15–16. — 15 Simon Peter and another disciple followed Jesus. Since that disciple was known to the high priest, he went with Jesus into the courtyard of the high priest, 16 but Peter was standing outside at the gate. So the other disciple, who was known to the high priest, went out, spoke to the woman who guarded the gate, and brought Peter in.

this would end.

Cf. 26:69–75

Cf. 26:67

Cf. 27:1 (§ 242, p. 193)

59 Now the chief priests and the
whole council were looking for
false testimony against Jesus so that
they might put him to death, 60 but
they found none, though many
false witnesses came forward.

At last two came forward
61 and said,
"This fellow said, 'I am able to
destroy the temple of God and

---

warming himself at the fire.

Cf. 14:66–72

Cf. 14:65

Cf. 15:1 (§ 242, p. 193)

55 Now the chief priests and the
whole council were looking for
testimony against Jesus
to put him to death; but
they found none. 56 For many gave
false testimony against him, and
their testimony did not agree.
57 Some stood up and gave false testimony against him, saying,
58 "We heard him say, 'I will
destroy this temple

---

56 Then a servant-girl, seeing him
in the firelight, stared at him and
said, "This man also was with
him." 57 But he denied it, saying,
"Woman, I do not know him."
58 A little later someone else, on
seeing him, said, "You also are
one of them." But Peter said,
"Man, I am not!" 59 Then about
an hour later still another kept in-
sisting, "Surely this man also was
with him; for he is a Galilean."
60 But Peter said, "Man, I do not
know what you are talking about!"
At that moment, while he was still
speaking, the cock crowed.
61 The Lord turned and looked at
Peter. Then Peter remembered the
word of the Lord, how he had said
to him, "Before the cock crows today, you will deny me three times."
62 And he went out and wept bitterly.
63 Now the men who were holding
Jesus began to mock him and beat
him; 64 they also blindfolded him
and kept asking him, "Prophesy!
Who is it that struck you?" 65 They
kept heaping many other insults on
him. 66 When day came, the assembly of the elders of the people,
both chief priests and scribes, gathered together, and they brought
him to their council.

• To MAT 26:59 = MAR 14:55 *cf.* JOH 18:19–24. • To MAT 26:61 = MAR 14:58 *cf.* JOH 2:19. — Jesus answered them, "Destroy this temple, and in three days I will raise it up."

◗ To MAT 26:61 = MAR 14:58 *cf.* **Gospel of Thomas, Logion 71.** — Jesus said, "I will destroy this house, and no one will be able to build it (again)."

to build it in three days.' "

62 The
high priest stood up
and said, "Have you no
answer? What is it that they testify
against you?" 63 But Jesus
was silent.
Then the high priest said to him,
"I put you under oath before the
living God, tell us if you are the
Messiah, the Son of
God."
64 Jesus said to him,
"You have said so.

But I tell you, From now on
you will see the Son of Man
seated at the right hand of
Power and coming on the
clouds of heaven."

65 Then the high priest tore his
clothes and said, "He has blasphemed! Why do we still need
witnesses? You have now
heard his blasphemy.
66 What is your verdict?"
They answered,
"He deserves death."
67 Then they
spat in his face and
struck him; and some slapped him,
68 saying,
"Prophesy to us, you Messiah!
Who is it that struck you?"

69 Now Peter was

---

that is made with hands, and
in three days I will build another,
not made with hands.' " 59 But
even on this point their testimony
did not agree. 60 Then the
high priest stood up before them
and asked Jesus, "Have you no
answer?" What is it that they testify
against you? 61 But he
was silent and did not answer.
Again the high priest asked him,

"Are you the
Messiah, the Son of
the Blessed One?"
62 Jesus said,
"I am; and

'you will see the Son of Man
seated at the right hand of
the Power,' and 'coming with the
clouds of heaven.' "

63 Then the high priest tore his
clothes and said,
"Why do we still need
witnesses? 64 You have
heard his blasphemy!
What is your decision?"
All of them
condemned him as deserving death.
65 Some began to
spit on him, to blindfold him, and
to strike him,
saying to him,
"Prophesy!"

The guards also took him over and
beat him. 66 While Peter was

---

67 They said,

"If you are the
Messiah,
tell us."
He replied,
"If I tell you, you will not believe;
68 and if I question you, you will not
answer. 69 But from now on
the Son of Man
will be seated at the right hand of
the power of God."

70 All of them asked, "Are you,
then, the Son of God?" He said to
them, "You say that I am."
71 Then they
said,
"What further
testimony do we need? We have
heard it ourselves from his own lips!"

△ *22:63–65 (repeated)*
*63 Now the men who were holding
Jesus began to mock him and
beat him; 64 they also blindfolded
him and kept asking him,
"Prophesy!
Who is it that struck you?"
65 They kept heaping many other insults on him.*

✧ MAT 26:64 (24:30) = MAR 14:62 (13:26) = LUK 22:69 (21:27) — DAN 7:13. ✧ MAT 26:65–66 = MAR 14:64 — LEV 24:16.

● To MAT 26:69*ff.* and parallels, *cf.* JOH 18:17, 25–27. — 17 The woman said to Peter, "You are not also one of this man's disciples, are you?" He said, "I am not." [18–24] 25 Now Simon Peter was standing and warming himself. They asked him, "You are not also one of his disciples, are you?" He denied it and said, "I am not." 26 One of the slaves of the high priest, a relative of the man whose ear Peter had cut off, asked, "Did I not see you in the garden with him?" 27 Again Peter denied it, and at that moment the cock crowed.

◗ To MAT 26:67 = MAR 14:65 *cf.* **Gospel of Peter 3:9.** — Others stood and spat in his eyes and still others slapped his cheeks; others pricked him with a reed, and some of them scourged him, saying, "With this honor let us honor the Son of God."

sitting outside in the courtyard. A servant-girl came to him	below in the courtyard, one of the servant-girls of the high priest came by. 67 When she saw Peter warming himself, she stared at him	Δ *22:56–62 (repeated)* *56 Then a servant-girl, seeing him in the firelight, stared at him*
and said, "You also were with Jesus the Galilean."	and said, "You also were with Jesus, the man from Nazareth."	*and said, "This man also was with him."*
70 But he denied it before all of them, saying, "I do not know what you are talking about."	68 But he denied it, saying, "I do not know or understand what you are talking about."	*57 But he denied it, saying, "Woman, I do not know him."*
71 When he went out to the porch,	And he went out into the forecourt. [G] Then the cock crowed.	*58 A little later*
another servant-girl saw him, and she said to the bystanders, "This man was with Jesus of Nazareth." 72 Again he denied it with an oath, "I do not know the man."	69 And the servant-girl, on seeing him, began again to say to the bystanders, "This man is one of them." 70 But again he denied it.	*someone else, on seeing him, said, "You also are one of them." But Peter said, "Man, I am not!"*
73 After a little while the bystanders came up and said to Peter, "Certainly you are also one of them, for your accent betrays you."	Then after a little while the bystanders again said to Peter, "Certainly you are one of them; for you are a Galilean."	*59 Then about an hour later still another kept insisting, "Surely this man also was with him; for he is a Galilean."*
74 Then he began to curse, and he swore an oath, "I do not know the man!" At that moment the cock crowed.	71 But he began to curse, and he swore an oath, "I do not know this man you are talking about." 72 At that moment the cock crowed for the second time. [H]	*60 But Peter said, "Man, I do not know what you are talking about!" At that moment, while he was still speaking, the cock crowed. 61 The Lord turned and looked at Peter.*
75 Then Peter remembered what Jesus had said: "Before the cock crows, you will deny me three times." And he went out and wept bitterly.	Then Peter remembered that Jesus had said to him, "Before the cock crows twice, you will deny me three times." And he broke down and wept.	*Then Peter remembered the word of the Lord, how he had said to him, "Before the cock crows today, you will deny me three times." 62 And he went out and wept bitterly.*

§ 242 JESUS DELIVERED TO PILATE

MAT 27:1–2	MAR 15:1	LUK 23:1 +
		Δ *22:66 (§ 241, p. 191)*
1 When morning came, all the chief priests and the elders of the	1 As soon as it was morning, the chief priests	*66 When day came, the assembly of the elders of the people, both chief priests and scribes,*

✦ [G] text: A C D Θ λ ø ℜ it vg sy^{p}; omit: *then the cock crowed*: S B W sy^{s} sa bo. ✦ [H] text: A B D W Θ λ ø ℜ it vg sy^{s} sy^{p} sa bo (*Cf.* MAR 14:68.); omit: *the second time*: S C. *Cf.* MAT 26:74; LUK 22:60; JOH 18:27.

• To § 242 *cf.* JOH 18:28–32.

◗ To MAT 26:74 *cf.* **Gospel of the Nazaraeans.** — The Jewish Gospel has: And he denied, and he swore (i.e., took an oath) and he cursed.

		gathered together, and they *brought him to their council.*
people conferred together against	held a consultation with the elders and scribes and the whole council.	23:1 Then the assembly rose as a body
Jesus in order to bring about his death. 2 They bound him, led him away, and handed him over to Pilate the governor.	They bound Jesus, led him away, and handed him over to Pilate.	and brought Jesus before Pilate.

§ 243 THE DEATH OF JUDAS

MAT 27:3–10	MAR	LUK
3 When Judas, his betrayer, saw that Jesus was condemned, he repented and brought back the thirty pieces of silver to the chief priests and the elders. 4 He said, "I have sinned by betraying innocent blood." But they said, "What is that to us? See to it yourself." 5 Throwing down the pieces of silver in the temple, he departed; and he went and hanged himself. 6 But the chief priests, taking the pieces of silver, said, "It is not lawful to put them into the treasury, since they are blood money." 7 After conferring together, they used them to buy the potter's field as a place to bury foreigners. 8 For this reason that field has been called the Field of Blood to this day. 9 Then was fulfilled what had been spoken through the prophet Jeremiah, "And they took the thirty pieces of silver, the price of the one on whom a price had been set, on whom some of the people of Israel had set a price, 10 and they gave them for the potter's field, as the Lord commanded me."		

§ 244 THE TRIAL BEFORE PILATE

MAT 27:11–14	MAR 15:2–5	LUK 23:2–5
		2 They began to accuse him, say- ing, "We found this man perverting our nation, forbidding us to pay taxes to the emperor, and saying that he himself is the Messiah, a king."
11 Now Jesus stood before the gov- ernor; and the governor asked him, "Are you the King of the Jews?" Jesus said, "You say so."	2 Pilate asked him, "Are you the King of the Jews?" He answered him, "You say so."	3 Then Pilate asked him, "Are you the king of the Jews?" He answered, "You say so."
12 But when he was accused by the chief priests and elders, he did not answer. 13 Then Pilate said to him, "Do you not hear how	3 Then the chief priests accused him of many things. 4 Pilate asked him again, "Have you no answer? See how	

✧ MAT 27:9–10 — ZEC 11:12–13; JER 18:2–3; 32:6–15.

• To § 243 *cf.* ACT 1:18–19. • To MAT 27:11*ff.* and parallels, *cf.* JOH 18:33–37.

MAT	MAR	LUK
many accusations they make against you?" 14 But he gave him no answer, not even to a single charge, so that the governor was greatly amazed.	many charges they bring against you." 5 But Jesus made no further reply, so that Pilate was amazed.	
		4 Then Pilate said to the chief priests and the crowds, "I find no basis for an accusation against this man." 5 But they were insistent and said, "He stirs up the people by teaching throughout all Judea, from Galilee where he began even to this place."

§ 245 JESUS BEFORE HEROD

MAT	MAR	LUK 23:6–16
Cf. 27:12 (§ 244, p. 194)	*Cf.* 15:3 (§ 244, p. 194)	6 When Pilate heard this, he asked whether the man was a Galilean. 7 And when he learned that he was under Herod's jurisdiction, he sent him off to Herod, who was himself in Jerusalem at that time. 8 When Herod saw Jesus, he was very glad, for he had been wanting to see him for a long time, because he had heard about him and was hoping to see him perform some sign. 9 He questioned him at some length, but Jesus gave him no answer. 10 The chief priests and the scribes stood by, vehemently accusing him. 11 Even Herod with his soldiers treated him with contempt and mocked him; then he put an elegant robe on him, and sent him back to Pilate. 12 That same day Herod and Pilate became friends with each other; before this they had been enemies. 13 Pilate then called together the chief priests, the leaders, and the people, 14 and said to them, "You brought me this man as one who was perverting the people; and here I have examined him in your presence and have not found this man guilty of any of your charges against him. 15 Neither has Herod, for he sent him back to us. Indeed, he has done nothing to deserve death. 16 I will therefore have him flogged and release him."

§ 246 THE SENTENCE OF DEATH

MAT 27:15–26	MAR 15:6–15	LUK 23:17–25
15 Now at the festival the governor was accustomed to release a	6 Now at the festival he used to release a	[17][I]

✦ [I] text: P^{75} A B sa bo; add verse 17, *Now he was obliged to release someone for them at the festival*: S W Θ λ ø 𝔎 it vg sy^{p}; verse 17 follows verse 19: D sy^{s} sy^{c}.

● To MAT 27:14; MAR 15:5 *cf.* JOH 19:9–10. — 9 He [Pilate] entered his headquarters again and asked Jesus, "Where are you from?" But Jesus gave him no answer. 10 Pilate therefore said to him, "Do you refuse to speak to me? Do you not know that I have power to release you, and power to crucify you?" ● To LUK 23:4–5 *cf.* JOH 19:6. — When the chief priests and the police saw him, they shouted, "Crucify him! Crucify him!" Pilate said to them, "Take him yourselves and crucify him; I find no case against him." ● To § 246 *cf.* JOH 18:38–40; 19:4–16.

prisoner for the crowd, anyone
whom they wanted. 16 At that time
they had a notorious prisoner,
called Jesus Barabbas.[J]
17 So
after they had gathered,
Pilate said to
them, "Whom do you want me to
release for you, Jesus Barabbas[J] or
Jesus who is called the Messiah?"
18 For he realized that it was out of
jealousy that they had
handed him over. 19 While he was
sitting on the judgment seat, his
wife sent word to him, "Have nothing to do with that innocent man,
for today I have suffered a great deal
because of a dream about him."
20 Now the chief priests and the elders persuaded the crowds to
ask for Barabbas and to have Jesus
killed. 21 The governor
again said to them, "Which of the
two do you want me to release for
you?" And they said,
"Barabbas."
22 Pilate
said to them,
"Then what should I do
with Jesus who is called the
Messiah?" All of them
said, "Let him be crucified!"
23 Then he asked,
"Why, what evil has he done?"

prisoner for them, anyone
for whom they asked. 7 Now
a man
called Barabbas was in prison with
the rebels who had committed murder during the insurrection. 8 So
the crowd came and began to ask
Pilate to do for them according to
his custom. 9 Then he answered
them, "Do you want me to
release for you
the King of the Jews?"
10 For he realized that it was out of
jealousy that the chief priests had
handed him over.
11 But the chief priests
stirred up the crowd to
have him release Barabbas for them
instead. 12 Pilate
spoke to them again,
"Then what do you wish me to do
with the man you call the
King of the Jews?" 13 They
shouted back, "Crucify him!"
14 Pilate asked them,
"Why, what evil has he done?"

Cf. 23:19

18 Then they all shouted out together, "Away with this fellow!
Release Barabbas for us!" 19 (This
was a man who had been put in
prison for an insurrection that had
taken place in the city, and for murder.) 20 Pilate, wanting to release
Jesus, addressed them again;
21 but they kept
shouting, "Crucify, crucify him!"
22 A third time he said to them,
"Why, what evil has he done? I
have found in him no ground for the

✦ [J] text: Θ λ sy[s] Origen; omit: *Jesus*: S A B D W ø 𝔐 it vg sy[p] sa bo.

● To MAT 27:23 and parallels, *cf.* JOH 19:6–7, 15. — 6 When the chief priests and the police saw him, they shouted, "Crucify him! Crucify him!" Pilate said to them, "Take him yourselves and crucify him; I find no case against him." 7 The Jews answered him, "We have a law, and according to that law he ought to die because he has claimed to be the Son of God." 15 They cried out, "Away with him! Away with him! Crucify him!" Pilate asked them, "Shall I crucify your King?" The chief priests answered, "We have no king but the emperor."

◗ To MAT 27:16 *cf.* **Gospel of the Nazaraeans** (in Jerome, *Commentary on Matthew 27:16*). — In the Gospel according to the Hebrews, Barabbas is interpreted as "son of their master (teacher?)." He had been condemned because of insurrection and murder.

		sentence of death; I will therefore have him flogged and then release him."
But they shouted all the more, "Let him be crucified!"	But they shouted all the more, "Crucify him!"	23 But they kept urgently demanding with loud shouts that he should be crucified; and their voices prevailed.
24 So when Pilate	15 So Pilate, wishing to satisfy the crowd,	24 So Pilate gave his verdict that their demand should be granted.
saw that he could do nothing, but rather that a riot was beginning, he took some water and washed his hands before the crowd, saying, "I am innocent of this man's blood; [K] see to it yourselves." 25 Then the people as a whole answered, "His blood be on us and on our children!"		
26 So he released Barabbas for them; and after flogging Jesus,	released Barabbas for them; and after flogging Jesus,	25 He released the man they asked for, the one who had been put in prison for insurrection and murder, and
he handed him over to be crucified.	he handed him over to be crucified.	he handed Jesus over as they wished.

§ 247 THE MOCKING BY THE SOLDIERS

MAT 27:27–31	MAR 15:16–20	LUK
27 Then the soldiers of the governor took Jesus into the governor's headquarters, and they gathered the whole cohort around him. 28 They stripped him and put a scarlet robe on him,	16 Then the soldiers led him into the courtyard of the palace (that is, the governor's headquarters); and they called together the whole cohort. 17 And they clothed him in a purple cloak;	
29 and after twisting some thorns into a crown, they put it on his head. They put a reed in his right hand and knelt before him and mocked him, saying, "Hail, King of the Jews!"	and after twisting some thorns into a crown, they put it on him. 18 And they began saluting him, "Hail, King of the Jews!"	
30 They spat on him, and took the reed and	19 They	

✧ MAT 27:24 — DEU 21:6–8.

✦ [K] text: B D Θ it (some MSS.) sy^{s} sa; *this righteous* (*innocent*) *man's blood*: S A W λ ø 𝔑 it (some MSS.) vg sy^{p} bo.

● To MAT 27:26 and parallels, *cf.* JOH 19:16. — Then he [Pilate] handed him [Jesus] over to them to be crucified. So they took Jesus. ● To § 247 *cf.* JOH 19:1–3.

◗ To MAT 27:24 *cf.* **Gospel of Peter 1:1–2.** — 1 None of the Jews washed their hands—neither Herod nor any of his judges; and as they would not wash, Pilate arose. 2 Then Herod the king commanded that the Lord be arrested, saying to them, "Do what I have commanded you." ◗ To MAT 27:26b–31 = MAR 15:15b–20 *cf.* **Gospel of Peter 2:5b–3:9.** — 2:5b And he delivered him to the people before the first day of Unleavened Bread, their feast day. 3:6 And having taken the Lord, they pushed him as they ran and said, "Let us drag away the Son of God now that we have power over him." 7 And they put a purple robe on him, and made him sit on the seat of judgment, saying, "Judge justly, king of Israel." 8 And one of them brought a crown of thorns and put it on the Lord's head; 9 and others stood and spat in his eyes and still others slapped his cheeks; others pricked him with a reed, and some of them scourged him, saying, "With this honor let us honor the Son of God."

struck him on the head. 31 After mocking him, they stripped him of the robe and put his own clothes on him. Then they led him away to crucify him.	struck his head with a reed, spat upon him, and knelt down in homage to him. 20 After mocking him, they stripped him of the purple cloak and put his own clothes on him. Then they led him out to crucify him.	*Cf.* 23:26

§ 248 SIMON OF CYRENE CARRIES JESUS' CROSS

MAT 27:32	MAR 15:21	LUK 23:26–32
32 As they went out, they came upon a man from Cyrene named Simon; they compelled	21 They	26 As they led him away, they seized a man, Simon of Cyrene,
	compelled a passer-by, who was coming in from the country,	who was coming from the country, and they laid the
this man to carry his cross.	to carry his cross; it was Simon of Cyrene, the father of Alexander and Rufus.	cross on him, and made him carry it
		behind Jesus. 27 A great number of the people followed him, and among them were women who were beating their breasts and wailing for him. 28 But Jesus turned to them and said, "Daughters of Jerusalem, do not weep for me, but weep for yourselves and for your children. 29 For the days are surely coming when they will say, 'Blessed are the barren, and the wombs that never bore, and the breasts that never nursed.' 30 Then they will begin to say to the mountains, 'Fall on us'; and to the hills, 'Cover us.' 31 For if they do this when the wood is green, what will
Cf. 27:38 (§ 249, p. 199)	*Cf.* 15:27 (§ 249, p. 199)	happen when it is dry?" 32 Two others also, who were criminals, were led away to be put to death with him.

✧ LUK 23:30 — HOS 10:8.

§ 249 THE CRUCIFIXION

MAT 27:33–44	MAR 15:22–32	LUK 23:33–43
33 And when they came to a place called Golgotha (which means Place of a Skull), 34 they offered him wine to drink, mixed with gall; but when he tasted it, he would not drink it. 35 And when they had crucified him, *Cf.* 27:38	22 Then they brought Jesus to the place called Golgotha (which means the place of a skull). 23 And they offered him wine mixed with myrrh; but he did not take it. 24 And they crucified him, *Cf.* 15:27	33 When they came to the place that is called The Skull, they crucified Jesus there with the criminals, one on his right and one on his left. 34 Then Jesus said, “Father, forgive them; for they do not know what they are doing.”[L]
35 they divided his clothes among themselves by casting lots;	24 and divided his clothes among them, casting lots to decide what each should take.	And they cast lots to divide his clothing.
36 then they sat down there and kept watch over him.		35 And the people stood by, watching;
	25 It was nine o'clock in the morning when they crucified him.	
37 Over his head they put the charge against him, which read, “This is Jesus, the King of the Jews.” 38 Then two bandits were crucified with him, one on his right and one on his left. 39 Those who passed by derided him, shaking their heads 40 and saying, “You who would destroy the temple and	26 The inscription of the charge against him read, “The King of the Jews.” 27 And with him they crucified two bandits, one on his right and one on his left.[M] 29 Those who passed by derided him, shaking their heads and saying, “Aha! You who would destroy the temple and	*Cf.* 23:38 *Cf.* 23:32–33

✧ MAT 27:34 = MAR 15:23 = LUK 23:36 — PSA 69:21. ✧ MAT 27:35 = MAR 15:24 = LUK 23:34b — PSA 22:18.
✧ MAT 27:39 = MAR 15:29 = LUK 23:35 — PSA 22:7.

✦ [L] text: S A C λ ø 𝔐 it vg sy^c sy^p Marcion, Irenaeus, Origen; omit: *Then Jesus said, “Father, forgive them; for they do not know what they are doing”*: P^{75} B D W Θ sy^s sa bo. ✦ [M] text: S A B C D sy^s sa bo; add verse 28: *And the scripture was fulfilled that says, “And he was counted among the lawless”*: Θ λ ø 𝔐 it vg sy^p. *Cf.* LUK 22:37; ISA 53:12.

• To MAT 27:33 and parallels, *cf.* JOH 19:17. — and carrying the cross by himself, he [Jesus] went out to what is called The Place of the Skull, which in Hebrew is called Golgotha. • To MAT 27:35 and parallels, *cf.* JOH 19:23–24. • To MAT 27:37 and parallels, *cf.* JOH 19:19. — Pilate also had an inscription written and put on the cross. It read, “Jesus of Nazareth, the King of the Jews.” • To MAT 27:38 and parallels, *cf.* JOH 19:18. — There they crucified him, and with him two others, one on either side, with Jesus between them.

◗ To MAT 27:33–44 *cf.* **Gospel of Peter 4:10–14.** — 10 And they brought two criminals and crucified the Lord between them; and he was silent, as one having no pain. 11 And when they had set up the cross, they wrote on it, “This is the King of Israel.” 12 And they laid Jesus' garments down, and divided them, and cast lots for them. 13 But one of those criminals reviled them, saying, “We have suffered in this way for the evils we have done; but in what way has this person injured you, who has become the people's Savior?” 14 And they were angry with Jesus and commanded that his legs should not be broken so that he might die in agony.
◗ To LUK 23:34 *cf.* **Gospel of the Nazaraeans** (in Haimo of Auxerre, *Commentary on Isaiah 53:12*). — As it is said in the Gospel of the Nazarenes: At this word of the Lord, many thousands of Jews standing around the cross believed.

build it in three days, save yourself! If you are the Son of God,
come down[N] from the cross.” 41 In
the same way the chief priests also,
along with the scribes and elders,
were mocking him,
saying, 42 “He saved
others; he cannot save himself.
He is the King of
Israel; let him come down from the
cross now, and we will
believe in him. 43 He trusts in God;
let God deliver him now, if he
wants to; for he said, ‘I am God’s
Son.’ ”

Cf. 27:48 (§ 250, p. 201)

Cf. 27:40

Cf. 27:37

44 The bandits
who were crucified with him
also taunted him in the same way.

---

build it in three days, 30 save yourself, and
come down from the cross!” 31 In
the same way the chief priests,
along with the scribes,
were also mocking him among
themselves and saying, “He saved
others; he cannot save himself.
32 Let the Messiah, the King of
Israel, come down from the
cross now, so that we may see and
believe.”

Cf. 15:36 (§ 250, p. 201)

Cf. 15:30

Cf. 15:26

Those
who were crucified with him
also taunted him.

Cf. 23:37

but the leaders
scoffed at him,
saying, “He saved
others; let him save himself if
he is the Messiah of
God, his chosen one!”

36 The soldiers also mocked him,
coming up and offering him sour
wine, 37 and saying, “If you are the
King of the Jews, save yourself!”
38 There was also an inscription over
him,[O] “This is the King of the
Jews.” 39 One of the criminals
who were hanged there
kept deriding him and saying, “Are
you not the Messiah? Save yourself and us!” 40 But the other
rebuked him, saying, “Do you not
fear God, since you are under the
same sentence of condemnation?
41 And we indeed have been condemned justly, for we are getting
what we deserve for our deeds, but
this man has done nothing wrong.”
42 Then he said, “Jesus, remember
me when you come into[P] your kingdom.” 43 He replied, “Truly I tell
you, today you will be with me in
Paradise.”

✧ MAT 27:43 — PSA 22:8.

✦ [N] text: B W Θ λ ø 𝔐 it (some MSS.) vg sa bo; *save yourself, if you are the Son of God, and come down*: S A D it (some MSS.) sy^{s} sy^{p}. ✦ [O] text: P^{75} B C sy^{c} sy^{s} sa bo; add: *in letters of Greek and Latin and Hebrew*: S A D W Θ λ ø 𝔐 it vg sy^{p}. *Cf.* JOH 19:20. ✦ [P] text: P^{75} B it (some MSS.) vg; *in your kingdom*: S A C it (some MSS.) sy^{c} sy^{s} sy^{p} sa bo.

§ 250 THE DEATH ON THE CROSS

MAT 27:45–56	MAR 15:33–41	LUK 23:44–49
45 From noon on, darkness came over the whole land[Q] until three in the afternoon.	33 When it was noon, darkness came over the whole land[Q] until three in the afternoon.	44 It was now about noon, and darkness came over the whole land[Q] until three in the afternoon, 45 while the sun's light failed;[R] and
Cf. 27:51a	*Cf.* 15:38	the curtain of the temple was torn in two.
46 And about three o'clock Jesus cried with a loud voice, "Eli, Eli, lema sabachthani?" that is, "My God, my God, why have you forsaken me?" 47 When some of the bystanders heard it, they said, "This man is calling for Elijah." 48 At once one of them ran and got a sponge, filled it with sour wine, put it on a stick, and gave it to him to drink. 49 But the others said, "Wait, let us see whether Elijah will come to save him."[S]	34 At three o'clock Jesus cried out with a loud voice, "Eloi, Eloi, lema sabachthani?" which means, "My God, my God, why have you forsaken me?" 35 When some of the bystanders heard it, they said, "Listen, he is calling for Elijah." 36 And someone ran, filled a sponge with sour wine, put it on a stick, and gave it to him to drink, saying, "Wait, let us see whether Elijah will come to take him down."	*Cf.* 23:36 (§ 249, p. 200)
50 Then Jesus cried again with a loud voice and	37 Then Jesus gave a loud cry and	46 Then Jesus, crying with a loud voice, said, "Father, into your hands I commend my spirit." Having said this,
breathed his last.	breathed his last.	he breathed his last.
51 At that moment the curtain of the temple was torn in two, from top to bottom. The earth shook, and the rocks were split. 52 The tombs also were opened, and many bodies of the saints who had fallen asleep were raised. 53 After his resurrec-	38 And the curtain of the temple was torn in two, from top to bottom.	*Cf.* 23:45

✧ MAT 27:46 = MAR 15:34 — PSA 22:1. ✧ MAT 27:48 = MAR 15:36 — PSA 69:21. ✧ LUK 23:46 — PSA 31:5.

✦ [Q] Or, *earth.* ✦ [R] text: B sa bo; *after the sun's light failed*: P[75] S C?; *and the sun was eclipsed*: A D W Θ λ ø ℜ it vg sy[c] sy[s] sy[p]. ✦ [S] text: A D W Θ λ ø ℜ it vg sy[s] sy[p] sa bo; add: *And another took a spear and pierced his side, and out came water and blood*: S B C. *Cf.* JOH 19:34.

• To MAT 27:48 and parallels, *cf.* JOH 19:29. — A jar full of sour wine was standing there. So they put a sponge full of the wine on a branch of hyssop and held it to his mouth. • To LUK 23:46 *cf.* JOH 19:30. — When Jesus had received the wine, he said, "It is finished." Then he bowed his head and gave up his spirit. *Cf.* JOH 19:31–37.

◗ To MAT 27:45–51 *cf.* **Gospel of Peter 5:15–20.** — 15 Now it was noon, and darkness covered over all Judea, and they were afraid and distressed for fear the sun had set while Jesus was still alive. For it is written for them that the sun should not set upon one put to death. 16 And one of them said, "Give him gall with vinegar to drink." And they mixed them and gave it to him. 17 And they fulfilled all things and brought their sins to an end upon their own heads. 18 And many went about with lamps, supposing it was night, and they went to bed. 19 And the Lord cried out, "My power, my power, you have forsaken me!" And saying this, Jesus was taken up. 20 In the same hour the curtain of the temple of Jerusalem was torn in two. ◗ To MAT 27:51 *cf.* **Gospel of the Nazaraeans** (in Jerome, *Letter 120 to Hedibia* and *Commentary on Matthew 27:51*). — In the Gospel that is written in Hebrew letters we read, not that the curtain of the temple was torn, but that the astonishingly large lintel of the temple collapsed.

tion they came out of the tombs and
entered the holy city and appeared
to many. 54 Now when the
centurion and those with him, who
were keeping watch over Jesus,
saw the earthquake and what took
place, they were terrified and said,
"Truly this man was God's Son!"[U]
55 Many women were also there,
looking on from a distance;
they had followed
Jesus from Galilee
and had provided for him.
56 Among them were Mary Magdalene, and Mary the mother of
James and Joseph, and the mother
of the sons of Zebedee.

39 Now when the
centurion, who
stood facing him,
saw that in this way[T] he breathed his
last, he said,
"Truly this man was God's Son!"[U]
40 There were also women
looking on from a distance; among
them were Mary Magdalene, and
Mary the mother of James the
younger and of Joses, and Salome.
41 These used to follow
him
and provided for him when he was
in Galilee; and
there were many other women who
had come up with him to Jerusalem.

47 When the
centurion
saw what had taken
place, he praised God and said,
"Certainly this man was innocent."
Cf. 8:3 (§ 84, p. 69)
Cf. 23:55 (§ 251, p. 203)
48 And when all the crowds who had
gathered there for this spectacle saw
what had taken place, they returned home, beating their breasts.
49 But all his acquaintances, including the women who had followed
him from Galilee, stood at a distance, watching these things.

✧ LUK 23:49 — PSA 38:11.

✦ [T] text: S B sa; *saw that he having thus cried out breathed his last*: A C λ ø ℜ it vgsy^{p}; *saw him having thus cried out and breathed his last*: D; *saw that he having cried out breathed his last*: W Θ sy^{s}; *saw that he breathed his last*: bo. ✦ [U] Or, *a son of God.*

• To MAT 27:55 and parallels, *cf.* JOH 19:25b. — Meanwhile, standing near the cross of Jesus were his mother, and his mother's sister, Mary the wife of Clopas, and Mary Magdalene.

◗ To MAT 27:55*ff.* and parallels, *cf.* Tatian, *Diatessaron* in Dura Parchment 24. — . . . of Zebedee and Salome, and the women who followed Jesus from Galilee seeing Jesus who had been crucified. It was the day of Preparation, and the sabbath was beginning. And when it was evening on the day of Preparation, that is, the day before the sabbath, a man named Joseph came from Erinmathaias, a city of Judea. Being a disciple of Jesus, he was good and righteous, but had been condemned secretly on account of the fear of the Jews, and he looked for the kingdom of God. He had not consented to the purpose . . . ◗ To LUK 23:48 *cf.* **Gospel of Peter 7:25.** — Then the Jews and the elders and the priests, when they perceived what great evil they had done to themselves, began to lament and to say, "Woe for our sins; the judgment and the end of Jerusalem has drawn near."

§ 251 THE BURIAL OF JESUS

MAT 27:57–61	MAR 15:42–47	LUK 23:50–56
57 When it was evening,	42 When evening had come, and since it was the day of Preparation, that is, the day before the sabbath,	
there came a rich man from Arimathea, named Joseph, who was also a disciple of Jesus.	43 Joseph of Arimathea, a respected	50 Now there was a good and righteous man named Joseph, who,
	member of the council,	though a member of the council, 51 had not agreed to their plan and action. He came from the Jewish
58 He went to Pilate and asked for the body of Jesus;	who was also himself waiting expectantly for the kingdom of God, went boldly to Pilate and asked for the body of Jesus. 44 Then Pilate wondered if he were already dead; and summoning the centurion, he asked him whether he had been dead for some time. 45 When he learned from the centurion that he was dead,	town of Arimathea, and he was waiting expectantly for the kingdom of God. 52 This man went to Pilate and asked for the body of Jesus.
then Pilate ordered it to be given to him. 59 So Joseph	he granted the body to Joseph. 46 Then Joseph bought a linen cloth, and	53 Then he
took the body and wrapped it in a clean linen cloth 60 and laid it in his own new tomb, which he had hewn in the rock.	taking down the body, wrapped it in the linen cloth, and laid it in a tomb that had been hewn out of the rock.	took it down, wrapped it in a linen cloth, and laid it in a rock-hewn tomb where no one had ever been laid. 54 It was the day of Preparation, and the sabbath was beginning.[V]
He then rolled a great stone to the door of the tomb and went away.	He then rolled a stone against the door of the tomb.	
61 Mary Magdalene and the other Mary were there, sitting opposite the tomb.	47 Mary Magdalene and Mary the mother of Joses saw where the body	55 The women who had come with him from Galilee followed, and they saw the tomb and how his body

✧ MAT 27:57–60 = MAR 15:43–46 = LUK 23:50–54 — DEU 21:22–23; EXO 34:25.

✦ [V] Greek: *was dawning.*

● To § 251 *cf.* JOH 19:38–42.

◗ To MAT 27:57*ff.* and parallels, *cf.* **Gospel of Peter 2:3–5a.** — 3 Joseph, the friend of Pilate and of the Lord, was standing there; and knowing that they were about to crucify Jesus, he went to Pilate and asked for the body of the Lord for burial. 4 And Pilate sent word to Herod and asked for the body. 5a And Herod responded, "Brother Pilate, even if no one asked for the body, we would bury it, since it is almost the sabbath. For it is written in the law, 'Let not the sun set on one who has been put to death.' "

◗ To MAT 27:57*ff.* and parallels, *cf.* **Gospel of Peter 6:21–24.** — 21 And then they drew out the nails from the hands of the Lord, and laid the body upon the earth. And the whole earth was shaken, and a great fear arose. 22 Then the sun shone and it was found to be the ninth hour. 23 The Jews rejoiced and gave Jesus' body to Joseph, to bury it, because he had seen all the good things that Jesus had done. 24 And Joseph took the body of the Lord, and washed it, and wrapped it in a linen shroud, and brought it to his own tomb, called the garden of Joseph.

MAT	MAR	LUK
	was laid. *Cf.* 16:1 (§ 253, p. 204)	was laid. 56 Then they returned, and prepared spices and ointments. On the sabbath they rested according to the commandment.

§ 252 THE GUARD AT THE TOMB

MAT 27:62–66	MAR	LUK
62 The next day, that is, after the day of Preparation, the chief priests and the Pharisees gathered before Pilate 63 and said, "Sir, we remember what that impostor said while he was still alive, 'After three days I will rise again.' 64 Therefore command the tomb to be made secure until the third day; otherwise his disciples may go and steal him away, and tell the people, 'He has been raised from the dead,' and the last deception would be worse than the first." 65 Pilate said to them, "You have a guard[W] of soldiers; go, make it as secure as you can."[X] 66 So they went with the guard and made the tomb secure by sealing the stone.		

§ 253 THE EMPTY TOMB

MAT 28:1–10	MAR 16:1–8	LUK 24:1–12
1 After the sabbath, as the first day of the week was dawning, Mary Magdalene	1 When the sabbath was over, Mary Magdalene,	*Cf.* 23:56b (§ 251, p. 204) 1 But on the first day of the week, at early dawn, they

---

◇ LUK 23:56 — EXO 12:16, 20:9–10; DEU 5:13–14.

✦ [W] Or, *Take a guard.* ✦ [X] Greek: *know how.*

● To § 253 *cf.* JOH 20:1-10.

▸ To MAT 27:62–66 *cf.* **Gospel of Peter 8:28–33.** — 28 When the scribes and Pharisees and elders had gathered with each other, . . . 29 they came to Pilate, begging him, 30 "Give us soldiers so that we can watch Jesus' tomb for three days, lest the disciples come and steal the body away, and the people suppose that Jesus has been raised from the dead, and will do evil things to us." 31 So Pilate gave them Petronius, the centurion, with soldiers, to watch the tomb. And the elders and scribes came with them to the tomb. 32 And when, with the centurion and the soldiers, they had rolled a great stone away and placed it against the door of the tomb, 33 and after they had spread seven wax seals on it and pitched a tent, they kept watch. ▸ To MAT 27:65 *cf.* **Gospel of the Nazaraeans,** as recorded in a marginal note of some manuscripts: The Jewish Gospel has: And he delivered armed men to them, that they might sit opposite the cave and guard it day and night. ▸ To MAT 28:1, 5–8 = MAR 16:1–8 = LUK 24:1–11 *cf.* **Gospel of Peter 12:50–54, 13:55–57.** — 50 Now early on the Lord's day Mary Magdalene, a disciple of the Lord, who was afraid because of the Jews (for they were inflamed with anger, and the women had not done at the tomb of the Lord the things that women usually do to their loved ones when they die) — 51 Mary took friends with her, and went to the tomb where Jesus was laid. 52 And they feared lest the Jews see them, and they said, "Even if we were not able to weep and lament for Jesus on the day of the crucifixion, yet let us now do so at the tomb. 53 But who will roll away for us the stone that is set against the door of the tomb, that we may enter and sit beside Jesus, and perform our obligations?" 54 For the stone was very large. "We fear lest some one see us. But if we cannot, then let us lay beside the door the things which we have brought in remembrance of Jesus, and we will weep and lament until we get home." 13:55 And they went and found the tomb open; and going near, they looked in, and saw there a young man sitting in the middle of the tomb, handsome, and dressed in a brilliant robe. And the angel said to them, 56 "Why have you come? Whom do you seek? Not the one who was crucified, for that one has risen and gone. But if you do not believe it, look in and see the place where the body lay, that it is not here. For Jesus has risen and gone to the place from which Jesus was sent." 57 Then the women were afraid and fled.

Matthew	Mark	Luke
and the other Mary	and Mary the mother of James, and Salome bought spices, so that they might go and anoint him. 2 And very early on the first day of the week, when the sun had risen,	
went to see the tomb.	they went to the tomb.	came to the tomb, taking the spices that they had prepared.
2 And suddenly there was a great earthquake; for an angel of the Lord, descending from heaven, came and rolled back the stone and sat on it. 3 His appearance was like lightning, and his clothing white as snow. 4 For fear of him the guards shook and became like dead men.		
	3 They had been saying to one another, "Who will roll away the stone for us from the entrance to the tomb?" 4 When they looked up, they saw that the stone, which was very large, had already been rolled back. 5 As they entered the tomb,	2 They found the stone rolled away from the tomb, 3 but when they went in, they did not find the body.[Y] 4 While they were perplexed about this, suddenly
	they saw a young man, dressed in a white robe, sitting on the right side; and they were alarmed.	two men in dazzling clothes stood beside them. 5 The women were terrified and bowed their faces to the ground,
5 But the angel said to the women,	6 But he said to them,	but the men said to them, "Why do you look for the living among the dead?
"Do not be afraid; I know that you are looking for Jesus who was crucified. 6 He is not here; for he has been raised, as he said. Come, see the place where he[A] lay. 7 Then go quickly and tell his disciples, 'He has been raised from the dead, and indeed he is going ahead of you to Galilee; there you will see him.' This is my message for you."	"Do not be alarmed; you are looking for Jesus of Nazareth, who was crucified. He has been raised; he is not here. Look, there is the place they laid him. 7 But go, tell his disciples and Peter that he is going ahead of you to Galilee; there you will see him, just as he told you."	He is not here, but has risen.[Z]
		6 Remember how he told you, while he was still in Galilee, 7 that the Son of Man must be handed over to sinners, and be crucified, and on the third day rise again."

✦ [Y] text: D it (some MSS.) Eusebius; add: *of Jesus*: sy^{c} sy^{s} sy^{p}; add: *of the Lord Jesus*: P^{75} S A B C W Θ λ ø ℜ it (some MSS.) vg sa bo. ✦ [Z] text: S A B C W Θ λ ø ℜ it (some MSS.) vg sy^{c} sy^{s} sy^{p}; omit: *He is not here, but has risen*: D it (some MSS.).
✦ [A] text: S B Θ sy^{s} sa bo; *the Lord*: A C D W λ ø ℜ it vg sy^{p}.

MAT	MAR	LUK
		8 Then they remembered his words, 9 and
8 So they left the tomb quickly with fear and great joy, and ran to tell his disciples.	8 So they went out and fled from the tomb, for terror and amazement had seized them; and they said nothing to anyone, for they were afraid.	returning from the tomb, they told all this to the eleven and to all the rest.
9 Suddenly Jesus met them and said, "Greetings!" And they came to him, took hold of his feet, and worshiped him. 10 Then Jesus said to them, "Do not be afraid; go and tell my brothers to go to Galilee; there they will see me."		
		10 Now it was Mary Magdalene, Joanna, Mary the mother of James, and the other women with them who told this to the apostles. 11 But these words seemed to them an idle tale, and they did not believe them. 12 But Peter got up and ran to the tomb; stooping and looking in, he saw the linen cloths by themselves; then he went home, amazed at what had happened.[B]

APPEARANCES OF THE RISEN LORD

The Matthean Narrative

Matthew 28:11–20

§ AA THE BRIBING OF THE SOLDIERS

MAT 28:11–15	MAR	LUK
11 While they were going, some of the guard went into the city and told the chief priests everything that had happened. 12 After the priests had assembled with the elders, they devised a plan to give a large sum of money to the soldiers, 13 telling		

✦ [B] text: P^{75} S A B W Θ λ φ ℜ it (some MSS.) vg sy^c sy^s sy^p sa bo (*Cf.* JOH 20:3–10); omit verse 12: D it (some MSS.).

◗ To MAT 28:11–15 *cf.* **Gospel of Peter 11:45–49.** — 45 When those who were with the centurion saw what had happened, they hurried to Pilate at night, leaving the tomb that they were guarding. And being greatly disturbed, they reported everything they had seen, saying, "Truly this one was a (the) son of God." 46 Pilate answered, "I am free from the blood of the son of God, but this seemed good to you." 47 And they all went and asked him and begged him to order the centurion and the soldiers to tell no one what they had seen. 48 "For it is better," they said, "to commit the greatest sin before God than to fall into the hands of the Jews and be stoned." 49 Then Pilate commanded the centurion and the soldiers to say nothing.

them, "You must say, 'His disciples came by night and stole him away while we
were asleep.' 14 If this comes to the governor's ears, we will satisfy him and keep
you out of trouble." 15 So they took the money and did as they were directed. And
this story is still told among the Jews to this day.

§ BB THE COMMISSIONING OF THE DISCIPLES

MAT 28:16–20	MAR	LUK
16 Now the eleven disciples went to Galilee, to the mountain to which Jesus had directed them. 17 When they saw him, they worshiped him; but some doubted. 18 And Jesus came and said to them, "All authority in heaven and on earth has been given to me. 19 Go therefore and make disciples of all nations, baptizing them in the name of the Father and of the Son and of the Holy Spirit, 20 and teaching them to obey everything that I have commanded you. And remember, I am with you always, to the end of the age."		

The Lucan Narrative

Luke 24:13–53

§ CC THE ROAD TO EMMAUS

MAT	MAR	LUK 24:13–35
		13 Now on that same day two of them were going to a village called Emmaus, about seven miles[C] from Jerusalem, 14 and talking with each other about all these things that had happened. 15 While they were talking and discussing, Jesus himself came near and went with them, 16 but their eyes were kept from recognizing him. 17 And he said to them, "What are you discussing with each other while you walk along?" They stood still, looking sad. 18 Then one of them, whose name was Cleopas, answered him, "Are you the only stranger in Jerusalem who does not know the things that have taken place there in these days?" 19 He asked them, "What things?" They replied, "The things about Jesus of Nazareth, who was a prophet mighty in deed and word before God and all the people, 20 and how our chief priests

✦ [C] Greek: (most MSS.) *sixty stadia; a hundred and sixty stadia*: S Θ.

• To MAT 28:20 *cf.* JOH 14:23b. — "Those who love me will keep my word, and my Father will love them, and we will come to them and make our home with them."

◗ To LUK 24:13–35 *cf.* **Gospel according to the Hebrews** (in Jerome, *On Illustrious Men, 2*). — The gospel called according to the Hebrews, which I recently translated into Greek and Latin, and which Origen often uses, records, after the resurrection of the Savior: The Lord, having given the linen cloth to the servant of the priest, went to James and appeared to him (for James had sworn that he would not eat bread from the time when he had drunk the Lord's cup until he saw the Lord risen from the dead). And shortly afterward the Lord said, "Bring a table and bread!" And immediately it is added, the Lord took bread, and blessed it, and broke it, and gave it to James the Just, and said to him, "My brother, eat your bread, for the Son of Man is raised from the dead."

and leaders handed him over to be condemned to death and crucified him. 21 But
we had hoped that he was the one to redeem Israel. Yes, and besides all this, it
is now the third day since these things took place. 22 Moreover, some women of
our group astounded us. They were at the tomb early this morning, 23 and when
they did not find his body there, they came back and told us that they had indeed
seen a vision of angels who said that he was alive. 24 Some of those who were with
us went to the tomb and found it just as the women had said; but they did not see
him." 25 Then he said to them, "Oh, how foolish you are, and how slow of heart
to believe all that the prophets have declared! 26 Was it not necessary that the
Messiah should suffer these things and then enter into his glory?" 27 Then beginning with Moses and all the prophets, he interpreted to them the things about
himself in all the scriptures.
28 As they came near the village to which they were going, he walked ahead as if
he were going on. 29 But they urged him strongly, saying, "Stay with us, because
it is almost evening and the day is now nearly over." So he went in to stay with
them. 30 When he was at the table with them, he took bread, blessed and broke
it, and gave it to them. 31 Then their eyes were opened, and they recognized him;
and he vanished from their sight. 32 They said to each other, "Were not our hearts
burning within us[D] while he was talking to us on the road, while he was opening
the scriptures to us?" 33 That same hour they got up and returned to Jerusalem;
and they found the eleven and their companions gathered together. 34 They were
saying, "The Lord has risen indeed, and he has appeared to Simon!" 35 Then they
told what had happened on the road, and how he had been made known to them in
the breaking of the bread.

§ DD JESUS APPEARS TO THE DISCIPLES

MAT	MAR	LUK 24:36–49

36 While they were talking about this, Jesus himself stood among them and said to
them, "Peace be with you."[E] 37 They were startled and terrified, and thought that
they were seeing a ghost. 38 He said to them, "Why are you frightened, and why
do doubts arise in your hearts? 39 Look at my hands and my feet; see that it is I
myself. Touch me and see; for a ghost does not have flesh and bones as you see
that I have." 40 And when he had said this, he showed them his hands and his feet.[F]
41 While in their joy they were disbelieving and still wondering, he said to them,
"Have you anything here to eat?" 42 They gave him a piece of broiled fish, 43 and
he took it and ate in their presence. 44 Then he said to them, "These are my words
that I spoke to you while I was still with you—that everything written about me in
the law of Moses, the prophets, and the psalms must be fulfilled." 45 Then he

✦ [D] text: S A λ ø ℜ vg sy^{p} sa bo; omit: *within us*: P^{75} B D sy^{c} sy^{s}. ✦ [E] text: P^{75} S A B Θ λ ø ℜ sy^{c} sy^{s} sa bo (*Cf.* JOH 20:19, 26.); omit: *and said to them, "Peace be with you"*: D it (some MSS.); *and he said to them, "Peace be with you; it is I, do not be afraid"*: it (some MSS.) vg sy^{p} (*Cf.* JOH 6:20.); *and he said to them, "It is I, do not be afraid; peace be with you"*: W. ✦ [F] text: P^{75} S A B W Θ λ ø ℜ it (some MSS.) vg sy^{p} sa bo. *Cf.* JOH 20:20. Omit verse 40: D it (some MSS.) sy^{c} sy^{s}.

● To § DD *cf.* JOH 20:19–23.

◗ To LUK 24:39 *cf.* Ignatius, *Epistle to the Smyrneans 3:2.* — Jesus, having gone to those with Peter, said to them, "Take hold of me, handle me, and see that I am not a bodiless spirit."

opened their minds to understand the scriptures, 46 and he said to them, "Thus it is
written, that the Messiah is to suffer and to rise from the dead on the third day,
47 and that repentance and forgiveness of sins is to be proclaimed in his name to all
nations,[G] beginning from Jerusalem. 48 You are witnesses of these things. 49 And
see, I am sending upon you what my Father promised; so stay here in the city until
you have been clothed with power from on high."

§ EE THE ASCENSION

MAT	MAR	LUK 24:50–53

50 Then he led them out as far as Bethany, and, lifting up his hands, he blessed
them. 51 While he was blessing them, he withdrew from them and was carried up
into heaven.[H] 52 And they worshiped him,[I] and returned to Jerusalem with great
joy; 53 and they were continually in the temple blessing God.

The Longer Ending of Mark

Mark 16:9–20

MAT	MAR 16:9–20	LUK

9 Now after he rose early on the first day of the week, he appeared first to Mary
Magdalene, from whom he had cast out seven demons. 10 She went out and told
those who had been with him, while they were mourning and weeping. 11 But
when they heard that he was alive and had been seen by her, they would not believe
it. 12 After this he appeared in another form to two of them, as they were walking
into the country. 13 And they went back and told the rest, but they did not believe
them.[1] 14 Later he appeared to the eleven themselves as they were sitting at the
table; and he upbraided them for their lack of faith and stubbornness, because they
had not believed those who saw him after he had risen. 15 And he said to them,
"Go into all the world and proclaim the good news to the whole creation. 16 The
one who believes and is baptized will be saved; but the one who does not believe

[1] MAR 16:12–13 — LUK 24:13–35.

✧ LUK 24:46 — HOS 6:2.

✦ [G] Or, *nations. Beginning from Jerusalem you are witnesses...* ✦ [H] text: P^{75} A B C W Θ λ ø 𝔐 it (some MSS.) vg sy^p sa bo; omit: *and was carried up into heaven*: S D it (some MSS.) sy^s. ✦ [I] text: P^{75} S A B C W Θ λ ø 𝔐 vg sy^p sa bo; omit: *and they worshiped him*: D it sy^s.

• To MAR 16:9–11 *cf.* JOH 20:11–18. • To MAR 16:14 *cf.* JOH 20:19–23.

◗ The Longer Ending is not found in: S B sy^s Clement, Origen; it is found in: A C D (to verse 16) W Θ λ ø 𝔐 it vg sy^c sy^p sa bo. ◗ The Shorter Ending, found only in a few manuscripts, reads as follows: And all that had been commanded them they told briefly to those around Peter. And afterward Jesus himself sent out out through them, from east to west, the sacred and imperishable proclamation of eternal salvation. ◗ After verse 14, W has a gloss, the so-called Freer Ending, the beginning of which is quoted in Latin by Jerome. An English translation of the Greek text of the gloss follows: And they excused themselves, saying, "This age of lawlessness and unbelief is under Satan, who does not allow the truth and power of God to prevail over the unclean things of the spirits. Therefore reveal your righteousness now" — thus they spoke to Christ. And Christ replied to them, "The term of years of Satan's power has been fulfilled, but other terrible things draw near. And for those who have sinned I was handed over to death, that they may return to the truth and sin no more, that they may inherit the spiritual and imperishable glory of righteousness that is in heaven."

will be condemned.[1] 17 And these signs will accompany those who believe: by
using my name they will cast out demons; they will speak in new tongues; 18 they
will pick up snakes in their hands, and if they drink any deadly thing, it will not
hurt them; they will lay their hands on the sick, and they will recover."
19 So then the Lord Jesus, after he had spoken to them, was taken up into heaven
and sat down at the right hand of God.[2] 20 And they went out and proclaimed the
good news everywhere, while the Lord worked with them and confirmed the
message by the signs that accompanied it.

---

[1] MAR 16:14–16 — MAT 28:16–20.
[2] MAR 16:19 — LUK 24:50–51.

SUBJECT INDEX